Bisby

Harnessing Hibernate

Other resources from O'Reilly

Related titles   Java in a Nutshell   Enterprise Java Beans 3.0
Java Power Tools   Java Pocket Guide
Learning Java

oreilly.com   *oreilly.com* is more than a complete catalog of O'Reilly books. You'll also find links to news, events, articles, weblogs, sample chapters, and code examples.

oreillynet.com is the essential portal for developers interested in open and emerging technologies, including new platforms, programming languages, and operating systems.

Conferences   O'Reilly Media, Inc. brings diverse innovators together to nurture the ideas that spark revolutionary industries. We specialize in documenting the latest tools and systems, translating the innovator's knowledge into useful skills for those in the trenches. Visit *conferences.oreilly.com* for our upcoming events.

Safari Bookshelf (*safari.oreilly.com*) is the premier online reference library for programmers and IT professionals. Conduct searches across more than 1,000 books. Subscribers can zero in on answers to time-critical questions in a matter of seconds. Read the books on your Bookshelf from cover to cover or simply flip to the page you need. Try it today for free.

Harnessing Hibernate

James Elliott, Ryan Fowler, and Tim O'Brien

O'REILLY®

Beijing · Cambridge · Farnham · Köln · Paris · Sebastopol · Taipei · Tokyo

Harnessing Hibernate

by James Elliott, Ryan Fowler, and Tim O'Brien

Published by O'Reilly Media, Inc., 1005 Gravenstein Highway North, Sebastopol, CA 95472

O'Reilly books may be purchased for educational, business, or sales promotional use. Online editions are also available for most titles (*http://safari.oreilly.com*). For more information, contact our corporate/institutional sales department: 800-998-9938 or *corporate@oreilly.com*.

Editor: Mike Loukides
Production Editor: Sarah Schneider
Production Services: nSight, Inc.

Indexer: Seth Maislin, Potomac Indexing, LLC
Cover Designer: Karen Montgomery
Interior Designer: David Futato
Illustrator: Robert Romano

Printing History:

April 2008:   First Edition

ISBN: 978-0-596-51772-4

[M]

1207939836

Table of Contents

Part II.   Playing Nice with Others

Preface

Hibernate is a lightweight object/relational mapping service for Java. What does that mean? It's a way to work easily and efficiently with information from a relational database in the form of natural Java objects. But that description doesn't come close to conveying how useful and exciting the technology is. I'm not the only person who thinks so: Hibernate 2.1 won *Software Development* magazine's 14th annual Jolt Award in the "Libraries, Frameworks, and Components" category. (And, with the hindsight afforded by the opportunity to write this updated and expanded version of *Hibernate: A Developer's Notebook*, I can say I was truly thrilled that the first edition of this book, which covered Hibernate 2, was itself a Productivity Winner in the 15th annual Awards.)

So, what's great about Hibernate? All nontrivial applications (and even many trivial ones) need to store and use information, and these days this usually involves a relational database. Worlds apart from Java objects, databases often involve people with different skills and specializations. Bridging these two worlds has been important for a while, but it used to be quite complex and tedious.

Most people start out struggling to write a few SQL queries, embedding these awkwardly as strings within Java code, and working with Java database connectivity (JDBC) to run them and process the results. JDBC has evolved into a rich and flexible database communication library, which now provides ways to simplify and improve upon this approach, but there is still a fair degree of tedium involved. People who work with data a great deal need more power—some way of moving the queries out of the code and making them act more like well-behaved components in an object-oriented world.

Such capabilities had been part of my own (even more) lightweight object/relational layer for years. It began with a Java database connection and query pooling system written by my colleague Eric Knapp for the Lands' End e-commerce site. Our pooler introduced the idea of external SQL templates that could be accessed by name and efficiently combined with runtime data to generate the actual database queries. Only later did it grow to include the ability to bind these templates directly to Java objects, by adding simple mapping directives to the templates.

Although far less powerful than a system like Hibernate, this approach proved valuable in many projects of different sizes and in widely differing environments. We continued to use it until the first version of this book, most recently in building IP telephony applications for Cisco's CallManager platform. However, we now use Hibernate for new projects, and once you work through this book, you'll understand why. You will probably make the same decision yourself. Hibernate does a tremendous amount for you, and does it so easily that you can almost forget you're working with a database. Your objects are simply there when you need them. This is how technology should work.

You may wonder how Hibernate relates to Enterprise JavaBeans™ (EJBs). Is it a competing solution? When would you use one over the other? In fact, you can use both. Not every application needs the complexity of EJBs; many can simply use Hibernate directly to interact with a database. On the other hand, EJBs are sometimes indispensable for very complex three-tier application environments. In such cases, Hibernate may be used by an EJB Session bean to persist data, or it might be used to persist BMP entity beans.

In fact, even the EJB committee was eventually sold on the power and convenience of Hibernate's "plain old Java objects" approach to persistence—the Java Persistence Architecture introduced in EJB version 3 (and usable outside of an EJB environment) was heavily influenced by Hibernate. In fact, Hibernate 3 can be used as an implementation of JPA in a fully portable way (although, as you'll see in Chapter 7, you'll probably still want to take advantage of Hibernate's extensions to JPA).

The development of Hibernate has clearly been a watershed event in the interaction between Java and relational databases. The Java world owes Gavin King and his intrepid cohorts a huge debt of thanks for making our lives easier. This book is intended to help you learn how take advantage of their achievement as quickly as possible.

How to Use This Book

This book started as part of O'Reilly's Developer's Notebook™ series, a new approach to helping readers rapidly come up to speed with useful new technologies. Although it has since been expanded to touch on more of the related technologies that Hibernate users might want to explore, it is not intended to be a comprehensive reference manual for Hibernate. Instead, it reflects the authors' own exploration of the system, from initial download and configuration through a series of projects that demonstrate how to accomplish a variety of practical goals.

By reading and following along with these examples, you'll be able to get your own Hibernate environment set up quickly and start using it for realistic tasks right away. It's as if you can "walk with us" through terrain we've mapped out, while we point out useful landmarks and tricky pitfalls along the way.

Although we certainly include some background materials and explanations of how Hibernate works and why, this is always in the service of a focused task. Sometimes we'll refer you to the reference documentation or other online resources if you'd like more depth about one of the underlying concepts or details about a related but different way to use Hibernate.

Once you're past the first few chapters, you don't need to read the rest in order; you can jump to topics that are particularly interesting or relevant to you. The examples do build on each other, but you can download the finished source code from the book's web site* (you may want to start with the previous chapter's files and follow along, making changes yourself to implement the examples you're reading). You can always jump back to the earlier examples if they turn out to be interesting because of how they relate to what you've just learned.

Font Conventions

This book follows certain conventions for font usage. Understanding these conventions upfront will make it easier to use this book.

Italic
> Used for filenames, file extensions, URLs, application names, emphasis, and introduction of new terms.

`Constant width`
> Used for Java class names, methods, variables, properties, data types, database elements, and snippets of code that appear in text.

`Constant width bold`
> Used for commands you enter at the command line and to highlight new code inserted in a running example.

`Constant width italic`
> Used to annotate output.

On the Web Site

The web site for this book, *http://www.oreilly.com/catalog/9780596517724/*, offers some important materials you'll want to know about. All the examples for this book can be found there, organized by chapter.

The examples are available as a ZIP archive and a compressed TAR archive.

In many cases, the same files are used throughout a series of chapters, and they evolve to include new features and capabilities from example to example. Each chapter folder

---

* *http://www.oreilly.com/catalog/9780596517724/*

in the downloadable archive contains a snapshot of the state of the example system, reflecting all the changes and new content introduced in that chapter.

How to Contact Us

Please address comments and questions concerning this book to the publisher:

O'Reilly Media, Inc.
1005 Gravenstein Highway North
Sebastopol, CA 95472
800-998-9938 (in the United States or Canada)
707-829-0515 (international or local)
707-829-0104 (fax)

O'Reilly's web site for this book, where we list errata, examples, or any additional information, can be accessed at:

http://www.oreilly.com/catalog/9780596517724/

To comment or ask technical questions about this book, send email to:

bookquestions@oreilly.com

For more information about our books, conferences, Resource Centers, and the O'Reilly Network, see our web site at:

http://www.oreilly.com

Acknowledgments

We're intensely grateful to Gavin King, Christian Bauer, Steve Ebersole, Max Andersen, and everyone else who has created and improved Hibernate. Our enthusiasm for how this tool has made our lives better as Java developers is why Jim wrote the *Developer's Notebook* in the first place, and why all three of us decided to produce this expanded and updated book. Hopefully it shows!

We're particularly indebted to our technical reviewers Michael Podrazik, Stefan Winz, and Henri Yandell for their careful, detailed, and helpful suggestions. They each contributed greatly to making this a better book.

We'd also like to thank Keith Fahlgren, Adam Witwer, and the other members of O'Reilly's production department who put in lots of work helping us come up to speed in the new DocBook XML authoring environment, and getting the book to look as good as it could.

The Stripes example includes code developed by Tim Fennell, under the Apache Software License. The license for Stripes is located at *ch14/stripes_license.txt* in the examples download.

James Elliott

Any list of thanks has to start with my parents for fostering my interest in computing even when we were living in countries that made that a major challenge, and with my partner Joe for putting up with it today when it has flowered into a major obsession. I'd also like to acknowledge my employer, Berbee, for giving me an opportunity to delve deeply into Java and build skills as an architect of reusable APIs; for letting me stay clear of the proprietary, platform-specific tar pit that is engulfing so much of the programming world; for surrounding me with such incredible colleagues; and for being supportive when I wanted to leverage these experiences in writing this book.

Ryan and Tim jumped in when I wanted some help expanding the second version to cover related technologies that have come up like Spring and Stripes. Their enthusiasm and expertise have been a major factor in getting this long-delayed update in motion.

Marc Loy got me connected with the wonderful folks at O'Reilly by inviting me to help with the second edition of *Java Swing*, and Mike Loukides has been patiently working with me ever since—encouraging me to write a book of my own. In Hibernate he found the perfect topic to get me started, and it turned out well enough that we came back to expand it. Deb Cameron, our revisions editor for the *Swing* effort, played a big role in turning my tentative authorial ambitions into a rewarding reality. I'm also grateful she was willing to "loan me out" from helping with the third edition of *Learning Emacs* to take on the Hibernate project.

I remain grateful to my technical reviewers for the first version of this book, Adrian Kellor and Curt Pederson. They looked at some very early drafts and helped set my tone and direction, as well as reinforcing my enthusiasm about the value of the project. As that book came together, Bruce Tate provided an important sanity check from someone actively using and teaching Hibernate, and offered some great advice and even more encouragement. Eric Knapp reviewed a large portion with an eye toward using the book in an instructional setting at a technical college, and reminded me to keep my feet on the ground. Tim Cartwright jumped in at the end, working with a nearly complete draft in an effort to understand Hibernate as a potential platform for future work, and providing a great deal of useful feedback about the content and presentation.

Ryan Fowler

I'd like to thank Jim for inviting me to help out on this book and for all the coaching he's given me on the book and in my day job. I'd like to thank Tim for providing technical help and consolation when I needed each. Thanks to Mike Loukides for being patient with me and for helping to provide some direction.

I'd also like to thank my wife, Sarah, for being so helpful, patient, and loving. Things could have turned ugly, and your support was the primary reason that didn't happen. Finally, I'd like to thank my parents for giving me the tools to get where I am now and wherever I'm going.

Timothy O'Brien

Thanks to Jim and Ryan for asking me to contribute to this book with the Spring and Maven chapters. Thanks to Mike Loukides for providing a good environment for writing and collaboration. Keith Fahlgren was an invaluable resource when it came to the logistics of writing. The O'Reilly publishing technology group went out of its way a number of times to help us all with various issues relating to DocBook markup and version control.

Thanks to Stefan Winz, Robert Sorkin, Ahmed Abu-Zayedeh, Bob Hartlaub, Rock Podrazik, and Jeff Leeman; you have all provided the necessary proving grounds and been unwitting guinea pigs for the code presented in both the Spring and Maven chapters. Thanks to my daughter Josephine Ann for providing essential and critical feedback on the Hibernate Annotations chapter; Josephine, you might only be two years old, but you've picked up Hibernate very quickly. Thanks for taking time off from watching *Blue's Clues* to catch those silly errors in my *pom.xml* file. Thanks to Susan, my wife, for being perfect.

## PART I

Hibernate in a Hurry

Our first goal is to get up to speed with Hibernate as quickly as possible. Most of the chapters in this part are updated versions of content from *Hibernate: A Developer's Notebook* (O'Reilly), reflecting the major changes that came about with Hibernate 3. The sample code now works with the latest versions of the tools we rely on to provide an easy yet realistic environment for working with Hibernate. There is also a new chapter covering the ability to use Java 5 annotations, rather than XML mapping files, to configure Hibernate mappings.

Getting started and following along with the examples is even easier in this new version of the book because we've adopted Maven to help download many of the tools and libraries. As we hope you will see, there's no excuse to avoid diving in and trying this stuff yourself!

Once you're comfortable with the fundamentals of Hibernate, Part II will demonstrate how to tie Hibernate into some other environments to make each more powerful than they are on their own.

All right, time to dive in....

> Of course, with any printed book about active open source projects, things will get out of date quickly! See Appendix E for the specific versions we discuss, and for ideas on how to cope with changes.

## CHAPTER 1

Installation and Setup

It continues to amaze me how many great, free, open source Java™ tools are out there. When I needed a lightweight object/relational mapping service for a JSP e-commerce project at the turn of the millennium, I had to build my own. It evolved over the years, developed some cool and unique features, and we've used it in a wide variety of different contexts. But, once I discovered Hibernate, we used that for new development instead of my own familiar system (toward which I'll cheerfully admit bias). That should tell you how compelling it is!

If you're looking at this book, you're likely interested in a powerful and convenient way to bridge the worlds of Java objects and relational databases. Hibernate fills that role very nicely, without being so complicated that learning it becomes a daunting challenge in itself. To demonstrate that, this chapter guides you to the point where you can play with Hibernate and see for yourself why it's so exciting.

Later chapters will look at using Hibernate as part of more complex environments such as Spring and Stripes, as well as using it with other databases. The goal of this first chapter is to show you how easy it is to put together a basic, self-contained environment in which you can explore Hibernate and do real things with it.

Getting an Ant Distribution

Although it might be surprising, the first few things you need to get Hibernate running have nothing to do with Hibernate itself. First, you must set up an environment in which the remaining examples work. This will have the pleasant side effect of building a solid foundation for any actual project you might be undertaking.

If you're not already using Ant to manage the building, testing, running, and packaging of your Java projects, now is the time to start. The examples in this book are Ant-driven, so you'll need a working Ant installation to run them and experiment with variations on your own system, which is the best way to learn.

First of all, get an Ant binary and install it.

Why do I care?

The examples use Apache Ant for several reasons. It's convenient and powerful; it's one of the standard build tools for Java-based development; it's free; and it's cross-platform. If you use Ant, the examples will work equally well anywhere there's a Java environment, which means readers of this book won't be frustrated or annoyed. Fortunately, it also means we can do many more cool things with less effort—especially since several Hibernate tools have explicit Ant support, which I'll show you how to leverage. (I should note that these days more complex Java projects often use Maven[*], which adds many other project management capabilities. Since I had to pick one, in the spirit of keeping things simple and true to what I find useful, I went with Ant for these examples.)

If you are currently using Maven as a build tool, you will notice that we are using Maven's Ant Tasks to manage dependencies from our Ant builds. Although Maven is gaining momentum, Ant continues to be the most widely used build tool in Java development. Every chapter's example code folder also has a Maven *pom.xml* file and can be compiled with Maven. In many cases, the Maven build file provides the same functionality as the Ant *build.xml* file by using the Maven Hibernate3 plug-in. In Chapter 12 you will find some guidance for building and deploying Hibernate applications using full-blown Maven, but the majority of the examples in this book focus on Ant as a build tool, using the Maven Ant Tasks to relieve the tedium of finding and downloading the various libraries we need, and the libraries on which they, in turn, rely.

To take advantage of all these capabilities, you need to have Ant installed and working on your system.

How do I do that?

You can download a binary release of Ant from *http://ant.apache.org/bindownload.cgi*. Scroll down to find the current release of Ant, and download the archive in a format that's convenient for you to work with. Pick an appropriate place for it to live, and expand the archive there.

> I used to wonder why people bothered with Ant when they could use Make. Now that I've seen how well Ant manages Java builds, I feel lost without it.

The directory into which you've expanded the archive is referred to as ANT_HOME. Let's say you've expanded the archive into the directory */usr/local/apache-ant-1.7.0*; you may want to create a symbolic link to make it easier to work with and to avoid the need to change any environment configuration when you upgrade to a newer version:

```
/usr/local % ln -s apache-ant-1.7.0 ant
```

Once Ant is situated, you need to do a couple of things to make it work correctly. You need to add its *bin* directory in the distribution (in this example, */usr/local/ant/bin*) to your command path. You also need to set the environment variable ANT_HOME to the top-level directory you installed (in this example, */usr/local/ant*). Details about how to

[*] *http://maven.apache.org/*

perform these steps under different operating systems can be found in the Ant manual (*http://ant.apache.org/manual/*) if you need them.

Check Your Java Version

Of course, I'm also assuming you've got a Java software development kit (SDK). These days you should be using Java 5 at the very least, since it gives you some useful new language features. Go with the most recent stable SDK if you can. Either Java 5 or Java 6 should work with all of the examples in this book. It *was* possible to use most of Hibernate 2 with Java 1.3, but you generally had to rebuild the Hibernate JAR file using your 1.3 compiler. We can only imagine more recent releases depend even more strongly on current Java versions, and Java 5 has been out long enough, and has enough benefits of its own, that we're not even going to investigate compatibility with prior JDKs. Our examples are written assuming you've got at least Java 5—and will need some serious tweaking if you don't:

```
% java -version
java version "1.6.0_02"
Java(TM) SE Runtime Environment (build 1.6.0_02-b06)
Java HotSpot(TM) Client VM (build 1.6.0_02-b06, mixed mode, sharing)
```

You should also be using a real licensed Java distribution (such as those from Sun or Apple); our technical reviewers found that the GNU "workalike" implementation did not run these tools and examples properly at the time of this writing. This GNU environment is the default Java shipped with many Linux distributions. If you're working with a Linux distribution, you may need to download Sun's JDK yourself and make sure it's the version you're invoking (by running *java -version*). Now that Sun has open sourced Java, this will hopefully improve in the future, and we'll get the Sun JRE and JDK by default even in purist distributions. Until that day, you may need to do some of your own downloading.

At the time of this writing, Debian-based distributions allow you to install a Sun JDK using their package management utilities (both 5 and 6 are available in Ubuntu's "Feisty Fawn" and "Gutsy Gibbon" releases). Red Hat–derived distributions still need to download Java directly from Sun Microsystems. Your mileage may vary.

Once you've got all this set up, you should be able to fire up Ant for a test run and verify that everything's right:

```
% ant -version
Apache Ant version 1.7.0 compiled on December 13 2006
```

What just happened?

Well, not much just yet, but you're now in a position where you'll be able to try out the examples we provide later on, and use them as a starting point for your actual Hibernate projects.

If you're new to Ant, it wouldn't be a bad idea to read the manual a little bit to get a sense of how it works and what it can do for you; this will help make sense of the *build.xml* files we start working with in our examples. If you decide (or already know) you like Ant, and want to dig deeper, you can read the manual[†] or pick up O'Reilly's *Ant: The Definitive Guide* (after you finish *this* book, of course)!

What about...

...Eclipse[‡], JBuilder[§], NetBeans[||], or some other Java IDE? Well, you can certainly use these, but you're on your own as far as what you need to do to get Ant integrated into the build process. (Several already use Ant, so you might be starting out ahead; for the others, you might have to jump through some hoops.) If all else fails, you can use the IDE to develop your own code but invoke Ant from the command line when you need to use one of our build scripts.

> If you are using Maven, you can generate Eclipse IDE project files by executing *mvn eclipse:eclipse* from any chapter's example directory, or in the top-level *examples* directory. If you run *mvn eclipse:eclipse* from the *examples* directory, Maven will generate an Eclipse project for each chapter's example set. In Chapter 12 you will find a more detailed recipe for building the examples in Maven, and Chapter 11 is an introduction to using Hibernate's Eclipse Tools more thoroughly.

Getting the Maven Tasks for Ant

Wait—didn't I just finish telling you that we're using Ant for the example projects in this book? I did. But that wasn't the whole story. Although Ant remains the foundation for the examples in this book, we've decided in this second version also to leverage Maven's excellent dependency management features via the Maven Tasks for Ant. The initial version of this book spent precious pages providing instructions for downloading and arranging a whole host of third-party libraries: everything from Jakarta Commons Lang to CGLIB. (And from your perspective, it meant you had to spend many precious

---

[†] *http://ant.apache.org/manual/*

[‡] *http://www.eclipse.org/*

[§] *http://www.borland.com/jbuilder/*

[||] *http://www.netbeans.org/*

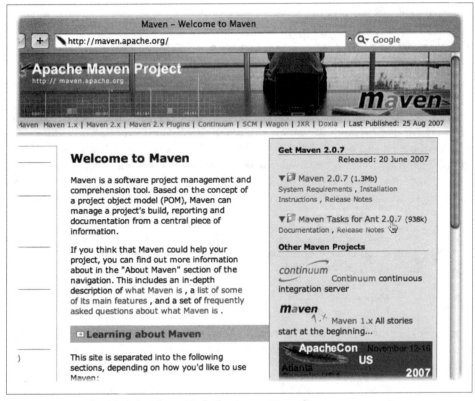

Figure 1-1. Download link for Maven Tasks for Ant on Maven site

minutes carefully and tediously following those instructions.) In this version, we're declaring our project's dependencies in our *build.xml* file and letting Maven take care of downloading and managing our dependencies. This saves a ton of steps and time. Now it's time to install the Maven Tasks for Ant.

How do I do that?

There are two ways to integrate the Maven Tasks for Ant: the first is to drop the required JAR in Ant's *lib* directory, and the second is to include the antlib via a `typedef` declaration in an Ant build file. We're going to use the former method, and drop the *maven-ant-tasks-2.0.8.jar* into Ant's *lib* directory because it requires the least amount of work in our example's *build.xml* file, and makes it easier to share between multiple projects. We'll get to creating *build.xml* later. First, let's download the necessary JAR file from the Maven web site[#]. On the front page you should see a link to download Maven Tasks for Ant (see Figure 1-1).

[#] *http://maven.apache.org/*

At the time of this writing, the Maven Tasks for Ant are at version 2.0.8. Clicking on the Maven Tasks for Ant 2.0.8 link and choosing a mirror will download a JAR file named *maven-ant-tasks-2.0.8.jar*. Save this file to a local directory.

Installing the Maven Tasks for Ant

Next, copy the *maven-ant-tasks-2.0.8.jar* file that you just downloaded to your *ANT_HOME/lib* directory. If you are following this chapter from start to finish, you just downloaded and installed Ant. You also should have set the environment variable ANT_HOME, and you should be familiar with where you just installed Ant. Once you've copied the *maven-ant-tasks-2.0.8.jar* to your *ANT_HOME/lib* directory, any *build.xml* file can include the appropriate namespace to use the Maven Tasks for Ant.

 If you are running these examples on a multiuser development machine, and you don't have administrative rights to put a JAR file into the *ANT_HOME/lib* directory, don't worry. You can put the *maven-ant-tasks-2.0.8.jar* file in the *~/.ant/lib* directory. Ant will also automatically look for any JAR files in this directory.

Once you've copied the *maven-ant-tasks-2.0.8.jar* to your *ANT_HOME/lib* directory, you should be able to run the following command to see if *maven-ant-tasks-2.0.8.jar* is included in the class path on Unix:

```
% ant -diagnostics | grep maven | grep bytes
maven-ant-tasks-2.0.8.jar (960232 bytes)
```

In Windows, run *ant -diagnostics* and inspect the output for the presence of *maven-ant-tasks-2.0.8.jar* in the list of libraries on the class path.

Using the HSQLDB Database Engine

Hibernate works with a great many relational databases; chances are, it will work with the one you are planning to use for your next project. We need to pick one to focus on in our examples, and luckily there's an obvious choice. The free, open source, 100% Java HSQLDB project is powerful enough that it forms the backing storage for several of our commercial software projects. Surprisingly, it's also incredibly self-contained and simple to install—so easy, in fact, that we can let Maven take care of it for us in this new version of the book—so it's perfect to discuss here. (If you've heard of Hypersonic-SQL, this is its current incarnation. Much of the Hibernate documentation uses the older name.)

Don't panic if you stumble across *http://hsql.sourceforge.net/* and it seems like the project has been shut down. That's the wrong address; it's talking about the predecessor to the current HSQLDB project. Figure 1-2 shows the correct home page of the current, quite lively project.

Why do I care?

Examples based on a database that everyone can download and easily experiment with mean you won't have to translate any of our SQL dialects or operating system commands to work with your available databases (and may even mean you can save a day or two learning how to download, install, and configure one of the more typical database environments). Finally, if HSQLDB is new to you, chances are good you'll be impressed and intrigued, and you may well end up using it in your own projects. As it says on the project home page:

> HSQLDB is the leading SQL relational database engine written in Java. It has a JDBC driver and supports a rich subset of ANSI-92 SQL (BNF tree format) plus SQL 99 and 2003 enhancements. It offers a small (less than 100 k in one version for applets), fast database engine which offers both in-memory and disk-based tables and supports embedded and server modes. Additionally, it includes tools such as a minimal web server, in-memory query and management tools (can be run as applets), and a number of demonstration examples.

How do I do that?

When you build the examples in this book, the Maven Ant Tasks will automatically download the HSQLDB JARs (and any other JARs you need) from the Maven repository at *http://repo1.maven.org/maven2/*. So if you want to just get right to playing, you can skip ahead to "Setting Up a Project Hierarchy." On the other hand, if you would like to download HSQLDB for your own purposes or to explore the documentation, online forum, or mailing list archives, visit the project page at *http://hsqldb.org/*. Click the link to manually download the "latest stable version" (which is 1.8.0.7 at the time of this writing, as highlighted in Figure 1-2). This will take you to a typical SourceForge downloads page with the current release selected. Pick your mirror and download the ZIP archive.

What about...

Go on, download HSQLDB. Heck, take two, they're small!

...some other common database? Don't worry, Hibernate can work with MySQL, PostgreSQL, Oracle, DB2, Sybase, Informix, Apache Derby, and others. (We'll talk about how you specify "dialects" for different databases later on, in Chapter 10 and Appendix C.) And, if you really want, you can try to figure out how to work with your favorite from the start, but it will mean extra work for you in following along with the examples, and you'll miss out on a great opportunity to discover HSQLDB.

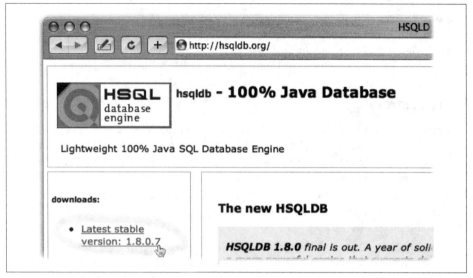

Figure 1-2. Latest stable version link on the HSQLDB home page

Using Hibernate Core

This section doesn't need much motivation! You picked up this book because you wanted to learn how to use Hibernate. The part that provides core object/relational mapping services for your applications is called, perhaps not too surprisingly, *Hibernate Core*. When you build the examples in this book, Hibernate and all of its dependencies are downloaded automatically. Even though this new version of the book's examples take care of getting Hibernate through the Maven Ant Tasks, you might want to download the latest Hibernate distribution yourself to explore the source, or just view the online documentation, forum, and other support materials. If you're ready to dive in to trying things out instead, you can skip to the next section, "Setting Up a Project Hierarchy."

How do I do that?

Start at the Hibernate home page at *http://hibernate.org/* and explore from there. To get a complete copy of the distribution, find the Download link, which is on the left side as shown in Figure 1-3.

The Binary Releases section will tell you which version of Hibernate Core is recommended for downloading; follow that advice. (If you want to be brave, you can try a Development release, but the safest bet is to stick with the latest Production version.) Once you've made your choice, click the Download link in the corresponding row (see Figure 1-4).

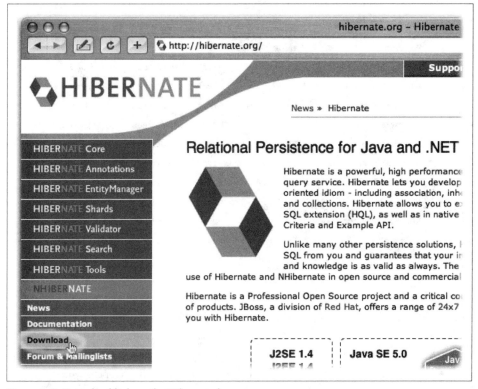

Figure 1-3. Download link on the Hibernate home page

This takes you to a SourceForge downloads page containing your chosen release, in a choice of archive formats. Pick your favorite and download it. The filename will look something like *hibernate-3.x.y.tar.gz* or *hibernate-3.x.y.zip*. (At the time of this writing, the filenames start with *hibernate-3.2.5.ga*, since the first generally available release of Hibernate 3.2.5 is the current production release.)

Pick a place that is suitable for keeping such items and expand the archive.

While you're on the Hibernate downloads page, you may also want to look at the Hibernate Tools (the Download link takes you to a page titled JBoss Tools, but you can still find the Hibernate Tools there). They offer several useful capabilities that aren't necessary for an application running Hibernate but are very helpful for developers creating such applications. We'll be using one to generate Java code for our first Hibernate experiment shortly. The Tools filename will look like *hibernatetools-3.x.y.zip* (it won't necessarily have the same version as Hibernate itself and seems usually to be available only as a beta; the Compatibility Matrix right below the Binary Releases section of Hibernate's downloads page displays a table showing which Hibernate pieces are compatible with each other).

Binary Releases

Package	Version	Release date	Category	
Hibernate Core	3.2.5.ga	31.07.2007	Production	*Download*
Hibernate Annotations	3.3.0 GA	20.03.2007	Production	*Download*
Hibernate EntityManager	3.3.1 GA	29.03.2007	Production	*Download*
Hibernate Validator	3.0.0 GA	20.03.2007	Production	*Download*
Hibernate Search	3.0.0 Beta4	1.08.2007	Development	*Download*
Hibernate Shards	3.0.0 Beta2	02.08.2007	Development	*Download*
Hibernate Tools	3.2.0 Beta9	13.01.2007	Development	*Download*
NHibernate	1.2.0.GA	03.05.2007	Production	*Download*
NHibernate Extensions	1.0.4	24.01.2007	Production	*Download*
JBoss Seam	1.2.0 Patch1	28.02.2007	Production	*Download*

Browse all Hibernate downloads, Browse all NHibernate downloads

Figure 1-4. Hibernate binary releases

Once again, download this file and expand it next to where you put Hibernate.

> If you have trouble with the download links, the site may be in a state of flux, and you may not see the files you expect. If that happens, you can fall back to clicking the "Browse all Hibernate downloads" link below the Binary Releases box and scroll through until you find what you're looking for. The project is so active that this happens more often than you might expect.

Setting Up a Project Hierarchy

Although we're going to start small in this walk-through, once we begin designing data structures and building Java classes and database tables that represent them, along with all the configuration and control files to glue them together and make useful things happen, we're going to end up with a lot of files. So, we want to make certain we are very organized from the beginning. Between the tools we've downloaded and their supporting libraries, there are already a significant number of files to organize. Luckily for us, the Maven Ant Tasks download and manage all of our external dependencies.

Why do I care?

If you end up building something cool by extending the examples in this book, and want to turn it into a real application, you'll be in good shape from the beginning. More to the point, if you set things up the way we describe here, the commands and instructions we give you throughout the examples will make sense and actually work; many examples build on one another throughout the book, so it's important to get on the right track from the beginning.

If you want to skip ahead to a later example, or just avoid typing some of the longer sample code and configuration files, you can download "finished" versions of the chapter examples from the book's web site[*]. These downloads will all be organized as described here. We strongly recommend that you download the examples and use them as a reference while you read this book.

How do I do that?

Here's how to set up an empty project hierarchy if you're not downloading the "finished" examples:

1. Pick a location on your hard drive where you want to work through these examples, and create a new folder, which we'll refer to from now on as your *project directory*.
2. Move into that directory, and create subdirectories called *src* and *data*. The hierarchy of Java source and related resources will be in the *src* directory. Our build process will compile it into a *classes* directory it creates, as well as copy any runtime resources there. The *data* directory is where we'll put the HSQLDB database.
3. The example classes we're going to create are all going to live in the `com.oreilly.hh` (harnessing Hibernate) package, and we'll have Hibernate generate our data beans in the `com.oreilly.hh.data` package to keep them separate from classes we write by hand, so create these directories under the *src* directory. On Linux and Mac OS X, you can use:

    ```
    mkdir -p src/com/oreilly/hh/data
    ```

    from within your project directory to accomplish this in one step.

At this point, your project directory should be structured as shown in Figure 1-5.

A quick test

> This is so much simpler than it was in the first book that it's almost not worth showing!

Before we get into actually rousing Hibernate to do some useful work, it's worth checking that the other supporting pieces are in place and ready to use. Let's start the Ant configuration file we'll be using throughout this project, tell Ant where we've put the files we're using, and have it fire up the HSQLDB graphical database interface. This will prove that the Maven Ant Tasks are able to find and download the libraries on which the examples will rely, and the ability to access the interface will be useful later when we want to look at the actual data that

---

[*] *http://www.oreilly.com/catalog/9780596517724/*

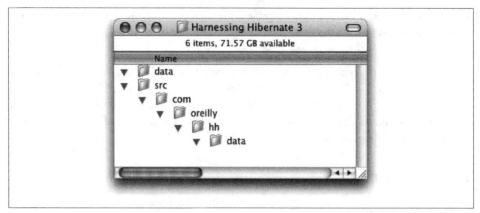

Figure 1-5. Initial project directory contents

Hibernate has been creating for us. For the moment this is primarily a sanity check that nothing is amiss and we're ready to move forward.

Fire up your favorite text editor, and create a file named *build.xml* at the top level inside your project directory. Type the content of Example 1-1 into the file.

Example 1-1. Ant build file

```
<?xml version="1.0"?> ❶
<project name="Harnessing Hibernate 3 (Developer's Notebook Second Edition)"
        default="db" basedir="."
        xmlns:artifact="antlib:org.apache.maven.artifact.ant"> ❷

    <!-- Set up properties containing important project directories --> ❸
    <property name="source.root" value="src"/>
    <property name="class.root" value="classes"/>
    <property name="data.dir" value="data"/>

    <artifact:dependencies pathId="dependency.classpath"> ❹
      <dependency groupId="hsqldb" artifactId="hsqldb" version="1.8.0.7"/>
      <dependency groupId="org.hibernate" artifactId="hibernate"
                version="3.2.5.ga">
        <exclusion groupId="javax.transaction" artifactId="jta"/>
      </dependency>
      <dependency groupId="org.hibernate" artifactId="hibernate-tools"
                version="3.2.0.beta9a"/>
      <dependency groupId="org.apache.geronimo.specs"
                artifactId="geronimo-jta_1.1_spec" version="1.1"/>
      <dependency groupId="log4j" artifactId="log4j" version="1.2.14"/>
    </artifact:dependencies>

    <!-- Set up the class path for compilation and execution -->
    <path id="project.class.path"> ❺
        <!-- Include our own classes, of course -->
        <pathelement location="${class.root}" /> ❻
        <!-- Add the dependencies classpath -->
        <path refid="dependency.classpath"/> ❼
    </path>
```

```
        <target name="db" description="Runs HSQLDB database management UI
    against the database file--use when application is not running"> ❽
            <java classname="org.hsqldb.util.DatabaseManager"
                  fork="yes">
                <classpath refid="project.class.path"/>
                <arg value="-driver"/>
                <arg value="org.hsqldb.jdbcDriver"/>
                <arg value="-url"/>
                <arg value="jdbc:hsqldb:${data.dir}/music"/>
                <arg value="-user"/>
                <arg value="sa"/>
            </java>
        </target>
    </project>
```

> Take care with punctuation if you're typing this, and pay special atten-
> tion to self-closing XML tags (those which end in "/>" rather than just
> ">"). If you get it wrong, you'll be rewarded with parse errors when you
> run Ant. Again, you can download all these files if you don't need the
> typing practice. If you're viewing this as a PDF on-screen, you can also
> cut and paste the code, but you will need to edit out the numbered
> callout bullets.

If you haven't seen an Ant build file before, here's a whirlwind introduction to help orient you. The documentation at *http://ant.apache.org/manual/index.html* is quite good if you want a bit more detail:

❶   The first line is simply a declaration that the type of the file is XML. If you've worked with XML in other contexts, you're used to seeing this. If not, you'll see it again. (Ant doesn't currently require this, but most XML parsers do, so it's a good habit to develop.)

❷   Ant's build files always contain a single **project** definition. The **default** attribute tells Ant which *target* (defined later) to build if you don't specify any on the command line. And the **basedir** attribute determines the directory relative to which all path calculations are done. We could have left this out since the default is to treat paths as being relative to the directory in which the *build.xml* is located, but it's a good habit to be explicit about fundamental settings like this. An important thing to note in this **project** element is the **xmlns:artifact** namespace definition for the Maven Ant Tasks. This namespace definition makes the Maven Ant Tasks available within this build file using the **artifact:** prefix (as you'll see used later).

❸   The next bit defines three *properties* that we can use by name throughout the rest of the build file. Essentially, we're defining symbolic names for the important directories used for different aspects of the project. This isn't necessary (especially when the directories are named so simply), but it's another good practice. For one thing, it means that if you need to change where one of these directories is located, you need to fix only one place in the build file, rather than conducting a tedious search and replace.

❹ The `artifact:dependencies` element is from the Maven Ant Tasks, which you (and Ant) can tell by the `artifact:` prefix. In this element we are defining a set of dependencies which the project needs for compilation and execution. These dependencies correspond to JAR files (or artifacts) in the central Maven 2 Repository at *http://repo1.maven.org/maven2*. Each artifact is uniquely identified by a `groupId`, `artifactId`, and a `version` number. In this project, we're depending on Hibernate, HSQLDB, Log4J, and the JTA API. When the Maven Ant Tasks encounter these dependency declarations, each artifact is downloaded from the central Maven 2 repository on an as-needed basis to your local Maven 2 repository (in *~/.m2/repository*). Don't worry if this section doesn't make much sense just yet; we're going to delve deeper into the details in a few pages.

This section is where you'd make changes to use a more recent version of one of these packages if you wanted to (since newer versions will likely become available after this book is printed), by changing the `version` values. But you can be confident the examples as printed in the book will continue to work, since the Maven repository guarantees the versions we tested against will continue to be available whenever you're exploring the examples. This in itself was a big reason we decided to adopt the Maven Ant Tasks for this book.

❺ The `class-path` section serves a clear purpose. This feature alone is why I almost never start Java projects anymore without setting up at least a simple Ant build for them. When you're using a lot of third-party libraries, which you're going to be doing for any serious project, there's a whole lot that needs to go into your class path, and you have to be sure to set it equivalently at compile time and runtime. Ant makes this very easy. We define a *path*, which is kind of like a property, but it knows how to parse and collect files and directories. Our path contains the *classes* directory in which we're going to be compiling our Java source (this directory doesn't exist yet; we'll add a step to the build process to create it in the next chapter), and it also contains all JAR files corresponding to the dependencies listed in the `artifact:dependencies` element. This is exactly what we need for compiling and running.

 Ant's understanding and manipulation of Java paths and class hierarchies is a big plus. It's worth learning in some depth.

❻ The syntax on this line looks like punctuation soup but can be broken down into pieces that make sense. Ant lets you use *substitution* to insert variable values into your rules. Where you see something like `"${class.root}"`, this means "look up the value of the property named `class.root` and stick it here." So, given the definition of the `class.root` property earlier, it's as if we had typed: `<pathelement location="classes"/>`. So, why do this? It lets you share a value throughout the file, so if you ever need to change it, there's only one place to worry about. In large, complex projects, this kind of organization and management is crucial.

❼ The `artifact:dependencies` element we saw earlier assembled all of the declared dependencies into a single path named `dependency.classpath` using its `pathId` attribute. Here, we are appending the contents of `dependency.classpath` to the `project.class.path` so all our Maven-fetched dependencies are available at compilation and runtime.

❽ Finally, with all this preamble out of the way, we can define our first *target*. A target is just a series of *tasks* that need to be executed in order to accomplish a project goal. Typical targets do things like compile code, run tests, package things up for distribution, and the like. Tasks are chosen from a rich set of capabilities built into Ant, and third-party tools like Hibernate can extend Ant to provide their own useful tasks, as we'll see in the next chapter. Our first target, **db**, is going to run HSQLDB's graphical interface so we can look at our example database. We can accomplish that using Ant's built-in `java` task, which can run a Java virtual machine for us, with whatever starting class, arguments, and properties we'd like.

In this case, the class we want to invoke is `org.hsqldb.util.DatabaseManager`, found in the HSQLDB JAR that the Maven Ant Tasks will manage for us. Setting the `fork` attribute to `yes` tells Ant to use a separate virtual machine, which isn't the default since it takes a little longer and isn't usually necessary. In this case, it's important since we want the database manager GUI to stay around until we dismiss it, and this doesn't happen when it runs in Ant's own VM.

 If your database GUI pops up and vanishes, double-check the `fork` attribute of your `java` task.

You can see how we're telling the `java` task about the class path we've set up; this will be a common feature of our targets. Then we supply a bunch of arguments to the database manager, telling it to use the normal HSQLDB JDBC driver, where to find the database, and what username to use. We've specified a database called *music* in the *data* directory. That directory is currently empty, so HSQLDB will create the database the first time we use it. The user **sa** is the default "system administrator" user for new databases, and it's configured not to need a password initially. Obviously, if you plan to make this database available over the network (which HSQLDB is capable of doing), you'll want to set a password. We aren't doing any such fancy things, so we can leave that out for now.

OK, let's try it! Save the file, and from a shell (command) prompt running in your top-level project directory (where you put *build.xml*), type the command:

ant db

(Or, since we've made db the default target, you can just type *ant*.) Once Ant starts running, if all goes well, you'll see output like this:

```
Buildfile: build.xml
Downloading: hsqldb/hsqldb/1.8.0.7/hsqldb-1.8.0.7.pom
Transferring OK
Downloading: org/hibernate/hibernate/3.2.5.ga/hibernate-3.2.5.ga.pom
Transferring 3K
Downloading: net/sf/ehcache/ehcache/1.2.3/ehcache-1.2.3.pom
Transferring 19K
Downloading: commons-logging/commons-logging/1.0.4/commons-logging-1.0.4.pom
Transferring 5K
Downloading: commons-collections/commons-collections/2.1/commons-collections-2.1
.pom
Transferring 3K
Downloading: asm/asm-attrs/1.5.3/asm-attrs-1.5.3.pom
Transferring OK
Downloading: dom4j/dom4j/1.6.1/dom4j-1.6.1.pom
Transferring 6K
Downloading: antlr/antlr/2.7.6/antlr-2.7.6.pom
Transferring OK
Downloading: cglib/cglib/2.1_3/cglib-2.1_3.pom
Transferring OK
Downloading: asm/asm/1.5.3/asm-1.5.3.pom
Transferring OK
Downloading: commons-collections/commons-collections/2.1.1/commons-collections-2
.1.1.pom
Transferring OK
Downloading: org/hibernate/hibernate-tools/3.2.0.beta9a/hibernate-tools-3.2.0.be
ta9a.pom
Transferring 1K
Downloading: org/hibernate/hibernate/3.2.0.cr5/hibernate-3.2.0.cr5.pom
Transferring 3K
Downloading: freemarker/freemarker/2.3.4/freemarker-2.3.4.pom
Transferring OK
Downloading: org/hibernate/jtidy/r8-20060801/jtidy-r8-20060801.pom
Transferring OK
Downloading: org/apache/geronimo/specs/geronimo-jta_1.1_spec/1.1/geronimo-jta_1.
1_spec-1.1.pom
Transferring 1K
Downloading: org/apache/geronimo/specs/specs/1.2/specs-1.2.pom
Transferring 2K
Downloading: org/apache/geronimo/genesis/config/project-config/1.1/project-confi
g-1.1.pom
Transferring 14K
Downloading: org/apache/geronimo/genesis/config/config/1.1/config-1.1.pom
Downloading: org/apache/geronimo/genesis/config/config/1.1/config-1.1.pom
Downloading: org/apache/geronimo/genesis/config/config/1.1/config-1.1.pom
Transferring OK
Downloading: org/apache/geronimo/genesis/genesis/1.1/genesis-1.1.pom
Downloading: org/apache/geronimo/genesis/genesis/1.1/genesis-1.1.pom
Downloading: org/apache/geronimo/genesis/genesis/1.1/genesis-1.1.pom
Transferring 6K
Downloading: org/apache/apache/3/apache-3.pom
```

```
Downloading: org/apache/apache/3/apache-3.pom
Downloading: org/apache/apache/3/apache-3.pom
Transferring 3K
Downloading: log4j/log4j/1.2.14/log4j-1.2.14.pom
Transferring 2K
Downloading: org/hibernate/hibernate-tools/3.2.0.beta9a/hibernate-tools-3.2.0.be
ta9a.jar
Transferring 352K
Downloading: org/hibernate/jtidy/r8-20060801/jtidy-r8-20060801.jar
Transferring 243K
Downloading: commons-collections/commons-collections/2.1.1/commons-collections-2
.1.1.jar
Transferring 171K
Downloading: commons-logging/commons-logging/1.0.4/commons-logging-1.0.4.jar
Transferring 37K
Downloading: antlr/antlr/2.7.6/antlr-2.7.6.jar
Transferring 433K
Downloading: org/apache/geronimo/specs/geronimo-jta_1.1_spec/1.1/geronimo-jta_1.
1_spec-1.1.jar
Transferring 15K
Downloading: net/sf/ehcache/ehcache/1.2.3/ehcache-1.2.3.jar
Transferring 203K
Downloading: asm/asm/1.5.3/asm-1.5.3.jar
Transferring 25K
Downloading: freemarker/freemarker/2.3.4/freemarker-2.3.4.jar
Transferring 770K
Downloading: dom4j/dom4j/1.6.1/dom4j-1.6.1.jar
Transferring 306K
Downloading: asm/asm-attrs/1.5.3/asm-attrs-1.5.3.jar
Transferring 16K
Downloading: cglib/cglib/2.1_3/cglib-2.1_3.jar
Transferring 275K
Downloading: hsqldb/hsqldb/1.8.0.7/hsqldb-1.8.0.7.jar
Transferring 628K
Downloading: log4j/log4j/1.2.14/log4j-1.2.14.jar
Transferring 358K
Downloading: org/hibernate/hibernate/3.2.5.ga/hibernate-3.2.5.ga.jar
Transferring 2202K

db:
```

This big list of downloads shows the Maven Ant Tasks doing their job of finding the pieces we told them we needed (including HSQLDB and Hibernate), along with all the libraries on which they, in turn, depend. This takes a little while to accomplish (depending on how fast your network connection is, and how loaded the servers are), but it will only need to happen once. The next time you fire up Ant, the Maven Ant Tasks will simply notice that your local repository already contains all these pieces, and will silently proceed with whatever else you wanted to accomplish.

Once all the downloading is accomplished, Ant prints db: to indicate that it's starting to execute the target you requested. A moment later, you should see the HSQLDB graphical interface, which will look something like Figure 1-6. There's nothing in our database yet, so there's not much to see beyond whether the command worked at all.

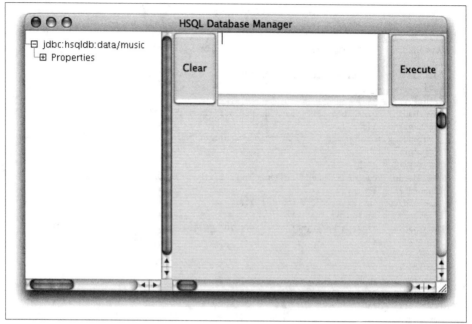

Figure 1-6. HSQLDB database manager interface

The tree view at the top left of the window is where the various tables and columns in our database can be explored. For now, just verify that the top reads *jdbc:hsqldb:data/ music.*

You can explore the menus a bit if you like, but don't make any changes to the database. Once you're done, choose File→Exit. The window will close, and Ant will report:

```
BUILD SUCCESSFUL
Total time: 56 seconds
```

The amount of time you spend playing may vary, of course. (Recall that Ant sticks around until the database shuts down because of the fork attribute we added to the java task.) At this point, if you look in the data directory, you'll find that HSQLDB has created some files to hold the database:

```
% ls data
music.log       music.properties music.script
```

You can even look at the contents of these files. Unlike most database systems, HSQLDB stores its data in a human-readable format by default. The properties file contains some basic settings, and the data itself goes in the script file, in the form of SQL statements. The log file is used to reconstruct a consistent database state if the application crashes or otherwise exits without gracefully closing the database. Right now, all you'll find in these files are the basic definitions that are entered by default, but as we start creating tables and adding data to them, you can view the file again and see the changes appear in it. This can be a useful debugging feature for basic sanity checks, and is even faster than firing up the graphical interface and running queries.

What just happened?

Now that we've successfully run the first example and set up our project's build file, it is probably time to explain how Ant retrieved all of the necessary dependencies for this project. Let's re-examine the `artifact:dependencies` element from the example's *build.xml* file (see Example 1-2).

Example 1-2. Our artifact:dependencies element

```
<artifact:dependencies pathId="dependency.classpath">
  <dependency groupId="hsqldb" artifactId="hsqldb" version="1.8.0.7"/>
  <dependency groupId="org.hibernate" artifactId="hibernate"
              version="3.2.5.ga">
    <exclusion groupId="javax.transaction" artifactId="jta"/>
  </dependency>
  <dependency groupId="org.hibernate" artifactId="hibernate-tools"
              version="3.2.0.beta9a"/>
  <dependency groupId="org.apache.geronimo.specs"
              artifactId="geronimo-jta_1.1_spec" version="1.1"/>
  <dependency groupId="log4j" artifactId="log4j" version="1.2.14"/>
</artifact:dependencies>
```

If you've never used Maven before, this probably looks very confusing. Let's start by defining some terminology. First there is an *artifact*. An artifact is a file that is produced by a project. An artifact can be any *type*—a WAR for a web application, an EAR for an enterprise application, or a JAR. For our purposes we are depending on JAR artifacts, and the default type if you don't specify it in the dependency element is `jar`, conveniently enough.

A specific artifact is identified by four attributes: `groupId`, `artifactId`, `version`, and `type`. For example, we are depending on version `3.2.5.ga` of the `hibernate` artifact in group `org.hibernate` and the implied type is `jar`. Maven will use these identifiers to locate the appropriate dependency in the central Maven 2 repository which is hosted at *http://repo1.maven.org/maven2/*. Using these values, Maven will attempt to locate the JAR for hibernate using the following pattern: *<repositoryUrl>/<groupId>/ <artifactId>/<version>/<artifactId>-<version>.<type>*, where periods in the `groupId` are converted to path separators for the URLs that, using this pattern, would be used to locate the JARs for the Hibernate and HSQLDB dependencies. See Example 1-3.

Example 1-3. URLs for project dependencies

```
http://repo1.maven.org/org/hibernate/hibernate/3.2.5.ga/hibernate-3.2.5.ga.jar
http://repo1.maven.org/hsqldb/hsqldb/1.8.0.7/hsqldb-1.8.0.7.jar
```

In our *build.xml* file, we are excluding the JTA dependency from the Hibernate dependency declaration. This is necessary because the Hibernate library depends on a nonfree JAR artifact not available on the public Maven 2 repository. Instead of using the standard Sun-supplied JTA API JAR, this project depends on a version of the JTA API created by the Apache Geronimo project. `geronimo-jta_1.1_spec` is a free, open source implementation of the Java Transaction API. This substitution is accomplished using the `exclusion` element within the dependency for Hibernate 3.2.5.ga, combined with the explicit dependency on the Geronimo JTA spec 1.1 later on.

All right, so we have some insight into how the Maven Ant Tasks retrieve the dependencies from the Maven repository, but where do they go once they've been downloaded? The Maven Ant Tasks download all dependencies to a local Maven repository. Maven maintains a local repository with a structure that mirrors the remote repository. When it needs to check for an artifact, it checks the local repository first before it requests the artifact from the remote repository. This means that if twenty projects all reference the same version of Hibernate, it is only downloaded from the remote repository once, and all twenty projects will refer to a single copy stored in the local Maven repository. So where is this magical local Maven repository? The easiest way to answer this question is to add a target to our *build.xml* file. Add the following target to the end of the Ant *build.xml* from earlier in the chapter, as shown in Example 1-4.

Example 1-4. Printing the dependency class path

```
<target name="print-classpath" description="Show the dependency class path">
  <property name="class.path" refid="dependency.classpath"/>
  <echo>${class.path}</echo>
</target>
```

Running this target will produce the following output results:

```
% ant print-classpath
Buildfile: build.xml

print-classpath:
    [echo] ~\.m2\repository\commons-logging\commons-logging\1.0.4\commons-logging-
1.0.4.jar;\
~\.m2\repository\dom4j\dom4j\1.6.1\dom4j-1.6.1.jar;\
~\.m2\repository\cglib\cglib\2.1_3\cglib-2.1_3.jar;\...
```

Try running this target. The output will vary depending on which operating system you are using, but you'll notice that the dependency class path refers to your local Maven repository. On a Windows XP machine this will likely be in *C:\Documents and Settings \Username\.m2\repository*; on Windows Vista this will likely be in *C:\Users\Username\.m2 \repository*; and on Unix and Macintosh this will be the *~/.m2/repository* directory.

You will also notice that there are more dependencies listed in the class path than were declared in the `artifact:dependencies` element in *build.xml*. These extra dependencies are called *transitive dependencies*, and they are dependencies of your explicitly declared dependencies. For example, Hibernate depends upon CGLib, EHCache, and Commons Collections, among other things. Although it is outside the scope of this book,

I'll give you a hint as to how the Maven Ant Tasks figure out the full set of dependencies for your project. If you explore your local repository after you've built one of the examples, you will notice that next to every JAR artifact sits a file with the extension *.pom*. *Project Object Model* files (or POMs) are the foundation of the Maven build system and repository. Each POM describes an artifact and that artifact's dependencies. The Maven Ant Tasks use this metadata to construct a tree of transitive dependencies. In other words, the Maven Ant Tasks don't just take care of downloading Hibernate, they download everything that Hibernate depends upon.

All you really need to know is that it works.

What's next?

Thanks to the Maven Ant Tasks, you had far fewer hoops to jump through to find, download, expand, and organize software than did readers of the previous version of this book. You're in a great position to start working with Hibernate and, as you'll see in the next chapter, we'll be moving very quickly. You'll be able to see Java code written for you! Database schemas created out of thin air (or, at least, out of the same XML mapping table that produced the Java)! Real tables and data appearing in the HSQLDB manager interface! (Or, at least, genuine faux sample data....)

Sound exciting? Well, compared to what you've done so far anyway? Then let's dig in to awakening the power of Hibernate.

Why didn't it work?

If, on the other hand, you saw no database manager window appear, and instead were greeted by error messages, try to figure out if they're due to problems in the build file, differences in the way you've set up Ant or your project hierarchy, difficulty accessing the Internet to download dependencies from the Maven repository, or something else. Double-check that all the pieces are arranged and installed as shown earlier, and consider downloading the sample code if you are having trouble with a version you typed in yourself.

CHAPTER 2

Introduction to Mapping

Now that we're in a position to work with Hibernate, it's worth pausing to reflect on the big picture, lest we remain lost in the reeds of installation and configuration. Object-oriented languages such as Java provide a powerful and convenient abstraction for working with information at runtime in the form of objects that instantiate classes. These objects can link up with each other in myriad ways and can embody rules and behavior as well as the raw data they represent. But when the program ends, all the objects swiftly and silently vanish away.

For information we need to keep around between runs or share between different programs and systems, relational databases have proven difficult to beat. They're scalable, reliable, efficient, and extremely flexible. So what we need is a means of taking information from a SQL database and turning it into Java objects, and vice versa.

There are many different ways of doing this, ranging from completely manual database design and coding to highly automated tools. The general problem is known as *Object/Relational Mapping*, and Hibernate is a lightweight O/R mapping service for Java.

The "lightweight" label means Hibernate is designed to be fairly simple to learn and use—and to place reasonable demands on system resources—compared to some of the other available tools. Despite this, it manages to be broadly useful and deep. The designers have done a good job of figuring out the kinds of things that real projects need to accomplish and supporting them well.

You can use Hibernate in many different ways, depending on what you're starting with. If you've got a database with which you need to interact, there are tools that can analyze the existing schema as a starting point for your mapping and help you write the Java classes to represent the data. If you've got classes that you want to store in a new database, you can start with the classes, get help building a mapping document, and generate an initial database schema.

In this book, we're going to show how you can start a brand-new project, with no existing classes or data, and have Hibernate help you build both. When starting from scratch like this, the most convenient place to begin is in the middle, with an abstract definition of the mapping we're going to make between program objects and the database tables that will store them. See Appendix E for some pointers about how to explore other approaches, and Chapter 11 if you'd like to use Hibernate with Eclipse.

People who are more used to working with Java objects than abstract schema representations may have a little trouble with this approach until they're used to it, and sometimes you just don't want to bother with an external XML file. Chapter 7 shows how to use Java 5 annotations to embed mapping information right inside your data model classes. It's important to get a handle on XML based mapping, though, so that is what we're starting with.

In our examples, we're going to be working with a database that could power an interface to a large personal collection of music, allowing users to search, browse, and listen in a natural way. (You might well have guessed this from the names of the database files that were created at the end of the first chapter.)

Writing a Mapping Document

Hibernate traditionally uses an XML document to track the mapping between Java classes and relational database tables. This *mapping document* is designed to be readable and hand-editable. You can also start by using graphical Computer Aided Software Engineering (CASE) tools (like Together[*], Rose[†], or Poseidon[‡]) to build UML diagrams representing your data model and feed these into AndroMDA[§], turning them into Hibernate mappings. The Hibernate Tools package mentioned earlier also gives you several of these capabilities (and Chapter 11 shows how easy some of them are to use in Eclipse).

Bear in mind that Hibernate and its extensions let you work in other ways, starting with classes or data if you've got them. We'll look at one of the newer approaches, *Hibernate Annotations*, which lets you do away with the XML mapping document entirely, in Chapter 7.

Here, we'll write an XML document by hand, showing it's quite practical. Let's start by creating a mapping for *tracks*, pieces of music that can be listened to individually, or as part of an album or playlist. To begin with, we'll keep track of the track's title, the path to the file containing the actual music, its playing time, the date on which it was added to the database, and the volume at which it should be played (in case the default volume isn't appropriate because it was recorded at a very different level than other music in the database).

---

[*] *http://www.borland.com/us/products/together/index.html*

[†] *http://www-306.ibm.com/software/awdtools/developer/technical/*

[‡] *http://gentleware.com/index.php*

[§] *http://www.andromda.org/*

Why do I care?

You might not have any need for a new system to keep track of your music, but the concepts and process involved in setting up this mapping will translate to the projects you actually want to tackle.

How do I do that?

Fire up your favorite text editor, and create the file *Track.hbm.xml* in the *src/com/oreilly/hh/data* directory you created in "Setting Up a Project Hierarchy." (If you skipped that section, you'll need to go back and follow it, because this example relies on the project structure and tools we set up there.) Type in the mapping document shown in Example 2-1.

> You may be thinking there's a lot of dense information in this file. That's true, and as you'll see, it can be used to create a bunch of useful project resources.

Example 2-1. The mapping document for tracks, Track.hbm.xml

```
<?xml version="1.0"?>
<!DOCTYPE hibernate-mapping PUBLIC "-//Hibernate/Hibernate Mapping DTD 3.0//EN"
          "http://hibernate.sourceforge.net/hibernate-mapping-3.0.dtd"> ❶

<hibernate-mapping>

  <class name="com.oreilly.hh.data.Track" table="TRACK"> ❷
    <meta attribute="class-description"> ❸
      Represents a single playable track in the music database.
      @author Jim Elliott (with help from Hibernate)
    </meta>

    <id name="id" type="int" column="TRACK_ID"> ❹
      <meta attribute="scope-set">protected</meta>
      <generator class="native"/> ❺
    </id>

    <property name="title" type="string" not-null="true"/> ❻

    <property name="filePath" type="string" not-null="true"/>

    <property name="playTime" type="time"> ❼
      <meta attribute="field-description">Playing time</meta>
    </property>

    <property name="added" type="date">
      <meta attribute="field-description">When the track was created</meta>
    </property>

    <property name="volume" type="short" not-null="true">
      <meta attribute="field-description">How loud to play the track</meta>
    </property>

  </class>
</hibernate-mapping>
```

❶ The first three lines are a required preamble to make this a valid XML document and announce that it conforms to the document type definition used by Hibernate for mappings. The actual mappings are inside the `hibernate-mapping` tag.

❷ We're defining a mapping for a single class, `com.oreilly.hh.data.Track`, and the name and package of this class are related to the name and location of the file we've created. This relationship isn't necessary; you can define mappings for any number of classes in a single mapping document and name it anything and place in any location you want, as long as you tell Hibernate how to find it. The advantage of following the convention of naming the mapping file after the class it maps, and placing it in the same place on the class path as that class, is that this allows Hibernate to automatically locate the mapping when you want to work with the class. This simplifies the configuration and use of Hibernate for a small number of classes.

 If you'll be working with a lot of classes, you probably want to use an XML-format configuration file for Hibernate, and reference all of the mapping documents from within it, rather than having to mention them all in example source code as we did in the first book—you'll see us switch to this approach starting with the next chapter. Also, when using XML-based configuration, it may make more sense to keep your mapping documents next to the Hibernate configuration file, rather than floating alongside the mapped classes.

In the opening of the `class` element, we have also specified that this class is stored in a database table named `TRACK`.

❸ This `meta` tag doesn't directly affect the mapping. Instead, it provides additional information that can be used by different tools. In this case, by specifying an attribute value of `class-description`, we are telling the Java code-generation tool what JavaDoc text we want associated with the `Track` class. This is entirely optional, and you'll see the result of including it in "Generating Some Class" later in this chapter.

❹ The remainder of the mapping sets up the pieces of information we want to keep track of, as properties in the class and their associated columns in the database table. Even though we didn't mention it in the introduction to this example, each track is going to need an *id*. Following database best practices, we'll use a meaningless surrogate key (a value with no semantic meaning, serving only to identify a specific database row). In Hibernate, the key/id mapping is set up using an `id` tag. We're choosing to use an `int` to store our `id` in the column `Track_id`. It contains another `meta` tag to communicate with the Java code generator, telling it that the `set` method for the `id` property should be protected; there's no need for application code to go changing track IDs.

❺ The `generator` tag determines how Hibernate creates `id` values for new instances. (Note that this tag relates to normal Object/Relational mapping operation, not to the Java code generator, which is often not even used; `generator` is more fundamental than the optional `meta` tags.) There are a number of different ID generation strategies to choose from, and you can even write your own. In this case, we're telling Hibernate to use whatever is most natural for the underlying database (we'll see later on how it learns what database we're using). In the case of HSQLDB, an identity column is used.

❻ After the ID, we just enumerate the various track properties we care about. The `title` is a string and cannot be `null`. The `filePath` has the same characteristics, while the remaining properties other than `volume` are allowed to be `null`.

❼ `playTime` is a time, `added` is a date, and `volume` is a `short`. These last three properties use a new kind of `meta` attribute, `field-description`, which specifies JavaDoc text for the individual properties, with some limitations in the current code generator.

So this mapping file contains a rigorous and compact specification of the data we want to use to represent a track of music, in a format with which Hibernate can work. Now let's see what Hibernate can actually do with it. (Hibernate can represent much more complex kinds of information, including relationships between objects, which we'll cover in upcoming chapters. Appendix E discusses ways you can learn even more than we can fit in the book.)

Generating Some Class

Our mapping contains information about both the database and the Java class between which it maps. We can use it to help us create both. Let's look at the class first.

How do I do that?

The Hibernate Tools you installed in Chapter 1 included a tool that can write Java source matching the specifications in a mapping document, and an Ant task that makes it easy to invoke from within an Ant build file. Edit *build.xml* to add the portions shown in bold in Example 2-2.

Example 2-2. The Ant build file updated for code generation

```
<?xml version="1.0"?>
<project name="Harnessing Hibernate 3 (Developer's Notebook Second Edition)"
        default="db" basedir="."
        xmlns:artifact="antlib:org.apache.maven.artifact.ant">

    <!-- Set up properties containing important project directories -->
    <property name="source.root" value="src"/>
    <property name="class.root" value="classes"/>
    <property name="data.dir" value="data"/>
```

```xml
<artifact:dependencies pathId="dependency.class.path">
  <dependency groupId="hsqldb" artifactId="hsqldb" version="1.8.0.7"/>
  <dependency groupId="org.hibernate" artifactId="hibernate"
              version="3.2.5.ga">
    <exclusion groupId="javax.transaction" artifactId="jta"/>
  </dependency>
  <dependency groupId="org.hibernate" artifactId="hibernate-tools"
              version="3.2.0.beta9a"/>
  <dependency groupId="org.apache.geronimo.specs"
              artifactId="geronimo-jta_1.1_spec" version="1.1"/>
  <dependency groupId="log4j" artifactId="log4j" version="1.2.14"/>
</artifact:dependencies>

<!-- Set up the class path for compilation and execution -->
<path id="project.class.path">
    <!-- Include our own classes, of course -->
    <pathelement location="${class.root}" />
    <!-- Add the dependencies classpath -->
    <path refid="dependency.class.path"/>
</path>

<!-- Teach Ant how to use the Hibernate Tools -->
<taskdef name="hibernatetool" ❶
         classname="org.hibernate.tool.ant.HibernateToolTask"
         classpathref="project.class.path"/>

<target name="db" description="Runs HSQLDB database management UI
against the database file--use when application is not running">
    <java classname="org.hsqldb.util.DatabaseManager"
          fork="yes">
      <classpath refid="project.class.path"/>
      <arg value="-driver"/>
      <arg value="org.hsqldb.jdbcDriver"/>
      <arg value="-url"/>
      <arg value="jdbc:hsqldb:${data.dir}/music"/>
      <arg value="-user"/>
      <arg value="sa"/>
    </java>
</target>

<!-- Generate the java code for all mapping files in our source tree -->
<target name="codegen" ❷
        description="Generate Java source from the O/R mapping files">
  <hibernatetool destdir="${source.root}">
    <configuration>
      <fileset dir="${source.root}">
        <include name="**/*.hbm.xml"/>
      </fileset>
    </configuration>
    <hbm2java/>
  </hibernatetool>
</target>

</project>
```

We added a new `taskdef` (task definition), and `target` to the build file:

❶ The task definition teaches Ant a new trick: it tells it how to use the `hibernate tool` task that is part of the Hibernate Tools, with the help of a class provided for this purpose. Note that it also specifies the class path to be used when invoking this tool, using the `project.class.path` definition which includes all the dependencies that the Maven Ant Tasks have managed for us. This is how the hibernate tools can be found by Ant when they are needed.

❷ The `codegen` target uses the Hibernate Tools `hbm2java` mode to run Hibernate's code generator on any mapping documents found in the *src* tree, writing the corresponding Java source. The pattern `**/*.hbm.xml` means "any file ending in *.hbm.xml*, within the specified directory, or any subdirectory, however deeply nested." Again, we have to tell the tool how to find the mapping files because we're not yet using an XML configuration file to more powerfully configure Hibernate; you'll see this change in the next chapter.

Let's try it! From within your project directory, type the following command:

```
ant codegen
```

You should see output like this (assuming you ran the *ant db* example in the previous chapter, which will have downloaded all the necessary dependencies; if you haven't, there will be a bunch more lines at the beginning as they are fetched):

```
Buildfile: build.xml

codegen:
[hibernatetool] Executing Hibernate Tool with a Standard Configuration
[hibernatetool] 1. task: hbm2java (Generates a set of .java files)
[hibernatetool] log4j:WARN No appenders could be found for logger (org.hibernate
.cfg.Environment).
[hibernatetool] log4j:WARN Please initialize the log4j system properly.

BUILD SUCCESSFUL
Total time: 2 seconds
```

The warnings are griping about the fact that we configured our build to install *log4j* in Chapter 1, but haven't yet taken the trouble to set up the configuration file that it expects. We'll see how to do that in "Cooking Up a Schema." For now, if you look in the directory *src/com/oreilly/hh/data*, you'll see that a new file named *Track.java* has appeared, with content similar to Example 2-3.

Example 2-3. Code generated from the Track mapping document

```
package com.oreilly.hh.data;
// Generated Sep 2, 2007 10:27:53 PM by Hibernate Tools 3.2.0.b9

import java.util.Date;

/**
 *       Represents a single playable track in the music database. ❶
 *       @author Jim Elliott (with help from Hibernate)
```

```
 *
 */
public class Track  implements java.io.Serializable {

    ❷
    private int id;
    private String title;
    private String filePath;
    /**
     * Playing time
     */
    private Date playTime;
    /**
     * When the track was created
     */
    private Date added;
    /**
     * How loud to play the track
     */
    private short volume;

    ❸
    public Track() {
    }

    public Track(String title, String filePath, short volume) {
        this.title = title;
        this.filePath = filePath;
        this.volume = volume;
    }
    public Track(String title, String filePath, Date playTime, Date added, short
volume) {
        this.title = title;
        this.filePath = filePath;
        this.playTime = playTime;
        this.added = added;
        this.volume = volume;
    }

    public int getId() {
        return this.id;
    }

    protected void setId(int id) {  ❹
        this.id = id;
    }
    public String getTitle() {
        return this.title;
    }

    public void setTitle(String title) {
        this.title = title;
    }
    public String getFilePath() {
        return this.filePath;
```

```
        }

        public void setFilePath(String filePath) {
            this.filePath = filePath;
        }
        /**
         *      * Playing time
         */
        public Date getPlayTime() {
            return this.playTime;
        }

        public void setPlayTime(Date playTime) {
            this.playTime = playTime;
        }
        /**
         *      * When the track was created
         */
        public Date getAdded() {
            return this.added;
        }

        public void setAdded(Date added) {
            this.added = added;
        }
        /**
         *      * How loud to play the track
         */
        public short getVolume() {
            return this.volume;
        }

        public void setVolume(short volume) {
            this.volume = volume;
        }

    }
```

How did this work? Ant found all files in our source tree ending in *.hbm.xml* (just one, so far) and fed them to the Hibernate code generator, which analyzed them and wrote a Java class meeting the specifications we provided for the Track mapping. Clearly this can save a lot of time and repetitive work!

You may find it worthwhile to compare the generated Java source with the mapping specification from which it arose (Example 2-1). The source starts out with the proper package declaration, which is easy for hbm2java to figure out from the fully qualified class name required in the mapping file:

> Hibernate can save a lot of time and fairly tedious activity. We were quickly spoiled by it.

❶   The class-level JavaDoc should look familiar, since it comes right from the class-description meta tag in our mapping document.

❷ The field declarations are derived from the `id` and `property` tags defined in the mapping. The Java types used are derived from the property types in the mapping document. To learn the full set of value types supported by Hibernate, look to the resources mentioned in Appendix E. For now, the relationship between the types in the mapping document and the Java types used in the generated code should be fairly clear.

❸ After the field declarations comes a trio of constructors. The first allows instantiation without any arguments (this is required if you want the class to be usable as a bean, such as on a Java Server Page, a very common use for data classes like this); the second fills in just the values we've indicated must not be `null`; and the last establishes values for all properties. Notice that none of the constructors set the value of `id`; this is the responsibility of Hibernate when we get the object out of the database, or insert it for the first time.

❹ Consistent with that, the `setId()` method is protected, as requested in our `id` mapping. The rest of the getters and setters are not surprising; this is all pretty much boilerplate code (which we've all written too many times), which is why it's so nice to be able to have the Hibernate tools generate it for us.

> If you want to use Hibernate's generated code as a starting point and then add some business logic or other features to the generated class, be aware that all your changes will be silently discarded the next time you run the code generator. In such a project, you will want to be sure the hand-tweaked classes are not regenerated by any Ant build target. One technique people use is to have their hand-tooled classes extend the Hibernate-generated ones. This fact is one of the reasons we have segregated our mapped classes into their own `data` package and subdirectory.

Even though we're having Hibernate generate our data classes in this example, it's important to point out that the getters and setters it creates are more than a nice touch. You need to put these in your persistent classes for any properties you want to persist, since Hibernate's fundamental persistence architecture is based on reflective access to JavaBeans–style properties. They don't need to be `public` if you don't want them to be —Hibernate has ways of getting at even properties declared `protected` or `private`—but they do need accessor methods. Think of it as enforcing good object design; the Hibernate team wants to keep the implementation details of actual instance variables cleanly separated from the persistence mechanism.

Cooking Up a Schema

That was pretty easy, wasn't it? You'll be happy to learn that creating database tables from the mapping is a very similar process. As with code generation, you've already done most of the work in coming up with the mapping document. All that's left is to set up and run the schema-generation tool.

How do I do that?

The first step is something we alluded to in Chapter 1. We need to tell Hibernate which database we're going to be using, so it knows the specific "dialect" of SQL to use. SQL is a standard, yes, but every database goes beyond it in certain directions and has a specific set of features and limitations that affect real-life applications. To cope with this reality, Hibernate provides a set of classes that encapsulate the unique features of common database environments, in the package `org.hibernate.dialect`. You just need to tell it which one you want to use. (And if you want to work with a database that isn't yet supported "out of the box," you can implement your own dialect.)

In our case, we're working with HSQLDB, so we want to use `HSQLDialect`. The easiest way to configure Hibernate is to create a properties file named *hibernate.properties* and put it at the root level in the class path. Create this file at the top level of your *src* directory, with the content shown in Example 2-4.

Example 2-4. Setting up hibernate.properties

```
hibernate.dialect=org.hibernate.dialect.HSQLDialect
hibernate.connection.driver_class=org.hsqldb.jdbcDriver
hibernate.connection.url=jdbc:hsqldb:data/music
hibernate.connection.username=sa
hibernate.connection.password=
hibernate.connection.shutdown=true
```

In addition to establishing the SQL dialect we are using, the properties file tells Hibernate how to establish a connection to the database using the JDBC driver that ships as part of the HSQLDB database JAR archive and that the data should live in the *data* directory we've created, in the database named `music`. The username and empty password (indeed, all these values) should be familiar from the experiment we ran at the end of Chapter 1. Finally, we tell Hibernate that it needs to shut down the database connection explicitly when it is done working with it; this is an artifact of working with HSQLDB in embedded mode. Without this shutdown, changes are not necessarily flushed when the tools exit, so your schema stays frustratingly empty.

 As noted earlier, you can use an XML format for the configuration information as well, but for the simple needs we have here, it doesn't buy us anything. We'll show you the XML configuration approach in Chapter 3.

You can put the properties file in other places and give it other names, or use entirely different ways of getting the properties into Hibernate, but this is the default place

Hibernate will look, so it's the path of least resistance (or, I guess, of least runtime configuration).

We also need to add some new pieces to our build file, as we'll show. Add the targets in Example 2-5 right before the closing **</project>** tag at the end of *build.xml.*

Example 2-5. Ant build file additions for schema generation

```
<!-- Create our runtime subdirectories and copy resources into them -->
<target name="prepare" description="Sets up build structures"> ❶
  <mkdir dir="${class.root}"/>

  <!-- Copy our property files and O/R mappings for use at runtime -->
  <copy todir="${class.root}" >
    <fileset dir="${source.root}" >
      <include name="**/*.properties"/>
      <include name="**/*.xml"/> ❷
    </fileset>
  </copy>
</target>

<!-- Generate the schemas for all mapping files in our class tree -->
<target name="schema" depends="prepare" ❸
        description="Generate DB schema from the O/R mapping files">

  <hibernatetool destdir="${source.root}">
    <configuration>
      <fileset dir="${class.root}">
        <include name="**/*.hbm.xml"/>
      </fileset>
    </configuration>
    <hbm2ddl drop="yes" /> ❹
  </hibernatetool>
</target>
```

❶ First we add a **prepare** target that is intended to be used by other targets more than from the command line. Its purpose is to create, if necessary, the *classes* directory into which we're going to compile Java code, and then copy any properties and mapping files found in the *src* directory hierarchy to corresponding directories in the *classes* hierarchy. This hierarchical copy operation (using the special **/* pattern) is a nice feature of Ant, enabling us to define and edit resources alongside the source files that use them, while making those resources available at runtime via the class loader.

❷ This copies all XML files it finds, not just mapping documents. Although it's more than we need right now, it will become important when we switch to XML-based configuration for Hibernate.

❸ The **schema** target depends on **prepare** to copy the mapping documents to the right place for runtime use. It invokes the Hibernate tools in **hbm2ddl** mode, telling them to generate the database schema associated with any mapping documents found in the *classes* tree. (As noted previously, this will get simpler when we change to using a more-powerful XML configuration file for Hibernate in the next chapter.)

❹ There are a number of parameters you can give the schema-generation tool to configure the way it works. In this example, we're telling it to get rid of any previous definition of the tables that might exist before generating a new one based on the mapping document (drop=yes). For more details about this and other configuration options, consult the Hibernate Tools reference manual[ǁ]. Hibernate can even look at an existing database and try to figure out how the schema needs to change to reflect a new mapping file.

With these additions, we're ready to generate the schema for our TRACK table. Hibernate is going to do a lot of fancy things for us to accomplish this, and it might be neat to see what they all are. It is fairly easy to watch; all we need to do is set up logging for the right messages. To achieve that, we need to configure *Log4j*, the logging environment used by Hibernate. The easiest way to do this is to make a *log4j.properties* file available at the root of the class path. We can take advantage of our existing prepare target to copy the properties file from the src to the classes directory at the same time Ant copies Hibernate's properties.

Create a file named *log4j.properties* in the *src* directory with the content shown in Example 2-6. (An easy way to do this is to copy the file out of the *doc/tutorial/src* directory in the Hibernate distribution you downloaded, since it's provided for use by the examples included in the distribution. If you're typing it in yourself, you can skip the blocks which are commented out; they are provided to suggest useful logging alternatives.)

Example 2-6. The logging configuration file, log4j.properties

```
### direct log messages to stdout ###
log4j.appender.stdout=org.apache.log4j.ConsoleAppender
log4j.appender.stdout.Target=System.out
log4j.appender.stdout.layout=org.apache.log4j.PatternLayout
log4j.appender.stdout.layout.ConversionPattern=%d{ABSOLUTE} %5p %c{1}:%L - %m%n

### direct messages to file hibernate.log ###
#log4j.appender.file=org.apache.log4j.FileAppender
#log4j.appender.file.File=hibernate.log
#log4j.appender.file.layout=org.apache.log4j.PatternLayout
#log4j.appender.file.layout.ConversionPattern=%d{ABSOLUTE} %5p %c{1}:%L - %m%n

### set log levels - for more verbose logging change 'info' to 'debug' ###

log4j.rootLogger=warn, stdout

log4j.logger.org.hibernate=info
#log4j.logger.org.hibernate=debug
```

ǁ *http://www.hibernate.org/hib_docs/tools/reference/en/html/*

```
### log HQL query parser activity
#log4j.logger.org.hibernate.hql.ast.AST=debug

### log just the SQL
#log4j.logger.org.hibernate.SQL=debug

### log JDBC bind parameters ###
log4j.logger.org.hibernate.type=info
#log4j.logger.org.hibernate.type=debug

### log schema export/update ###
log4j.logger.org.hibernate.tool.hbm2ddl=debug

### log HQL parse trees
#log4j.logger.org.hibernate.hql=debug

### log cache activity ###
#log4j.logger.org.hibernate.cache=debug

### log transaction activity
#log4j.logger.org.hibernate.transaction=debug

### log JDBC resource acquisition
#log4j.logger.org.hibernate.jdbc=debug

### enable the following line if you want to track down connection ###
### leakages when using DriverManagerConnectionProvider ###
#log4j.logger.org.hibernate.connection.DriverManagerConnectionProvider=trace
```

 With the log configuration in place, you might want to edit the code gen target in *build.xml* so that it, too, depends on our new prepare target. This will ensure logging is configured and the hibernate configuration is available whenever codegen is invoked, eliminating the gripe we saw when first using it.

Time to make a schema! From the project directory, execute the command *ant prepare* and then follow it up with *ant schema*. You'll see output similar to Example 2-7 as the *classes* directory is created and populated with resources; then the schema generator is run.

Example 2-7. Building the schema using HSQLDB's embedded database server
```
% ant prepare
Buildfile: build.xml

prepare:
    [mkdir] Created dir: /Users/jim/svn/oreilly/hib_dev_2e/current/examples/ch02
/classes
     [copy] Copying 3 files to /Users/jim/svn/oreilly/hib_dev_2e/current/example
s/ch02/classes

BUILD SUCCESSFUL
Total time: 0 seconds
```

```
% ant schema
Buildfile: build.xml

prepare:

schema:
[hibernatetool] Executing Hibernate Tool with a Standard Configuration
[hibernatetool] 1. task: hbm2ddl (Generates database schema)
[hibernatetool] 22:38:21,858  INFO Environment:514 - Hibernate 3.2.5
[hibernatetool] 22:38:21,879  INFO Environment:532 - loaded properties from reso
urce hibernate.properties: {hibernate.connection.username=sa, hibernate.connecti
on.password=****, hibernate.dialect=org.hibernate.dialect.HSQLDialect, hibernate
.connection.shutdown=true, hibernate.connection.url=jdbc:hsqldb:data/music, hibe
rnate.bytecode.use_reflection_optimizer=false, hibernate.connection.driver_class
=org.hsqldb.jdbcDriver}
[hibernatetool] 22:38:21,897  INFO Environment:681 - Bytecode provider name : cg
lib
[hibernatetool] 22:38:21,930  INFO Environment:598 - using JDK 1.4 java.sql.Time
stamp handling
[hibernatetool] 22:38:22,108  INFO Configuration:299 - Reading mappings from fil
e: /Users/jim/Documents/Work/OReilly/svn_hibernate/current/examples/ch02/classes
/com/oreilly/hh/data/Track.hbm.xml
[hibernatetool] 22:38:22,669  INFO HbmBinder:300 - Mapping class: com.oreilly.hh
.data.Track -> TRACK
[hibernatetool] 22:38:22,827  INFO Dialect:152 - Using dialect: org.hibernate.di
alect.HSQLDialect
[hibernatetool] 22:38:23,186  INFO SchemaExport:154 - Running hbm2ddl schema exp
ort
[hibernatetool] 22:38:23,194 DEBUG SchemaExport:170 - import file not found: /im
port.sql
[hibernatetool] 22:38:23,197  INFO SchemaExport:179 - exporting generated schema
 to database
[hibernatetool] 22:38:23,232  INFO DriverManagerConnectionProvider:41 - Using Hi
bernate built-in connection pool (not for production use!)
[hibernatetool] 22:38:23,234  INFO DriverManagerConnectionProvider:42 - Hibernat
e connection pool size: 20
[hibernatetool] 22:38:23,241  INFO DriverManagerConnectionProvider:45 - autocomm
it mode: false
[hibernatetool] 22:38:23,255  INFO DriverManagerConnectionProvider:80 - using dr
iver: org.hsqldb.jdbcDriver at URL: jdbc:hsqldb:data/music
[hibernatetool] 22:38:23,258  INFO DriverManagerConnectionProvider:86 - connecti
on properties: {user=sa, password=****, shutdown=true}
[hibernatetool] drop table TRACK if exists;
[hibernatetool] 22:38:23,945 DEBUG SchemaExport:303 - drop table TRACK if exists
;
[hibernatetool] create table TRACK (TRACK_ID integer generated by default as ide
ntity (start with 1), title varchar(255) not null, filePath varchar(255) not nul
l, playTime time, added date, volume smallint not null, primary key (TRACK_ID));
[hibernatetool] 22:38:23,951 DEBUG SchemaExport:303 - create table TRACK (TRACK_
ID integer generated by default as identity (start with 1), title varchar(255) n
ot null, filePath varchar(255) not null, playTime time, added date, volume small
int not null, primary key (TRACK_ID));
```

```
[hibernatetool] 22:38:23,981  INFO SchemaExport:196 - schema export complete
[hibernatetool] 22:38:23,988  INFO DriverManagerConnectionProvider:147 - cleanin
g up connection pool: jdbc:hsqldb:data/music

BUILD SUCCESSFUL
Total time: 2 seconds
```

Toward the end of the schema export section, you can see the actual SQL used by Hibernate to create the TRACK table. If you look at the *music.script* file in the data directory, you'll see it's been incorporated into the database. For a slightly more friendly (and perhaps convincing) way to see it, execute *ant db* to fire up the HSQLDB graphical interface, as shown in Figure 2-1.

Alert readers are probably wondering why Ant was invoked twice, to first run prepare and then run schema, when the schema target already depends on prepare. This is one of those bootstrapping issues that comes up only the first time you're creating an environment. The problem is that Ant decides what goes into the project class path during startup when it processes that property definition. Until prepare is run at least once, the *classes* directory doesn't exist and doesn't contain *hibernate.properties*, so it's not included in the class path. Once prepare is run, this file is in the right place to be in the class path from now on, but Ant won't re-evaluate the property definition until the next time it is run. So if you try running schema in one step the very first time, Hibernate will fail, complaining that you didn't specify a database dialect, because it can't find its configuration properties. This kind of situation can lead to a lot of frustrated head scratching. However, from now on, it's safe to run schema and rely on it invoking prepare to copy in new versions of the property file as they are needed, because they will be on the class path from the beginning.

What just happened?

We were able to use Hibernate to create a data table in which we can persist instances of the Java class it created for us. We didn't have to type a single line of SQL or Java! Of course, the table is still empty at this point. Let's change that! Chapter 3 will look at the stuff you probably want to see the most: using Hibernate from within a Java program to turn objects into database entries and vice versa.

Before diving into that cool task, it's worth taking a moment to reflect on how much we've been able to accomplish with a couple of XML and properties files. Hopefully you're starting to see the power and convenience that make Hibernate so exciting.

What about...

...other approaches to ID generation? Keys that are globally unique across a database or the world? Hibernate can support a variety of methods for picking the keys for objects it stores in the database. This is controlled using the generator tag, bullet 5 in Example 2-1. In this example we told Hibernate to use the most natural kind of keys for the

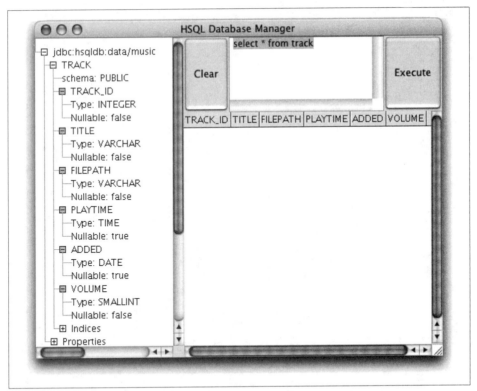

Figure 2-1. Database interface with our new TRACK table expanded, and a query

type of database that it happens to be using. Other alternatives include the popular `hi/lo` algorithm, global UUIDs, leaving it entirely up to your Java code, and more. See the "generator" section in the *Basic O/R Mapping* chapter of the Hibernate reference documentation for details. And, as usual, if none of the built-in choices are perfect for your needs, you can supply your own class to do it exactly how you'd like, implementing the interface `org.hibernate.id.IdentifierGenerator` and supplying your class name in the `generator` tag.

If you want to see an example of connecting Hibernate to a database you may be more familiar with, Chapter 10 shows how to work with MySQL.

## CHAPTER 3

Harnessing Hibernate

All right, we've set up a whole bunch of infrastructure, defined an object/relational mapping, and used it to create a matching Java class and database table. But what does that buy us? It's time to see how easy it is to work with persistent data from your Java code.

Configuring Hibernate

Before we can continue working with Hibernate, we need to get some busy work out of the way. In the previous chapter, we configured Hibernate's JDBC connection using a *hibernate.properties* file in the *src* directory. In this chapter we introduce a way to configure the JDBC connection, SQL dialect, and much more, using a Hibernate XML Configuration file. Just like the *hibernate.properties* file, we'll place this file in the *src* directory. Enter the content shown in Example 3-1 into a file called *hibernate.cfg.xml* within *src*, and delete the *hibernate.properties* file.

Example 3-1. Configuring Hibernate using XML: hibernate.cfg.xml

```
<?xml version="1.0" encoding="utf-8"?>
<!DOCTYPE hibernate-configuration PUBLIC
        "-//Hibernate/Hibernate Configuration DTD 3.0//EN"
        "http://hibernate.sourceforge.net/hibernate-configuration-3.0.dtd">

<hibernate-configuration>
  <session-factory>
    <!-- SQL dialect -->
    <property name="dialect">org.hibernate.dialect.HSQLDialect</property>  ❶

    <!-- Database connection settings -->  ❷
    <property name="connection.driver_class">org.hsqldb.jdbcDriver</property>
    <property name="connection.url">jdbc:hsqldb:data/music</property>
    <property name="connection.username">sa</property>
    <property name="connection.password"></property>
    <property name="connection.shutdown">true</property>

    <!-- JDBC connection pool (use the built-in one) -->
    <property name="connection.pool_size">1</property>  ❸
```

```
<!-- Enable Hibernate's automatic session context management -->
<property name="current_session_context_class">thread</property>

<!-- Disable the second-level cache --> ❹
<property
 name="cache.provider_class">org.hibernate.cache.NoCacheProvider</property>

<!-- disable batching so HSQLDB will propagate errors correctly. -->
<property name="jdbc.batch_size">0</property> ❺

<!-- Echo all executed SQL to stdout -->
<property name="show_sql">true</property> ❻

<!-- List all the mapping documents we're using --> ❼
<mapping resource="com/oreilly/hh/data/Track.hbm.xml"/>
</session-factory>
</hibernate-configuration>
```

As you can see, *hibernate.cfg.xml* configures the dialect, the JDBC parameters, the connection pool, and the cache provider. This XML document also references the mapping document we wrote in the previous chapter, eliminating the need to reference the mapping documents from within our Java source. Let's go through the details of this configuration file one section at a time:

❶ Just like the *hibernate.properties* file from the previous chapter, we're defining the dialect needed to work with HSQLDB. You might notice that the **property** element's **name** attribute is **dialect,** which is similar to the name of the property in the properties file, **hibernate.dialect.** When you configure Hibernate using the XML configuration file, you are passing the same properties to Hibernate. In the XML you can omit the **hibernate.** prefix from the name of the property. This section (dialect) and the next section (connection) are the same set of properties that were configured by the *hibernate.properties* file we used in Chapter 2.

❷ The properties used to configure the JDBC connection from Hibernate—**connection.driver_class,** **connection.url,** **connection.username,** **connection.password,** and **connection.shutdown**—match the properties set in *hibernate.properties* in Example 2-4.

❸ The **connection.pool_size** property is set to a value of **1.** This means that Hibernate will create a JDBC Connection pool with only one connection. Connection pooling is important in larger applications that need to scale, but for the purposes of this book, we can safely configure Hibernate to use the built-in connection pool with a single JDBC connection. Hibernate allows for a great deal of flexibility when it comes to connection pool implementations; it is very easy to configure Hibernate to use other connection pool implementations such as Apache Commons DBCP and C3P0.

❹ As things stand, when we start telling Hibernate to perform actual persistence operations for us, it is going to warn us that we haven't properly configured its second-level caching systems. For a simple application like this, we don't need any at all; this line turns off the second-level caching and sends every operation to the database.

❺ Here we are turning off Hibernate's JDBC batching feature. This reduces efficiency slightly—although far less so for an in-memory database like HSQLDB—but is necessary for usable error reporting in current HSQLDB releases. With batching turned on, if any statement in the batch has a problem, the only exception you get from HSQLDB is a `BatchUpdateException` telling you that the batch failed. This makes it almost impossible to debug your program. The author of HSQLDB reports that this problem will be fixed in the next major release; until then, we have to live without batching when using HSQLDB, for our sanity's sake.

❻ The `show_sql` property is a useful property to set when developing and debugging a program that uses Hibernate. Setting `show_sql` to `true` tells Hibernate to print out every statement it executes against a database. Set this property to `false` if you do not want to see the SQL statements printed out to the console.

❼ This final section lists all of the mapping documents in our project. Note that the path contains forward slashes and is relative to the *src* directory. This path addresses the *.hbm.xml* files on the class path as resources. By listing these files here, we no longer need to explicitly find them within *build.xml* targets that manipulate mapped classes (as you'll see later), nor load them from within each `main( )` method in our example source code, as we did in the previous version of the book. We think you'll agree it's nicer to keep this all in one place.

In addition to the *hibernate.cfg.xml* file in the *src* directory, you will also need to alter your *build.xml* to reference the XML configuration file. Change the `configuration` elements within the `codegen` and `schema` targets to look like the boldfaced lines in Example 3-2.

Example 3-2. Changes to build.xml to use XML configuration for Hibernate

```
...

    <!-- Generate the java code for all mapping files in our source tree -->
    <target name="codegen" depends="prepare"
            description="Generate Java source from the O/R mapping files">
      <hibernatetool destdir="${source.root}">
        <configuration configurationfile="${source.root}/hibernate.cfg.xml"/>
        <hbm2java/>
      </hibernatetool>
    </target>

...

    <!-- Generate the schemas for all mapping files in our class tree -->
    <target name="schema" depends="prepare"
            description="Generate DB schema from the O/R mapping files">

      <hibernatetool destdir="${source.root}">
```

```
  <configuration configurationfile="${source.root}/hibernate.cfg.xml"/>
    <hbm2ddl drop="yes" />
  </hibernatetool>
</target>
```

  ...

These two lines tell the Hibernate Tools Ant tasks where to look for the Hibernate XML configuration, and they find all the information they need within that configuration (including the mapping documents we're working with; recall that in Chapter 2 we had to explicitly build Ant `fileset` elements inside our `configuration` elements to match all mapping files found within the project source tree). We will be using the Hibernate XML configuration throughout the remainder of this book, which makes it easier to pass all kinds of information to all the Hibernate-related tools.

Now that we've successfully configured Hibernate, let's return to our main task for the chapter: making some persistent objects.

Creating Persistent Objects

Let's start by creating some new `Track` instances and persisting them to the database, so we can see how they turn into rows and columns for us. Because of the way we've organized our mapping document and configuration file, it's extremely easy to configure the Hibernate session factory and get things rolling.

How do I do that?

This discussion assumes you've created the schema and generated Java code by following the preceding examples. If you haven't, you can start by downloading the examples archive from this book's web site[*], jumping into the *ch03* directory, and using the commands *ant prepare* and *ant codegen*[†] followed by *ant schema* to automatically fetch the Hibernate and HSQLDB libraries and set up the generated Java code and database schema on which this example is based. (As with the other examples, these commands should be issued in a shell whose current working directory is the top of your project tree, containing Ant's *build.xml* file.)

We'll start with a simple example class, `CreateTest`, containing the necessary imports and housekeeping code to bring up the Hibernate environment and create some `Track` instances that can be persisted using the XML mapping document with which we started. Type the source of Example 3-3 in the directory *src/com/oreilly/hh*.

---

[*] *http://www.oreilly.com/catalog/9780596517724/*

[†] Even though the `codegen` target depends on the `prepare` target, the very first time you're working with one of the example directories you need to create the proper classpath structure for Ant to be happy by running `prepare` explicitly first, as discussed in "Cooking Up a Schema" back in Chapter 2.

Example 3-3. Data creation test, CreateTest.java

```java
package com.oreilly.hh;

import org.hibernate.*; ❶
import org.hibernate.cfg.Configuration;

import com.oreilly.hh.data.*;

import java.sql.Time;
import java.util.Date;

/**
 * Create sample data, letting Hibernate persist it for us.
 */
public class CreateTest {

    public static void main(String args[]) throws Exception {
        // Create a configuration based on the XML file we've put
        // in the standard place.
        Configuration config = new Configuration(); ❷
        config.configure();

        // Get the session factory we can use for persistence
        SessionFactory sessionFactory = config.buildSessionFactory(); ❸

        // Ask for a session using the JDBC information we've configured
        Session session = sessionFactory.openSession(); ❹
        Transaction tx = null;
        try {
            // Create some data and persist it
            tx = session.beginTransaction(); ❺

            Track track = new Track("Russian Trance",
                                "vol2/album610/track02.mp3",
                                Time.valueOf("00:03:30"), new Date(),
                                (short)0);
            session.save(track);

            track = new Track("Video Killed the Radio Star",
                        "vol2/album611/track12.mp3",
                        Time.valueOf("00:03:49"), new Date(),
                        (short)0);
            session.save(track);


            track = new Track("Gravity's Angel",
                        "vol2/album175/track03.mp3",
                        Time.valueOf("00:06:06"), new Date(),
                        (short)0);
            session.save(track);

            // We're done; make our changes permanent
            tx.commit(); ❻

        } catch (Exception e) {
```

```
        if (tx != null) {
            // Something went wrong; discard all partial changes
            tx.rollback();
        }
        throw new Exception("Transaction failed", e);
    } finally {
        // No matter what, close the session
        session.close();
    }

    // Clean up after ourselves
    sessionFactory.close(); ❼
  }
}
```

The first part of *CreateTest.java* needs a little explanation:

❶   We import some useful Hibernate classes, including `Configuration`, which is used to set up the Hibernate environment. We also want to import any and all data classes that Hibernate has generated for us based on our mapping documents; these will all be found in our **data** package. The `Time` and `Date` classes are used in our data objects to represent track playing times and creation timestamps. The only method we implement in `CreateTest` is the `main( )` method that supports invocation from the command line.

❷   When this class is run, it starts by creating a Hibernate `Configuration` object. Since we don't tell it otherwise, Hibernate looks for a file named *hibernate.cfg.xml* at the root level in the classpath. It finds the one we created earlier, which tells it we're using HSQLDB and how to find the database. This XML configuration file also references the Hibernate Mapping XML document for the `Track` object. Calling `config.configure( )` automatically adds the mapping for the `Track` class.

❸   That's all the configuration we need in order to create and persist track data, so we're ready to create the `SessionFactory`. Its purpose is to provide us with `Session` objects, the main avenue for interaction with Hibernate. The `SessionFactory` is thread-safe, and you need only one for your entire application. (To be more precise, you need one for each database environment for which you want persistence services; most applications therefore need only one.) Creating the session factory is a pretty expensive and slow operation, so you'll definitely want to share it throughout your application. It's trivial in a one-class application like this one, but the reference documentation provides some good examples of ways to do it in more realistic scenarios.

❹   When it comes time to actually perform persistence, we ask the SessionFactory to open a Session for us, which establishes a JDBC connection to the database and provides us with a context in which we can create, obtain, manipulate, and delete persistent objects. As long as the session is open, a connection to the database is maintained, and changes to the persistent objects associated with the session are tracked so they can be applied to the database when the session is closed. Conceptually, you can think of a session as a "large-scale transaction" between the persistent objects and the database, which may encompass several database-level transactions. As with a database transaction, though, you should not think about keeping your Hibernate session open over long periods of application existence (such as while you're waiting for user input). A single session is used for a specific and bounded operation in the application, something like populating the user interface or making a change that has been committed by the user. The next operation will use a new session. Also note that Session objects themselves are not thread-safe, so they cannot be shared between threads. Each thread needs to obtain its own session from the factory.

> It's worth getting a solid understanding of the purposes and lifecycles of these objects. This book gives you just enough information to get started; you'll want to spend some time with the reference documentation and understand the examples in depth.

It's worth going into a bit more depth about the lifecycle of mapped objects in Hibernate and how this relates to sessions because the terminology is rather specific and the concepts are quite important. A mapped object, such as an instance of our Track class, moves back and forth between two states with respect to Hibernate: *transient* and *persistent*. An object that is transient is not associated with any session. When you first create a Track instance using new( ), it is transient; unless you tell Hibernate to persist it, the object will vanish when your application terminates.

Passing a transient mapped object to a Session's save( ) method causes it to become persistent. It will survive past its scope in the Java VM, until it is explicitly deleted later. If you've got a persistent object and you call Session's delete( ) method on it, the object transitions back to transient state. The object still exists as an instance in your application, but it is no longer going to stay around unless you change your mind and save it again. On the other hand, if you haven't deleted it (so it's still persistent) and you make changes to the object, there's no need to save it again in order for those changes to be reflected. Hibernate automatically tracks changes to any persistent objects and flushes those changes to the database at appropriate times. When you close the session, any pending changes are flushed.

An important but subtle point concerns the status of persistent objects with which you worked in a session that has been closed, such as after you run a query to find all entities matching some criteria (you'll see how to do this in "Finding Persistent Objects" later in this chapter). As noted earlier, you don't want to keep this session around longer than necessary to perform the database operation, so you close it once your queries are finished. What's the deal with the mapped objects you've loaded at this point? Well, they were persistent while the session was around, but once they are no longer associated with an active session (in this case, because the session has been closed), they are not persistent any longer. Now, this doesn't mean that they no longer exist in the database; indeed, if you run the query again (assuming nobody has changed the data in the meantime), you'll get back the same set of objects. It simply means that there is not currently an active correspondence being maintained between the state of the objects in your virtual machine and the database; they are *detached*. It is perfectly reasonable to carry on working with the objects. If you later need to make changes to the objects and you want the changes to stick, you will open a new session and use it to save the changed objects. Because each entity has a unique ID, Hibernate has no problem figuring out how to link the transient objects back to the appropriate persistent state in the new session.

> Hang in there, we'll be back to the example soon!

 Of course, as with any environment in which you're making changes to an offline copy of information backed by a database, you need to think about application-level data-integrity constraints. You may need to devise some higher-level locking or versioning protocol to support them. Hibernate can offer help with this task, too, but the design and detailed implementation is up to you. The reference manual does strongly recommend the use of a version field, and there are several approaches available.

❺ Armed with these concepts and terms, the remainder of the example is easy enough to understand. We set up a database transaction using our open session. Within that, we create a few Track instances containing sample data and save them in the session, turning them from transient instances into persistent entities.

❻ Finally, we commit our transaction, atomically (as a single, indivisible unit) making all the database changes permanent. The try/catch/finally block wrapped around all this shows an important and useful idiom for working with transactions. If anything goes wrong, the catch block will roll back the transaction and then bubble out the exception, leaving the database the way we found it. The session is closed in the finally portion, ensuring that this takes place whether we exit through the "happy path" of a successful commit or via an exception that caused rollback. Either way, it gets closed as it should.

⑦   At the end of our method we also close the session factory itself. This is something you'd do in the "graceful shutdown" section of your application. In a web application environment, it would be in the appropriate lifecycle event handler. In this simple example, when the `main( )` method returns, the application is ending.

With all we've got in place, by now it's quite easy to tell Ant how to compile and run this test. Add the targets shown in Example 3-4 right before the closing `</project>` tag at the end of *build.xml*.

Example 3-4. Ant targets to compile all Java source and invoke data creation test

```
<!-- Compile the java source of the project -->
<target name="compile" depends="prepare" ❶
        description="Compiles all Java classes">
  <javac srcdir="${source.root}"
         destdir="${class.root}"
         debug="on"
         optimize="off"
         deprecation="on">
    <classpath refid="project.class.path"/>
  </javac>
</target>

<target name="ctest" description="Creates and persists some sample data"
        depends="compile"> ❷
  <java classname="com.oreilly.hh.CreateTest" fork="true">
    <classpath refid="project.class.path"/>
  </java>
</target>
```

❶   The aptly named `compile` target uses the built-in `javac` task to compile all the Java source files found in the *src* tree to the *classes* tree. Happily, this task also supports the project class path we've set up, so the compiler can find all the libraries we're using. The `depends=prepare` attribute in the target definition tells Ant that before running the `compile` target, `prepare` must be run. Ant manages dependencies so that when you're building multiple targets with related dependencies, they are executed in the right order, and each dependency gets executed only once, even if it is mentioned by multiple targets.

If you're accustomed to using shell scripts to compile a lot of Java source, you'll be surprised by how quickly the compilation happens. Ant invokes the Java compiler within the same virtual machine that it is using, so there is no process startup delay for each compilation.

❷   The `ctest` target uses `compile` to make sure the class files are built and then creates a new Java virtual machine to run our `CreateTest` class.

All right, we're ready to create some data! Example 3-5 shows the results of invoking the new `ctest` target. Its dependency on the `compile` target ensures the `CreateTest` class gets compiled before we try to use it. The output for `ctest` itself shows the logging emitted by Hibernate as the environment and mappings are set up and the connection is shut back down.

Example 3-5. Invoking the CreateTest class

```
% ant ctest
prepare:

compile:
    [javac] Compiling 2 source files to /Users/jim/svn/oreilly/hib_dev_2e/curren
t/examples/ch03/classes

ctest:
    [java] 00:21:45,833  INFO Environment:514 - Hibernate 3.2.5
    [java] 00:21:45,852  INFO Environment:547 - hibernate.properties not found
    [java] 00:21:45,864  INFO Environment:681 - Bytecode provider name : cglib
    [java] 00:21:45,875  INFO Environment:598 - using JDK 1.4 java.sql.Timestam
p handling
    [java] 00:21:46,032  INFO Configuration:1426 - configuring from resource: /
hibernate.cfg.xml
    [java] 00:21:46,034  INFO Configuration:1403 - Configuration resource: /hib
ernate.cfg.xml
    [java] 00:21:46,302  INFO Configuration:553 - Reading mappings from resourc
e : com/oreilly/hh/data/Track.hbm.xml
    [java] 00:21:46,605  INFO HbmBinder:300 - Mapping class: com.oreilly.hh.dat
a.Track -> TRACK
    [java] 00:21:46,678  INFO Configuration:1541 - Configured SessionFactory: n
ull
    [java] 00:21:46,860  INFO DriverManagerConnectionProvider:41 - Using Hibern
ate built-in connection pool (not for production use!)
    [java] 00:21:46,862  INFO DriverManagerConnectionProvider:42 - Hibernate co
nnection pool size: 1
    [java] 00:21:46,864  INFO DriverManagerConnectionProvider:45 - autocommit m
ode: false
    [java] 00:21:46,879  INFO DriverManagerConnectionProvider:80 - using driver
: org.hsqldb.jdbcDriver at URL: jdbc:hsqldb:data/music
    [java] 00:21:46,891  INFO DriverManagerConnectionProvider:86 - connection p
roperties: {user=sa, password=****, shutdown=true}
    [java] 00:21:47,533  INFO SettingsFactory:89 - RDBMS: HSQL Database Engine,
 version: 1.8.0
    [java] 00:21:47,538  INFO SettingsFactory:90 - JDBC driver: HSQL Database E
ngine Driver, version: 1.8.0
    [java] 00:21:47,613  INFO Dialect:152 - Using dialect: org.hibernate.dialec
t.HSQLDialect
    [java] 00:21:47,638  INFO TransactionFactoryFactory:31 - Using default tran
saction strategy (direct JDBC transactions)
    [java] 00:21:47,646  INFO TransactionManagerLookupFactory:33 - No Transacti
onManagerLookup configured (in JTA environment, use of read-write or transaction
al second-level cache is not recommended)
    [java] 00:21:47,649  INFO SettingsFactory:143 - Automatic flush during befo
reCompletion(): disabled
    [java] 00:21:47,650  INFO SettingsFactory:147 - Automatic session close at
end of transaction: disabled
    [java] 00:21:47,657  INFO SettingsFactory:154 - JDBC batch size: 15
    [java] 00:21:47,659  INFO SettingsFactory:157 - JDBC batch updates for vers
ioned data: disabled
```

```
    [java] 00:21:47,664  INFO SettingsFactory:162 - Scrollable result sets: ena
bled
    [java] 00:21:47,666  INFO SettingsFactory:170 - JDBC3 getGeneratedKeys(): d
isabled
    [java] 00:21:47,668  INFO SettingsFactory:178 - Connection release mode: au
to
    [java] 00:21:47,671  INFO SettingsFactory:205 - Default batch fetch size: 1
    [java] 00:21:47,678  INFO SettingsFactory:209 - Generate SQL with comments:
 disabled
    [java] 00:21:47,680  INFO SettingsFactory:213 - Order SQL updates by primar
y key: disabled
    [java] 00:21:47,681  INFO SettingsFactory:217 - Order SQL inserts for batch
ing: disabled
    [java] 00:21:47,684  INFO SettingsFactory:386 - Query translator: org.hiber
nate.hql.ast.ASTQueryTranslatorFactory
    [java] 00:21:47,690  INFO ASTQueryTranslatorFactory:24 - Using ASTQueryTran
slatorFactory
    [java] 00:21:47,694  INFO SettingsFactory:225 - Query language substitution
s: {}
    [java] 00:21:47,695  INFO SettingsFactory:230 - JPA-QL strict compliance: d
isabled
    [java] 00:21:47,702  INFO SettingsFactory:235 - Second-level cache: enabled
    [java] 00:21:47,704  INFO SettingsFactory:239 - Query cache: disabled
    [java] 00:21:47,706  INFO SettingsFactory:373 - Cache provider: org.hiberna
te.cache.NoCacheProvider
    [java] 00:21:47,707  INFO SettingsFactory:254 - Optimize cache for minimal
puts: disabled
    [java] 00:21:47,709  INFO SettingsFactory:263 - Structured second-level cac
he entries: disabled
    [java] 00:21:47,724  INFO SettingsFactory:283 - Echoing all SQL to stdout
    [java] 00:21:47,731  INFO SettingsFactory:290 - Statistics: disabled
    [java] 00:21:47,732  INFO SettingsFactory:294 - Deleted entity synthetic id
entifier rollback: disabled
    [java] 00:21:47,734  INFO SettingsFactory:309 - Default entity-mode: pojo
    [java] 00:21:47,735  INFO SettingsFactory:313 - Named query checking : enab
led
    [java] 00:21:47,838  INFO SessionFactoryImpl:161 - building session factory
    [java] 00:21:48,464  INFO SessionFactoryObjectFactory:82 - Not binding fact
ory to JNDI, no JNDI name configured
    [java] Hibernate: insert into TRACK (TRACK_ID, title, filePath, playTime, a
dded, volume) values (null, ?, ?, ?, ?, ?)
    [java] Hibernate: call identity()
    [java] Hibernate: insert into TRACK (TRACK_ID, title, filePath, playTime, a
dded, volume) values (null, ?, ?, ?, ?, ?)
    [java] Hibernate: call identity()
    [java] Hibernate: insert into TRACK (TRACK_ID, title, filePath, playTime, a
dded, volume) values (null, ?, ?, ?, ?, ?)
    [java] Hibernate: call identity()
    [java] 00:21:49,365  INFO SessionFactoryImpl:769 - closing
    [java] 00:21:49,369  INFO DriverManagerConnectionProvider:147 - cleaning up
 connection pool: jdbc:hsqldb:data/music

BUILD SUCCESSFUL
Total time: 2 seconds
```

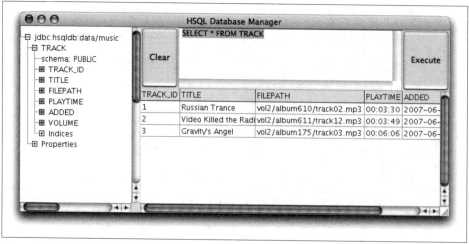

Figure 3-1. Test data persisted into the TRACK table

What just happened?

If you scan through all the messages Hibernate prints out because we've turned on "info" logging, you can see that our test class fired up Hibernate, loaded the mapping information for the Track class, opened a persistence session to the associated HSQLDB database, and used that to create some instances and persist them in the TRACK table. Then it shut down the session and closed the database connection, ensuring the data was saved.

After running this test, you can use *ant db* to take a look at the contents of the database. You should find three rows in the TRACK table now, as shown in Figure 3-1. (Type your query in the text box at the top of the window and click the Execute button. You can get a command skeleton and syntax documentation by choosing Command→Select in the menu bar.)

At this point, it's worth pausing a moment to reflect on the fact that we wrote no code to connect to the database or issue SQL commands. Looking back to the preceding sections, we didn't even have to create the table ourselves, nor the Track object that encapsulates our data. Yet the query output in Figure 3-1 shows nicely readable data representing the Java objects created and persisted by our short, simple test program. Hopefully you'll agree that this reflects very well on the power and convenience of Hibernate as a persistence service. For being free and lightweight, Hibernate can certainly do a lot for you, quickly and easily.

If you have been using JDBC directly, especially if you're pretty new to it, you may be used to relying on the "auto-commit" mode in the database driver rather than always using database transactions. Hibernate is rightly opinionated that this is the wrong way to structure application code; the only place it makes sense is in database console experimentation by humans. So, you'll always need to use transactions around your persistence operations in Hibernate.

As noted in Chapter 1, you can also look directly at the SQL statements creating your data in the *music.script* file in the *data* directory as shown in Example 3-6.

Example 3-6. Looking at the raw database script file

```
% cat data/music.script
CREATE SCHEMA PUBLIC AUTHORIZATION DBA
CREATE MEMORY TABLE TRACK(TRACK_ID INTEGER GENERATED BY DEFAULT AS IDENTITY(STAR
T WITH 1) NOT NULL PRIMARY KEY,TITLE VARCHAR(255) NOT NULL,FILEPATH VARCHAR(255)
 NOT NULL,PLAYTIME TIME,ADDED DATE,VOLUME SMALLINT NOT NULL)
ALTER TABLE TRACK ALTER COLUMN TRACK_ID RESTART WITH 4
CREATE USER SA PASSWORD ""
GRANT DBA TO SA
SET WRITE_DELAY 10
SET SCHEMA PUBLIC
INSERT INTO TRACK VALUES(1,'Russian Trance','vol2/album610/track02.mp3','00:03:3
0','2007-06-17',0)
INSERT INTO TRACK VALUES(2,'Video Killed the Radio Star','vol2/album611/track12.
mp3','00:03:49','2007-06-17',0)
INSERT INTO TRACK VALUES(3,'Gravity''s Angel','vol2/album175/track03.mp3','00:06
:06','2007-06-17',0)
```

The final three statements show our **TRACK** table rows. The top contains the schema and the user that gets provided by default when creating a new database. (Of course, in a real application environment, you'd want to change these credentials, unless you were only enabling in-memory access.)

Tempted to learn more about HSQLDB? We won't try to stop you!

What about...

...objects with relationships to other objects? Collections of objects? You're right—these are cases where persistence gets more challenging (and, if done right, valuable). Hibernate can handle associations like this just fine. In fact, there isn't any special effort involved on our part. We'll discuss this in Chapter 4. For now, let's look at how to retrieve objects that were persisted in earlier sessions.

Finding Persistent Objects

It's time to throw the giant lever into reverse and look at how you load data from a database into Java objects.

Let's see how it works, using Hibernate Query Language to get an object-oriented view of the contents of mapped database tables. These might have started out as objects persisted in a previous session or might be data that came from completely outside your application code.

How do I do that?

Example 3-7 shows a program that runs a simple query using the test data we just created. The overall structure will look very familiar because all the Hibernate setup is the same as in the previous program.

Example 3-7. Data retrieval test, QueryTest.java

```java
package com.oreilly.hh;

import org.hibernate.*;
import org.hibernate.cfg.Configuration;

import com.oreilly.hh.data.*;

import java.sql.Time;
import java.util.*;

/**
 * Retrieve data as objects
 */
public class QueryTest {

    /**
     * Retrieve any tracks that fit in the specified amount of time.
     *
     * @param length the maximum playing time for tracks to be returned.
     * @param session the Hibernate session that can retrieve data.
     * @return a list of {@link Track}s meeting the length restriction.
     */
    public static List tracksNoLongerThan(Time length, Session session) {   ❶
        Query query = session.createQuery("from Track as track " +
                                          "where track.playTime <= ?");
        query.setParameter(0, length, Hibernate.TIME);
        return query.list();
    }

    /**
     * Look up and print some tracks when invoked from the command line.
     */
    public static void main(String args[]) throws Exception {
        // Create a configuration based on the properties file we've put
        // in the standard place.
```

```
        Configuration config = new Configuration();
        config.configure();

        // Get the session factory we can use for persistence
        SessionFactory sessionFactory = config.buildSessionFactory();

        // Ask for a session using the JDBC information we've configured
        Session session = sessionFactory.openSession();
        try { ❷
            // Print the tracks that will fit in five minutes
            List tracks = tracksNoLongerThan(Time.valueOf("00:05:00"),
                                             session);
            for (ListIterator iter = tracks.listIterator() ;
                 iter.hasNext() ; ) {
                Track aTrack = (Track)iter.next();
                System.out.println("Track: \"" + aTrack.getTitle() +
                                   "\", " + aTrack.getPlayTime());
            }
        } finally {
            // No matter what, close the session
            session.close();
        }

        // Clean up after ourselves
        sessionFactory.close();
    }
}
```

Once again, we add a target, shown in Example 3-8, at the end of *build.xml* (right before the closing **project** tag) to run this test.

Example 3-8. Ant target to invoke our query test

```
<target name="qtest" description="Run a simple Hibernate query"
        depends="compile">
  <java classname="com.oreilly.hh.QueryTest" fork="true">
    <classpath refid="project.class.path"/>
  </java>
</target>
```

With this in place, we can simply type *ant qtest* to retrieve and display some data, with the results shown in Example 3-9. To save space in the output, we've edited *log4j.properties* to turn off all the "info" messages, since they're no different than in the previous example. You can do this yourself by changing the line:

```
log4j.logger.org.hibernate=info
```

to replace the word info with warn:

```
log4j.logger.org.hibernate=warn
```

Example 3-9. Running the query test

```
% ant qtest
Buildfile: build.xml
```

```
prepare:
    [copy] Copying 1 file to /Users/jim/svn/oreilly/hib_dev_2e/current/examples
/ch03/classes

compile:
    [javac] Compiling 1 source file to /Users/jim/svn/oreilly/hib_dev_2e/current
/examples/ch03/classes

qtest:
    [java] Hibernate: select track0_.TRACK_ID as TRACK1_0_, track0_.title as ti
tle0_, track0_.filePath as filePath0_, track0_.playTime as playTime0_, track0_.a
dded as added0_, track0_.volume as volume0_ from TRACK track0_ where track0_.pla
yTime<=?
    [java] Track: "Russian Trance", 00:03:30
    [java] Track: "Video Killed the Radio Star", 00:03:49

BUILD SUCCESSFUL
Total time: 2 seconds
```

What just happened?

❶ We started out by defining a utility method, `tracksNoLongerThan( )`, which performs the actual Hibernate query. It retrieves any tracks whose playing time is
less than or equal to the amount specified as a parameter. Notice that HQL,
Hibernate's SQL-inspired query language, supports parameter placeholders,
much like `PreparedStatement` in JDBC. And, just like in that environment, using
them is preferable to putting together queries through string manipulation (especially since this protects you from SQL injection attacks). As you'll see,
however, Hibernate offers even better ways of working with queries in Java.

The query itself looks a little strange. It starts with **from** rather than **select**
something, as you might expect. While you can certainly use the more familiar
format, and will do so when you want to pull out individual properties from an
object in your query, if you want to retrieve entire objects, you can use this more
abbreviated syntax.

Also note that the query is expressed in terms of the mapped Java *objects* and
properties, rather than the tables and columns. It's not obvious in this case, since
the object and table have the same name, as do the property and column, but it
is true. Keeping the names consistent is a fairly natural choice and will always be
the case when you're using Hibernate to generate the schema and the data objects,
unless you tell it explicitly to use different column names.

> When you're working with preexisting databases and objects, it's
> important to realize that HQL queries refer to object properties
> rather than to database table columns.

Also, just as in SQL, you can alias a column or table to another name. In HQL, you alias classes in order to select or constrain their properties. This won't come up in this simple introduction, but if you dig into the resources mentioned in Appendix E, you'll encounter it.

❷ The rest of the program should look mighty familiar from the previous example. Our `try` block is simplified because we don't need explicit access to our transaction, as we're not changing any data. We still use `try` so that we can have a `finally` clause to close our session cleanly. The body is quite simple, calling our query method to request any tracks whose playing time is five minutes or less, and then iterating over the resulting `Track` objects, printing their titles and playing times.

Also, now that we've turned off "info" level logging from within Hibernate, the SQL debugging output we configured in *hibernate.cfg.xml* is much easier to spot—the first line in the `"qtest:"` section of the output is not something we wrote ourselves in *QueryTest.java*; it's Hibernate showing us the SQL it generated to implement the HQL query we requested. Interesting... and if you ever get sick of seeing it, remember that you can set the `show_sql` property value to `false`.

What about...

...deleting objects? If you've made changes to your data-creation script and want to start with a "clean slate" in the form of an empty database so you can test them, all you need to do is run *ant schema* again. This will drop and recreate the `Track` table in a pristine and empty state. Don't do it unless you mean it!

If you want to be more selective about what you delete, you can either do it through SQL commands in the HSQLDB UI (*ant db*), or you can make a variant of the querytest example that retrieves the objects you want to get rid of. Once you've got a reference to a persistent object, passing it to the `Session`'s `delete( )` method will remove it from the database:

```
session.delete(aTrack);
```

You've still got at least one reference to it in your program, until `aTrack` goes out of scope or gets reassigned, so conceptually the easiest way to understand what `delete( )` does is to think of it as turning a persistent object back into a transient one.

Another way to delete is to write an HQL deletion query that matches multiple objects. This lets you delete many persistent objects at once, whether or not you have them as objects in memory, without writing your own loop. A Java-based alternative to *ant schema*, and a slightly less violent way of clearing out all the tracks, would therefore be something like this:

```
Query query = session.createQuery("delete from Track");
query.executeUpdate();
```

Don't forget that regardless of which of these approaches you use, you'll need to wrap the data-manipulation code inside a Hibernate transaction and commit the transaction if you want your changes to stick.

Better Ways to Build Queries

As mentioned earlier in this chapter, HQL lets you go beyond the use of JDBC-style query placeholders to get parameters conveniently into your queries. You can use *named parameters* and *named queries* to make your programs much easier to read and maintain.

Why do I care?

Named parameters make code easier to understand because the purpose of the parameter is clear both within the query itself and within the Java code that is setting it up. This self-documenting nature is valuable in itself, but it also reduces the potential for error by freeing you from counting commas and question marks, and it can modestly improve efficiency by letting you use the same parameter more than once in a single query.

Named queries let you move the queries completely out of the Java code. Keeping queries out of your Java source makes them much easier to read and edit because they aren't giant concatenated series of Java strings spread across multiple lines and interwoven with extraneous quotation marks, backslashes, and other Java punctuation. Typing them the first time is bad enough, but if you've ever had to perform significant surgery on a query embedded in a program in this way, you will have had your fill of moving quotation marks and plus signs around to try to get the lines to break in nice places again.

How do I do that?

The key to both of these capabilities in Hibernate is the `Query` interface. We already began using this interface in Example 3-7 because, starting with Hibernate 3, it is the only nondeprecated way of performing queries. So today it's even less of an effort than it used to be to use the nice features described in this section.

We'll start by changing our query to use a named parameter, as shown in Example 3-10. (This isn't nearly as big a deal for a query with a single parameter like this one, but it's worth getting into the habit right away. You'll be very thankful when you start working with the light-dimming queries that power your real projects!)

Example 3-10. Revising our query to use a named parameter
```
    public static List tracksNoLongerThan(Time length, Session session) {
        Query query = session.createQuery("from Track as track " +
                                          "where track.playTime <= :length");
        query.setTime("length", length);
```

```
    return query.list();
}
```

Named parameters are identified within the query body by prefixing them with a colon. Here, we've changed the ? to :length. The Session object provides a createQuery( ) method that gives us back an implementation of the Query interface with which we can work. Query has a full complement of type-safe methods for setting the values of named parameters. Here we are passing in a Time value, so we use setTime( ). Even in a simple case like this, the syntax is more natural and readable than the original version of our query. If we had been passing in anonymous arrays of values and types (as would have been necessary with more than one parameter), the improvement would be even more significant. And we've added a layer of compile-time type checking, always a welcome change.

Running this version produces exactly the same output as our original program.

So, how do we get the query text out of the Java source? Again, this query is short enough that the need to do so isn't as pressing as usual in real projects, but it's the best way to do things, so let's start practicing! As you may have predicted, the place we can store queries is inside the mapping document. Example 3-11 shows what this looks like. We have to use the somewhat clunky CDATA construct, since our query contains characters (like <) that could otherwise confuse the XML parser.

Example 3-11. Our query in the mapping document

```
<query name="com.oreilly.hh.tracksNoLongerThan">
  <![CDATA[
      from Track as track
      where track.playTime <= :length
  ]]>
</query>
```

Put this just after the closing tag of the class definition in *Track.hbm.xml* (right before the </hibernate-mapping> line). Then we can revise *QueryTest.java* one last time, as shown in Example 3-12. Once again, the program produces exactly the same output as the initial version. It's just better organized now, and we're in great shape if we ever want to make the query more complex.

Example 3-12. Final version of our query method

```
public static List tracksNoLongerThan(Time length, Session session) {
    Query query = session.getNamedQuery(
                    "com.oreilly.hh.tracksNoLongerThan");
    query.setTime("length", length);
    return query.list();
}
```

The Query interface has other useful capabilities beyond what we've examined here. You can use it to control how many rows (and which specific rows) you retrieve. If your JDBC driver supports scrollable ResultSets, you can access this capability as well. Check the JavaDoc or the Hibernate reference manual for more details.

What about...

...avoiding a SQL-like language altogether? Or diving into HQL and exploring more complex queries? These are both options that are covered later in this book.

Chapter 8 discusses criteria queries, an interesting mechanism that lets you express the constraints on the entities you want, using a natural Java API. This lets you build Java objects to represent the data you want to find, which is easier for people who aren't database experts to understand; lets you leverage your IDE's code completion as a memory aid; and even gives you compile-time checking of your syntax. It also supports a form of "query by example," where you can supply objects that are similar to the ones you're searching for, which is particularly handy for implementing search interfaces in an application.

SQL veterans who'd like to see more tricks with HQL can jump to Chapter 9, which explores more of its capabilities and unique features.

For now, we'll continue our exploration of mapping by looking at how to cope with objects that are linked to each other, which you will need in any nontrivial program.

Collections and Associations

No, this isn't about taxes or politics. Now that we've seen how easy it is to get individual objects into and out of a database, it's time to see how to work with groups and relationships between objects. Happily, it's no more difficult.

Mapping Collections

In any real application you'll be managing lists and groups of things. Java provides a healthy and useful set of library classes to help with this: the Collections utilities. Hibernate provides natural ways for mapping database relationships onto Collections, which are usually very convenient. You do need to be aware of a couple semantic mismatches, generally minor. The biggest is the fact that Collections don't provide "bag" semantics, which might frustrate some experienced database designers. This gap isn't Hibernate's fault, and it even makes some effort to work around the issue.

Enough abstraction! The Hibernate reference manual does a good job of discussing the whole bag issue, so let's leave it and look at a working example of mapping a collection where the relational and Java models fit nicely. It might seem natural to build on the Track examples from Chapter 2 and group them into albums, but that's not the simplest place to start, because organizing an album involves tracking additional information, like the disc on which the track is found (for multidisc albums), and other such finicky details. So let's add artist information to our database.

> Bags are like sets, except that the same value can appear more than once.

The information of which we need to keep track for artists is, at least initially, pretty simple. We'll start with just the artist's name. And each track can be assigned a set of artists, so we know who to thank or blame for the music, and you can look up all tracks by an artist you like. (It really is critical to allow more than one artist to be assigned to a track, yet so few music management programs get this right. The task of adding a separate link to keep track of composers is left as a useful exercise for the reader after understanding this example.)

> As usual, the examples assume you followed the steps in the previous chapters. If you did not, download the example source as a starting point.

How do I do that?

For now, our `Artist` class doesn't need anything other than a name property (and its key, of course). Setting up a mapping document for it will be easy. Create the file *Artist.hbm.xml* in the same directory as the `Track` mapping document, with the contents shown in Example 4-1.

Example 4-1. Mapping document for the Artist class

```xml
<?xml version="1.0"?>
<!DOCTYPE hibernate-mapping PUBLIC "-//Hibernate/Hibernate Mapping DTD 3.0//EN"
          "http://hibernate.sourceforge.net/hibernate-mapping-3.0.dtd">

<hibernate-mapping>

  <class name="com.oreilly.hh.data.Artist" table="ARTIST">
    <meta attribute="class-description">
     Represents an artist who is associated with a track or album.
     @author Jim Elliott (with help from Hibernate)
    </meta>

    <id name="id" type="int" column="ARTIST_ID">
      <meta attribute="scope-set">protected</meta>
      <generator class="native"/>
    </id>

    <property name="name" type="string"> ❶
      <meta attribute="use-in-tostring">true</meta>
      <column name="NAME" not-null="true" unique="true" index="ARTIST_NAME"/>
    </property>

    <set name="tracks" table="TRACK_ARTISTS" inverse="true"> ❷
      <meta attribute="field-description">Tracks by this artist</meta> ❸
      <key column="ARTIST_ID"/>
      <many-to-many class="com.oreilly.hh.data.Track" column="TRACK_ID"/>
    </set>

  </class>

</hibernate-mapping>
```

❶   Our mapping for the `name` property introduces a couple of refinements to both the code generation and schema generation phases. The `use-in-tostring` meta tag causes the generated class to include a custom `toString()` method that shows the artist's name as well as the cryptic hash code when it is printed, as an aid for debugging (you can see the result near the bottom of Example 4-4). And expanding the `column` attribute into a full-blown tag allows us finer-grained control over the nature of the column, which we use in this case to add an index for efficient lookup and sorting by name.

❷   Notice that we can represent the fact that an artist is associated with one or more tracks quite naturally in this file. This mapping tells Hibernate to add a property named `tracks` to our `Artist` class, whose type is an implementation of `java.util.Set`. This will use a new table named `TRACK_ARTISTS` to link to the `Track` objects for which this `Artist` is responsible. The attribute `inverse=true` is explained later in the discussion of Example 4-3, where the bidirectional nature of this association is examined.

The `TRACK_ARTISTS` table we just called into existence will contain two columns: `TRACK_ID` and `ARTIST_ID`. Any rows appearing in this table will mean that the specified `Artist` object has something to do with the specified `Track` object. The fact that this information lives in its own table means that there is no restriction on how many tracks can be linked to a particular artist, nor how many artists are associated with a track. That's what is meant by a "many-to-many" association[*].

On the flip side, since these links are in a separate table you have to perform a join query in order to retrieve any meaningful information about either the artists or the tracks. This is why such tables are often called "join tables." Their whole purpose is to join other tables together.

Finally, notice that unlike the other tables we've set up in our schema, `TRACK_ARTISTS` does not correspond to any mapped Java object. It is used only to implement the links between `Artist` and `Track` objects, as reflected by `Artist`'s `tracks` property.

❸ The `field-description` `meta` tag can be used to provide JavaDoc descriptions for collections and associations as well as plain old value fields. This is handy in situations where the field name isn't completely self-documenting.

The tweaks and configuration choices provided by the mapping document, especially when aided by `meta` tags, give you a great deal of flexibility over how the source code and database schema are built. Nothing can quite compare to the control you can obtain by writing them yourself, but most common needs and scenarios appear to be within reach of the mapping-driven generation tools. This is great news, because they can save you a lot of tedious typing!

Once we've created *Artist.hbm.xml* we need to add it to the list of mapping resources in our *hibernate.cfg.xml*. Open up the *hibernate.cfg.xml* file in *src*, and add the line shown in bold in Example 4-2.

Example 4-2. Adding Artist.hbm.xml to the Hibernate configuration

```
<?xml version='1.0' encoding='utf-8'?>
<!DOCTYPE hibernate-configuration PUBLIC
        "-//Hibernate/Hibernate Configuration DTD 3.0//EN"
```

---

[*] If concepts like join tables and many-to-many associations aren't familiar, spending some time with a good data modeling introduction would be worthwhile. It will help a lot when it comes to designing, understanding, and talking about data-driven projects. George Reese's *Java Database Best Practices* (O'Reilly) has such an introduction, and you can even view the chapter online at *http://www.oreilly.com/catalog/javadtabp/chapter/ch02.pdf*.

```
              "http://hibernate.sourceforge.net/hibernate-configuration-3.0.dtd">

      <hibernate-configuration>
        <session-factory>

      ...
          <mapping resource="com/oreilly/hh/data/Track.hbm.xml"/>
          <mapping resource="com/oreilly/hh/data/Artist.hbm.xml"/>

        </session-factory>
      </hibernate-configuration>
```

With that in place, let's also add the collection of **Artists** to our **Track** class. Edit *Track.hbm.xml* to include the new **artists** property as shown in Example 4-3 (the new content is shown in bold).

Example 4-3. Adding an artist collection to the Track mapping file

```
      ...

      <property name="playTime" type="time">
        <meta attribute="field-description">Playing time</meta>
      </property>

      <set name="artists" table="TRACK_ARTISTS">
        <key column="TRACK_ID"/>
        <many-to-many class="com.oreilly.hh.data.Artist" column="ARTIST_ID"/>
      </set>

      <property name="added" type="date">
        <meta attribute="field-description">When the track was created</meta>
      </property>

      ...
```

This adds a similar **Set** property named **artists** to the **Track** class. It uses the same **TRACK_ARTISTS** join table introduced earlier in Example 4-1 to link to the **Artist** objects we mapped there. This sort of bidirectional association is very useful. It's important to let Hibernate know explicitly what's going on by marking one end of the association as *inverse*. In the case of a many-to-many association like this one, the choice of which side to call the inverse mapping isn't crucial, although it does affect when Hibernate will decide to automatically update the join table. The fact that the join table is named "track artists" makes the link from artists back to tracks the best choice for the inverse end, if only from the perspective of people trying to understand the database.

Hibernate itself doesn't care which end we choose, as long as we mark one of the directions as inverse. That's why we did so in Example 4-1. With this configuration, if we make changes to the **artists** set in a **Track** object, Hibernate will know it needs to update the **TRACK_ARTISTS** table. If we make changes to the **tracks** set in an **Artist** object, this will not automatically happen.

While we're enhancing the Track mapping document we might as well flesh out the title property similar to how we fleshed out name in Artist:

```
...

<property name="title" type="string">
  <meta attribute="use-in-tostring">true</meta>
  <column name="TITLE" not-null="true" index="TRACK_TITLE"/>
</property>

...
```

With the new and updated mapping files in place, we're ready to rerun *ant codegen* to update the Track source code, and create the new **Artist** source. If you do that and look at *Track.java*, you'll see the new Set-valued property artists has been added, as has a new toString( ) method. Example 4-4 shows the content of the new *Artist.java*.

Example 4-4. Code generated for the Artist class

```
package com.oreilly.hh.data;
// Generated Sep 3, 2007 10:12:45 PM by Hibernate Tools 3.2.0.b9

import java.util.HashSet;
import java.util.Set;

/**
 *         Represents an artist who is associated with a track or album.
 *         @author Jim Elliott (with help from Hibernate)
 */
public class Artist  implements java.io.Serializable {

    private int id;
    private String name;
    /**
     * Tracks by this artist
     */
    private Set tracks = new HashSet(0);

    public Artist() {
    }

    public Artist(String name) {
        this.name = name;
    }

    public Artist(String name, Set tracks) {
        this.name = name;
        this.tracks = tracks;
    }

    public int getId() {
        return this.id;
    }

    protected void setId(int id) {
```

```
        this.id = id;
    }

    public String getName() {
        return this.name;
    }

    public void setName(String name) {
        this.name = name;
    }

    /**
     *      * Tracks by this artist
     */
    public Set getTracks() {
        return this.tracks;
    }

    public void setTracks(Set tracks) {
        this.tracks = tracks;
    }

    /**
     * toString
     * @return String
     */
    public String toString() {
        StringBuffer buffer = new StringBuffer();

      buffer.append(getClass().getName()).append("@").append(
        Integer.toHexString(hashCode())).append(" [");
      buffer.append("name").append("='").append(getName()).append("' ");
      buffer.append("]");

      return buffer.toString();
    }
}
```

Why didn't it work?

If you see Hibernate complaining about something along these lines, don't despair:

```
[hibernatetool] An exception occurred while running exporter
#2:hbm2java (Generates a set of .java files)
[hibernatetool] To get the full stack trace run ant with -verbose
[hibernatetool] org.hibernate.MappingNotFoundException: resource:
com/oreilly/hh/data/Track.hbm.xml not found
[hibernatetool] A resource located at com/oreilly/hh/data/Track.hbm.xml was not
found.
[hibernatetool] Check the following:
[hibernatetool]
[hibernatetool] 1) Is the spelling/casing correct ?
[hibernatetool] 2)       Is com/oreilly/hh/data/Track.hbm.xml available via the c
```

Anyone looking for a popcorn project to pitch in on Hibernate? How about changing the tools' code generation to use a StringBuilder rather than a StringBuffer in toString( )?

```
lasspath ?
[hibernatetool] 3) Does it actually exist ?

BUILD FAILED
```

This just means you were starting from a fresh download of the sample directory, and you've run into the kind of Ant premature classpath calcification issues we mentioned in "Cooking Up a Schema" back in Chapter 2. If you try it a second time (or if you had manually run *ant prepare* once before trying it in the first place), it should work fine.

What about...

...modern (Java 5) considerations of type-safety? These classes are using nongeneric versions of the Collections classes, and will cause compiler warnings like the following when code is compiled against them with current Java compilers:

```
[javac] Note: /Users/jim/svn/oreilly/hib_dev_2e/current/scratch/ch04/src/com
/oreilly/hh/CreateTest.java uses unchecked or unsafe operations.
[javac] Note: Recompile with -Xlint:unchecked for details.
```

It'd sure be nice if there was a way to generate code that used Java Generics, to tighten up the things we can put in the tracks Set and thereby avoid these warnings and all the tedious type casting that used to mar the Collections experience. Well, we're in luck, because it's actually pretty easy to do so, by modifying the way we invoke hbm2java. Edit *build.xml* and change the hbm2java line so that it looks like this:

```
<hbm2java jdk5="true"/>
```

This tells the tool that we're in a Java 5 (or later) environment, so we'd like to take advantage of its useful new capabilities. After this change, run *ant codegen* again, and notice the changes in the generated code, which are highlighted in Example 4-5.

Example 4-5. Improvements to generated Artist class in jdk5 mode

```
...
    private Set<Track> tracks = new HashSet<Track>(0);
...
    public Artist(String name, Set<Track> tracks) {
        this.name = name;
        this.tracks = tracks;
    }
...
    public Set<Track> getTracks() {
        return this.tracks;
    }

    public void setTracks(Set<Track> tracks) {
        this.tracks = tracks;
    }
...
```

This is the code I was hoping to see—nice type-safe use of the Java Generics capabilities added to Collections in Java 5. Similar treatment was given to the artists property in

Track.java. Let's take a peek at the new "full" constructor as an example, and so we can see how to invoke it later in Example 4-9:

```
public Track(String title, String filePath, Date playTime,
        Set<Artist> artists, Date added, short volume) {
    ...
    }
```

Our schema change has created a new parameterized `Set` argument for the artists property between `playTime` and `Date added`.

Now that the classes are created (or updated), we can use *ant schema* to build the new database schema that supports them.

> Ah, much better. It's amazing how much benefit you can get from one little configuration parameter.

 Of course you should watch for error messages when generating your source code and building your schema, in case there are any syntax or conceptual errors in the mapping document. Not all exceptions that show up are signs of real problems you need to address, though. In experimenting with evolving this schema, I ran into some exception reports because Hibernate tried to drop foreign key constraints that hadn't been set up by previous runs. The schema generation continued past them, scary as they looked, and worked correctly. This may improve in later versions (of Hibernate or HSQLDB, or perhaps just the SQL dialect implementation), but the behavior has been around for several years now.

The generated schema contains the tables we'd expect, along with indices and some clever foreign key constraints. As our object model gets more sophisticated, the amount of work (and expertise) being provided by Hibernate is growing nicely. The full output from the schema generation is rather long, but Example 4-6 shows the highlights.

Example 4-6. Excerpts from our new schema generation

```
[hibernatetool] drop table ARTIST if exists;
[hibernatetool] drop table TRACK if exists;
[hibernatetool] drop table TRACK_ARTISTS if exists;

[hibernatetool] create table ARTIST (ARTIST_ID integer generated by default
    as identity (start with 1), NAME varchar(255) not null,
    primary key (ARTIST_ID), unique (NAME));

[hibernatetool] create table TRACK (TRACK_ID integer generated by default as
    identity (start with 1), TITLE varchar(255) not null,
    filePath varchar(255) not null, playTime time, added date,
    volume smallint not null, primary key (TRACK_ID));

[hibernatetool] create table TRACK_ARTISTS (ARTIST_ID integer not null,
    TRACK_ID integer not null, primary key (TRACK_ID, ARTIST_ID));

[hibernatetool] create index ARTIST_NAME on ARTIST (NAME);
[hibernatetool] create index TRACK_TITLE on TRACK (TITLE);
```

```
[hibernatetool] alter table TRACK_ARTISTS add constraint
  FK72EFDAD8620962DF foreign key (ARTIST_ID) references ARTIST;

[hibernatetool] alter table TRACK_ARTISTS add constraint
  FK72EFDAD82DCBFAB5 foreign key (TRACK_ID) references TRACK;
```

Figure 4-1 shows HSQLDB's tree view representation of the schema after these additions. I'm not sure why two separate indices are used to establish the uniqueness constraint on artist names, but that seems to be an implementation quirk in HSQLDB, and this approach will work just fine.

> Cool! I didn't even know how to do some of that stuff in HSQLDB!

What just happened?

We've set up an object model that allows our Track and Artist objects to keep track of an arbitrary set of relationships to each other. Any track can be associated with any number of artists, and any artist can be responsible for any number of tracks. Getting this set up right can be challenging, especially for people who are new to object-oriented code or relational databases (or both!), so it's nice to have the help of Hibernate. But just wait until you see how easy it is to work with data in this setup.

It's worth emphasizing that the links between artists and tracks are not stored in the ARTIST or TRACK tables themselves. Because they are in a many-to-many association, meaning that an artist can be associated with many tracks, and many artists can be associated with a track, these links are stored in a separate join table called TRACK_ARTISTS. Rows in this table pair an ARTIST_ID with a TRACK_ID, to indicate that the specified artist is associated with the specified track. By creating and deleting rows in this table, we can set up any pattern of associations we need. (This is how many-to-many relationships are always represented in relational databases; the chapter of George Reese's *Java Database Best Practices* cited earlier is a good introduction to data models like this.)

Keeping this in mind, you will also notice that our generated classes don't contain any code to manage the TRACK_ARTISTS table. Nor will the upcoming examples that create and link persistent Track and Artist objects. They don't have to, because Hibernate's special Collection classes take care of all those details for us, based on the mapping information we added to Examples 4-1 and 4-3.

All right, let's create some tracks and artists.

Persisting Collections

Our first task is to enhance the CreateTest class to take advantage of the new richness in our schema, creating some artists and associating them with tracks.

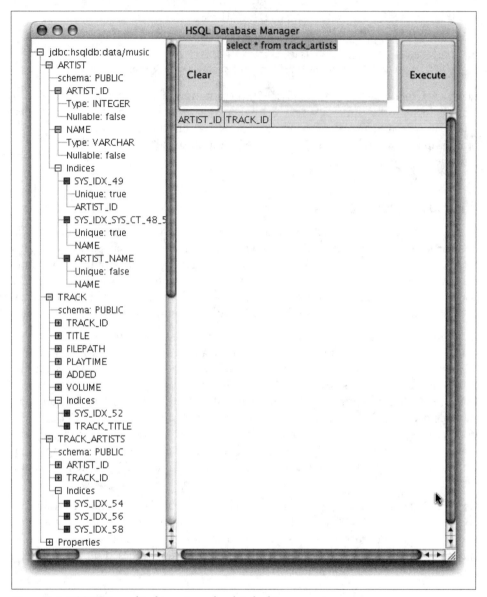

Figure 4-1. HSQLDB graphical tree view of updated schema

How do I do that?

To begin with, add some helper methods to *CreateTest.java* to simplify the task, as shown in Example 4-7 (with changes and additions in bold).

Example 4-7. Utility methods to help find and create artists, and link them to tracks

```
package com.oreilly.hh;

import org.hibernate.*;
import org.hibernate.cfg.Configuration;

import com.oreilly.hh.data.*;

import java.sql.Time;
import java.util.*; ❶

/**
 * Create more sample data, letting Hibernate persist it for us.
 */
public class CreateTest {

  /**
   * Look up an artist record given a name.
   * @param name the name of the artist desired.
   * @param create controls whether a new record should be created if
   *        the specified artist is not yet in the database.
   * @param session the Hibernate session that can retrieve data
   * @return the artist with the specified name, or <code>null</code> if no
   *         such artist exists and <code>create</code> is <code>false</code>.
   * @throws HibernateException if there is a problem.
   */
  public static Artist getArtist(String name, boolean create, Session session) ❷
  {
    Query query = session.getNamedQuery("com.oreilly.hh.artistByName");
    query.setString("name", name);
    Artist found = (Artist)query.uniqueResult(); ❸
    if (found == null && create) { ❹
      found = new Artist(name, new HashSet<Track>());
      session.save(found);
    }
    return found;
  }

  /**
   * Utility method to associate an artist with a track
   */
  private static void addTrackArtist(Track track, Artist artist) { ❺
    track.getArtists().add(artist);
  }
```

As is so often the case when working with Hibernate, this code is pretty simple and self-explanatory:

❶ We used to import `java.util.Date`, but we're now importing the whole util package to work with `Collections`. The "*" is bold to highlight this, but it's easy to miss when scanning the example.

❷ We'll want to reuse the same artists if we create multiple tracks for them—that's the whole point of using an **Artist** object rather than just storing strings—so our getArtist( ) method does the work of looking them up by name.

❸ The uniqueResult( ) method is a convenience feature of the **Query** interface, perfect in situations like this, where we know we'll either get one result or none. It saves us the trouble of getting back a list of results, checking the length and extracting the first result if it's there. We'll either get back the single result or **null** if there were none. (We'll be thrown an exception if there is more than one result—you might think our **unique** constraint on the column would prevent that, but SQL is case-sensitive, and our query is matching insensitively, so it's up to us to be sure we always call getArtist( ) to see if an artist exists before creating a new record.)

❹ So all we need to do is check for **null** and create a new **Artist** if we didn't find one and the create flag indicates we're supposed to.

 If we left out the session.save( ) call, our artists would remain transient. (Itinerant painters? Sorry.) Hibernate is helpful enough to throw an exception if we try to commit our transaction in this state, by detecting references from persistent **Track** instances to transient **Artist** instances. You may want to review the lifecycle discussion in Chapter 3, and "Lifecycle Associations" in Chapter 5, which explores this in more depth.

❺ The addTrackArtist( ) method is almost embarrassingly simple. It's just ordinary Java **Collections** code that grabs the **Set** of artists belonging to a **Track** and adds the specified **Artist** to it. Can that really do everything we need? Where's all the database manipulation code we normally have to write? Welcome to the wonderful world of object/relational mapping tools!

You might have noticed that getArtist( ) uses a named query to retrieve the **Artist** record. In Example 4-8, we will add that at the end of *Artist.hbm.xml*. (Actually, we could put it in any mapping file, but this is the most sensible place, since it relates to **Artist** records.)

Example 4-8. Artist lookup query to be added to the artist mapping document

```
<query name="com.oreilly.hh.artistByName">
    <![CDATA[
        from Artist as artist
        where upper(artist.name) = upper(:name)
    ]]>
</query>
```

We use the upper( ) function to perform a case-insensitive comparison of artists' names, so that we retrieve the artist even if the capitalization is different during lookup than what's stored in the database. This sort of case-insensitive but preserving architecture, a user-friendly concession to the way humans like to work, is worth implementing whenever possible. Databases other than HSQLDB may have a different name for the function that converts strings to uppercase, but there should be one available. And we'll see a nice Java-oriented, database-independent way of doing this sort of thing in Chapter 8.

Now we can use this infrastructure to actually create some tracks with linked artists. Example 4-9 shows the remainder of the CreateTest class with the additions marked in bold. Edit your copy to match (or download it to save the typing).

Example 4-9. Revisions to main() in CreateTest.java to add artist associations

```
public static void main(String args[]) throws Exception {
  // Create a configuration based on the XML file we've put
  // in the standard place.
  Configuration config = new Configuration();
  config.configure();

  // Get the session factory we can use for persistence
  SessionFactory sessionFactory = config.buildSessionFactory();

  // Ask for a session using the JDBC information we've configured
  Session session = sessionFactory.openSession();
  Transaction tx = null;
  try {
    // Create some data and persist it
    tx = session.beginTransaction();

    Track track = new Track("Russian Trance",
                        "vol2/album610/track02.mp3",
                        Time.valueOf("00:03:30"),
                        new HashSet<Artist>(), ❶
                        new Date(), (short)0);
    addTrackArtist(track, getArtist("PPK", true, session));
    session.save(track);

    track = new Track("Video Killed the Radio Star",
                    "vol2/album611/track12.mp3",
                    Time.valueOf("00:03:49"), new HashSet<Artist>(),
                    new Date(), (short)0);
    addTrackArtist(track, getArtist("The Buggles", true, session));
    session.save(track);

    track = new Track("Gravity's Angel",
                    "vol2/album175/track03.mp3",
                    Time.valueOf("00:06:06"), new HashSet<Artist>(),
                    new Date(), (short)0);
    addTrackArtist(track, getArtist("Laurie Anderson", true, session));
    session.save(track);

    track = new Track("Adagio for Strings (Ferry Corsten Remix)", ❷
                    "vol2/album972/track01.mp3",
                    Time.valueOf("00:06:35"), new HashSet<Artist>(),
                    new Date(), (short)0);
    addTrackArtist(track, getArtist("William Orbit", true, session));
    addTrackArtist(track, getArtist("Ferry Corsten", true, session));
```

```
          addTrackArtist(track, getArtist("Samuel Barber", true, session));
          session.save(track);

          track = new Track("Adagio for Strings (ATB Remix)",
                          "vol2/album972/track02.mp3",
                          Time.valueOf("00:07:39"), new HashSet<Artist>(),
                          new Date(), (short)0);
          addTrackArtist(track, getArtist("William Orbit", true, session));
          addTrackArtist(track, getArtist("ATB", true, session));
          addTrackArtist(track, getArtist("Samuel Barber", true, session));
          session.save(track);

          track = new Track("The World '99",
                          "vol2/singles/pvw99.mp3",
                          Time.valueOf("00:07:05"), new HashSet<Artist>(),
                          new Date(), (short)0);
          addTrackArtist(track, getArtist("Pulp Victim", true, session));
          addTrackArtist(track, getArtist("Ferry Corsten", true, session));
          session.save(track);

          track = new Track("Test Tone 1", ❸
                          "vol2/singles/test01.mp3",
                          Time.valueOf("00:00:10"), new HashSet<Artist>(),
                          new Date(), (short)0);
          session.save(track);

          // We're done; make our changes permanent
          tx.commit();

        } catch (Exception e) {
          if (tx != null) {
            // Something went wrong; discard all partial changes
            tx.rollback();
          }
          throw new Exception("Transaction failed", e);
        } finally {
          // No matter what, close the session
          session.close();
        }

        // Clean up after ourselves
        sessionFactory.close();
      }
    }
```

The changes to the existing code are pretty minimal:

❶   The lines that created the three tracks from Chapter 3 need only a single new
      parameter each to supply an initially empty set of **Artist** associations. Each also
      gets a new follow-up line establishing an association to the artist for that track.
      We could have structured this code differently, by writing a helper method to
      create the initial **HashSet** containing the artist, so we could do this all in one line.
      The approach we actually used scales better to multiartist tracks, as the next
      section illustrates.

---

❷ The largest chunk of new code simply adds three new tracks to show how multiple artists per track are handled. If you like electronica and dance remixes (or classical for that matter), you know how important an issue that can be. Because we set the links up as collections, it's simply a matter of adding each artist link to the tracks.

❸ Finally, we add a track with no artist associations to see how that behaves. Now you can run *ant ctest* to create the new sample data containing tracks, artists, and associations between them.

 If you're making changes to your test data creation program and you want to try it again starting from an empty database, issue the command *ant schema ctest*. This useful trick tells Ant to run the schema and ctest targets one after the other. Running schema blows away any existing data; then ctest gets to create it anew.

What just happened?

There's no visible output from running ctest beyond the SQL statements Hibernate is using (if you still have show_sql set to true in *hibernate.cfg.xml*) and those aren't very informative; look at *data/music.script* to see what got created or fire up *ant db* to look at it via the graphical interface. Take a look at the contents of the three tables. Figure 4-2 shows what ended up in the join table that represents associations between artists and tracks. The raw data is becoming cryptic.

> Of course, in real life you'd be getting this data into the database in some other way—through a user interface, or as part of the process of importing the actual music. But your unit tests might look like this.

If you're used to relational modeling, this query shows you everything worked. If you're mortal like me, the next section is more convincing; it's certainly more fun.

Retrieving Collections

You might expect that getting the collection information back out of the database is similarly easy. You'd be right! Let's enhance our QueryTest class so it shows us the artists associated with the tracks it displays. Example 4-10 shows the appropriate changes and additions in bold. Little new code is needed.

Example 4-10. QueryTest.java enhanced to display artists associated with tracks

```
package com.oreilly.hh;

import org.hibernate.*;
import org.hibernate.cfg.Configuration;

import com.oreilly.hh.data.*;

import java.sql.Time;
```

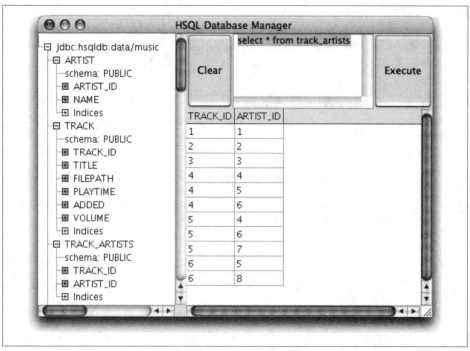

Figure 4-2. Artist and track associations created by the new version of CreateTest

```java
import java.util.*;

/**
 * Retrieve data as objects
 */
public class QueryTest {

    /**
     * Retrieve any tracks that fit in the specified amount of time.
     *
     * @param length the maximum playing time for tracks to be returned.
     * @param session the Hibernate session that can retrieve data.
     * @return a list of {@link Track}s meeting the length restriction.
     */
    public static List tracksNoLongerThan(Time length, Session session) {
        Query query = session.getNamedQuery(
                        "com.oreilly.hh.tracksNoLongerThan");
        query.setTime("length", length);
        return query.list();
    }

    /**
     * Build a parenthetical, comma-separated list of artist names.
     * @param artists the artists whose names are to be displayed.
     * @return the formatted list, or an empty string if the set was empty.
     */
    public static String listArtistNames(Set<Artist> artists) { ❶
```

```
        StringBuilder result = new StringBuilder();
        for (Artist artist : artists) {
            result.append((result.length() == 0) ? "(" : ", ");
            result.append(artist.getName());
        }
        if (result.length() > 0) {
            result.append(") ");
        }
        return result.toString();
    }

    /**
     * Look up and print some tracks when invoked from the command line.
     */
    public static void main(String args[]) throws Exception {
        // Create a configuration based on the XML file we've put
        // in the standard place.
        Configuration config = new Configuration();
        config.configure();

        // Get the session factory we can use for persistence
        SessionFactory sessionFactory = config.buildSessionFactory();

        // Ask for a session using the JDBC information we've configured
        Session session = sessionFactory.openSession();
        try {
            // Print the tracks that will fit in seven minutes
            List tracks = tracksNoLongerThan(Time.valueOf("00:07:00"), ❷
                                             session);
            for (ListIterator iter = tracks.listIterator() ;
                 iter.hasNext() ; ) {
                Track aTrack = (Track)iter.next();
                System.out.println("Track: \"" + aTrack.getTitle() + "\" " +
                                    listArtistNames(aTrack.getArtists()) + ❸
                                    aTrack.getPlayTime());
            }
        } finally {
            // No matter what, close the session
            session.close();
        }

        // Clean up after ourselves
        sessionFactory.close();
    }
}
```

❶   The first thing we add is a little utility method to format the set of artist names nicely, as a comma-delimited list inside parentheses, with proper spacing, or as nothing at all if the set of artists is empty.

❷   Since all the interesting new multiartist tracks are longer than five minutes, we increase the cutoff in our query to seven minutes so we can see some results.

❸ Finally, we call `listArtistNames()` at the proper position in the `println()` statement describing the tracks found.

At this point, it's time to get rid of Hibernate's query debugging output, because it will prevent us from seeing what we want to see. Edit *hibernate.cfg.xml* in the *src* directory, and change the `show_sql` property value to `false`:

```
...
    <!-- Echo all executed SQL to stdout -->
    <property name="show_sql">false</property>
...
```

With this done, Example 4-11 shows the new output from *ant qtest*.

Example 4-11. QueryTest output with artist information

```
% ant qtest
Buildfile: build.xml

prepare:

compile:
    [javac] Compiling 1 source file to /Users/jim/svn/oreilly/hib_dev_2e/current
/scratch/ch04/classes

qtest:
    [java] Track: "Russian Trance" (PPK) 00:03:30
    [java] Track: "Video Killed the Radio Star" (The Buggles) 00:03:49
    [java] Track: "Gravity's Angel" (Laurie Anderson) 00:06:06
    [java] Track: "Adagio for Strings (Ferry Corsten Remix)" (Ferry Corsten, Wi
lliam Orbit, Samuel Barber) 00:06:35
    [java] Track: "Test Tone 1" 00:00:10

BUILD SUCCESSFUL
Total time: 2 seconds
```

You'll notice two things. First, you'll see that this is much easier to interpret than the columns of numbers in Figure 4-2, and second, it worked! Even in the "tricky" case of the test tone track without any artist mappings, Hibernate takes the friendly approach of creating an empty artists `Set`, sparing us from peppering our code with the `null` checks we'd otherwise need to avoid crashing with `NullPointerException`s.

> But wait, there's more! No additional code needed....

Using Bidirectional Associations

In our creation code, we established links from tracks to artists, simply by adding Java objects to appropriate collections. Hibernate did the work of translating these associations and groupings into the necessary cryptic entries in a join table it created for that purpose. It allowed us with easy, readable code to establish and probe these relationships. But, remember that we made this association bidirectional—the `Artist` class has a collection of `Track` associations, too. We didn't bother to store anything in there.

The great news is that we don't have to. Because we marked this as an inverse mapping in the Artist mapping document, Hibernate understands that when we add an Artist association to a Track, we're implicitly adding that Track as an association to the Artist at the same time.

 This convenience works only when you make changes to the "primary" mapping, in which case they propagate to the inverse mapping. If you make changes only to the inverse mapping—in our case, the Set of tracks in the Artist object—they will not be persisted. This unfortunately means your code must be sensitive to which mapping is the inverse.

Let's build a simple interactive graphical application that can help us check whether the artist-to-track links really show up. When you type in an artist's name, it will show you all the tracks associated with that artist. A lot of the code is very similar to our first query test. Create the file *QueryTest2.java* and enter the code shown in Example 4-12.

Example 4-12. Source for QueryTest2.java

```java
package com.oreilly.hh;

import org.hibernate.*;
import org.hibernate.cfg.Configuration;

import com.oreilly.hh.data.*;

import java.sql.Time;
import java.util.*;
import java.awt.*;
import java.awt.event.*;
import javax.swing.*;

/**
 * Provide a user interface to enter artist names and see their tracks.
 */
public class QueryTest2 extends JPanel {

    JList list;  // Will contain tracks associated with current artist
    DefaultListModel model; // Lets us manipulate the list contents

    /**
     * Build the panel containing UI elements
     */
    public QueryTest2() {
        setLayout(new BorderLayout());
        model = new DefaultListModel();
        list = new JList(model);
        add(new JScrollPane(list), BorderLayout.SOUTH);

        final JTextField artistField = new JTextField(28);
        artistField.addKeyListener(new KeyAdapter() { ❶
                public void keyTyped(KeyEvent e) { ❷
```

```
                    SwingUtilities.invokeLater(new Runnable() { ❸
                        public void run() {
                            updateTracks(artistField.getText());
                        }
                    });
                }
            });
    add(artistField, BorderLayout.EAST);
    add(new JLabel("Artist: "), BorderLayout.WEST);
}


/**
 * Update the list to contain the tracks associated with an artist
 */
private void updateTracks(String name) { ❹
    model.removeAllElements();  // Clear out previous tracks
    if (name.length() < 1) return;   // Nothing to do
    try {
        // Ask for a session using the JDBC information we've configured
        Session session = sessionFactory.openSession(); ❺
        try {
            Artist artist = CreateTest.getArtist(name, false, session);
            if (artist == null) {  // Unknown artist
                model.addElement("Artist not found");
                return;
            }
            // List the tracks associated with the artist
            for (Track aTrack : artist.getTracks()) { ❻
                model.addElement("Track: \"" + aTrack.getTitle() +
                                 "\", " + aTrack.getPlayTime());
            }
        } finally { ❼
            // No matter what, close the session
            session.close();
        }
    } catch (Exception e) {
        System.err.println("Problem updating tracks:" + e);
        e.printStackTrace();
    }
}

private static SessionFactory sessionFactory;  // Used to talk to Hibernate

/**
 * Set up Hibernate, then build and display the user interface.
 */
public static void main(String args[]) throws Exception {
    // Load configuration properties, read mappings for persistent classes
    Configuration config = new Configuration(); ❽
    config.configure();

    // Get the session factory we can use for persistence
    sessionFactory = config.buildSessionFactory();

    // Set up the UI
```

```
        JFrame frame = new JFrame("Artist Track Lookup"); ❾
        frame.setDefaultCloseOperation(JFrame.EXIT_ON_CLOSE);
        frame.setContentPane(new QueryTest2());
        frame.setSize(400, 180);
        frame.setVisible(true);
    }
}
```

The bulk of the novel code in this example deals with setting up a Swing user interface. It's actually a rather primitive interface, and won't resize nicely, but dealing with such details would make the code larger, and really falls outside the scope of this book. If you want examples of how to build rich, quality, Swing interfaces, check out our *Java Swing*, Second Edition (O'Reilly). It's much thicker so it has room for all that good stuff.

> Yes, this is a shameless plug.

❶ The only item I want to highlight in the constructor is the KeyListener that gets added to artistField. This rather tricky bit of code creates an anonymous class whose keyTyped( ) method is invoked whenever the user types in the artist text field.

❷ That method tries to update the track display by checking whether the field now contains a recognized artist name.

❸ Unfortunately, at the time the method gets invoked, the text field has not yet been updated to reflect the latest keystroke, so we're forced to defer the actual display update to a second anonymous class (this Runnable instance) via the invokeLater( ) method of SwingUtilities. This technique causes the update to happen when Swing "gets around to it," which in our case means the text field will have finished updating itself.

❹ The updateTracks( ) method that gets called at that point is where the interesting Hibernate stuff happens. It starts by clearing the list, discarding any tracks it might have previously been displaying. If the artist name is empty, that's all it does.

❺ Otherwise, it opens a Hibernate session and tries to look up the artist using the getArtist( ) method we wrote in CreateTest. This time we tell it *not* to create an artist if it can't find the one for which we asked, so we'll get back a null if the user hasn't typed the name of a known artist. If that's the case, we just display a message to that effect.

❻ If we do find an Artist record, on the other hand, we iterate over any Track records found in the artist's set of associated tracks, and display information about each one. All this will test whether the inverse association has worked the way we'd like it to.

❼ Finally (no pun intended), we make sure to close the session when we're leaving the method, even through an exception. You don't want to leak sessions—that's a good way to bog down and crash your whole database environment.

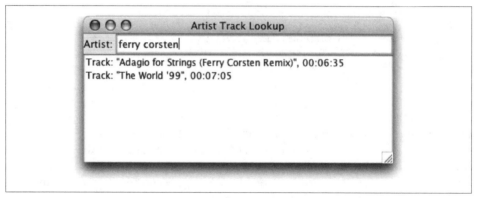

Figure 4-3. A very simple artist tracks browser

❽ The `main( )` method starts out with the same Hibernate configuration steps we've seen before.

❾ It then creates and displays the user interface frame, and sets the interface up to end the program when it's closed. After displaying the frame, `main( )` returns. From that point on, the Swing event loop is in control.

Once you've created (or downloaded) this source file, you also need to add a new target, shown in Example 4-13, to the end of *build.xml* (the Ant build file) to invoke this new class.

Example 4-13. Ant target for running the new query test

```
<target name="qtest2" description="Run a simple Artist exploration GUI"
        depends="compile">
  <java classname="com.oreilly.hh.QueryTest2" fork="true">
    <classpath refid="project.class.path"/>
  </java>
</target>
```

> This is very similar to the existing qtest target; copy and tweak that.

Now you can fire it up by typing *ant qtest2* and playing with it yourself. Figure 4-3 shows the program in action, displaying tracks for one of the artists in our sample data.

Working with Simpler Collections

The collections we've been looking at so far have all contained associations to other objects, which is appropriate for a chapter titled "Collections and Associations," but these aren't the only kind you can use with Hibernate. You can also define mappings for collections of simple values, like strings, numbers, and nonpersistent value classes.

How do I do that?

Suppose we want to be able to record some number of comments about each track in the database. We want a new property called comments to contain the `String` values of each associated comment. The new mapping in *Track.hbm.xml* looks a lot like what we did for artists, only a bit simpler[†]:

```
<set name="comments" table="TRACK_COMMENTS">
    <key column="TRACK_ID"/>
    <element column="COMMENT" type="string"/>
</set>
```

(You can put this right before the closing `</class>` tag in the mapping file—and you need to if you want the `Track` constructor to work with the rest of this example.)

Since we're able to store an arbitrary number of comments for each `Track`, we're going to need a new table in which to put them. Each comment will be linked to the proper `Track` through the track's id property.

Rebuilding the databases with *ant schema* shows how this gets built in the database:

```
[hibernatetool] create table TRACK_COMMENTS (TRACK_ID integer not null, COMMENT
varchar(255));
...
[hibernatetool] 16:16:55,876 DEBUG SchemaExport:303 - alter table TRACK_COMMENTS
 add constraint FK105B26882DCBFAB5 foreign key (TRACK_ID) references TRACK;
```

After updating the `Track` class via *ant codegen*, we need to add another `Set` at the end of each constructor invocation in *CreateTest.java*, for the comments. For example:

> Data modeling junkies will recognize this as a "one-to-many" relationship.

```
track = new Track("Test Tone 1",
"vol2/singles/test01.mp3",
Time.valueOf("00:00:10"), new HashSet<Artist>(),
                new Date(), (short)0, new HashSet<String>());
```

Then we can assign a comment on the following line:

```
track.getComments().add("Pink noise to test equalization");
```

A quick *ant ctest* will compile and run this (making sure you've not forgotten to add the second `HashSet` of strings to any tracks), and you can check *data/music.script* to see how it's stored in the database. Or, add another loop after the track `println()` in *QueryTest.java* to print the comments for the track that was just displayed:

```
for (String comment : aTrack.getComments()) {
                System.out.println("  Comment: " + comment);
}
```

[†] If you're porting these examples to Oracle, you'll have to change the name of the COMMENT column, which turns out to be a reserved word in the world of Oracle SQL. Standards—gotta love them—there are so many to choose from!

Then *ant qtest* will give you output like this:

```
...
[java] Track: "Test Tone 1" 00:00:10
[java]    Comment: Pink noise to test equalization
```

It's nice when tools make simple things easier. In the next chapter we'll see that more complex things are possible, too.

## CHAPTER 5

Richer Associations

Yes, wealthy friends would be nice. But we can't propose an easy way to get any, so instead let's look at relationships between objects that carry more information than simple grouping. In this chapter we'll look at the tracks that make up an album. We put that off in Chapter 4 because organizing an album involves more than simply grouping some tracks; you also need to know the order in which the tracks occur, as well as things like which disc they're on, if you want to support multidisc albums. That goes beyond what you can achieve with an automatically generated join table, so we'll design our own `AlbumTrack` object and table, and let albums link to these.

Eager and Lazy Associations

First rich, then eager and lazy? It sure sounds like we're anthropomorphizing our data model. But this really is an object/relational mapping topic of some importance. As your data model grows, adding associations between objects and tables, your program gains power, which is great. But you often end up with a large fraction of your objects somehow linked to each other. So, what happens when you load one of the objects that is part of a huge interrelated cluster? Since, as you've seen, you can move from one object to its associated objects just by traversing properties, it seems you'd have to load all the associated objects when you load any of them. For small databases, this is fine (and indeed, the HSQLDB databases we've been playing with in the examples exist entirely in memory at runtime), but in general application design your database will often hold a *lot* more than the memory available to your program. Uh oh! And, even if it could all fit, rarely will you actually access most of those objects, so it'd be a waste to load them all.

Luckily, this problem was anticipated by the designers of object/relational mapping software, including Hibernate. The trick is to allow associations to be "lazy," so that associated objects aren't loaded until they're actually referenced. Hibernate will instead make a note of the linked object's identity and put off loading it until you actually try to access it. This is especially important for collections like those we've been using.

How do I do that?

Prior to Hibernate 3, the default was for associations *not* to be lazy, so you needed to set the `lazy` attribute in the mapping declaration. However, since it is almost always the best practice to use lazy associations, this default was reversed in Hibernate 3 (which required careful attention on the part of people migrating their applications; backward-incompatible changes like this are never undertaken lightly).

When their associations are lazy, Hibernate uses its own special lazy implementations of Collections classes that don't load their contents from the database until you actually try to use them. This is done completely transparently, so you don't even notice it's taking place in your code.

Well, if it's that simple, and avoids problems with loading giant snarls of interrelated objects, why would you ever turn it off? The problem is that the transparency breaks down once you've closed your Hibernate session. At that point, if you try to access content from a lazy collection that hasn't been initialized (even if you've assigned the collection to a different variable, or returned it from a method call), the Hibernate-provided proxy collection can no longer access the database to perform the deferred loading of its contents, and it is forced to throw a `LazyInitializationException`. (And, as we'll discuss in a few pages, you do want to close your sessions quickly.)

Because this can lead to unexpected crashes far away from the Hibernate-specific code, you can turn it off in cases where the effort of making sure anything you might need to use outweighs the potential cost of loading more than you really need. It's your responsibility to think carefully about situations in which you need to disable it, and ensure that you are using your lazily-loaded objects safely. The Hibernate reference manual goes into a bit of detail about strategies to consider.

> Conservation of complexity seems almost like a law of thermodynamics.

For example, if we wanted to avoid having to worry about lazy initialization, our track artists mapping could look like Example 5-1.

Example 5-1. Eagerly initializing the track artist associations

```
<set name="artists" table="TRACK_ARTISTS" lazy="false">
  <key column="TRACK"/>
  <many-to-many class="com.oreilly.hh.data.Artist" column="ARTIST_ID"/>
</set>
```

What about...

...laziness outside of collections? Caching and clustering?

It's easy to see how lazy collections can be supported, since Hibernate can provide its own special implementations of the various `Collection` interfaces. But what about other kinds of associations? They might benefit from on-demand loading as well.

In fact, Hibernate does support this, and almost as easily (at least from our perspective as users of its services). Again, starting with Hibernate 3, this is enabled by default but you can turn it off by marking an entire persistent class as `lazy=false` (this attribute goes right in the `class` tag of the mapping document).

When your classes are being mapped in a lazy fashion, Hibernate will generate a proxy class that extends (and poses as) your data class. This lazy proxy puts off actually loading the data until it is needed. Any other objects with associations to the lazy class will sneakily be given these proxy objects, rather than references to your actual data object. The first time any of the methods of the proxy object are used, it will load the real data object and delegate the method call to it. Once the data object is loaded, the proxy simply continues delegating all method calls to it.

If you want to get fancier, you can specify a specific class (or interface) to be extended (or implemented) by the proxy class, using the `proxy` attribute. The `lazy` attribute is shorthand for specifying the persistent class itself as the type to be proxied. (If this is all incomprehensible, don't worry; that just means you don't yet need this capability. By the time you do, you'll understand it!)

Naturally, the same caveats about taking care to load anything you'll need to use before closing the session also apply to this kind of lazy initialization. You can use it, but do so with care and planning.

The Hibernate reference documentation discusses these considerations in more depth in its chapter *Improving Performance*[*]. Also introduced there is the fact that Hibernate can be integrated with JVM-level or even clustered object caches to boost the performances of large, distributed applications, by reducing the bottleneck of database access. When plugged in to such a cache, the mapping document lets you configure the cache behavior of classes and associations using (appropriately enough) `cache` tags. These configurations go well beyond what we cover in this book, but you should be aware that they're possible in case your application would benefit from them.

My head hurts

You may not have enjoyed even skimming that discussion. Frankly, these issues of understanding the boundaries of the set of objects your code will need to access along any path it might execute, and trying to optimize the ones that are loaded without wasting too much memory or developer energy, are among the most difficult tradeoffs and challenges that exist in object/relational mapping. Not even a nice library like Hibernate can completely shield you from them.

Fortunately, there are techniques for structuring your data access code to essentially avoid the whole problem in many common application scenarios, and you can probably understand why they are so popular. Remember that lazy associations can bite you only

[*] *http://www.hibernate.org/hib_docs/v3/reference/en/html/performance.html*

when you try to traverse the association after you have already closed the Hibernate session. If you do all your data manipulation while you have the session open, lazy associations always work perfectly and you don't have to think about them.

OK, great, let's just open a session at the start of the application, and close it when the user quits, right? Well, no, not so fast. A session includes a database transaction, and databases are shared resources. The longer you keep open a transaction, the more you bog down the database, the longer you hide your activities from other users and processes that probably should see them, and the more likely you'll run into a conflict with some other transaction when you finally try to commit it. You would *never* keep a transaction open while waiting for the user to do something.

So are we stuck in a catch-22? It's not as bad as all that. Often the overall structure of an application makes it very clear when data access is taking place, and provides natural boundaries for the Hibernate session to begin and end. For example, in a web application, it makes great sense to open a Hibernate session for the duration of processing an incoming request. In fact, people often set up Servlet filters to do just that automatically. And, if there are background tasks which periodically work with the data (for example to send out mailings overnight), they can use their own separate sessions with similarly well-defined boundaries. So, it's tricky and important, but not insurmountable. We provide more concrete examples of good approaches in Chapters 13 and 14.

Ordered Collections

That was a pretty big digression about object lifecycles, and an important one. But this chapter is meant to teach you how to do other fancy tricks with mapped collections, so let's get back to that fun stuff! Our first goal will be to store the tracks that make up an album, keeping them in the right order. Later we'll add information like the disc on which a track is found, and its position on that disc, so we can gracefully handle multidisc albums.

How do I do that?

> Oh, right, that's what we were going to try....

The task of keeping a collection in a particular order is actually quite straightforward. If that's all we cared about in organizing album tracks, we'd need only tell Hibernate to map a `List` or an `Array`. In our `Album` mapping we'd use something like what's shown in Example 5-2.

Example 5-2. Simple ordered mapping of tracks for an album

```
<list name="tracks" table="ALBUM_TRACKS">
  <key column="ALBUM_ID"/>
  <list-index column="LIST_POS"/>
  <many-to-many class="com.oreilly.hh.data.Track" column="TRACK_ID"/>
</list>
```

This is very much like the set mappings we've used so far (although it uses a different tag to indicate that it's an ordered list and therefore maps to a `java.util.List`). But notice that we also need to add a `list-index` tag to establish the ordering of the list, and we need to add a column to hold the value controlling the ordering in the database. Hibernate will manage the contents of this column for us, and use it to ensure that when we get the list out of the database in the future, its contents will be in the same order in which we stored them. The column is created as an integer, and if possible, it is used as part of a composite key for the table. The mapping in Example 5-2, when used to generate a HSQLDB database schema, produces the table shown in Example 5-3.

Example 5-3. Our simple track list realized as an HSQLDB schema

```
[hibernatetool] create table ALBUM_TRACKS (ALBUM_ID INTEGER not null,
                TRACK_ID INTEGER not null, LIST_POS INTEGER not null,
                primary key (ALBUM_ID, LIST_POS))
```

It's important to understand why the `LIST_POS` column is necessary. We need to control the order in which tracks appear in an album, and there aren't any properties of the tracks themselves we can use to keep them sorted in the right order. (Imagine how annoyed you'd be if your jukebox system could only play the tracks of an album in, say, alphabetical order, regardless of the intent of the artists who created it!) The fundamental nature of relational database systems is that you get results in whatever order the system finds convenient, unless you tell it how to sort them. The `LIST_POS` column gives Hibernate a value under its control that can be used to ensure that our list is always sorted in the order in which we created it. Another way to think about this is that the order of the entries is one of the independent pieces of information of which we want to keep track, so Hibernate needs a place to store it.

The corollary is also important. If there are values in your data that provide a natural order for traversal, there is no need for you to provide an index column; you don't even have to use a `list`. The `set` and `map` collection mappings can be configured to be sorted in Java by providing a `sort` attribute, or within the database itself by providing a SQL `order-by` attribute[†]. In either case, when you iterate over the contents of the collection, you'll get them in the specified order.

The values in the `LIST_POS` column will always be the same values you'd use as an argument to the `tracks.get( )` method in order to obtain the value at a particular position in the tracks list.

[†] The `order-by` attribute and SQL sorting of collections is only available if you're using version 1.4 or later of the Java SDK, since it relies on the `LinkedHashSet` or `LinkedHashMap` classes introduced in that release.

Augmenting Associations in Collections

All right, we've got a handle on what we need to do if we want our albums' tracks to be kept in the right order. What about the additional information we'd like to keep, such as the disc on which the track is found? When we map a collection of associations, we've seen that Hibernate creates a join table in which to store the relationships between objects. And we've just seen how to add an index column to the ALBUM_TRACKS table to maintain an ordering for the collection. Ideally, we'd like to have the ability to augment that table with more information of our own choosing, in order to record the other details we'd like to know about album tracks.

As it turns out, we can do just that, and in a very straightforward way.

How do I do that?

Up to this point we've seen two ways of getting tables into our database schema. The first was by explicitly mapping properties of a Java object onto columns of a table. The second was defining a collection (of values or associations), and specifying the table and columns used to manage that collection. As it turns out, there's nothing that prevents us from using a single table in both ways. Some of its columns can be used directly to map to our own objects' properties, while the others can manage the mapping of a collection. This lets us achieve our goals of recording the tracks that make up an album in an ordered way, augmented by additional details to support multidisc albums.

We'll want a new data object, AlbumTrack, to contain information about how a track is used on an album. Since we've already seen several examples of how to map full-blown entities with independent existence, and there really isn't a need for our AlbumTrack object to exist outside the context of an Album entity, this is a good opportunity to look at mapping a *component*. Recall that in Hibernate jargon an entity is an object that stands on its own in the persistence mechanism: it can be created, queried, and deleted independently of any other objects, and therefore has its own persistent identity (as reflected by its mandatory id property). A component, in contrast, is an object that can be saved to and retrieved from the database, but only as a subordinate part of some other entity. In this case, we'll define a list of AlbumTrack objects as a component part of our Album entity. Example 5-4 shows a mapping for the Album class that achieves this.

> This flexibility takes a little getting used to, but it makes sense, especially if you think about mapping objects to an existing database schema.

Example 5-4. Album.hbm.xml, the mapping definition for an album

```xml
<?xml version="1.0"?>
<!DOCTYPE hibernate-mapping PUBLIC "-//Hibernate/Hibernate Mapping DTD 3.0//EN"
        "http://hibernate.sourceforge.net/hibernate-mapping-3.0.dtd">

<hibernate-mapping>
  <class name="com.oreilly.hh.data.Album" table="ALBUM">
    <meta attribute="class-description">
```

```
            Represents an album in the music database, an organized list of tracks.
            @author Jim Elliott (with help from Hibernate)
        </meta>

        <id column="ALBUM_ID" name="id" type="int">
            <meta attribute="scope-set">protected</meta>
            <generator class="native" />
        </id>

        <property name="title" type="string">
            <meta attribute="use-in-tostring">true</meta>
            <column index="ALBUM_TITLE" name="TITLE" not-null="true" />
        </property>

        <property name="numDiscs" type="integer" />

        <set name="artists" table="ALBUM_ARTISTS">
            <key column="ALBUM_ID" />
            <many-to-many class="com.oreilly.hh.data.Artist" column="ARTIST_ID" />
        </set>

        <set name="comments" table="ALBUM_COMMENTS">
            <key column="ALBUM_ID" />
            <element column="COMMENT" type="string" />
        </set>

        <list name="tracks" table="ALBUM_TRACKS"> ❶
            <meta attribute="use-in-tostring">true</meta>
            <key column="ALBUM_ID" />
            <index column="LIST_POS" />
            <composite-element class="com.oreilly.hh.data.AlbumTrack"> ❷
                <many-to-one class="com.oreilly.hh.data.Track" name="track"> ❸
                    <meta attribute="use-in-tostring">true</meta>
                    <column name="TRACK_ID" />
                </many-to-one>
                <property name="disc" type="integer" /> ❹
                <property name="positionOnDisc" type="integer" /> ❺
            </composite-element>
        </list>

        <property name="added" type="date">
            <meta attribute="field-description">
                When the album was created
            </meta>
        </property>

    </class>
</hibernate-mapping>
```

Once we've created the file *Album.hbm.xml*, we need to add it to the list of mapping resources in *hibernate.cfg.xml*. Open up the *hibernate.cfg.xml* file in *src*, and add the line highlighted in bold in Example 5-5.

Example 5-5. Adding Album.hbm.xml to the Hibernate configuration

```xml
<?xml version='1.0' encoding='utf-8'?>
<!DOCTYPE hibernate-configuration PUBLIC
        "-//Hibernate/Hibernate Configuration DTD 3.0//EN"
        "http://hibernate.sourceforge.net/hibernate-configuration-3.0.dtd">

<hibernate-configuration>

    <session-factory>

...
            <mapping resource="com/oreilly/hh/data/Track.hbm.xml"/>
            <mapping resource="com/oreilly/hh/data/Artist.hbm.xml"/>
            <mapping resource="com/oreilly/hh/data/Album.hbm.xml"/>

    </session-factory>

</hibernate-configuration>
```

A lot of this is similar to mappings we've seen before, but the tracks list is worth some careful examination. The discussion gets involved, so let's step back a minute and recall exactly what we're trying to accomplish.

We want our album to keep an ordered list of the tracks that make it up, along with additional information about each track that tells which disc it's on (in case the album has multiple discs) and the track's position within the disc. This conceptual relationship is shown in the middle of Figure 5-1. The association between albums and tracks is mediated by an "Album Tracks" object that adds disc and position information, as well as keeping them in the right order. The model of the tracks themselves is familiar (we're leaving out artist and comment information in this diagram, in an effort to keep it simple). This model is what we've captured in the album mapping document, Example 5-4. Let's examine the details of how it was done. Later we'll look at how Hibernate turns this specification into Java code (the bottom part of Figure 5-1) and a database schema (the top part).

All right, armed with this reminder and elaboration of the conceptual framework, we're ready to look at the details of Example 5-4:

❶   If you compare the list definition with one of the set mappings in the preceding chapter, you'll see a lot of similarity. It looks even more like Example 5-2, except that the association mapping has been moved inside a new composite-element mapping.

❷   This element introduces the new AlbumTrack object we use to group the disc, position, and Track link needed to organize an album's tracks.

❸   Also, rather than being a many-to-many mapping (because an album generally has multiple tracks, and a given track file might be shared between several albums), the association between AlbumTrack and Track is many-to-one: several AlbumTrack objects (from different albums) might refer to the same Track file if

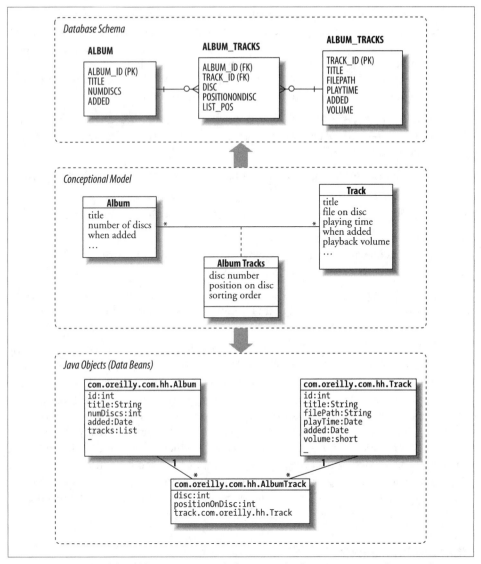

Figure 5-1. Models of the tables, concepts, and objects involved in representing album tracks

we're trying to save disk space, but each `AlbumTrack` object is concerned with only one `Track`. The `list` tag that contains `AlbumTrack` is implicitly one-to-many. (If you're still having trouble with these data modeling concepts, don't struggle too hard just now—the source code and schema coming up shortly will hopefully help you see what is happening here.)

OK, back to considering this new `composite-element` definition as a whole. It specifies that we want to use a new `AlbumTrack` class as the values that appear in our `Album` data bean's tracks list. The body of the `composite-element` tag defines the properties of AlbumTrack, which group all the information we need about a track on an album. The syntax for these nested properties is no different than that of the outer mappings for Album's own properties. They can even include their own nested composite elements, collections, or (as seen here) meta elements. This gives us tremendous flexibility to set up fine-grained mappings that retain a healthy degree of object-oriented encapsulation.

Inside our composite AlbumTrack mapping, we are recording an association with the actual Track (the many-to-one element we just examined) to be played at each position within the Album.

❹ The composite mapping also keeps track of the disc number on which that track is found.

❺ And finally it stores this entry's position on that disc (for example, track 3 of disc 2).

This mapping achieves the goals with which we started with illustrates how arbitrary information can be attached to a collection of associations.

The source for the component class itself can be found in Example 5-6, and it might help clarify this discussion. Compare this source code with its graphical representation at the bottom of Figure 5-1.

You may have noticed that we chose an explicit column name of TRACK_ID to use for the many-to-one link to the TRACK table. We've actually been doing this in a number of places, but previously it didn't require an entire separate line. It's worth talking about the reasoning behind this choice. Without this instruction, Hibernate will just use the property name (track) for the column name. You can use any names you want for your columns, but *Java Database Best Practices* encourages naming foreign key columns the same as the primary keys in the original tables to which they refer. This helps data modeling tools recognize and display the "natural joins" the foreign keys represent, which makes it easier for people to understand and work with the data. This consideration is also why I included the table names as part of the primary keys' column names.

What just happened?

I was all set to explain that by choosing to use a composite element to encapsulate our augmented track list, we'd have to write the Java source for AlbumTrack ourselves. I was sure this went far beyond the capabilities of the code generation tool. Much to my delight, when I tried *ant codegen* to see what sort of errors would result, the command reported success, and both *Album.java* and *AlbumTrack.java* appeared in the source directory!

It was at this point that I went back and added the use-in-tostring meta element for the track's many-to-one mapping inside the component. I

Sometimes it's *nice* to be proved wrong.

wasn't sure this would work either, because the only examples of its use I'd found in the reference manual were attached to actual **property** tags. But work it did, exactly as I had hoped.

The Hibernate best practices encourage using fine-grained classes and mapping them as components. Given how easily the code generation tool allows you to create them from your mapping documents, there is absolutely no excuse for ignoring this advice. Example 5-6 shows the source generated for our nested composite mapping.

Example 5-6. Code generated for AlbumTrack.java

```
package com.oreilly.hh.data;
// Generated Jun 21, 2007 11:11:48 AM by Hibernate Tools 3.2.0.b9

/**
 *       Represents an album in the music database, an organized list of tracks.
 *       @author Jim Elliott (with help from Hibernate)
 */
public class AlbumTrack  implements java.io.Serializable {

    private Track track;
    private Integer disc;
    private Integer positionOnDisc;

    public AlbumTrack() {
    }

    public AlbumTrack(Track track, Integer disc, Integer positionOnDisc) {
        this.track = track;
        this.disc = disc;
        this.positionOnDisc = positionOnDisc;
    }

    public Track getTrack() {
        return this.track;
    }

    public void setTrack(Track track) {
        this.track = track;
    }

    public Integer getDisc() {
        return this.disc;
    }

    public void setDisc(Integer disc) {
        this.disc = disc;
    }

    public Integer getPositionOnDisc() {
        return this.positionOnDisc;
    }

    public void setPositionOnDisc(Integer positionOnDisc) {
```

```java
        this.positionOnDisc = positionOnDisc;
    }

    /**
     * toString
     * @return String
     */
    public String toString() {
        StringBuffer buffer = new StringBuffer();

      buffer.append(getClass().getName()).append("@").append(
          Integer.toHexString(hashCode())).append(" [");
      buffer.append("track").append("='").append(getTrack()).append("' ");
      buffer.append("]");

      return buffer.toString();
    }
}
```

This looks similar to the generated code for entities we've seen in previous chapters, but it lacks an `id` property, which makes sense. Component classes don't need identifier fields, and they need not implement any special interfaces. The class JavaDoc is shared with the `Album` class, in which this component is used. The source of the `Album` class itself is a typical generated entity, so there's no need to reproduce it here.

At this point we can build the schema for these new mappings, via *ant schema*. Example 5-7 shows highlights of the resulting schema creation process. This is the concrete HSQLDB representation of the schema modeled at the top of Figure 5-1.

Example 5-7. Additions to the schema caused by our new album mapping

```
...
[hibernatetool] create table ALBUM (ALBUM_ID integer generated by default
                as identity (start with 1), TITLE varchar(255) not null,
                numDiscs integer, added date, primary key (ALBUM_ID));
...
[hibernatetool] create table ALBUM_ARTISTS (ALBUM_ID integer not null,
                ARTIST_ID integer not null,
                primary key (ALBUM_ID, ARTIST_ID));
...
[hibernatetool] create table ALBUM_COMMENTS (ALBUM_ID integer not null,
                COMMENT varchar(255));
...
[hibernatetool] create table ALBUM_TRACKS (ALBUM_ID integer not null,
                TRACK_ID integer, disc integer, positionOnDisc integer,
                LIST_POS integer not null,
                primary key (ALBUM_ID, LIST_POS));
...
[hibernatetool] create index ALBUM_TITLE on ALBUM (TITLE);
...
[hibernatetool] alter table ALBUM_ARTISTS add constraint FK7BA403FC620962DF
                foreign key (ARTIST_ID) references ARTIST;
[hibernatetool] alter table ALBUM_ARTISTS add constraint FK7BA403FC3C553835
                foreign key (ALBUM_ID) references ALBUM;
```

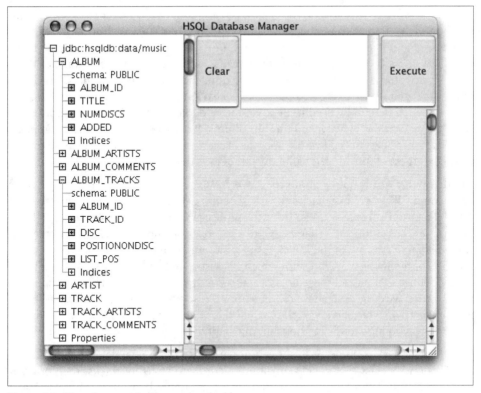

Figure 5-2. The schema with album-related tables

```
[hibernatetool] alter table ALBUM_COMMENTS add constraint FK1E2C21E43C553835
                foreign key (ALBUM_ID) references ALBUM;
[hibernatetool] alter table ALBUM_TRACKS add constraint FKD1CBBC782DCBFAB5
                foreign key (TRACK_ID) references TRACK;
[hibernatetool] alter table ALBUM_TRACKS add constraint FKD1CBBC783C553835
                foreign key (ALBUM_ID) references ALBUM;
...
```

 You may find that making radical changes to the schema causes problems for Hibernate or the HSQLDB driver. When I switched to this new approach for mapping album tracks, I ran into trouble because the first set of mappings established database constraints that Hibernate didn't know to drop before trying to build the revised schema. This prevented it from dropping and recreating some tables. If this ever happens to you, you can delete the database file (*music.script* in the *data* directory) and start from scratch, which should work fine. Recent versions of Hibernate also seem more robust in scenarios like this.

Figure 5-2 shows our enriched schema in HSQLDB's graphical management interface.

You might wonder why we use the separate Track class at all, rather than simply embedding all that information directly in our enhanced AlbumTrack collection. The simple answer is that not all tracks are part of an album—some might be singles, downloads, or otherwise independent. Given that we need a separate table to keep track of these anyway, it would be a poor design choice to duplicate its contents in the AlbumTracks table rather than associating with it. There is also a more subtle advantage to this approach, which is actually used in my own music database: this structure allows us to share a single track file between multiple albums. If the exact same recording appears on an album, a "best of" collection, and one or more period collections or sound tracks, linking all these albums to the same track file saves disk space.

Another point worth noting about the ALBUM_TRACK schema is that there is no obvious ID column. If you look back at the schema definition Hibernate emitted for ALBUM_TRACK in Example 5-7, you'll see the phrase primary key (ALBUM_ID, LIST_POS). Hibernate has noticed that, given the relationships we've requested in *Album.hbm.xml*, a row in the ALBUM_TRACK table can be uniquely identified by a combination of the ID of the Album with which it's associated and the index within the list it's modeling, so it has set these up as a *composite key* for the table. This is a nice little optimization we didn't even have to think about. Also notice that one of those columns is a property of the AlbumTrack class while the other is not. We'll look at a slightly different way to model this relationship in Chapter 7.

Let's look at some sample code showing how to use these new data objects. Example 5-8 shows a class that creates an album record and its list of tracks, then prints it out to test the debugging support that we've configured through the toString( ) method.

Example 5-8. Source of AlbumTest.java

```
package com.oreilly.hh;

import org.hibernate.*;
import org.hibernate.cfg.Configuration;

import com.oreilly.hh.data.*;

import java.sql.Time;
import java.util.*;

/**
 * Create sample album data, letting Hibernate persist it for us.
 */
public class AlbumTest {

    /**
     * Quick and dirty helper method to handle repetitive portion of creating
     * album tracks. A real implementation would have much more flexibility.
     */
    private static void addAlbumTrack(Album album, String title, String file,
                                      Time length, Artist artist, int disc,
```

```
                                      int positionOnDisc, Session session) { ❶
    Track track = new Track(title, file, length, new HashSet<Artist>(),
                            new Date(), (short)0, new HashSet<String>());
    track.getArtists().add(artist); ❷
    session.save(track);
    album.getTracks().add(new AlbumTrack(track, disc, positionOnDisc)); ❸
}

public static void main(String args[]) throws Exception {
    // Create a configuration based on the properties file we've put
    // in the standard place.
    Configuration config = new Configuration();
    config.configure();

    // Get the session factory we can use for persistence
    SessionFactory sessionFactory = config.buildSessionFactory();

    // Ask for a session using the JDBC information we've configured
    Session session = sessionFactory.openSession();
    Transaction tx = null;
    try {
        // Create some data and persist it
        tx = session.beginTransaction();

        Artist artist = CreateTest.getArtist("Martin L. Gore", true,
                                             session);
        Album album = new Album("Counterfeit e.p.", 1,
            new HashSet<Artist>(), new HashSet<String>(),
            new ArrayList<AlbumTrack>(5), new Date());
        album.getArtists().add(artist);
        session.save(album);

        addAlbumTrack(album, "Compulsion", "vol1/album83/track01.mp3",
                      Time.valueOf("00:05:29"), artist, 1, 1, session);
        addAlbumTrack(album, "In a Manner of Speaking",
                      "vol1/album83/track02.mp3", Time.valueOf("00:04:21"),
                      artist, 1, 2, session);
        addAlbumTrack(album, "Smile in the Crowd",
                      "vol1/album83/track03.mp3", Time.valueOf("00:05:06"),
                      artist, 1, 3, session);
        addAlbumTrack(album, "Gone", "vol1/album83/track04.mp3",
                      Time.valueOf("00:03:32"), artist, 1, 4, session);
        addAlbumTrack(album, "Never Turn Your Back on Mother Earth",
                      "vol1/album83/track05.mp3", Time.valueOf("00:03:07"),
                      artist, 1, 5, session);
        addAlbumTrack(album, "Motherless Child", "vol1/album83/track06.mp3",
                      Time.valueOf("00:03:32"), artist, 1, 6, session);

        System.out.println(album);

        // We're done; make our changes permanent
        tx.commit();

        // This commented out section is for experimenting with deletions.
        //tx = session.beginTransaction();
```

```
          //album.getTracks().remove(1);
          //session.update(album);
          //tx.commit();

          //tx = session.beginTransaction();
          //session.delete(album);
          //tx.commit();

      } catch (Exception e) {
          if (tx != null) {
              // Something went wrong; discard all partial changes
              tx.rollback();
          }
          throw new Exception("Transaction failed", e);
      } finally {
          // No matter what, close the session
          session.close();
      }

      // Clean up after ourselves
      sessionFactory.close();
  }
}
```

❶   The addAlbumTrack( ) method creates and persists a Track object given the speci-
     fied parameters.

❷   Next it associates the new track with a single Artist.

❸   Finally, it adds the track to the supplied Album, recording the disc it's on and its
     position within that disc.

In this simple example we're creating an album with just one disc. This quick-and-dirty
method can't cope with many variations, but it does allow the example to be compressed nicely.

We also need a new target at the end of *build.xml* to invoke the class. Add the lines of
Example 5-9 at the end of the file (but inside the project element, of course).

Example 5-9. New target to run our album test class
```
<target name="atest" description="Creates and persists some album data"
        depends="compile">
  <java classname="com.oreilly.hh.AlbumTest" fork="true">
    <classpath refid="project.class.path"/>
  </java>
</target>
```

With this in place, assuming you've generated the schema, run *ant ctest* followed by
ant atest. (Running ctest first is optional, but having some extra data in there to begin
with makes the album data somewhat more interesting. Recall that you can run these
targets in one command as *ant ctest atest*, and if you want to start by erasing the contents
of the database first, you can invoke *ant schema ctest atest*.) The debugging output
produced by this command is shown in Example 5-10. Although admittedly cryptic,

you should be able to see that the album and tracks have been created, and the order of the tracks has been maintained.

Example 5-10. Output from running the album test

```
atest:
     [java] com.oreilly.hh.data.Album@5bcf3a [title='Counterfeit e.p.' tracks='[
com.oreilly.hh.data.AlbumTrack@6a346a [track='com.oreilly.hh.data.Track@973271 [
title='Compulsion' volume='Volume[left=100, right=100]' sourceMedia='CD' ]' ], c
om.oreilly.hh.data.AlbumTrack@8e0e1 [track='com.oreilly.hh.data.Track@e3f8b9 [ti
tle='In a Manner of Speaking' volume='Volume[left=100, right=100]' sourceMedia='
CD' ]' ], com.oreilly.hh.data.AlbumTrack@de59f0 [track='com.oreilly.hh.data.Trac
k@e2d159 [title='Smile in the Crowd' volume='Volume[left=100, right=100]' source
Media='CD' ]' ], com.oreilly.hh.data.AlbumTrack@1e5a36 [track='com.oreilly.hh.da
ta.Track@b4bb65 [title='Gone' volume='Volume[left=100, right=100]' sourceMedia='
CD' ]' ], com.oreilly.hh.data.AlbumTrack@7b1683 [track='com.oreilly.hh.data.Trac
k@3171e [title='Never Turn Your Back on Mother Earth' volume='Volume[left=100, r
ight=100]' sourceMedia='CD' ]' ], com.oreilly.hh.data.AlbumTrack@e2e4d7 [track='
com.oreilly.hh.data.Track@1dfc6e [title='Motherless Child' volume='Volume[left=1
00, right=100]' sourceMedia='CD' ]' ]]' ]
```

If we run our old query test, we can see both the old and new data, as in Example 5-11.

Example 5-11. All tracks less than seven minutes long, whether from albums or otherwise

```
% ant qtest
Buildfile: build.xml
...
qtest:
     [java] Track: "Russian Trance" (PPK) 00:03:30
     [java] Track: "Video Killed the Radio Star" (The Buggles) 00:03:49
     [java] Track: "Gravity's Angel" (Laurie Anderson) 00:06:06
     [java] Track: "Adagio for Strings (Ferry Corsten Remix)" (Ferry Corsten, Sa
muel Barber, William Orbit) 00:06:35
     [java] Track: "Test Tone 1" 00:00:10
     [java]    Comment: Pink noise to test equalization
     [java] Track: "Compulsion" (Martin L. Gore) 00:05:29
     [java] Track: "In a Manner of Speaking" (Martin L. Gore) 00:04:21
     [java] Track: "Smile in the Crowd" (Martin L. Gore) 00:05:06
     [java] Track: "Gone" (Martin L. Gore) 00:03:32
     [java] Track: "Never Turn Your Back on Mother Earth" (Martin L. Gore) 00:03
:07
     [java] Track: "Motherless Child" (Martin L. Gore) 00:03:32

BUILD SUCCESSFUL
Total time: 2 seconds
```

Finally, Figure 5-3 shows a query in the HSQLDB interface that examines the contents of the ALBUM_TRACKS table.

What about…

…deleting, rearranging, and otherwise manipulating these interrelated pieces of information? This is actually supported fairly automatically, as the next section illustrates.

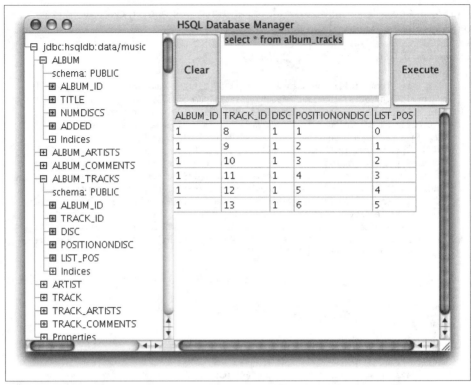

Figure 5-3. Our augmented collection of associations in action

Lifecycle Associations

Hibernate is completely responsible for managing the ALBUM_TRACKS table, adding and deleting rows (and, if necessary, renumbering LIST_POS values) as entries are added to or removed from Album beans' tracks properties. You can test this by writing a test program to delete the second track from our test album and see the result. A very quick-and-dirty way to do this would be to add the following four lines (shown in Example 5-12) right after the existing tx.commit( ) line in Example 5-8, and then run *ant schema ctest atest db*.

Example 5-12. Deleting our album's second track
```
tx = session.beginTransaction();
album.getTracks().remove(1);
session.update(album);
tx.commit();
```

Doing so changes the contents of ALBUM_TRACKS as shown in Figure 5-4 (compare this with the original contents in Figure 5-3). The second record has been removed (remember that Java list elements are indexed starting with zero), and LIST_POS has been

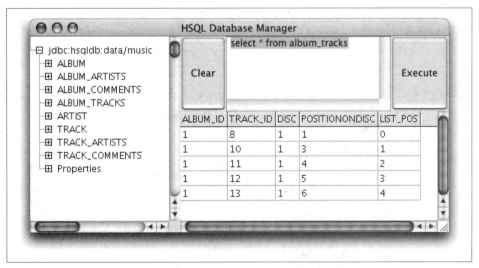

Figure 5-4. Album track associations after deleting our album's second track

adjusted so that it retains its consecutive nature, corresponding to the indices of the list elements (the values you'd use when calling `tracks.get( )`).

This happens because Hibernate understands that this list is "owned" by the Album record, and that the lifecycles of the two objects are intimately connected. This notion of lifecycle becomes more clear if you consider what happens if the entire Album is deleted: all of the associated records in ALBUM_TRACKS will be deleted as well. (Go ahead and modify the test program to try this if you're not convinced.)

Contrast this with the relationship between the ALBUM table and the TRACK table. Tracks are sometimes associated with albums, but they are sometimes independent. Removing a track from the list got rid of a row in ALBUM_TRACKS, eliminating the link between the album and track, but didn't get rid of the row in TRACK, so it didn't delete the persistent Track object itself. Similarly, deleting the Album would eliminate all the associations in the collection, but none of the actual Tracks. It's the responsibility of our code to take care of that when appropriate (probably after consulting the user, in case any of the track records might be shared across multiple albums, as discussed earlier).

If we don't need the flexibility of sharing the same track between albums—disk space is pretty cheap lately given the size of compressed audio—we can let Hibernate manage the TRACK records for the album in the same way it does the ALBUM_TRACKS collection. It won't assume it should do this, because Track and Album objects can exist independently, but we can establish a lifecycle relationship between them in the album mapping document.

How do I do that?

By now you're probably not surprised that there's a way to automate this.

Example 5-13 shows (in bold) the changes we'd make to the tracks property mapping in *Album.hbm.xml*.

Example 5-13. Establishing a lifecycle relationship between an album and its tracks

```
<list name="tracks" table="ALBUM_TRACKS" cascade="all">
  <meta attribute="use-in-tostring">true</meta>
  <key column="ALBUM_ID" />
  <index column="LIST_POS" />
  <composite-element class="com.oreilly.hh.AlbumTrack">
    <many-to-one class="com.oreilly.hh.Track" name="track"
                 cascade="all">
      <meta attribute="use-in-tostring">true</meta>
      <column name="TRACK_ID" />
    </many-to-one>
    <property name="disc" type="integer" />
    <property name="positionOnDisc" type="integer" />
  </composite-element>
</list>
```

The cascade attribute tells Hibernate that you want operations performed on a "parent" object to be transitively applied to its "child" or "dependent" objects. It's applicable to all forms of collections and associations. There are several possible values from which to choose. The most common are none (the default), save-update, delete, and all (which combines save-update and delete). You can also change the default from none to save-update throughout your entire mapping document by supplying a default-cascade attribute in the hibernate-mapping tag itself.

In our example, we want the tracks owned by an album to be automatically managed by the album, so that when we delete the album, its tracks are deleted. Note that we need to apply the cascade attribute both to the **tracks** collection and its constituent **track** element to achieve this. Also, by using a cascade value of all, we eliminate the need to explicitly save any Track objects we create for the album—the addAlbumTrack( ) method of Example 5-8 no longer needs the line:

```
session.save(track);
```

By telling Hibernate that it's fully responsible for the relationship between an album and its track, we enable it to persist tracks when they're added to the album as well as delete them when the album itself is deleted.

Delegating this sort of bookkeeping to the mapping layer can be very convenient, freeing you to focus on more abstract and important tasks, so it is worth using when appropriate. It's reminiscent of the liberation provided by Java's pervasive garbage collection, but it can't be as comprehensive because there is no definitive way to know when you're finished with persistent data by performing reachability analysis; you need to indicate it by calling delete( ) and establishing lifecycle connections. The trade-off between flexibility and simple automation is yours to make, based on the nature of your data and the needs of your project.

 Hibernate's management of lifecycle relationships is not fool-proof—or perhaps it's more accurate to say it's not all-encompassing. For example, if you use the `Collections` methods to remove a `Track` from an `Album`'s `tracks` property, this breaks the link between the `Album` and `Track` but does *not* actually delete the `Track` record. Even if you later delete the entire `Album`, this `Track` will remain, because it wasn't linked to the `Album` at the time it was deleted. Try some of these experiments by modifying *AlbumTest.java* appropriately and look at the resulting data in the tables!

And, actually, there are certain special cases where Hibernate can take care of even this level of detail. As long as you are using a many-to-one mapping in a parent-child relationship, you can mark it with a `cascade` value of `delete-orphan`. More details about this sort of thing can be found in the *Transitive persistence*[‡] section of the online reference manual.

Reflexive Associations

It's also possible for objects and tables to have associations back to themselves. This supports persistent recursive data structures like trees, in which nodes link to other nodes. Tracing through a database table storing such relationships using a SQL query interface is a major chore. Luckily, once it's mapped to Java objects, the process is much more readable and natural.

One way we might use a reflexive link in our music database is to allow alternate names for artists. This is useful more often than you might expect, because it makes it very easy to let the user find either "The Smiths" or "Smiths, The" depending on how they're thinking of the group, with little code, and in a language-independent way.

How do I do that?

All you need to do is add another field to the `Artist` mapping in *Artist.hbm.xml*, establishing a link back to `Artist`. Example 5-14 shows one option.

Example 5-14. Supporting a reflexive association in the Artist class

```
<many-to-one name="actualArtist" class="com.oreilly.hh.data.Artist">
  <meta attribute="use-in-tostring">true</meta>
</many-to-one>
```

> I mean human language here— English versus Spanish or something else. Put the links in the data rather than trying to write tricky code to guess when an artist name should be permuted.

[‡] *http://www.hibernate.org/hib_docs/v3/reference/en/html/objectstate.html#objectstate-transitive*

This gives us an `actualArtist` property that we can set to the id of the "definitive" `Artist` record when we're setting up an alternate name. For example, our "The Smiths" record might have id 5, and its `actualArtist` field would be `null` since it is definitive. Then we can create an "alias" `Artist` record with the name "Smiths, The" at any time, and set the actualArtist field in that record to point to record 5.

 This kind of reflexive link is one instance where a column containing a foreign key can't be named the same as the key column to which it is a link. We are associating a row in `ARTIST` with another row in `ARTIST`, and of course the table already has a column named `ARTIST_ID`.

Why is this association set up as many-to-one? There might be many alias records that point to one particular definitive `Artist`. So, each nickname needs to store the id of the actual artist record for which it is an alternative name. This is, in the language of data modeling, a many-to-one relationship.

Code that looks up artists just needs to check the `actualArtist` property before returning. If it's `null`, all is well. Otherwise, it should return the record indicated by actualArtist. Example 5-15 shows how we could extend the `getArtist( )` method in `CreateTest` to support this new feature (additions are in bold). Notice that the `Artist` constructor gets a new argument for setting `actualArtist`, which means we had to update the other places that call it in `CreateTest` too, even though we aren't showing them here.

Example 5-15. Artist lookup method supporting resolution of alternate names

```
public static Artist getArtist(String name, boolean create, Session session) {
    Query query = session.getNamedQuery("com.oreilly.hh.artistByName");
    query.setString("name", name);
    Artist found = (Artist)query.uniqueResult();
    if (found == null && create) {
        found = new Artist(name, new HashSet(), null);
        session.save(found);
    }
    if (found != null && found.getActualArtist() != null) {
        return found.getActualArtist();
    }
    return found;
}
```

Hopefully this chapter has given you a feel for the rich and powerful ways you can use associations and collections in Hibernate. As should be obvious from the way you can nest and combine these capabilities, there are far more variations than we can hope to cover in a book like this.

The good news is that Hibernate seems well equipped to handle almost any kind of relationship your application might need, and it can even do the drudge work of building the data classes and database schema for you. This works much more effectively and deeply than I ever expected it would when I started creating these examples.

## CHAPTER 6

Custom Value Types

Defining a User Type

Hibernate supports a wealth of Java types—both simple values and objects—as you can see by skimming Appendix A. By setting up mapping specifications, you can persist even highly complex, nested object structures to arbitrary database tables and columns. With all this power and flexibility, you might wonder why you'd ever need to go beyond the built-in type support.

One situation that might motivate you to customize Hibernate's type support is if you want to use a different SQL column type to store a particular Java type than Hibernate normally chooses. The reference documentation cites the example of persisting Java `BigInteger` values into `VARCHAR` columns, which might be necessary to accommodate a legacy database schema.

Another scenario that is very common involves persisting enumerated type values. Prior to Java 5, there was no built-in language support for enumerations, so although Joshua Bloch's excellent pattern presented in *Effective Java Programming Language Guide* (Addison-Wesley) was a de facto standard, Hibernate had to be agnostic about how to support the concept. The `PersistentEnum` interface that it provided prior to Hibernate 3 wasn't suited to the native `enum` support introduced in Java 5, so it has gone away. Unfortunately, nothing has arisen to replace it within Hibernate itself, so we'll show you how to leverage the user type support for this purpose.

Another scenario that requires the ability to tweak the type system is when you have a single property value that needs to be split into more than one database column—maybe the `Address` object in your company's mandated reuse library stores ZIP+4 codes as a single string, but the database to which you're integrating contains a required five digit column and a separate nullable four digit column for the two components. Or, maybe it's the other way around, and you need to separate a single database column into more than one property.

Luckily, in situations like this, Hibernate lets you take over the details of the persistence mapping so you can fit square pegs into round holes when you really need to.

You might also want to build a custom value type even in some cases where it's not strictly necessary. If you've got a composite type that is used in many places throughout your application (a vector, complex number, address, or the like), you can certainly map each of these occurrences as components, but it might be worth encapsulating the details of the mapping in a shared, reusable Java class rather than propagating the details throughout each of the mapping documents. That way, if the details of the mapping ever need to change for any reason, you've only got one class to fix rather than many individual component mappings to hunt down and adjust.

> Continuing in the spirit of making simple things easy and complex things possible....

In all of these scenarios, the task is to teach Hibernate a new way to translate between a particular kind of in-memory value and its persistent database representation.

How do I do that?

Hibernate lets you provide your own logic for mapping values in situations that need it, by implementing one of two interfaces: `org.hibernate.usertype.UserType` or `org.hibernate.usertype.CompositeUserType`.

It's important to realize that what is being created is a *translator* for a particular kind of value, not a new kind of value that knows how to persist itself. In other words, in our ZIP code example, it's not the ZIP code property that would implement `UserType`. Instead, we'd create a new class implementing `UserType`, and in our mapping document, specify this class as the Java type used to map the ZIP code property. Because of this, I think the terminology of "user types" is a little confusing.

Let's look at a concrete example. As noted above, a very common goal is to persist an enumerated type, and though Hibernate doesn't natively support this, we can leverage the `UserType` mechanism to achieve it fairly easily. Later in this chapter we'll look at a more complex mapping example involving multiple properties and columns.

Defining a Persistent Enumerated Type

An *enumerated type* is a common and useful programming abstraction allowing a value to be selected from a fixed set of named choices. These were originally well represented in Pascal, but C took such a minimal approach (essentially just letting you assign symbolic names to interchangeable integer values) that early Java releases reserved C's `enum` keyword but declined to implement it. A better, object-oriented approach known as the "typesafe enum pattern" evolved and was popularized in Joshua Bloch's *Effective Java*. This approach required a fair amount of boilerplate coding, but it lets you do all kinds of interesting and powerful things. One of the many delightful innovations in the Java 5 specification was the ability to resuscitate the `enum` keyword as an easy way to get the power of typesafe enumerations without all the tedious boilerplate coding, and it provides other nifty benefits.

Regardless of how you implement an enumerated type, you're some-times going to want to be able to persist such values to a database. And even though there is now a standard way to do it in Java, Hibernate doesn't offer any built-in support. So let's see how to implement a User Type that can persist an enum for us.

C-style numeric "enumerations" still appear too often in Java. Older parts of the Sun API contain many of them.

Let's suppose we want to be able to specify whether our tracks came from cassette tapes, vinyl, VHS tapes, CDs, a broadcast, an Internet download site, or a digital audio stream. (We could go really nuts and distinguish between Internet streams and satellite radio services like Sirius or XM, or radio versus television broad-cast, but this is plenty to demonstrate the important ideas.)

Without any consideration of persistence, our typesafe enumeration class might look something like Example 6-1. (The JavaDoc has been compressed to take less printed space, but the downloadable version is formatted normally.)

Example 6-1. SourceMedia.java, our initial typesafe enumeration

```java
package com.oreilly.hh;

/**
 * This is a typesafe enumeration that identifies the media on which an
 * item in our music database was obtained.
 */
public enum SourceMedia {
    /** Music obtained from magnetic cassette tape. */
    CASSETTE("Audio Cassette Tape"),

    /** Music obtained from a vinyl record. */
    VINYL("Vinyl Record"),

    /** Music obtained from VHS tapes. */
    VHS("VHS Videocassette tape"),

    /** Music obtained from a broadcast. */
    BROADCAST("Analog Broadcast"),

    /** Music obtained from a digital compact disc. */
    CD("Compact Disc"),

    /** Music obtained as an Internet download. */
    DOWNLOAD("Internet Download"),

    /** Music obtained from a digital audio stream. */
    STREAM("Digital Audio Stream");

    /**
     * Stores the human-readable description of this instance, by which it is
     * identified in the user interface.
     */
    private final String description;

    /**
```

```
 * Enum constructors are always private since they can only be accessed
 * through the enumeration mechanism.
 *
 * @param description human readable description of the source for the
 *           audio, by which it is presented in the user interface.
 */
private SourceMedia(String description) {
    this.description = description;
}

/**
 * Return the description associated with this enumeration instance.
 *
 * @return the human-readable description by which this value is
 *           identified in the user interface.
**/
public String getDescription() {
    return description;
}
}
```

Of course, the beauty of working with Hibernate is that we don't need to change our normal Java classes to add support for persistence. Even though we've not thought about persistence in designing this enum, we will be able to use it as-is. Now that we no longer have to consider using the deprecated PersistentEnum interface, defining a persistent enumerated type is no different than defining any other enumerated type.

So how do we teach Hibernate to persist values of our enumeration?

Using a Custom Type Mapping

As noted in the introduction to this chapter, we are going to create a class that Hibernate can use when it needs to persist our enumeration. We'll call our new class SourceMediaType. Our next decision is whether it needs to implement UserType or CompositeUserType. The reference documentation doesn't provide much guidance on this question, but the API documentation confirms the hint contained in the interface names: the CompositeUserType interface is only needed if your custom type implementation wants to expose internal structure in the form of named properties that can be accessed individually in queries (as in our ZIP code example). For SourceMedia, a simple UserType implementation is sufficient. The source for a mapping manager meeting our needs is shown in Example 6-2.

> The PersistentEnum interface did require you to change your enumerations for persistence. That was probably an even bigger reason why it was deprecated than the fact that it did not mesh well with the *Effective Java* persistent enumeration pattern or the Java 5 enum keyword.

Example 6-2. SourceMediaType.java, our custom type mapping handler

```
package com.oreilly.hh;

import java.io.Serializable;
import java.sql.PreparedStatement;
import java.sql.ResultSet;
import java.sql.SQLException;
```

```java
import java.sql.Types;

import org.hibernate.Hibernate;
import org.hibernate.HibernateException;
import org.hibernate.usertype.UserType;

/**
 * Manages persistence for the {@link SourceMedia} typesafe enumeration.
 */
public class SourceMediaType implements UserType {

    /**
     * Indicates whether objects managed by this type are mutable.
     *
     * @return <code>false</code>, since enumeration instances are immutable
     *         singletons.
     */
    public boolean isMutable() {
        return false;
    }

    /**
     * Return a deep copy of the persistent state, stopping at
     * entities and collections.
     *
     * @param value the object whose state is to be copied.
     * @return the same object, since enumeration instances are singletons.
     */
    public Object deepCopy(Object value) {
        return value;
    }

    /**
     * Compare two instances of the class mapped by this type for persistence
     * "equality".
     *
     * @param x first object to be compared.
     * @param y second object to be compared.
     * @return <code>true</code> iff both represent the same SourceMedia type.
     * @throws ClassCastException if x or y isn't a {@link SourceMedia}.
     */
    public boolean equals(Object x, Object y) {
        // We can compare instances, since SourceMedia are immutable singletons
        return (x == y);
    }

    /**
     * Determine the class that is returned by {@link #nullSafeGet}.
     *
     * @return {@link SourceMedia}, the actual type returned
     * by {@link #nullSafeGet}.
     */
    public Class returnedClass() {
        return SourceMedia.class;
    }
```

```
/**
 * Determine the SQL type(s) of the column(s) used by this type mapping.
 *
 * @return a single VARCHAR column.
 */
public int[] sqlTypes() { ❶
    // Allocate a new array each time to protect against callers changing
    // its contents.
    int[] typeList = new int[1];
    typeList[0] = Types.VARCHAR;
    return typeList;
}

/**
 * Retrieve an instance of the mapped class from a JDBC {@link ResultSet}.
 *
 * @param rs the results from which the instance should be retrieved.
 * @param names the columns from which the instance should be retrieved.
 * @param owner the entity containing the value being retrieved.
 * @return the retrieved {@link SourceMedia} value, or <code>null</code>.
 * @throws SQLException if there is a problem accessing the database.
 */
public Object nullSafeGet(ResultSet rs, String[] names, Object owner)
    throws SQLException ❷
{
    // Start by looking up the value name
    String name = (String) Hibernate.STRING.nullSafeGet(rs, names[0]);
    if (name == null) {
        return null;
    }
    // Then find the corresponding enumeration value
    try {
        return SourceMedia.valueOf(name); ❸
    }
    catch (IllegalArgumentException e) {
        throw new HibernateException("Bad SourceMedia value: " + name, e); ❹
    }
}

/**
 * Write an instance of the mapped class to a {@link PreparedStatement},
 * handling null values.
 *
 * @param st a JDBC prepared statement.
 * @param value the SourceMedia value to write.
 * @param index the parameter index within the prepared statement at which
 *        this value is to be written.
 * @throws SQLException if there is a problem accessing the database.
 */
public void nullSafeSet(PreparedStatement st, Object value, int index)
    throws SQLException ❺
{
    String name = null;
    if (value != null)
```

```java
        name = ((SourceMedia)value).toString();
        Hibernate.STRING.nullSafeSet(st, name, index);
}

/**
 * Reconstruct an object from the cacheable representation. At the very least this
 * method should perform a deep copy if the type is mutable. (optional operation)
 *
 * @param cached the object to be cached
 * @param owner the owner of the cached object
 * @return a reconstructed object from the cachable representation
 */
public Object assemble(Serializable cached, Object owner) {
    return cached;
}

/**
 * Transform the object into its cacheable representation. At the very least this
 * method should perform a deep copy if the type is mutable. That may not be enough
 * for some implementations, however; for example, associations must be cached as
 * identifier values. (optional operation)
 *
 * @param value the object to be cached
 * @return a cachable representation of the object
 */
public Serializable disassemble(Object value) {
    return (Serializable)value;
}

/**
 * Get a hashcode for an instance, consistent with persistence "equality".
 * @param x the instance whose hashcode is desired.
 */
public int hashCode(Object x) {
    return x.hashCode();
}

/**
 * During merge, replace the existing (target) value in the entity we are merging to
 * with a new (original) value from the detached entity we are merging. For immutable
 * objects, or null values, it is safe to simply return the first parameter. For
 * mutable objects, it is safe to return a copy of the first parameter. For objects
 * with component values, it might make sense to recursively replace component values.
 *
 * @param original the value from the detached entity being merged
 * @param target the value in the managed entity
 * @return the value to be merged
 */
public Object replace(Object original, Object target, Object owner)
    throws HibernateException
{
    return original;
}
}
```

Although it may look daunting, don't panic. All of the methods in this class are required by the UserType interface. Our implementations are quite brief and straightforward, as befits the simple mapping we've undertaken. The first three methods don't need any discussion beyond what's in the JavaDoc and inline comments. Here are some notes about the interesting bits:

❶ The sqlTypes( ) method reports to Hibernate the number of columns that will be needed to store values managed by this custom type and the SQL types of those columns. We indicate that our type uses a single VARCHAR column.

Since the API specifies that this information is to be returned as an array, safe coding practices dictate that we create and return a new array on each call, to protect against malicious or buggy code that might manipulate the contents of the array. (Java has no support for immutable arrays. It would have been preferable if the UserType interface declared this method to return a Collection or List, since these can be immutable.)

❷ In nullSafeGet( ) we translate database results into the corresponding MediaSource enumeration value. Since we know we stored the value as a string in the database, we can delegate the actual retrieval to Hibernate's utility method for loading strings from database results. You'll be able to do something like this in most cases.

❸ Then it's just a matter of using the enumeration's own instance lookup capability.

❹ HibernateException is a RuntimeException thrown by Hibernate when there is a problem performing a mapped operation. We're "freeloading" on the exception here since our issue arguably relates to mapping. If we wanted to get fancy we could define our own exception type to provide more details, but it might still make sense to have that extend HibernateException, especially when working in the context of an abstraction framework like Spring, as we'll explore in Chapter 13.

❺ Mapping the other direction is handled by nullSafeSet( ). Once again we can rely on built-in features of the Java 5 enum mechanism to translate from a SourceMedia instance to its name, and then use Hibernate's utilities to store this string in the database.

In all the methods dealing with values, it's important to write your code in a way that will not crash if any of the arguments are null, as they often will be. The "nullSafe" prefix in some method names is a reminder of this, but even the equals( ) method must be used carefully. Blindly delegating to x.equals(y) would blow up if x is null.

And the rest of the methods are trivial implementations of the interface, because when dealing with immutable singletons, as enumeration values are, the potentially tricky facets of persistence management are avoided.

All right, we've created a custom type persistence handler, and it wasn't so bad! Now it's time to actually use it to persist our enumeration data.

How do I do that?

This is actually almost embarrassingly easy. Once we've got the value class, `SourceMedia`, and the persistence manager, `SourceMediaType`, in place, all we need to do is use our custom persistence manager class rather than the raw value type, whenever we want to map it.

> That's it. No, really!

We'll walk through an example of using our source media enumeration to illustrate this. But before diving into it, let's step back for a minute and think about generalizing our implementation for use in a bigger project.

What about...

...if there is more than one enumeration that you want to persist? If you've thought about it, you probably realized there was essentially nothing in Example 6-2 that was deeply tied to our `SourceMedia` enumeration. There are only a handful of places (even fewer if you discount the JavaDoc) where the type is even mentioned. Wouldn't it be pretty easy to parameterize this and support any `enum` type with a single implementation?

Indeed, that's pretty easy, and it would have been nice if a simple but flexible implementation had been built into Hibernate. There are a number that you can choose from on the Hibernate wiki (way more than you may want to sort through, on several different pages), so perhaps we should adopt Gavin King's *Enhanced UserType* found on the *Java 5 EnumUserType*[*] page as our unofficial "official choice" since he's the author of so much of Hibernate itself. It seems fairly full-featured without going overboard. At least consider comparing it to Example 6-2 to see the kind of work needed to generalize our solution.

But now, back to concrete examples—let's see how to actually use our enumeration!

> I can hear some exclamations of "it's about time!"

Working with Persistent Enumerations

You may have noticed that we never defined a persistence mapping for the `SourceMedia` class in the first part of this chapter. That's because our enumerated type

---

[*] *http://www.hibernate.org/272.html*

is a *value* that gets persisted as part of one or more entities, rather than being an entity unto itself.

In that light, it's not surprising that we've not yet done any mapping. That happens when it's time to actually use the persistent enumeration—which is to say, now.

How do I do that?

Recall that we wanted to keep track of the source media for the music tracks in our jukebox system. That means we want to use the `SourceMedia` enumeration in our `Track` mapping. We can simply add a new `property` tag to the `class` definition in *Track.hbm.xml*, as shown in Example 6-3.

Example 6-3. Adding the sourceMedia property to the track mapping document

```
...
<property name="volume" type="short">
  <meta attribute="field-description">How loud to play the track</meta>
</property>

<property name="sourceMedia" type="com.oreilly.hh.SourceMediaType">
  <meta attribute="field-description">Media on which track was obtained</meta>
  <meta attribute="use-in-tostring">true</meta>
</property>

<set name="comments" table="TRACK_COMMENTS">
...
```

Notice that we've told Hibernate that the type of this property is our `UserType` implementation, not the raw enumeration type that it is responsible for helping persist. Because the `type` of our `sourceMedia` property names a class that implements the `UserType` interface, Hibernate knows to delegate to that class to perform persistence, as well as for discovering the Java and SQL types associated with the mapping.

Now, running *ant codegen* updates our `Track` class to include the new property....

Not so fast!

During development of this chapter, I ran into a strange problem where suddenly my code wouldn't compile anymore, due to complaints about constructors not being found. At first it seemed to be somehow related to adopting the Maven Ant Tasks for dependency management, because it first happened when I was testing that. Even looking closely at the code, it took me a while to see what was wrong, because it was subtle. The sourceMedia property in `Track` was being assigned the type `SourceMediaType` (the mapping manager), rather than `SourceMedia` like it should be.

After we all flailed around for a while and I posted a confused bug report to the Hibernate Tools team, which they quite rightly reported being unable to reproduce, I figured out what was happening. The build was broken: the Hibernate Tools need to be able to find the compiled SourceMediaType class in order to make sense of the mapping document and realize that it is a user type. As I was writing the text, I had written and compiled SourceMediaType first, so it was there when I updated the mapping to look like Example 6-3 and invoked the codegen target. But when I came back and was testing with the Maven ant tasks, I was starting with no compiled classes, just like you would after downloading the code examples archive, and the creation and query tests had already been updated as described in the next few sections. However, in that context, running codegen before compile leaves you in a situation where the classes are inconsistent and can't compile. And you can't run compile before codegen because those test classes are dependent on the existence of the generated data classes.

This kind of head-spinning circular dependency problem is, sadly, not uncommon when you've not been paying attention to maintaining your build instructions. I'd introduced a new dependency for the codegen target without encoding it in the *build.xml*. We wasted a fair amount of time barking up the wrong trees, but it did give me a chance to describe the problem and the solution, so hopefully you will be smarter if you find yourself in a similar situation.

> Sure sounds like a classic catch-22.

Once the problem was clearly understood, it wasn't difficult to solve. Example 6-4 shows the changes needed in *build.xml*.

Example 6-4. Expressing the UserType dependencies in the build process

```
<!-- Compile the UserType definitions so they can be used in the code
     generation phase. -->
<target name="usertypes" depends="prepare" ❶
        description="Compile custom type definitions needed in by codegen">
  <javac srcdir="${source.root}"
         includes="com/oreilly/hh/*Type.java"
         destdir="${class.root}"
         debug="on"
         optimize="off"
         deprecation="on">
    <classpath refid="project.class.path"/>
  </javac>
</target>

<!-- Generate the java code for all mapping files in our source tree -->
<target name="codegen" depends="usertypes" ❷
        description="Generate Java source from the O/R mapping files">
```

❶ We create a target named usertypes for compiling just the user type definitions, right before the existing codegen target. These don't refer to any generated classes, so they can be compiled before the codegen target is run. The easiest way to select them is to take advantage of the fact that they reside in the com.oreilly.hh package, and the naming convention we're using here (which Hibernate itself uses for its type mapping classes), in which their filenames end in "*Type.java*" (e.g., *SourceMediaType.java*, and later in this chapter, *StereoVolumeType.java*).

If you don't have such a convention, you can explicitly list all the files here, or put them in their own separate package. This approach happens to work well for our needs.

❷ Then we update the codegen target to list usertypes as its dependency. This will ensure that the custom type mappings needed by the code generation task are always compiled and available before it runs. (We no longer need to list prepare as a dependency here, since it is now a dependency of the usertypes target.)

With these additions in place, running *ant codegen* now correctly updates our Track class to include the new property. The signature of the full-blown Track constructor now looks like this:

<table><tr><td>Phew!</td></tr></table>

```
public Track(String title, String filePath, Date playTime,
             Set<Artist> artists, Date added, short volume,
             SourceMedia sourceMedia, Set<String> comments) { ... }
```

We need to make corresponding changes in *CreateTest.java*:

```
Track track = new Track("Russian Trance",
                        "vol2/album610/track02.mp3",
                        Time.valueOf("00:03:30"),
                        new HashSet<Artist>(),
                        new Date(), (short)0, SourceMedia.CD,
                        new HashSet<String>());

...

track = new Track("Video Killed the Radio Star",
                  "vol2/album611/track12.mp3",
                  Time.valueOf("00:03:49"), new HashSet<Artist>(),
                  new Date(), (short)0, SourceMedia.VHS,
                  new HashSet<String>());
```

And so on. To get the results shown in Figure 6-1, we mark the rest as coming from CDs, except for "The World '99," which comes from a stream, and give "Test Tone 1" a null sourceMedia value. At this point, run *ant schema* to rebuild the database schema with support for the new property, and run *ant ctest* to create the sample data.

What just happened?

Our TRACK table now contains a column to store the sourceMedia property. We can see its values by looking at the contents of the table after creating the sample data (the easiest way is to run a query within *ant db*, as shown in Figure 6-1).

We can verify that the values persisted to the database are correct by cross-checking the codes assigned to our persistent enumeration. Leveraging Java 5's enum features allows even this raw query to be pretty meaningful.

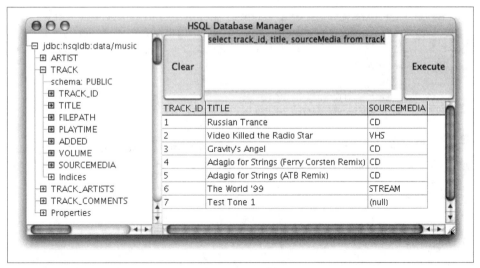

Figure 6-1. Source media information in the TRACK table

Why didn't it work?

By introducing these custom types to our mapping documents, we've introduced another new dependency that we have not yet reflected in *build.xml*. So, if you weren't following along carefully, and failed to run *ant compile* before *ant schema*, you will have received some complaints like this from Hibernate:

```
[hibernatetool] INFO: Using dialect: org.hibernate.dialect.HSQLDialect
[hibernatetool] An exception occurred while running exporter #2:hbm2ddl (Generat
es database schema)
[hibernatetool] To get the full stack trace run ant with -verbose
[hibernatetool] org.hibernate.MappingException: Could not determine type for: co
m.oreilly.hh.StereoVolumeType, for columns: [org.hibernate.mapping.Column(VOL_LE
FT), org.hibernate.mapping.Column(VOL_RIGHT)]

BUILD FAILED
/Users/jim/Documents/Work/OReilly/svn_hibernate/current/examples/ch07/build.xml:
81: org.hibernate.MappingException: Could not determine type for: com.oreilly.hh
.StereoVolumeType, for columns: [org.hibernate.mapping.Column(VOL_LEFT), org.hib
ernate.mapping.Column(VOL_RIGHT)]

Total time: 3 seconds
```

This is because, without compiling our new custom types, Hibernate can't find or use them, so the mappings don't make sense. As a quick fix, just run *ant compile* and then try *ant schema* again. We should also fix this in *build.xml* so that it can't bite anyone else in the future:

```
<!-- Generate the schemas for all mapping files in our class tree -->
<target name="schema" depends="compile"
        description="Generate DB schema from the O/R mapping files">
...
```

It doesn't matter that the compile target comes later in the file than schema; Ant will sort this out just fine. If it bothers you, feel free to swap them. To be completely thorough about this we can also make compile depend on codegen, to ensure that the data classes are generated before we try to compile everything:

```
<!-- Compile the java source of the project -->
<target name="compile" depends="codegen"
        description="Compiles all Java classes">
...
```

With that set of chained dependencies, you can start with a bare source directory, and generate and compile everything in one fell swoop:

```
% ant compile
Buildfile: build.xml

prepare:
     [copy] Copying 3 files to /Users/jim/svn/oreilly/hib_dev_2e/current/example
s/ch07/classes

usertypes:
    [javac] Compiling 2 source files to /Users/jim/svn/oreilly/hib_dev_2e/curren
t/examples/ch07/classes

codegen:
[hibernatetool] Executing Hibernate Tool with a Standard Configuration
[hibernatetool] 1. task: hbm2java (Generates a set of .java files)

compile:
    [javac] Compiling 8 source files to /Users/jim/svn/oreilly/hib_dev_2e/curren
t/examples/ch07/classes

BUILD SUCCESSFUL
Total time: 3 seconds
```

OK, let's get back to learning about custom types....

We can see an even more friendly version of the information (and incidentally test the retrieval half of our custom persistence helper) by slightly enhancing the query test to print the descriptions associated with this property for the tracks it retrieves. The necessary changes are shown in bold in Example 6-5.

Example 6-5. Displaying source media in QueryTest.java

```
...
// Print the tracks that will fit in seven minutes
List tracks = tracksNoLongerThan(Time.valueOf("00:07:00"),
                                 session);
for (ListIterator iter = tracks.listIterator() ;
     iter.hasNext() ; ) {
    Track aTrack = (Track)iter.next();
    String mediaInfo = "";
    if (aTrack.getSourceMedia() != null) {
        mediaInfo = ", from " +
            aTrack.getSourceMedia().getDescription();
```

```
    }
    System.out.println("Track: \"" + aTrack.getTitle() + "\" " +
                    listArtistNames(aTrack.getArtists()) +
                    aTrack.getPlayTime() + mediaInfo);
    ...
```

With these enhancements, running *ant qtest* yields the output shown in Example 6-6.
Tracks with non-null source media values now have "from" and the appropriate media
description displayed at the end.

Example 6-6. Human-oriented display of source media information

```
    ...
    qtest:
        [java] Track: "Russian Trance" (PPK) 00:03:30, from Compact Disc
        [java] Track: "Video Killed the Radio Star" (The Buggles) 00:03:49, from VH
    S Videocassette tape
        [java] Track: "Gravity's Angel" (Laurie Anderson) 00:06:06, from Compact Di
    sc
        [java] Track: "Adagio for Strings (Ferry Corsten Remix)" (William Orbit, Fe
    rry Corsten, Samuel Barber) 00:06:35, from Compact Disc
        [java] Track: "Test Tone 1" 00:00:10
        [java]    Comment: Pink noise to test equalization
```

Note that if we hadn't decided to do our own fancy formatting of a subset of the tracks'
properties in QueryTest and instead relied on the toString( ) method in Track, we would
not have needed to make any changes to QueryTest to see this new information, although we'd have seen the same minimalist version of the enumeration names as in the
database query. Our mapping document specified that the sourceMedia property
should be included in the toString( ) result, which would have taken care of it. You
can inspect the generated toString( ) source to check this, or write a simple test program to see what the toString( ) output looks like. An excellent strategy would be to
fix *AlbumTest.java* so it will compile and run after our changes to Track. The easiest fix
is to simply hard-code the addAlbumTrack( ) method to assume everything comes from
CDs, as in Example 6-7 (the JavaDoc already excuses such shameful rigidity).

Example 6-7. Fixing AlbumTest.java to support source media

```
    /**
     * Quick and dirty helper method to handle repetitive portion of creating
     * album tracks. A real implementation would have much more flexibility.
     */
    private static void addAlbumTrack(Album album, String title, String file,
                                  Time length, Artist artist, int disc,
                                  int positionOnDisc, Session session) {
        Track track = new Track(title, file, length, new HashSet<Artist>(),
                        new Date(), (short)0, SourceMedia.CD,
                        new HashSet<String>());
        track.getArtists().add(artist);
        // session.save(track);
        album.getTracks().add(new AlbumTrack(track, disc, positionOnDisc));
    }
```

With this fix in place, running *ant atest* shows that the source media information propagates all the way up to `Album`'s own `toString()` method:

```
[java] com.oreilly.hh.data.Album@ccad9c [title='Counterfeit e.p.' tracks='[
com.oreilly.hh.data.AlbumTrack@9c0287 [track='com.oreilly.hh.data.Track@6a21b2 [
title='Compulsion' sourceMedia='CD' ]' ], com.oreilly.hh.data.AlbumTrack@aa8eb7
[track='com.oreilly.hh.data.Track@7fc8a0 [title='In a Manner of Speaking' source
Media='CD' ]' ], com.oreilly.hh.data.AlbumTrack@4cadc4 [track='com.oreilly.hh.da
ta.Track@243618 [title='Smile in the Crowd' sourceMedia='CD' ]' ], com.oreilly.h
h.data.AlbumTrack@5b644b [track='com.oreilly.hh.data.Track@157e43 [title='Gone'
sourceMedia='CD' ]' ], com.oreilly.hh.data.AlbumTrack@1483a0 [track='com.oreilly
.hh.data.Track@cdae24 [title='Never Turn Your Back on Mother Earth' sourceMedia=
'CD' ]' ], com.oreilly.hh.data.AlbumTrack@63dc28 [track='com.oreilly.hh.data.Tra
ck@ae511 [title='Motherless Child' sourceMedia='CD' ]' ]]' ]
```

With a little work, Hibernate lets you extend your typesafe enumerations to support persistence. And once you've invested that effort, you can persist them as easily as any other value type for which native support exists.

It would be nice if the native type support in Hibernate evolved to take advantage of the robust `enum` keyword support in Java 5 out of the box, though I don't hold out much hope since Java 5 has been out for a while now. But, as far as gripes go, this is a mild one, and you can take your pick of `enum`-supporting user type implementations on the Hibernate wiki.

Now let's move into mappings that are complex and idiosyncratic enough that nobody would expect Hibernate to build in support for them.

Building a Composite User Type

Recall that in our `Track` object we have a property that determines our preferred playback volume for the track. Suppose we'd like the jukebox system to be able to adjust the *balance* of tracks for playback, rather than just their volume. To accomplish this we'd need to store separate volumes for the left and right channels. The quick solution would be to edit the `Track` mapping to store these as separate mapped properties.

If we're serious about object-oriented architecture, we might want to encapsulate these two values into a `StereoVolume` class. This class could then simply be mapped as a `composite-element`, as the `AlbumTrack` component was in Example 5-4. This is still fairly straightforward.

There is a drawback, however, to this simple approach. It's likely we will discover other places in our system where we want to represent `StereoVolume` values. If we build a playlist mechanism that can override a track's default playback options, and also want to be able to assign volume control to entire albums, suddenly we have to recreate the composite mapping in several places, and we might not do it consistently everywhere (this is more likely to be an issue with a more complex compound type, but you get the idea). The Hibernate reference documentation says that it's a good practice to use a composite user type in situations like this, and I agree.

How do I do that?

Let's start by defining the StereoVolume class. There's no reason for this to be an entity (to have its own existence independent of some other persistent object), so we'll write it as an ordinary (and rather simple) Java object. See Example 6-8.

Example 6-8. StereoVolume.java, a value class representing a stereo volume level

<aside>The JavaDoc in this example has been compressed to take less space. We're trusting you not to do this in real projects. The downloadable version is more complete.</aside>

```java
package com.oreilly.hh;

import java.io.Serializable;

/**
 * A simple structure encapsulating a stereo volume level.
 */
public class StereoVolume implements Serializable {

    /** The minimum legal volume level. */
    public static final short MINIMUM = 0;

    /** The maximum legal volume level. */
    public static final short MAXIMUM = 100;

    /** Stores the volume of the left channel. */
    private short left;

    /** Stores the volume of the right channel. */
    private short right;

    /** Default constructor sets full volume in both channels. */
    public StereoVolume() { ❶
        this(MAXIMUM, MAXIMUM);
    }

    /** Constructor that establishes specific volume levels. */
    public StereoVolume(short left, short right) {
        setLeft(left);
        setRight(right);
    }

    /**
     * Helper method to make sure a volume value is legal.
     * @param volume the level that is being set.
     * @throws IllegalArgumentException if it is out of range.
     */
    private void checkVolume(short volume) {
        if (volume < MINIMUM) {
            throw new IllegalArgumentException("volume cannot be less than " +
                                               MINIMUM);
        }
        if (volume > MAXIMUM) {
            throw new IllegalArgumentException("volume cannot be more than " +
                                               MAXIMUM);
        }
    }
}
```

```
/** Set the volume of the left channel. */
public void setLeft(short volume) { ❷
    checkVolume(volume);
    left = volume;
}

/** Set the volume of the right channel. */
public void setRight(short volume) {
    checkVolume(volume);
    right = volume;
}

/** Get the volume of the left channel */
public short getLeft() {
    return left;
}

/** Get the volume of the right channel. */
public short getRight() {
    return right;
}

/** Format a readable version of the volume levels, for debugging. */
public String toString() {
    return "Volume[left=" + left + ", right=" + right + ']';
}

/**
 * Compare whether another object is equal to this one.
 * @param obj the object to be compared.
 * @return true if obj is also a StereoVolume instance, and represents
 *         the same volume levels.
 */
public boolean equals(Object obj) { ❸
    if (obj instanceof StereoVolume) {
        StereoVolume other = (StereoVolume)obj;
        return other.getLeft() == getLeft() &&
            other.getRight() == getRight();
    }
    return false;  // It wasn't a StereoVolume
}

/**
 * Returns a hash code value for the StereoVolume. This method must be
 * consistent with the {@link #equals} method.
 */
public int hashCode() {
    return (int)getLeft() * MAXIMUM * 10 + getRight();
}
}
```

❶   Since we want to be able to persist this with Hibernate, we provide a default constructor...

❷ ...and property accessors.

❸ Correct support for the Java `equals( )` and `hashCode( )` contracts is also important, since this is a mutable value object.

To let us persist this as a composite type, rather than defining it as a nested compound object each time we use it, we build a custom user type to manage its persistence. A lot of what we need to provide in our custom type is the same as what we put in `SourceMediaType` (Example 6-2, shown earlier in this chapter). We'll focus on the new and interesting stuff. Example 6-9 shows one way to persist `StereoVolume` as a composite user type.

Example 6-9. StereoVolumeType.java, a composite user type to persist StereoVolume

```java
package com.oreilly.hh;

import java.io.Serializable;
import java.sql.PreparedStatement;
import java.sql.ResultSet;
import java.sql.SQLException;

import org.hibernate.Hibernate;
import org.hibernate.engine.SessionImplementor;
import org.hibernate.type.Type;
import org.hibernate.usertype.CompositeUserType;

/**
 * Manages persistence for the {@link StereoVolume} composite type.
 */
public class StereoVolumeType implements CompositeUserType {

    /**
     * Get the names of the properties that make up this composite type, and
     * that may be used in a query involving it.
     */
    public String[] getPropertyNames() { ❶
        // Allocate a new response each time, because arrays are mutable
        return new String[] { "left", "right" };
    }

    /**
     * Get the types associated with the properties that make up this composite
     * type.
     *
     * @return the types of the parameters reported by {@link #getPropertynames},
     *         in the same order.
     */
    public Type[] getPropertyTypes() {
        return new Type[] { Hibernate.SHORT, Hibernate.SHORT };
    }

    /**
     * Look up the value of one of the properties making up this composite type.
     *
```

```
 * @param component a {@link StereoVolume} instance being managed.
 * @param property the index of the desired property.
 * @return the corresponding value.
 * @see #getPropertyNames
 */
public Object getPropertyValue(Object component, int property) { ❷
    StereoVolume volume = (StereoVolume)component;
    short result;

    switch (property) {

    case 0:
        result = volume.getLeft();
        break;

    case 1:
        result = volume.getRight();
        break;

    default:
        throw new IllegalArgumentException("unknown property: " + property);
    }

    return new Short(result);
}

/**
 * Set the value of one of the properties making up this composite type.
 *
 * @param component a {@link StereoVolume} instance being managed.
 * @param property the index of the desired property.
 * @object value the new value to be established.
 * @see #getPropertyNames
 */
public void setPropertyValue(Object component, int property, Object value) {
    StereoVolume volume = (StereoVolume)component;
    short newLevel = ((Short)value).shortValue();
    switch (property) {

    case 0:
        volume.setLeft(newLevel);
        break;

    case 1:
        volume.setRight(newLevel);
        break;

    default:
        throw new IllegalArgumentException("unknown property: " + property);
    }
}

/**
 * Determine the class that is returned by {@link #nullSafeGet}.
 *
```

```
 * @return {@link StereoVolume}, the actual type returned by
 *          {@link #nullSafeGet}.
 */
public Class returnedClass() {
    return StereoVolume.class;
}


/**
 * Compare two instances of the class mapped by this type for persistence
 * "equality".
 *
 * @param x first object to be compared.
 * @param y second object to be compared.
 * @return <code>true</code> iff both represent the same volume levels.
 * @throws ClassCastException if x or y isn't a {@link StereoVolume}.
 */
public boolean equals(Object x, Object y) { ❸
    if (x == y) { // This is a trivial success
        return true;
    }
    if (x == null || y == null) { // Don't blow up if either is null!
        return false;
    }
    // Now it's safe to delegate to the class' own sense of equality
    return ((StereoVolume)x).equals(y);
}


/**
 * Return a deep copy of the persistent state, stopping at entities and
 * collections.
 *
 * @param value the object whose state is to be copied.
 * @return a copy representing the same volume levels as the original.
 * @throws ClassCastException for non {@link StereoVolume} values.
 */
public Object deepCopy(Object value) { ❹
    if (value == null)
        return null;
    StereoVolume volume = (StereoVolume)value;
    return new StereoVolume(volume.getLeft(), volume.getRight());
}


/**
 * Indicates whether objects managed by this type are mutable.
 *
 * @return <code>true</code>, since {@link StereoVolume} is mutable.
 */
public boolean isMutable() {
    return true;
}


/**
 * Retrieve an instance of the mapped class from a JDBC {@link ResultSet}.
 *
 * @param rs the results from which the instance should be retrieved.
```

```
 * @param names the columns from which the instance should be retrieved.
 * @param session an extension of the normal Hibernate session interface
 *          that gives you much more access to the internals.
 * @param owner the entity containing the value being retrieved.
 * @return the retrieved {@link StereoVolume} value, or <code>null</code>.
 * @throws SQLException if there is a problem accessing the database.
 */
public Object nullSafeGet(ResultSet rs, String[] names, ❺
                          SessionImplementor session, Object owner)
        throws SQLException {
    Short left = (Short)Hibernate.SHORT.nullSafeGet(rs, names[0]);
    Short right = (Short)Hibernate.SHORT.nullSafeGet(rs, names[1]);

    if (left == null || right == null) {
        return null; // We don't have a specified volume for the channels
    }

    return new StereoVolume(left.shortValue(), right.shortValue());
}

/**
 * Write an instance of the mapped class to a {@link PreparedStatement},
 * handling null values.
 *
 * @param st a JDBC prepared statement.
 * @param value the StereoVolume value to write.
 * @param index the parameter index within the prepared statement at which
 *          this value is to be written.
 * @param session an extension of the normal Hibernate session interface
 *          that gives you much more access to the internals.
 * @throws SQLException if there is a problem accessing the database.
 */
public void nullSafeSet(PreparedStatement st, Object value, int index,
                        SessionImplementor session)
        throws SQLException {
    if (value == null) {
        Hibernate.SHORT.nullSafeSet(st, null, index);
        Hibernate.SHORT.nullSafeSet(st, null, index + 1);
    } else {
        StereoVolume vol = (StereoVolume)value;
        Hibernate.SHORT.nullSafeSet(st, new Short(vol.getLeft()), index);
        Hibernate.SHORT.nullSafeSet(st, new Short(vol.getRight()),
                index + 1);
    }
}

/**
 * Reconstitute a working instance of the managed class from the cache.
 *
 * @param cached the serializable version that was in the cache.
 * @param session an extension of the normal Hibernate session interface
 *          that gives you much more access to the internals.
 * @param owner the entity containing the value being retrieved.
 * @return a copy of the value as a {@link StereoVolume} instance.
 */
```

```java
public Object assemble(Serializable cached, SessionImplementor session, ❻
                       Object owner) {
    // Our value type happens to be serializable, so we have an easy out.
    return deepCopy(cached);
}

/**
 * Translate an instance of the managed class into a serializable form to be
 * stored in the cache.
 *
 * @param session an extension of the normal Hibernate session interface
 *         that gives you much more access to the internals.
 * @param value the StereoVolume value to be cached.
 * @return a serializable copy of the value.
 */
public Serializable disassemble(Object value, SessionImplementor session) {
    return (Serializable)deepCopy(value);
}

/**
 * Get a hashcode for the instance, consistent with persistence "equality"
 */
public int hashCode(Object x) { ❼
    return x.hashCode(); // Can delegate to our well-behaved object
}

/**
 * During merge, replace the existing (target) value in the entity we are
 * merging to with a new (original) value from the detached entity we are
 * merging. For immutable objects, or null values, it is safe to simply
 * return the first parameter. For mutable objects, it is safe to return a
 * copy of the first parameter. However, since composite user types often
 * define component values, it might make sense to recursively replace
 * component values in the target object.
 *
 * @param original value being merged from.
 * @param target value being merged to.
 * @param session the  hibernate session into which the merge is happening.
 * @param owner the containing entity.
 * @return an independent value that can safely be used in the new context.
 */
public Object replace(Object original, Object target, ❽
                       SessionImplementor session, Object owner) {
    return deepCopy(original);
}
}
```

❶ Due to the getPropertyNames( ) and getPropertyTypes( ) methods, Hibernate knows the "pieces" that make up the composite type. These are the values that are available when you write HQL queries using the type. In our case they correspond to the properties of the actual StereoVolume class we're persisting, but that isn't required. This is our opportunity, for example, to provide a friendly property interface to some legacy object that wasn't designed for persistence at all.

❷ The translation between the virtual properties provided by the composite user type and the real data on which they are based is handled by the getPropertyValue( ) and setPropertyValue( ) methods. In essence, Hibernate hands us an instance of the type we're supposed to manage, about which it makes no assumptions at all, and says, "hey, give me the second property," or, "set the first property to this value." You can see how this lets us do any work needed to add a property interface to old or third-party code. In this case, since we don't actually need that power, the hoops we need to jump through to pass the property manipulation on to the underlying StereoVolume class are just boilerplate.

The next lengthy stretch of code consists of methods we've seen before in Example 6-2. Some of the differences in this version are interesting. Most of the changes have to do with the fact that, unlike SourceMedia, our StereoVolume class is mutable—it contains values that can be changed. So we have to come up with full implementations for some methods we finessed last time.

❸ We need to provide a meaningful way of comparing instances in equals( ),

❹ and of making independent copies in deepCopy( ).

❺ The actual persistence methods, nullSafeGet( ) and nullSafeSet( ), are quite similar to Example 6-2, with one difference we didn't need to exploit. They both have a SessionImplementor parameter, which gives you some really deep access to the gears and pulleys that make Hibernate work. This is only needed for truly complex persistence challenges, and it is well outside the scope of this book. If you need to use SessionImplementor methods, you're doing something quite tricky, and you must have a profound understanding of the architecture of Hibernate. You're essentially writing an extension to the system, and you probably need to study the source code to develop the requisite level of expertise.

❻ The assemble( ) and disassemble( ) methods allow custom types to support caching of values that aren't already Serializable. They give our persistence helper a place to copy any important values into another object that is capable of being serialized, using any means necessary. Since it was trivial to make Stereo Volume serializable in the first place, we don't need this flexibility either. Our implementation can just make copies of the serializable StereoVolume instances for storing in the cache. (We make copies because, again, our data class is mutable, and it wouldn't do to have cached values mysteriously changing.)

❼ The hashCode( ) method was added in Hibernate 3, requiring changes to CompositeUserType implementations, but it helps with efficiency. In our case, we have an object that already implements this method to which we can delegate, but, again, if we were wrapping some crufty legacy data structures, this is an opportunity to put a nice Java wrapper on them.

❽ Finally, the replace( ) method is another new Hibernate 3 requirement. Again, since we have a handy object to copy, we can take an easy way out. Alternatively, we could have manually copied all the nested property values from the original object to the target object.

All right, we've created this beast, how do we use it? Example 6-10 shows how to enhance the volume property in the Track mapping document to use the new composite type. Let's also take this opportunity to add it to Track's toString( ) method so we can see it in test output.

> That may seem like a lot of work for a simple value class, but it shows you all you'll need to know when you have more complex values to model.

Example 6-10. Changes to Track.hbm.xml to use StereoVolume

```
...
<property name="volume" type="com.oreilly.hh.StereoVolumeType">
    <meta attribute="field-description">How loud to play the track</meta>
    <meta attribute="use-in-tostring">true</meta>
    <column name="VOL_LEFT"/>
    <column name="VOL_RIGHT"/>
</property>
...
```

Notice again that we supply the name of our custom user type, responsible for managing persistence, rather than the raw type that it is managing. This is just like Example 6-3. Also, our composite type uses two columns to store its data, so we need to supply two column names here.

Now when we regenerate the Java source for Track by running *ant codegen*, we get the results shown in Example 6-11.

Example 6-11. Changes to the generated Track.java source

```
...

/**
 * How loud to play the track
 */
private StereoVolume volume;
...

public Track(String title, String filePath, Date playTime,
             Set<Artist> artists, Date added,
             StereoVolume volume, SourceMedia sourceMedia,
             Set<String> comments) {
...
}
...
/**
 * How loud to play the track
 */
public StereoVolume getVolume() {
    return this.volume;
}

public void setVolume(StereoVolume volume) {
    this.volume = volume;
}
```

```
...
public String toString() {
    StringBuffer buffer = new StringBuffer();

    buffer.append(getClass().getName()).append("@").append(Integer.toHexString
(hashCode())).append(" [");
    buffer.append("title").append("='").append(getTitle()).append("' ");

    buffer.append("volume").append("='").append(getVolume()).append("' ");

    buffer.append("sourceMedia").append("='").append(getSourceMedia()).append(
"' ");
    buffer.append("]");

    return buffer.toString();
}
...
```

At this point we are ready to run *ant schema* to recreate the database tables. Example 6-12 shows the relevant output.

Example 6-12. Creation of the track schema from the new mapping

```
...
[hibernatetool] create table TRACK (TRACK_ID integer generated by default as
    identity (start with 1), TITLE varchar(255) not null,
    filePath varchar(255) not null, playTime time, added date,
    VOL_LEFT smallint, VOL_RIGHT smallint, sourceMedia varchar(255),
    primary key (TRACK_ID));
...
```

Let's beef up the data creation test so it can work with the new **Track** structure. Example 6-13 shows the kind of changes we need.

Example 6-13. Changes required to CreateTest.java to test stereo volumes

```
...
// Create some data and persist it
tx = session.beginTransaction();
StereoVolume fullVolume = new StereoVolume();

Track track = new Track("Russian Trance",
                        "vol2/album610/track02.mp3",
                        Time.valueOf("00:03:30"),
                        new HashSet<Artist>(),
                        new Date(), fullVolume, SourceMedia.CD,
                        new HashSet<String>());
addTrackArtist(track, getArtist("PPK", true, session));
session.save(track);
...
// The other tracks created use fullVolume too, until...
...
track = new Track("Test Tone 1",
                  "vol2/singles/test01.mp3",
                  Time.valueOf("00:00:10"), new HashSet<Artist>(),
                  new Date(), new StereoVolume((short)50, (short)75),
```

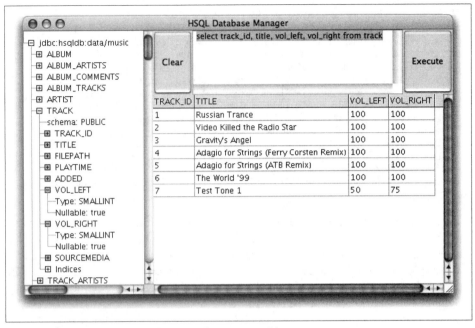

Figure 6-2. Stereo volume information in the TRACK table

```
                    null, new HashSet<String>());
    track.getComments().add("Pink noise to test equalization");
    session.save(track);
    ...
```

Now if we execute *ant ctest* and look at the results with *ant db*, we'll find values like those shown in Figure 6-2.

We only need to make the single change, shown in Example 6-14, to `AlbumTest` to make it compatible with this new `Track` format.

Example 6-14. Change to AlbumTest.java to support stereo track volumes

```
    ...
    private static void addAlbumTrack(Album album, String title, String file,
                                      Time length, Artist artist, int disc,
                                      int positionOnDisc, Session session) {
        Track track = new Track(title, file, length, new HashSet<Artist>(),
                        new Date(), new StereoVolume(), SourceMedia.CD,
                        new HashSet<String>());
    ...
```

This lets us run *ant atest* and see the stereo volume information, shown by the new version of `Track`'s `toString( )` method in Example 6-15.

Example 6-15. An album with stereo track information

```
[java] com.oreilly.hh.data.Album@ccad9c [title='Counterfeit e.p.' tracks='[
com.oreilly.hh.data.AlbumTrack@9c0287 [track='com.oreilly.hh.data.Track@6a21b2 [
title='Compulsion' volume='Volume[left=100, right=100]' sourceMedia='CD' ]' ], c
om.oreilly.hh.data.AlbumTrack@aa8eb7 [track='com.oreilly.hh.data.Track@7fc8a0 [t
itle='In a Manner of Speaking' volume='Volume[left=100, right=100]' sourceMedia=
'CD' ]' ], com.oreilly.hh.data.AlbumTrack@4cadc4 [track='com.oreilly.hh.data.Tra
ck@243618 [title='Smile in the Crowd' volume='Volume[left=100, right=100]' sourc
eMedia='CD' ]' ], com.oreilly.hh.data.AlbumTrack@5b644b [track='com.oreilly.hh.d
ata.Track@157e43 [title='Gone' volume='Volume[left=100, right=100]' sourceMedia=
'CD' ]' ], com.oreilly.hh.data.AlbumTrack@1483a0 [track='com.oreilly.hh.data.Tra
ck@cdae24 [title='Never Turn Your Back on Mother Earth' volume='Volume[left=100,
 right=100]' sourceMedia='CD' ]' ], com.oreilly.hh.data.AlbumTrack@63dc28 [track
='com.oreilly.hh.data.Track@ae511 [title='Motherless Child' volume='Volume[left=
100, right=100]' sourceMedia='CD' ]' ]]' ]
```

Well, we may have gone into more depth about creating custom types than you wanted right now, but someday you might come back and mine this example for the exact nugget you're looking for. In the meantime, let's change gears and look at something new, simple, and completely different. Chapter 7 shows an alternative to using XML mapping documents at all, and Chapter 8 introduces criteria queries, a unique and very programmer-friendly capability in Hibernate.

What about...

...other fancy tricks in mapping custom types? All right, if this hasn't been too much information, you can explore the other interfaces in the **org.hibernate.usertype** package, which include **EnhancedUserType** (which lets your custom type act as an entity's **id** and do other tricks) and **ParameterizedUserType** (that can be configured to support mapping multiple different types) among others. The reusable mappings for Java 5 enums discussed on the *Java 5 EnumUserType*[†] page of the Hibernate wiki illustrate good uses of both of these, but they go beyond the scope of this book.

[†] *http://www.hibernate.org/272.html*

## CHAPTER 7

The Annotations Alternative

So far, we've been working with the XML mapping document as the starting point for our examples. In cases where you're starting with just a concept and can leave the details of creating data tables and data objects to Hibernate, that remains a great option. The advent of Java 5's flexible Annotation support opened up a very interesting alternate approach, however, especially for the common case where you've already got some objects written by the time that you're thinking about how to save them to a database.

Hibernate Annotations

If you haven't started using annotations yet, the code examples in this chapter will look a little strange, so it's worth spending a minute or two to discuss the history and purpose of Java annotations. Basically, an annotation is a way to add information about a piece of code (in the Java world, typically a class, field, or method) to help tools understand how the code is being used, or to enable automation that saves you work. Rather than having a separate file, like a persistence mapping, to maintain in parallel with your source code, you would put that information right in the source code it affected. This way you are in no danger of a file separate from your source code becoming out of synch. Before Java 5 included robust support for this style of coding, people found a "back door" way of achieving it, by leveraging the extensible nature of the JavaDoc tools.

JavaDoc was a form of annotation that existed in Java from the beginning, with the purpose of enabling developers to produce quality documentation of their classes and APIs without having to maintain a set of files separate from the source code, and it worked very well, so much so that people wanted to be able to use it for other things. The XDoclet project[*] was a popular and sophisticated framework that extended the JavaDoc framework in many interesting ways, and a rich set of Hibernate XDoclet tags were developed.

---

[*] *http://xdoclet.sourceforge.net/xdoclet/index.html*

The power of this approach was so evident that Sun built full general-purpose annotation support right into Java 5, eliminating the need for tricky tools that leveraged JavaDoc comments. Now the Java compiler itself can process annotations (and uses some of its own to let you control specific warnings within individual classes, methods or even fields). Reflection can report on annotations (if they're configured to stick around in compiled classes), and you can define your own annotation classes very easily. So naturally Hibernate adopted Java 5's native annotations.

Convergent evolution went even farther than that, though—the power of using annotations to configure mapping for classes has such appeal that Hibernate's own tags strongly influenced the EJB 3 specification. They also were impressed by how useful Hibernate-style persistence could be outside a full-blown Java Enterprise Edition (EE) environment, so they defined the Java Persistence API (often referred to as the *JPA*) as a stand-alone component which can be used for persistence in a normal Java Standard Edition (SE) environment. As the specifications firmed up, Hibernate adapted to support them directly, so you can now use many of Hibernate's features through the EJB 3 and JPA interfaces and annotations, without making your application dependent on (or aware of) Hibernate at all.

We're not going to go that far, since several of the features we're already using in Hibernate require use of its own tags. In fact, once you get used to Hibernate, and its very flexible and powerful philosophy of "persist any old Java object, any way you need to," you'll find the effort of warping your code to fit the limits of the JPA specification too confining to consider except in cases where there is a strong mandate to stay agnostic about persistence implementations (and you will probably try to avoid such projects). Yet, even if you know you're using Hibernate, sometimes it's nice to use annotations to configure your mappings instead of XML files.

Why do I care?

Once you're used to annotation syntax (and IDEs like Eclipse already have surprisingly sophisticated abilities to understand, document, and autocomplete annotations—even custom ones you may come up with for your own use, a technique we'll use in Chapter 14), ditching mapping documents means there's one less file format you need to remember how to set up and read.

As noted earlier, if you can keep your object and mapping specifications in one file, they're less likely to get out of synch, and readers will have a more immediate understanding of what's going on. It's a form of self-documenting code. The reasonable defaults provided by the annotations often allow you to get away with specifying less configuration as well. Even when you specify everything, you'll find the annotation syntax much more compact than the XML file, so you have less to type, or to read through once your IDE has helped type it.

> What, the introduction didn't sell you on how cool they are?

This approach is most likely to work well when you have direct control over the database and it is strongly coupled to your object model (or if you are designing objects to work with a specific, fixed database structure, which yields the same kind of strong coupling). This means that cases where you need to adapt an object model to multiple databases aren't good candidates for use of annotations; in that kind of situation, the separate nature of an external mapping file is actually an advantage, since you can have multiple separate mapping file sets without affecting your Java source.

Many other Java tools are adopting annotations for configuration and integration, as you'll see starting in Chapter 13. When working with such tools it is often most convenient to use annotations with Hibernate as well—indeed, the other tools may depend on them. Had we not already wanted to show you how to use annotations in this new version of the book, the Spring chapter would have forced the issue.

 One criticism of annotations is that database details get lost in the shuffle of Java source code. Luckily, there are some useful Hibernate tools available that will generate Hibernate Mapping documentation from both Hibernate XML mapping files and Hibernate Annotations. For more information about hbm2doc, see "Generating Hibernate mapping documentation" in Chapter 12.

How do I do that?

The first thing we need to do is update our Maven dependencies to retrieve the Hibernate annotations. Edit *build.xml* so the dependencies look like Example 7-1 (the additions are shown in bold).

Example 7-1. Obtaining the Hibernate Annotations

```
<artifact:dependencies pathId="dependency.class.path">
    <dependency groupId="hsqldb" artifactId="hsqldb" version="1.8.0.7"/>
    <dependency groupId="org.hibernate" artifactId="hibernate"
            version="3.2.5.ga">
      <exclusion groupId="javax.transaction" artifactId="jta"/>
    </dependency>
    <dependency groupId="org.hibernate" artifactId="hibernate-tools"
            version="3.2.0.beta9a"/>
    <dependency groupId="org.hibernate" artifactId="hibernate-annotations"
            version="3.3.0.ga"/>
    <dependency groupId="org.hibernate"
            artifactId="hibernate-commons-annotations"
            version="3.3.0.ga"/>
    <dependency groupId="org.apache.geronimo.specs"
            artifactId="geronimo-jta_1.1_spec" version="1.1"/>
    <dependency groupId="log4j" artifactId="log4j" version="1.2.14"/>
</artifact:dependencies>
```

While in the file, delete the **usertypes** and **codegen** targets. Working with annotations, we are not going to generate Java code. Instead, we'll be starting with Java and using that to define the Hibernate mapping (and the database schema). So those targets are obsolete (and dangerous) in this chapter.

As you might expect, the schema target itself needs a little tweaking to work in this new way, as highlighted in Example 7-2.

Example 7-2. Generating the schema using annotations

```
<!-- Generate the schemas for annotated classes --> ❶
<target name="schema" depends="compile"
        description="Generate DB schema from the annotated model classes">

    <hibernatetool destdir="${source.root}">
      <classpath refid="project.class.path"/> ❷
      <annotationconfiguration
          configurationfile="${source.root}/hibernate.cfg.xml"/> ❸
      <hbm2ddl drop="yes"/>
    </hibernatetool>
</target>
```

❶   The comment and target description needed to be updated to reflect the way things now work.

❷   We need a reference to the compiled classes, so the annotations within them can be found by the schema generation tool. Note that this means we need the classes to be compiled before a schema can be generated, which was not the case in most earlier versions of this target, but we added that dependency in Chapter 6, so our schema target already depends on the compile target.

❸   Finally, we tell the tool to configure itself using annotations. We still supply an overall Hibernate configuration file, so the tool knows what database we're using and such. And that file also must list the annotated classes with which we want to work, which we'll tackle after one last build adjustment.

Our compile target used to depend on the code-generation target we've deleted, so it won't work until we remove that dependency. In our new approach, all that's needed to support compilation is for our basic prepare target to have run. Edit the compile target to reflect the changes highlighted in Example 7-3.

Example 7-3. Simpler compilation dependencies

```
<!-- Compile the java source of the project -->
<target name="compile" depends="prepare"
        description="Compiles all Java classes">
    <javac srcdir="${source.root}"
           destdir="${class.root}"
           debug="on" optimize="off" deprecation="on">
      <classpath refid="project.class.path"/>
    </javac>
</target>
```

As noted earlier, we need to update the Hibernate configuration to list the annotated classes with which we want to work instead of the mapping documents we used to use.

Delete those documents, and change the end of *hibernate.cfg.xml* in the *src* directory to look like Example 7-4 (as usual, the changes are highlighted in bold).

Example 7-4. Configuring Hibernate to work with annotations

```
...
    <!-- Don't echo all executed SQL to stdout -->
    <property name="show_sql">false</property>

    <!-- disable batching so HSQLDB will propagate errors correctly. -->
    <property name="jdbc.batch_size">0</property>

    <!-- List all the annotated classes we're using -->
    <mapping class="com.oreilly.hh.data.Album"/>
    <mapping class="com.oreilly.hh.data.AlbumTrack"/>
    <mapping class="com.oreilly.hh.data.Artist"/>
    <mapping class="com.oreilly.hh.data.Track"/>

  </session-factory>
</hibernate-configuration>
```

Why do I have to?

You might wonder why it's necessary to list the annotated classes in the configuration file. Can't Hibernate find them by their annotations? Well, it can, and if you change your coding style to fully rely on the JPA interfaces (using Hibernate's implementation of the JPA `EntityManager` instead of a Hibernate `Session`), it will quite happily look for your annotated classes without being told where to find them. But, as noted earlier, we're not going that far in this book. When you stick with Hibernate's native interfaces, it wants explicit declaration of the classes for which you want it to perform persistence, even when you're using annotations to control that persistence.

We're almost ready to show this working, except we need the annotated classes that form the core of this approach! So it's time to get to the really interesting part of this chapter, and show you what annotated Java source code for data objects looks like, and how it controls Hibernate mappings.

Annotating Model Objects

Annotations can be applied to a variety of Java elements. When working with Hibernate, you'll most often be concerned with annotating classes and their fields, to specify how a model object is to be mapped to a database schema. This is analogous to the way our XML mapping documents were structured around mapped classes and their properties. That's enough background and explanation—let's dive right in and make this concrete. Time to map the classes from the examples (as fully developed in Chapter 6) using annotations!

How do I do that?

Example 7-5 shows one way you could annotate the `Artist` class. This chapter will explain the basics of Hibernate Annotations, but if you would like a more thorough description of some of these annotations, please refer to the Hibernate Annotations project web site at *http://annotations.hibernate.org*[†]. To save pages, the listings of annotated classes are compressed slightly from what you'll find in the source download —whitespace is condensed and the JavaDoc is omitted. Since these are hand-written classes, not code-generated ones as they were in prior chapters, there is room for much more comprehensive JavaDoc, so it's worthwhile to take a look at the downloadable versions, too.

Example 7-5. Annotating the Artist class

```
package com.oreilly.hh.data;

import java.util.*;
import javax.persistence.*; ❶
import org.hibernate.annotations.Index;

@Entity ❷
@Table(name="ARTIST")
@NamedQueries({
    @NamedQuery(name="com.oreilly.hh.artistByName",
        query="from Artist as artist where upper(artist.name) = upper(:name)")
})
public class Artist {

    @Id ❸
    @Column(name="ARTIST_ID")
    @GeneratedValue(strategy=GenerationType.AUTO)
    private Integer id;

    @Column(name="NAME",nullable=false,unique=true) ❹
    @Index(name="ARTIST_NAME",columnNames={"NAME"}) ❺
    private String name;

    @ManyToMany ❻
    @JoinTable(name="TRACK_ARTISTS",
            joinColumns={@JoinColumn(name="TRACK_ID")},
            inverseJoinColumns={@JoinColumn(name="ARTIST_ID")})
    private Set<Track> tracks;

    @ManyToOne ❼
    @JoinColumn(name="actualArtist")
    private Artist actualArtist;

    public Artist() {}
```

[†] If you've skipped ahead to this chapter, you will probably get more out of it if you learn about the classes and relationships we're discussing by going back and at least skimming from Chapter 3 onward before proceeding.

```
public Artist(String name, Set<Track> tracks, Artist actualArtist) {
  this.name = name;
  this.tracks = tracks;
  this.actualArtist = actualArtist;
}

public Integer getId() { return id; }
public void setId(Integer id) {
  this.id = id;
}

public String getName() { return name; }
public void setName(String name) {
  this.name = name;
}

public Artist getActualArtist() { return actualArtist; }
public void setActualArtist(Artist actualArtist) {
  this.actualArtist = actualArtist;
}

public Set<Track> getTracks() { return tracks; }
public void setTracks(Set<Track> tracks) {
  this.tracks = tracks;
}

/**
 * Produce a human-readable representation of the artist.
 *
 * @return a textual description of the artist.
 */
public String toString() {
  StringBuilder builder = new StringBuilder();

  builder.append(getClass().getName()).append("@");
  builder.append(Integer.toHexString(hashCode())).append(" [");
  builder.append("name").append("=").append(getName()).append("' ");
  builder.append("actualArtist").append("=").append("'").append(getActualArtist());
  builder.append("' ").append("]");

  return builder.toString();
}

}
```

❶ In order to use annotations that aren't core to the Java language itself, such as the persistence-related ones we're discussing here, you need to import them. Annotations are just Java classes (albeit ones which implement a particular interface, and which are declared in an interesting way that's beyond the scope of this chapter, but which you can see in Chapter 14), so you import them using ordinary import statements like these.

As discussed in the history earlier, most of the annotations we need are the standard EJB 3 variety, which are defined in the javax.persistence package. We do need one Hibernate-specific annotation in order to be able to request a specific index. The Java Persistence API was downloaded and made available to us automatically by Maven because it's a dependency of the Hibernate Annotations we requested in the updated *build.xml*. We can use the Java Persistence API on its own like this because it was designed to be usable by itself within a Java SE environment like ours, as well as part of the EJB support built into Java EE. You may want to learn more about it, and its home page[‡] is a good starting point.

❷ This cluster of annotations applies to the `Artist` class as a whole. The `Entity` annotation marks the class as capable of persistence. The `Table` annotation is optional; the annotation processor will make very reasonable default assumptions for mappings, but we wanted to show how to explicitly state a table name, in case you're connecting to an existing database with strange names.

> This query language relationship shows Hibernate really did influence the direction of EJB 3 in a deep way.

And what is our query doing back in the Java source? Alas, this is another drawback to using Hibernate-native interfaces with annotations: there's nowhere else to put the named queries. If we were using the JPA `EntityManager`, we could put named queries in a *persistence.xml* file, and retain the advantages of keeping them outside of Java source code. Since we're sticking with the `Session` interface in this book, we lose one of the advantages of named queries when we use annotations instead of XML mapping files. But, we can still write them in HQL, and use all its features. Switching to the JPA interfaces would require us to use JPAQL instead, which is a subset of HQL.

❸ Here's how you annotate a mapped property. This is a special case, because the property is also the unique identifier for the object, as indicated by the `@Id` annotation. You can specify different kinds of ID generation strategies with the annotations, just as you can with Hibernate's XML mapping documents. (The annotations were intended to be a full replacement for the capabilities of existing O/R layers, and between the standard JPA choices and Hibernate's own, you really can do almost anything you need.) Choosing `AUTO` for the generation style is the annotations-based equivalent of specifying `<generator class="native"/>` in XML. It tells Hibernate to use whatever approach is most natural for the database being used.

As with the entity-level annotations, if you omit some choices like the column name, the defaults chosen are quite reasonable, but we wanted to illustrate how to be specific when you need to. In fact, you don't need to annotate the properties at all—the JPA will assume that all properties of an entity are to be mapped, unless instructed otherwise (through annotations, naturally: `@Transient` serves this purpose).

[‡] *http://java.sun.com/javaee/technologies/persistence.jsp*

Also note that we've attached the annotations to the actual field, rather than to an accessor method. This tells Hibernate to access the field directly, which you might want to do in a class where the accessors are good for providing abstractions to other classes at runtime, but not compatible with persistence. In many cases, you'll want to have Hibernate use the accessors, which you'd achieve by putting the annotations on the getter or setter method. You need to pick one approach or the other—mixing and matching from property to property is not allowed (by JPA, although Hibernate has extensions... but it may confuse others even if you can do it).

❹ When mapping a column, there are a number of optional attributes you can supply to control things such as nullability, uniqueness constraints, and so on, just like when you're doing it in an XML mapping file.

❺ The ability to specify that a column should have an index (and how that index should be set up) is one reason we added the Hibernate annotations to the mix. This @Index tag is not part of the standard JPA annotations; it's a useful Hibernate extension. Relying on it makes our code dependent on Hibernate, but beyond the fact that this is a book *about* Hibernate, as we noted earlier (and you'll see later), there are a lot of reasons why you'll often make the same choice.

❻ As with mapping documents, there are more options when it comes to associations. In this case we're describing a many-to-many relationship with Track objects, and explicitly spelling out how that relationship is represented in the database.

❼ Sometimes there really isn't much you need to say, even when you're being explicit. This is an example of how the annotation approach can be significantly more concise than XML mapping files. We do use an @JoinColumn annotation to keep the column name the same as it was in our XML-based approach. It works fine without this, but the default column name is the slightly more verbose ACTUALARTIST_ARTIST_ID.

Other than that, there isn't much to say about the class—it's a simple data bean, very similar to the one that was generated from our mapping document in earlier chapters. The JavaDoc in the downloadable version explains the fields and methods better than was possible in generated code.

This annotated class produces the same ARTIST table we achieved with the *Artist.hbm.xml* mapping document we developed in the preceding chapters.

Annotating Track

The annotated Artist class references the Track class. Example 7-6 shows the annotations on Track, which introduce some new issues.

Example 7-6. Annotating the Track class

```
package com.oreilly.hh.data;

import java.sql.Time;
import java.util.*;
import javax.persistence.*;
import org.hibernate.annotations.CollectionOfElements;
import org.hibernate.annotations.Index;

@Entity
@Table(name="TRACK")
@NamedQueries({
        @NamedQuery(name="com.oreilly.hh.tracksNoLongerThan",
                        query="from Track as track where track.playTime <= :length")
})
public class Track {

  @Id
  @Column(name="TRACK_ID")
  @GeneratedValue(strategy=GenerationType.AUTO)
  private Integer id;

  @Column(name="TITLE",nullable=false)
  @Index(name="TRACK_TITLE",columnNames={"TITLE"})
  private String title;

  @Column(nullable=false)
  private String filePath;

  @Temporal(TemporalType.TIME) ❶
  private Date playTime;

  @ManyToMany
  @JoinTable(name="TRACK_ARTISTS",
              joinColumns={@JoinColumn(name="ARTIST_ID")},
              inverseJoinColumns={@JoinColumn(name="TRACK_ID")})
  private Set<Artist> artists;

  @Temporal(TemporalType.DATE) ❷
  private Date added;

  @CollectionOfElements ❸
  @JoinTable(name="TRACK_COMMENTS",
              joinColumns = @JoinColumn(name="TRACK_ID"))
  @Column(name="COMMENT")
  private Set<String> comments;

  @Enumerated(EnumType.STRING) ❹
  private SourceMedia sourceMedia;

  @Embedded ❺
  @AttributeOverrides({ ❻
    @AttributeOverride(name = "left", column = @Column(name = "VOL_LEFT")),
    @AttributeOverride(name = "right", column = @Column(name = "VOL_RIGHT"))
  })
```

```
StereoVolume volume;

public Track() {}

public Track(String title, String filePath) {
  this.title = title;
  this.filePath = filePath;
}

public Track(String title, String filePath, Time playTime,
             Set<Artist> artists, Date added, StereoVolume volume,
             SourceMedia sourceMedia, Set<String> comments) {
  this.title = title;
  this.filePath = filePath;
  this.playTime = playTime;
  this.artists = artists;
  this.added = added;
  this.volume = volume;
  this.sourceMedia = sourceMedia;
  this.comments = comments;
}

public Date getAdded() { return added; }
public void setAdded(Date added) {
  this.added = added;
}

public String getFilePath() { return filePath; }
public void setFilePath(String filePath) {
  this.filePath = filePath;
}

public Integer getId() { return id; }
public void setId(Integer id) {
  this.id = id;
}

public Date getPlayTime() { return playTime; }
public void setPlayTime(Date playTime) {
  this.playTime = playTime;
}

public String getTitle() { return title; }
public void setTitle(String title) {
  this.title = title;
}

public Set<Artist> getArtists() { return artists; }
public void setArtists(Set<Artist> artists) {
  this.artists = artists;
}

public Set<String> getComments() { return comments; }
public void setComments(Set<String> comments) {
  this.comments = comments;
```

```
  }

  public SourceMedia getSourceMedia() { return sourceMedia; }
  public void setSourceMedia(SourceMedia sourceMedia) {
    this.sourceMedia = sourceMedia;
  }

  public StereoVolume getVolume() { return volume; }
  public void setVolume(StereoVolume volume) {
    this.volume = volume;
  }

  public String toString() { ❼
    StringBuilder builder = new StringBuilder();
    builder.append(getClass().getName()).append("@");
    builder.append(Integer.toHexString(hashCode())).append(" [");
    builder.append("title").append("='").append(getTitle()).append("' ");
    builder.append("volume").append("='").append(getVolume()).append("' ");
    builder.append("sourceMedia").append("='").append(getSourceMedia());
    builder.append("' ").append("]");
    return builder.toString();
  }
}
```

❶ Since Java lacks distinct classes for representing times of day as compared to dates (or timestamps which include both), we need a way of declaring how a Date class is being used. The @Temporal annotation provides that clarity. In this case we are annotating the fact that playTime corresponds to a TIME column in SQL. If this annotation is omitted, the default column type used is TIMESTAMP.

❷ The added property, though it shares the same Date type with playTime, corresponds to a DATE column.

❸ The @CollectionOfElements annotation is another Hibernate extension, which gives us a simpler way to control the table and column in which an association to a collection of a simple value type is mapped. This is one of the biggest reasons to break out of the standard annotations. With pure JPA, you can't directly map collections of simple value types like String or Integer at all. You need to declare a full-blown entity class to hold such values, and then map that. For people who are used to Hibernate's flexibility in mapping Plain Old Java Objects, this would be a big step backwards.

To learn about all Hibernate's extensions to the mapping annotations, you can take advantage of the fact that they are all listed nicely in a section of the online manual§.

❹ On the other hand, the JPA has robust support for mapping enumerations built right in, one advantage it gained by coming out *after* the Java 5 enum (and the widespread adoption of the type-safe enumeration pattern that led to this

§ *http://www.hibernate.org/hib_docs/annotations/reference/en/html/entity.html#entity-hibspec*

language feature). This annotation is a lot easier than the work we had to go through in Chapter 6!

❺ This is the standard JPA annotation for mapping a composite user type, the equivalent of Example 6-10. The JPA spec requires that when we do this we also mark the StereoVolume class as embeddable:

```
package com.oreilly.hh.data;

import java.io.Serializable;
import javax.persistence.Embeddable;

/**
 * A simple structure encapsulating a stereo volume level.
 */
@Embeddable
public class StereoVolume implements Serializable {
    ...
}
```

(In fact, Hibernate is happy to map the embedded class without us doing this, but a future release might be more stringent about sticking to the spec, and there is no harm in being well-behaved.)

❻ Once again we've added more annotations than are really needed, in order to end up with exactly the same database schema we had in the XML-mapped version of the examples. Without the @AttributeOverrides, the columns used to store the two pieces of the volume would be just LEFT and RIGHT (the names of the properties in the StereoVolume class), rather than VOL_LEFT and VOL_RIGHT.

❼ In order for our test programs to print out the same information as they did using the old approach, we've copied over the toString( ) implementations Hibernate's code generator created for us. Note that we took the opportunity to upgrade them to use StringBuilder rather than the unnecessarily thread-safe[‖] (and therefore slower) StringBuffer.

This set of annotations causes the creation of the TRACK, TRACK_ARTISTS, and TRACK_COMMENTS tables, with the same schema that we achieved using *Track.hbm.xml* as it evolved in Examples 2-1 through 6-10.

Annotating Album

The Album class is the core model class of the rest of the examples we've built so far. Example 7-7 shows how to annotate it to recreate the database schema and mappings with which we've been working, and introduces a few more concepts worth noting.

[‖] The variable builder is local to the method, so there's no way more than one thread can be messing with it.

Example 7-7. Annotating the Album class

```java
package com.oreilly.hh.data;

import java.util.*;
import javax.persistence.*;
import org.hibernate.annotations.CollectionOfElements; ❶
import org.hibernate.annotations.Index;
import org.hibernate.annotations.IndexColumn;

@Entity
@Table(name="ALBUM")
public class Album {

@Id
@Column(name="ALBUM_ID")
@GeneratedValue(strategy=GenerationType.AUTO)
private Integer id;

  @Column(name="TITLE",nullable=false)
  @Index(name="ALBUM_TITLE",columnNames={"TITLE"})
  private String title;

  @Column(nullable=false)
  private Integer numDiscs;

  @ManyToMany(cascade=CascadeType.ALL)
  @JoinTable(name="ALBUM_ARTISTS",
              joinColumns=@JoinColumn(name="ARTIST_ID"),
              inverseJoinColumns=@JoinColumn(name="ALBUM_ID"))
  private Set<Artist> artists;

  @CollectionOfElements
  @JoinTable(name="ALBUM_COMMENTS",
              joinColumns = @JoinColumn(name="ALBUM_ID"))
  @Column(name="COMMENT")
  private Set<String> comments;

  @Temporal(TemporalType.DATE)
  private Date added;

  @CollectionOfElements ❷
  @IndexColumn(name="LIST_POS") ❸
  @JoinTable(name="ALBUM_TRACKS",
              joinColumns = @JoinColumn(name="ALBUM_ID"))
  private List<AlbumTrack> tracks;

  public Album() {}

  public Album(String title, int numDiscs, Set<Artist> artists,
              Set<String> comments, List<AlbumTrack> tracks,
              Date added) {
    this.title = title;
    this.numDiscs = numDiscs;
    this.artists = artists;
    this.comments = comments;
```

```
        this.tracks = tracks;
        this.added = added;
    }

    public Date getAdded() { return added; }
    public void setAdded(Date added) {
        this.added = added;
    }

    public Integer getId() { return id; }
    public void setId(Integer id) {
        this.id = id;
    }

    public Integer getNumDiscs() { return numDiscs; }
    public void setNumDiscs(Integer numDiscs) {
        this.numDiscs = numDiscs;
    }

    public String getTitle() { return title; }
    public void setTitle(String title) {
        this.title = title;
    }

    public List<AlbumTrack> getTracks() { return tracks; }
    public void setTracks(List<AlbumTrack> tracks) {
        this.tracks = tracks;
    }

    public Set<Artist> getArtists() { return artists; }
    public void setArtists(Set<Artist> artists) {
        this.artists = artists;
    }

    public Set<String> getComments() { return comments; }
    public void setComments(Set<String> comments) {
        this.comments = comments;
    }

    public String toString() {
        StringBuilder builder = new StringBuilder();
        builder.append(getClass().getName()).append("@");
        builder.append(Integer.toHexString(hashCode())).append(" [");
        builder.append("title").append("='").append(getTitle()).append("' ");
        builder.append("tracks").append("='").append(getTracks()).append("' ");
        builder.append("]");
        return builder.toString();
    }
}
```

❶ Yup, we keep being unable to do without Hibernate-specific extensions. No fewer than three in this class.

❷ AlbumTrack is not an entity (it doesn't have an ID property, and instances can't be looked up on their own outside the context of an Album record), so we map the association using @CollectionOfElements (as we do for basic types) rather than @OneToMany, which we'd use for an entity.

❸ JPA and EJB only support set-like semantics for mapped collections. As we saw in Chapter 5, being able to keep rows in a particular order is important, which is why we use data structures like Lists and arrays, and Hibernate makes it easy to map them. You can't in pure JPA, however! Hibernate's @IndexColumn extension is the way around that.

The combination of this annotation and the @JoinColumn information that follows causes Hibernate to produce exactly the schema we had based on *Album.hbm.xml* in Example 5-4, in which the ALBUM_TRACKS table has a composite key formed from ALBUM_ID and LIST_POS.

Album is closely related to the AlbumTrack class, which gets annotated as shown in Example 7-8 to round out the recreation of our example schema.

Example 7-8. Annotating the AlbumTrack class

```
package com.oreilly.hh.data;

import java.io.Serializable;
import javax.persistence.*;

@Embeddable ❶
public class AlbumTrack {

    @ManyToOne(cascade=CascadeType.ALL) ❷
    @JoinColumn(name="TRACK_ID", nullable=false)
    private Track track;

    private Integer disc; ❸
    private Integer positionOnDisc;

    public AlbumTrack() {}

    public AlbumTrack(Track track, Integer disc, Integer positionOnDisc) {
        this.track = track;
        this.disc = disc;
        this.positionOnDisc = positionOnDisc;
    }

    public Track getTrack() { return track; }
    public void setTrack(Track track) {
        this.track = track;
    }

    public Integer getDisc() { return disc; }
    public void setDisc(Integer disc) {
        this.disc = disc;
    }

    public Integer getPositionOnDisc() { return positionOnDisc; }
    public void setPositionOnDisc(Integer positionOnDisc) {
```

```
        this.positionOnDisc = positionOnDisc;
    }

    public String toString() {
        StringBuilder builder = new StringBuilder();
        builder.append(getClass().getName()).append("@");
        builder.append(Integer.toHexString(hashCode())).append(" [");
        builder.append("track").append("='").append(getTrack()).append("' ");
        builder.append("]");
        return builder.toString();
    }
}
```

❶   As described earlier in the discussion of the `Album` mapping, this class is not an entity capable of standing on its own, so we map it with `@Embeddable`, as we did `StereoVolume`.

❷   Even though it's not an entity, we need to tell Hibernate how to handle the `track` property, which does refer to an entity. Without this annotation, attempts to build the schema will fail. This also gives us the ability to retain the same column name we had in the XML-based approach. Unfortunately, the request to cascade through to the `Track` class isn't enough to automatically save tracks when creating a new album, so we'll need to go back to an earlier version of the `AlbumTest` class, as shown later. In "An Alternate Approach" later in this chapter, we'll explore a variation on the schema which regains this automation.

❸   These last two properties illustrate the fact that when using annotations, sometimes you don't need to supply any annotations at all. These two properties *do* get mapped, naked though they look, and the defaults provided by the annotation processor are just what we want them to be.

The rest of the class is straightforward, and shorter than the others we've looked at, as there's no ID property to manage, and only a handful of other properties.

As mentioned in the discussion earlier, this mapping requires us to reclaim the responsibility for saving tracks when creating new albums. With the final version of the mapping in *Album.hbm.xml* in Example 5-13, we commented out the line that called `session.save(track)` in the `addAlbumTrack( )` method of `AlbumTest.java`. We need to uncomment that line so the method looks the way it did in Example 5-8.

Does it work?

With all this in place, we can create the schema. Example 7-9 shows most of the result of running *ant schema* with the annotations-based approach we've now set up. A few less-interesting stretches have been omitted to save space, and the table-creation lines have been reformatted for better readability.

Example 7-9. Highlights from creating the schema using annotated classes

```
% ant schema
Buildfile: build.xml
Downloading: org/hibernate/hibernate-annotations/3.3.0.ga/hibernate-annotations-
3.3.0.ga.pom ❶
Transferring 1K
Downloading: org/hibernate/hibernate/3.2.1.ga/hibernate-3.2.1.ga.pom
Transferring 3K
Downloading: javax/persistence/persistence-api/1.0/persistence-api-1.0.pom
Transferring 1K
Downloading: org/hibernate/hibernate-commons-annotations/3.3.0.ga/hibernate-comm
ons-annotations-3.3.0.ga.pom
Transferring 1K
Downloading: org/hibernate/hibernate-annotations/3.3.0.ga/hibernate-annotations-
3.3.0.ga.jar
Transferring 258K
Downloading: javax/persistence/persistence-api/1.0/persistence-api-1.0.jar
Transferring 50K
Downloading: org/hibernate/hibernate-commons-annotations/3.3.0.ga/hibernate-comm
ons-annotations-3.3.0.ga.jar
Transferring 64K

prepare:
    [copy] Copying 1 file to /Users/jim/svn/oreilly/hibernate/current/examples/
ch07/classes

compile:
    [javac] Compiling 10 source files to /Users/jim/svn/oreilly/hibernate/curren
t/examples/ch07/classes

schema:
[hibernatetool] Executing Hibernate Tool with a Hibernate Annotation/EJB3 Config
uration ❷
[hibernatetool] 1. task: hbm2ddl (Generates database schema)
[hibernatetool] alter table ALBUM_ARTISTS drop constraint FK7BA403FCB99A6003;
...
[hibernatetool] alter table TRACK_COMMENTS drop constraint FK105B2688E424525B;
[hibernatetool] drop table ALBUM if exists;
...
[hibernatetool] drop table TRACK_COMMENTS if exists;
[hibernatetool] create table ALBUM (ALBUM_ID integer generated by default
                as identity (start with 1), added date, numDiscs integer,
                TITLE varchar(255) not null,
                primary key (ALBUM_ID)); ❸
[hibernatetool] create table ALBUM_ARTISTS (ARTIST_ID integer not null,
                ALBUM_ID integer not null,
                primary key (ARTIST_ID, ALBUM_ID));
[hibernatetool] create table ALBUM_COMMENTS (ALBUM_ID integer not null,
                COMMENT varchar(255));
[hibernatetool] create table ALBUM_TRACKS (ALBUM_ID integer not null,
                disc integer, positionOnDisc integer, TRACK_ID integer,
                LIST_POS integer not null,
                primary key (ALBUM_ID, LIST_POS));
[hibernatetool] create table ARTIST (ARTIST_ID integer generated by default
                as identity (start with 1), NAME varchar(255) not null,
```

```
                actualArtist integer,
                primary key (ARTIST_ID), unique (NAME));
[hibernatetool] create table TRACK (TRACK_ID integer generated by default
                as identity (start with 1), added date,
                filePath varchar(255) not null, playTime time,
                sourceMedia varchar(255), TITLE varchar(255) not null,
                VOL_LEFT smallint, VOL_RIGHT smallint,
                primary key (TRACK_ID));
[hibernatetool] create table TRACK_ARTISTS (ARTIST_ID integer not null,
                TRACK_ID integer not null,
                primary key (TRACK_ID, ARTIST_ID));
[hibernatetool] create table TRACK_COMMENTS (TRACK_ID integer not null,
                COMMENT varchar(255));
[hibernatetool] create index ALBUM_TITLE on ALBUM (TITLE);
[hibernatetool] alter table ALBUM_ARTISTS add constraint FK7BA403FCB99A6003 fore
ign key (ARTIST_ID) references ALBUM;
...
[hibernatetool] alter table TRACK_COMMENTS add constraint FK105B2688E424525B for
eign key (TRACK_ID) references TRACK;
[hibernatetool] 9 errors occurred while performing <hbm2ddl>. ❹
[hibernatetool] Error #1: java.sql.SQLException: Table not found: ALBUM_ARTISTS
in statement [alter table ALBUM_ARTISTS]
...

BUILD SUCCESSFUL
Total time: 5 seconds
```

❶ Since this is the first time we've asked the Maven Ant Tools for the Hibernate Annotations, they are downloaded along with their dependencies.

❷ Here's where you can see that annotations are being used to drive the creation of the schema.

❸ If you compare this with the corresponding line in Example 5-7, you'll see that the column definitions are identical, although they show up in a different order. The same is true for the definitions of ALBUM_ARTISTS, ALBUM_COMMENTS, and, most challengingly, ALBUM_TRACKS. We've successfully recreated our original schema.

❹ These are the normal errors you see in creating a schema when the database didn't exist at all at the time. They don't abort the build, and it is considered successful despite them.

You may also want to run *ant db* simultaneously in this chapter's folder with another copy running in the folder for Chapter 5, as an easier visual way of comparing schema definitions. Also, looking at actual data might be nice. Example 7-10 shows the two small changes we need to make to *CreateTest.java* to get it working with annotation-based mappings. We need to import the AnnotationConfiguration class, and then use it where we previously used the Configuration class.

Example 7-10. Tweaks to the test classes needed to work with annotations
```
package com.oreilly.hh;
```

```
import org.hibernate.*;
import org.hibernate.cfg.AnnotationConfiguration;
import org.hibernate.cfg.Configuration;

...

    public static void main(String args[]) throws Exception {
        // Create a configuration based on the annotations in our
        // model classes.
        Configuration config = new AnnotationConfiguration();
        config.configure();

...
```

Once that's done, you can run *ant ctest* to create sample data and perform the same side-by-side comparison using multiple instances of *ant db*.

The same changes need to be made to *QueryTest.java*, *QueryTest2.java*, and *AlbumTest.java*. We won't show the output from running *ant qtest* or *ant qtest2* since it's the same as in the previous chapter. But we will show the output from AlbumTest because it relies on the entire schema, and so will be a good sanity check. This also acts at a verification that the track-saving line was uncommented successfully as described in the discussion after Example 7-8. The output from running *ant atest* with our annotations-based schema is shown in Example 7-11.

Example 7-11. Running AlbumTest using annotations

```
atest:
     [java] com.oreilly.hh.data.Album@27d19d [title='Counterfeit e.p.' tracks='[
com.oreilly.hh.data.AlbumTrack@bf4c80 [track='com.oreilly.hh.data.Track@2e3919 [
title='Compulsion' volume='Volume[left=100, right=100]' sourceMedia='CD' ]' ], c
om.oreilly.hh.data.AlbumTrack@3778cf [track='com.oreilly.hh.data.Track@f4d063 [t
itle='In a Manner of Speaking' volume='Volume[left=100, right=100]' sourceMedia=
'CD' ]' ], com.oreilly.hh.data.AlbumTrack@dc696e [track='com.oreilly.hh.data.Tra
ck@a5dac0 [title='Smile in the Crowd' volume='Volume[left=100, right=100]' sourc
eMedia='CD' ]' ], com.oreilly.hh.data.AlbumTrack@8dbef1 [track='com.oreilly.hh.d
ata.Track@c4b579 [title='Gone' volume='Volume[left=100, right=100]' sourceMedia=
'CD' ]' ], com.oreilly.hh.data.AlbumTrack@f2f761 [track='com.oreilly.hh.data.Tra
ck@8cd64 [title='Never Turn Your Back on Mother Earth' volume='Volume[left=100,
right=100]' sourceMedia='CD' ]' ], com.oreilly.hh.data.AlbumTrack@4f1541 [track=
'com.oreilly.hh.data.Track@c042ba [title='Motherless Child' volume='Volume[left=
100, right=100]' sourceMedia='CD' ]' ]]' ]
```

Apart from the differences in memory addresses where Java happens to have loaded classes, this is identical to the output we saw in Example 5-10, just as we hoped.

> It worked! It all worked!

An Alternate Approach

This exercise has shown that annotations are clearly a viable way of mapping model classes. By jumping through a few hoops we were able to maintain the exact schema we'd evolved in the preceding chapters, though we lost the ability to cascade creation of `Tracks` during the creation of an `Album`. There's another approach we could have taken in the schema which would maintain that automatic cascade, and give us some other abilities, as well, if we think about the `AlbumTrack` class slightly differently.

Mapping `AlbumTrack` as a full-blown entity gives us places to put cascade annotations that Hibernate will honor all the way from the `Album` definition to the embedded `Track` reference. It also gives us a few new complications to think about, but some of those can be seen as opportunities. First of all, `AlbumTrack` as an entity will need an ID. And since we will then be able to get our hands on `AlbumTrack` objects without starting from an `Album`, the `AlbumTrack` model ought to be enhanced to expose the link back to the `ALBUM` table from the `ALBUM_TRACKS` table (which used to be hidden in Hibernate's composite key). We'd achieve that by adding an `album` property. Example 7-12 shows the key parts of the `AlbumTrack` mapping as they would differ in this approach.

Example 7-12. Annotating the AlbumTrack class as an entity

```
package com.oreilly.hh.data;

import java.io.Serializable;
import javax.persistence.*;
@Entity ❶
@Table(name="ALBUM_TRACKS")
public class AlbumTrack {

    @Id ❷
    @GeneratedValue(strategy=GenerationType.AUTO)
    private Integer id;

    @ManyToOne
    @JoinColumn(name="ALBUM_ID", insertable=false, updatable=false, ❸
                nullable=false)
    private Album album;

    @ManyToOne(cascade=CascadeType.ALL) ❹
    @JoinColumn(name="TRACK_ID", nullable=false)
    private Track track;
...

    public Integer getId() {
        return id;
    }

    public void setId(Integer id) {
        this.id = id;
    }

    public Album getAlbum() {
        return album;
    }
    ❺
    public Track getTrack() {
...
}
```

❶ Obviously, we change the class annotation from @Embeddable to @Entity, and we choose the table name here rather than in the Album source.

❷ Here is where we diverge the most from the schema in the XML-based examples. Previously our ALBUM_TRACK table used a composite key, taking advantage of the fact that there can only ever be one row with a particular combination of ALBUM_ID and TRACK_ID. That saved us from needing a separate ID column in the ALBUM_TRACK table. And this composite key was achieved effortlessly, due to the way we mapped the association.

While it would be possible to retain that database schema even after making AlbumTrack an entity, it would require significant effort. The JPA requires all composite keys to be mapped to a separate class that exposes the components of the key. So, in order to preserve our database schema, we'd have to make even more radical changes to our model classes, creating a new class for the sole purpose of holding AlbumTrack keys.

Changing the schema slightly instead, by adding an (admittedly, pretty useless) ID column to ALBUM_TRACKS seems like a less disruptive option. In any case, this is an interesting illustration of the tradeoffs one faces when changing mapping approaches.

❸ The mapping back to Album is @ManyToOne, which we've seen before, but we need some extra parameters to make it work the way we want. This incantation is used to recreate the situation we achieved with *Album.hbm.xml*, in which Hibernate is completely in charge of maintaining the ALBUM_ID column in the ALBUM_TRACKS table. Without the insertable and updatable attributes on the @JoinColumn annotation, we'd have to change AlbumTest to explicitly set the album property for each AlbumTrack object, which means missing out on some of the automation we want from Hibernate.

This is a pattern you will want to remember when you're using indexed mappings to entities (with either @IndexColumn or @MapKey).

❹ Now that AlbumTrack is an entity, Hibernate can honor the cascade setting for its track property.

❺ We can enforce the notion that Hibernate is managing the links to albums by omitting a setAlbum( ) method.

There would be a small difference in the way the relationship is mapped in *Album.java*, as well, of course. This is shown in Example 7-13.

Example 7-13. The AlbumTracks entity mapping in Album.java

```
...
    @OneToMany(cascade=CascadeType.ALL)
    @IndexColumn(name="LIST_POS")
    @JoinColumn(name="ALBUM_ID", nullable=false)
    private List<AlbumTrack> tracks;
...
```

The `cascade` setting in the `@OneToMany` annotation sets up the same unbroken cascade from `Album` through to its embedded `Track` references we had in the final version of *Album.hbm.xml*, developed in Example 5-13, in which albums manage their tracks' life cycles. This lets us comment out the track-saving line in the `addAlbumTrack( )` method of `AlbumTest` again. So we've recreated the old functionality with a different schema. If we were willing to go to the trouble of creating a class to manage a composite key, we could keep both the functionality and database schema intact.

As with many other parts of the Hibernate API (and with object-oriented modeling in general), there are a great many ways to reach your goals.

What now?

Hopefully this chapter has given you a feel for how to use annotations to express data mappings, and will serve as a good starting point when you want to explore that option in your own projects. As with the rest of the book, we've not tried to list all the details and features available—that's what the reference documentation is for, although it can seem a bit sparse at times, so hopefully some of the issues we sorted out in this discussion will also serve as examples of how to resolve ambiguity. If all else fails, just keep trying variations and pasting error messages into Google! Or, if you're a good citizen, delve into the source code and post questions on the Hibernate forum, to lay down a trail of crumbs for future users, and help highlight where the documentation could stand shoring up.

We'll be going back to the XML-based world for the next few chapters as we explore more ways to query for data. But keep the annotations concepts at the back of your mind—they'll be put to good use again in the Spring and Stripes chapters at the end of the book.

## CHAPTER 8

Criteria Queries

Relational query languages like HQL (and SQL, on which HQL is based) are extremely flexible and powerful, but they take a long time to truly master. Many application developers get by with a rudimentary understanding, cribbing similar examples from past projects, and calling in database experts when they need to come up with something truly new, or to understand a particularly cryptic query expression.

It can also be awkward to mix a query language's syntax with Java code. The section "Better Ways to Build Queries" in Chapter 3 showed how to at least keep the queries in a separate file so they can be seen and edited in one piece, free of Java string escape sequences and concatenation syntax. Even with that technique, though, the HQL isn't parsed until the mapping document is loaded, which means that any syntax errors it might harbor won't be caught until the application is running.

Hibernate offers an unusual solution to these problems in the form of criteria queries. They provide a way to create and connect simple Java objects that act as filters for picking your desired results. You can build up nested, structured expressions. The mechanism also allows you to supply example objects to show what you're looking for, with control over which details matter and which properties to ignore.

As you'll see, this can be quite convenient. To be fair, it has its own (very minor) disadvantages. Expanding long query expressions into a Java API makes them take up more room, and they'll be less familiar to experienced database developers than a SQL-like query. The most serious deficiencies that existed in the API when the first version of this book was written have been solved in Hibernate 3. Formerly there were some things you simply couldn't express using the criteria API, such as *projection* (retrieving a subset of the properties of a class, e.g., "`select title, id from com.oreilly.hh.Track`" rather than "`select * from com.oreilly.hh.Track`") and *aggregation* (summarizing results, e.g., getting the sum, average, or count of a property). We'll show you how you now can do these things. The next chapter shows how to accomplish similar tasks using Hibernate's object-oriented query language.

Regardless of which approach you use to formulate queries with Hibernate, what comes out in the end are database-specific SQL statements which implement your intentions.

This can be blissfully invisible to you, or if you're interested in such nuts and bolts, you can turn on SQL logging using the show_sql property discussed in Example 3-1, or play with an interactive SQL preview within Eclipse, which will be shown in Chapter 11.

Using Simple Criteria

Let's start by building a criteria query to find tracks shorter than a specified length, replacing the HQL we used in Example 3-11 and updating the code of Example 3-12.

How do I do that?

The first thing we need to figure out is how to specify the kind of object we're interested in retrieving. There is no query language involved in building criteria queries. Instead, you build up a tree of Criteria objects describing what you want. The Hibernate Session acts as a factory for these criteria, and you start, conveniently enough, by specifying the type of objects you want to retrieve.

Edit *QueryTest.java*, replacing the contents of the tracksNoLongerThan( ) method with those shown in Example 8-1.

Example 8-1. The beginnings of a criteria query

```
public static List tracksNoLongerThan(Time length, Session session) {
    Criteria criteria = session.createCriteria(Track.class);
    return criteria.list();
}
```

> These examples assume the database has been set up as described in the preceding chapters. If you don't want to go through all that, download the sample code, then jump into this chapter and run the codegen, schema, and ctest targets. Even if you've been following along, running schema and ctest will make sure you've got just the data these examples show.

The session's createCriteria( ) method builds a criteria query that will return instances of the persistent class you supply as an argument—easy enough. If you run the example at this point, of course, you'll see all the tracks in the database, since we haven't gotten around to expressing any actual *criteria* to limit our results yet (see Example 8-2).

Example 8-2. Our fledgling criteria query returns all tracks

```
% ant qtest
...
qtest:
    [java] Track: "Russian Trance" (PPK) 00:03:30, from Compact Disc
    [java] Track: "Video Killed the Radio Star" (The Buggles) 00:03:49, from VH
S Videocassette tape
    [java] Track: "Gravity's Angel" (Laurie Anderson) 00:06:06, from Compact Di
sc
    [java] Track: "Adagio for Strings (Ferry Corsten Remix)" (Ferry Corsten, Wi
lliam Orbit, Samuel Barber) 00:06:35, from Compact Disc
    [java] Track: "Adagio for Strings (ATB Remix)" (William Orbit, ATB, Samuel
Barber) 00:07:39, from Compact Disc
    [java] Track: "The World '99" (Ferry Corsten, Pulp Victim) 00:07:05, from D
igital Audio Stream
```

```
[java] Track: "Test Tone 1" 00:00:10
[java]    Comment: Pink noise to test equalization
```

OK, easy enough. How about picking the tracks we want? Also easy! Add a new import statement at the top of the file:

```
import org.hibernate.criterion.*;
```

Then just add one more line to the method, as shown in Example 8-3.

Example 8-3. Criteria query that fully replaces the HQL version from Chapter 3

```
public static List tracksNoLongerThan(Time length, Session session) {
    Criteria criteria = session.createCriteria(Track.class);
    criteria.add(Restrictions.le("playTime", length));
    return criteria.list();
}
```

The Restrictions class acts as a factory for obtaining Criterion instances that can specify different kinds of constraints on your query. Its le( ) method creates a criterion that constrains a property to be less than or equal to a specified value. In this case we want the Track's playTime property to be no greater than the value passed in to the method. We add this to our set of desired criteria.

> Just like HQL, expressions are always in terms of object properties, not table columns.

We'll look at some other Criterion types available through Restrictions in the next section. Appendix B lists them all, and you can create your own implementations of the Criterion interface if you've got something new you want to support.

Running the query this time gives us just the tracks that are no more than seven minutes long, as requested by the main( ) method (see Example 8-4).

Example 8-4. Results of our complete simple criteria query

```
% ant qtest
...
qtest:
    [java] Track: "Russian Trance" (PPK) 00:03:30, from Compact Disc
    [java] Track: "Video Killed the Radio Star" (The Buggles) 00:03:49, from VH
S Videocassette tape
    [java] Track: "Gravity's Angel" (Laurie Anderson) 00:06:06, from Compact Di
sc
    [java] Track: "Adagio for Strings (Ferry Corsten Remix)" (Ferry Corsten, Sa
muel Barber, William Orbit) 00:06:35, from Compact Disc
    [java] Track: "Test Tone 1" 00:00:10
    [java]    Comment: Pink noise to test equalization
```

A surprising number of the queries used to retrieve objects in real applications are very simple, and criteria queries are an extremely natural and compact way of expressing them in Java. Our new tracksNoLongerThan( ) method is actually shorter than it was in Example 3-12, and that version required a separate query (Example 3-11) to

> While I revised this example for the new book, the "Adagio for Strings" remix started randomly playing in iTunes.

be added to the mapping document, as well! Both approaches lead to the same patterns of underlying database access, so they are equally efficient at runtime.

If possible, however, to make the code even more compact. The `add()` and `createCriteria()` methods return the `Criteria` instance, so you can continue to manipulate it in the same Java statement. Taking advantage of that, we can boil the method down to the version shown in Example 8-5.

Example 8-5. An even more compact version of our criteria query

```
public static List tracksNoLongerThan(Time length, Session session) {
    return session.createCriteria(Track.class).
        add(Restrictions.le("playTime", length)).list();
}
```

The style you choose is a trade-off between space and readability (although some people may find the compact, run-on version even more readable).

What about...

...sorting the list of results, or retrieving a subset of all matching objects? Like the `Query` interface, the `Criteria` interface lets you limit the number of results you get back (and choose where to start) by calling `setMaxResults()` and `setFirstResult()` as well as a variety of other scrolling and manipulation methods. It also lets you control the order in which results are returned (which you'd do using an `order by` clause in an HQL query), as shown in Example 8-6.

Example 8-6. Sorting the results by title

```
public static List tracksNoLongerThan(Time length, Session session) {
    Criteria criteria = session.createCriteria(Track.class);
    criteria.add(Restrictions.le("playTime", length));
    criteria.addOrder(Order.asc("title").ignoreCase());
    return criteria.list();
}
```

The `Order` class is just a way of representing orderings. It has two static factory methods, `asc()` and `desc()`, for creating ascending or descending orderings respectively. Each takes the name of the property to be sorted. If you call the `ignoreCase()` method on an `Order` instance, it will sort capital and lowercase letters together, which is often what you want for display. The results of running this version are in Example 8-7.

Example 8-7. The sorted results

```
% ant qtest
...
qtest:
     [java] Track: "Adagio for Strings (Ferry Corsten Remix)" (Ferry Corsten, Sa
muel Barber, William Orbit) 00:06:35, from Compact Disc
     [java] Track: "Gravity's Angel" (Laurie Anderson) 00:06:06, from Compact Di
sc
     [java] Track: "Russian Trance" (PPK) 00:03:30, from Compact Disc
```

```
[java] Track: "Test Tone 1" 00:00:10
[java]    Comment: Pink noise to test equalization
[java] Track: "Video Killed the Radio Star" (The Buggles) 00:03:49, from VH
S Videocassette tape
```

You can add more than one `Order` to the `Criteria`, and it will sort by each of them in turn (the first gets priority, and then if there are any results with the same value for that property, the second ordering is applied to them, and so on).

Compounding Criteria

As you might expect, you can add more than one `Criterion` to your query, and all of them must be satisfied for objects to be included in the results. This is equivalent to building a compound criterion using `Restrictions.conjunction()`, described in Appendix B. As shown in Example 8-8, we can restrict our results so that the tracks also have to contain a capital "A" somewhere in their title by adding another line to our method.

Example 8-8. A pickier list of short tracks
```
Criteria criteria = session.createCriteria(Track.class);
criteria.add(Restrictions.le("playTime", length));
criteria.add(Restrictions.like("title", "%A%"));
criteria.addOrder(Order.asc("title").ignoreCase());
return criteria.list();
```

With this in place, we get fewer results, as Example 8-9 shows.

Example 8-9. Tracks of seven minutes or less containing a capital "A" in their titles
```
qtest:
    [java] Track: "Adagio for Strings (Ferry Corsten Remix)" (Samuel Barber, Fe
rry Corsten, William Orbit) 00:06:35, from Compact Disc
    [java] Track: "Gravity's Angel" (Laurie Anderson) 00:06:06, from Compact Di
sc
```

If you don't even want to remember (or learn) the SQL "%" syntax for string matching with `like`, Hibernate provides a variation of the factory you can call to express in Java the kind of matching you want—in this case, it would be `Restrictions.like("title", "A", MatchMode.ANYWHERE)`. If you want to do case-insensitive matching, use `ilike` instead of `like`.

If you want to find any objects matching *any one* of your criteria, rather than requiring them to fit *all* criteria, you need to explicitly use `Restrictions.disjunction()` to group them. You can build up combinations of such groupings, and other complex hierarchies, using the criteria factories offered by the `Restrictions` class. Check Appendix B for the details. Example 8-10 shows how we'd change the sample query to give us tracks that *either* met the length restriction or contained a capital "A."

Example 8-10. Picking tracks more leniently

```
Criteria criteria = session.createCriteria(Track.class);
Disjunction any = Restrictions.disjunction();
any.add(Restrictions.le("playTime", length));
any.add(Restrictions.like("title", "%A%"));
criteria.add(any);
criteria.addOrder(Order.asc("title").ignoreCase());
return criteria.list();
```

This results in us picking up a new version of "Adagio for Strings" (see Example 8-11).

Example 8-11. Tracks whose title contains the letter "A," or whose length is seven minutes or less

```
qtest:
    [java] Track: "Adagio for Strings (ATB Remix)" (ATB, William Orbit, Samuel
Barber) 00:07:39, from Compact Disc
    [java] Track: "Adagio for Strings (Ferry Corsten Remix)" (Ferry Corsten, Wi
lliam Orbit, Samuel Barber) 00:06:35, from Compact Disc
    [java] Track: "Gravity's Angel" (Laurie Anderson) 00:06:06, from Compact Di
sc
    [java] Track: "Russian Trance" (PPK) 00:03:30, from Compact Disc
    [java] Track: "Test Tone 1" 00:00:10
    [java]    Comment: Pink noise to test equalization
    [java] Track: "Video Killed the Radio Star" (The Buggles) 00:03:49, from VH
S Videocassette Tape
```

Finally, note that it's still possible, thanks to the clever return values of these methods, to consolidate our method into a single expression (see Example 8-12).

Example 8-12. Taking code compactness a bit too far

```
return session.createCriteria(Track.class).add(Restrictions.disjunction().
        add(Restrictions.le("playTime", length)).
        add(Restrictions.like("title", "%A%"))).
    addOrder(Order.asc("title").ignoreCase()).list();
```

Although this yields the same results, I hope you agree it doesn't do good things for the readability of the method (except perhaps for LISP experts)!

You can use the facilities in **Restrictions** to build up a wide variety of multipart criteria. Some things still require HQL, and past a certain threshold of complexity, you may be better off in that environment. But, you can do a lot with criteria queries, and they're often the right way to go.

Projection and Aggregation with Criteria

If you're familiar with SQL, you know what this section title means. If not, fear not; it's actually pretty simple. *Projection* simply means that you don't need all of the information available in a table, so you want to request just part of it. In the case of an object-oriented environment like Hibernate, it means that you don't need to retrieve an entire object, just one or two of its properties. *Aggregation* similarly involves identifying properties, but then allows you to ask for statistical information about those properties, such as counting values, or finding maximum, minimum, or average values.

Before Hibernate 3, neither of these were possible without using HQL, so they are a nice addition to the Criteria API. Let's look at some examples. Starting simply, suppose we want to print all the track titles that contain the letter "v" without bothering to load any entire Track objects.

How do I do that?

Example 8-13 shows a method that uses the projection capability of the criteria API to achieve this.

Example 8-13. Simple projection on a single property

```
/**
 * Retrieve the titles of any tracks that contain a particular text string.
 *
 * @param text the text to be matched, ignoring case, anywhere in the title.
 * @param session the Hibernate session that can retrieve data.
 * @return the matching titles, as strings.
 */
public static List titlesContainingText(String text, Session session) {
    Criteria criteria = session.createCriteria(Track.class);
    criteria.add(Restrictions.like("title", text, MatchMode.ANYWHERE). ❶
            ignoreCase());
    criteria.setProjection(Projections.property("title")); ❷
    return criteria.list();
}
```

❶ This is an illustration of using the MatchMode interface to avoid having to perform string manipulation or remember the "%" character for specifying the kind of string matching desired.

❷ This use of the Projections class is how we tell the criteria we want a projection, and that we're specifically interested in retrieving the title property of the tracks we find.

So this method, like our other criteria queries, returns a List. But a list of what, exactly? The criteria are created on the Track class, but it wouldn't make sense to construct and return Track objects since we are only retrieving the title property. In fact, in situations like this where you project on a single property, you get a list of whatever class is associated with that property. In this case, since it is a string property, you get a List of String instances.

That makes sense!

We can easily check this by adding this method to *QueryTest.java* and changing main( ) to call it as follows:

```
System.out.println(titlesContainingText("v", session));
```

Running this version produces the following output:

```
qtest:
    [java] [Video Killed the Radio Star, Gravity's Angel]
```

It should be clear that projections can retrieve a different property than the one(s) you use in the restrictions. If we retrieved the track lengths instead, like so:

```
criteria.setProjection(Projections.property("playTime"));
```

we'd get this output:

```
qtest:
    [java] [00:03:49, 00:06:06]
```

Of course, the method name would be wrong then, and the output is kind of cryptic. What if we wanted to retrieve both the titles and lengths? It turns out that's almost as easy, as shown in Example 8-14.

Example 8-14. Projection on two properties

```
/**
 * Retrieve the titles and play times of any tracks that contain a
 * particular text string.
 *
 * @param text the text to be matched, ignoring case, anywhere in the title.
 * @param session the Hibernate session that can retrieve data.
 * @return the matching titles and times wrapped in object arrays.
 */
public static List titlesContainingTextWithPlayTimes(String text,
                                                     Session session) {
    Criteria criteria = session.createCriteria(Track.class);
    criteria.add(Restrictions.like("title", text, MatchMode.ANYWHERE)
            .ignoreCase());
    criteria.setProjection(Projections.projectionList(). ❶
            add(Projections.property("title")). ❷
            add(Projections.property("playTime")));
    return criteria.list();
}
```

❶   The projectionList( ) method creates a ProjectionList instance that can contain multiple projection choices for a single criteria query. Note that we're using the compact chaining notation introduced in Example 8-5 to avoid the need to declare a variable to hold this instance.

❷   Then we just add all the projections we want to the ProjectionList, and that gets passed to the query's setProjection( ) method.

The trickiest part here is what gets returned from the query. As always, it is a List, but now each element is going to contain more than one value, of potentially different types. Hibernate chooses to return a list of Object arrays. This makes the code for display somewhat more awkward:

```
for (Object o : titlesContainingTextWithPlayTimes("v", session)) {
    Object[] array = (Object[])o;
```

```
            System.out.println("Title: " + array[0] +
                    " (Play Time: " + array[1] + ')');
    }
```

This produces the following output:

```
qtest:
    [java] Title: Video Killed the Radio Star (Play Time: 00:03:49)
    [java] Title: Gravity's Angel (Play Time: 00:06:06)
```

But really, the code is ugly; you'd never really use projection this way. The whole point of an object/relational mapping system is that you can just return the object, and then use that to get at the properties you want when you want more than one of them.

So, why would projection support multiple values? Well, there is actually a good reason, and it has to do with that notion of aggregation that we introduced at the start of this section. Most of the time you are interested in using projection, you will be getting values that aren't directly object properties at all, but that are based on those properties. Example 8-15 shows a method that prints out, for each type of media represented in the database, the number of tracks that came from that media, and the longest play time of any track from that media.

Example 8-15. Projection with aggregation

```
/**
 * Print statistics about various media types.
 *
 * @param session the Hibernate session that can retrieve data.
 */
public static void printMediaStatistics(Session session) {
    Criteria criteria = session.createCriteria(Track.class);
    criteria.setProjection(Projections.projectionList(). ❶
            add(Projections.groupProperty("sourceMedia")). ❷
            add(Projections.rowCount()). ❸
            add(Projections.max("playTime"))); ❹

    for (Object o : criteria.list()) { ❺
        Object[] array = (Object[])o;
        System.out.println(array[0] + " track count: " + array[1] +
                "; max play time: " + array[2]);
    }
}
```

This example builds on many of the things we've seen so far:

❶ As before, we are creating a `ProjectionList` to hold the various items we want our query to return.

> Now we're doing interesting things with the power of the database!

❷ The `groupProperty( )` method is similar to the `property( )` method we've used so far, but it tells Hibernate to group all rows with the same value for the specified property into a single row in our results. This is the key to performing aggregation, and allows us to add aggregate values to the projection.

❸ The `rowCount( )` projection doesn't need any arguments, because it just returns the number of rows that were grouped into the current set of results (based on the value of our `groupProperty( )`, `sourceMedia`). This is how we count the tracks for each media type.

❹ The `max( )` projection returns the largest value found for its property in each grouped set of results.

❺ Finally, we have an output loop like the one we created for the previous example, which loops over the `List` of `Object` arrays returned by the criteria query, and prints them out.

Setting up `main( )` in *QueryTest.java* to call this method is simple:

```
printMediaStatistics(session);
```

And it produces the following output:

```
qtest:
    [java] CD track count: 4; max play time: 00:07:39
    [java] VHS track count: 1; max play time: 00:03:49
    [java] STREAM track count: 1; max play time: 00:07:05
    [java] null track count: 1; max play time: 00:00:10
```

That should give you a sense of the real value of projection and aggregation. (That `null` media type was our test tone.)

Notice that this output is not sorted in any particular order, though. We might want to do that, but how do you sort on a projection? To answer that we need to look at another refinement in the Criteria API. You can assign *aliases* to objects and properties with which you're working (just as you can for tables and columns in database query languages), whether they come directly from the database, or from projection and aggregation. So to get things sorted nicely by source media, we need to start by adding an alias to our grouped property:

```
add(Projections.groupProperty("sourceMedia").as("media")).
```

This declares the alias `media` which we can then use for sorting, as we did previously with ordinary object properties:

```
criteria.addOrder(Order.asc("media"));
```

With these changes, we see sorted output:

```
qtest:
    [java] null track count: 1; max play time: 00:00:10
    [java] CD track count: 4; max play time: 00:07:39
    [java] STREAM track count: 1; max play time: 00:07:05
    [java] VHS track count: 1; max play time: 00:03:49
```

There are other reasons for using aliases, and more things you can do with projection, but it's time to look at other aspects of criteria. We'll show you where you can learn more about all this at the end of the chapter.

Applying Criteria to Associations

So far we've been looking at the properties of a single class in forming our criteria. Of course, in our real systems, we've got a rich set of associations between objects, and sometimes the details we want to use to filter our results come from these associations. Fortunately, the criteria query API provides a straightforward way of performing such searches.

How do I do that?

Let's suppose we're interested in finding all the tracks associated with particular artists. We'd want our criteria to look at the values contained in each Track's artists property, which is a collection of associations to Artist objects. Just to make it a bit more fun, let's say we want to be able to find tracks associated with artists whose name property matches a particular substring pattern.

Let's add a new method to *QueryTest.java* to implement this. Add the method shown in Example 8-16 after the end of the tracksNoLongerThan( ) method.

Example 8-16. Filtering tracks based on their artist associations

```
/**
 * Retrieve any tracks associated with artists whose name matches a SQL
 * string pattern.
 *
 * @param namePattern the pattern which an artist's name must match
 * @param session the Hibernate session that can retrieve data.
 * @return a list of {@link Track}s meeting the artist name restriction.
 */
public static List tracksWithArtistLike(String namePattern, Session session)
{
    Criteria criteria = session.createCriteria(Track.class);
    Criteria artistCriteria = criteria.createCriteria("artists");  ❶
    artistCriteria.add(Restrictions.like("name", namePattern));  ❷
    artistCriteria.addOrder(Order.asc("name").ignoreCase());  ❸
    return criteria.list();
}
```

❶ Things started out looking familiar, but this line creates a second Criteria instance, attached to the one we're using to select tracks, by following the tracks' artists property. This means we can add constraints to either criteria (which would apply to the properties of the Track itself), or to artistCriteria, which causes them to apply to the properties of the Artist entities associated with the track.

❷ In this case, we are only interested in features of the artists, so we restrict our results to tracks associated with at least one artist whose name matches the specified pattern. (Again, by applying constraints to both Criteria, we could have restricted by both

> Finally, in this version of the book, we can see the output I'd originally hoped for.

Track and Artist properties.)

❸ We request sorting by artist name. This is another improvement Hibernate 3 offers over the experimental Criteria API that was available when the first version of this book was written. Back then, you could only sort the outermost criteria, not the subcriteria you created for associations. If you tried, you were rewarded with an UnsupportedOperationException.

To see all this in action, we need to make one more change. Modify the main( ) method so that it invokes this new query, as shown in Example 8-17.

Example 8-17. Calling the new track artist name query

```
...
// Ask for a session using the JDBC information we've configured
Session session = sessionFactory.openSession();
try {
    // Print tracks associated with an artist whose name ends with "n"
    List tracks = tracksWithArtistLike("%n", session);
    for (ListIterator iter = tracks.listIterator() ;
...
```

Running *ant qtest* now gives the results shown in Example 8-18.

Example 8-18. Tracks associated with an artist whose name ends with the letter "n"

```
qtest:
    [java] Track: "The World '99" (Pulp Victim, Ferry Corsten) 00:07:05, from D
igital Audio Stream
    [java] Track: "Adagio for Strings (Ferry Corsten Remix)" (William Orbit, Sa
muel Barber, Ferry Corsten) 00:06:35, from Compact Disc
    [java] Track: "Gravity's Angel" (Laurie Anderson) 00:06:06, from Compact Di
sc
```

What just happened?

If you look at the lists of artists for each of the three tracks that were found, you'll see that at least one of them has a name ending in "n" as we requested (they're in bold type for easier recognition in this printing). Also notice that we have access to all the artists associated with each track, not just the ones that matched the name criterion. This is what you'd expect and want, given that we've retrieved the actual Track entities. You can run criteria queries in a different mode, by calling setResultTransformer(Criteria.ALIAS_TO_ENTITY_MAP), which causes it to return a list of hierarchical Maps in which the criteria at each level have filtered the results. This goes beyond the scope of this book, but there are some examples of it in the reference and API documentation.

> You can also create aliases for the associations with which you're working, and use those aliases in expressions. This starts getting complex but it's useful. Explore it someday.

If the table from which you're fetching objects might contain duplicate entries, you can achieve the equivalent of SQL's "select distinct" by calling setResultTransformer(Criteria.DISTINCT_ROOT_ENTITY) on your criteria.

Querying by Example

If you don't want to worry about setting up expressions and criteria, but you've got an object that shows what you're looking for, you can use it as an example and have Hibernate build the criteria for you.

How do I do that?

Let's add another query method to *QueryTest.java*. Add the code of Example 8-19 to the top of the class where the other queries are.

Example 8-19. Using an example entity to populate a criteria query

```
/**
 * Retrieve any tracks that were obtained from a particular source media
 * type.
 *
 * @param media the media type of interest.
 * @param session the Hibernate session that can retrieve data.
 * @return a list of {@link Track}s meeting the media restriction.
 */
public static List tracksFromMedia(SourceMedia media, Session session) {
    Track track = new Track();                              ❶
    track.setSourceMedia(media);
    Example example = Example.create(track);                ❷

    Criteria criteria = session.createCriteria(Track.class); ❸
    criteria.add(example);
    criteria.addOrder(Order.asc("title"));
    return criteria.list();
}
```

❶ We start by creating the example Track and set the sourceMedia property to represent what we're looking for.

❷ Then we wrap it in an Example object. This object gives you some control over which properties will be used in building criteria and how strings are matched. The default behavior is that null properties are ignored, and that strings are compared in a case-sensitive and literal way. You can call example's excludeZeroes( ) method if you want properties with a value of zero to be ignored, too, or excludeNone( ) if even null properties are to be matched. An excludeProperty( ) method lets you explicitly ignore specific properties by name, but that's starting to get a lot like building criteria by hand. To tune string handling, there are `ignoreCase( )` and `enableLike( )` methods, which do just what they sound like.

❸   Then we create a criteria query, just like our other examples in this chapter, except that we add our `example` to it instead of using `Restrictions` to create a `Criterion`. Hibernate takes care of translating `example` into the corresponding criteria. The remaining lines are just like our previous query methods: setting up a sort order, running the query, and returning the list of matching entities.

Once again we need to modify the `main( )` method to call our new query. Let's find the tracks that came from CDs. Make the changes shown in Example 8-20.

Example 8-20. Changes to main() to call our example-driven query method

```
...
// Ask for a session using the JDBC information we've configured
Session session = sessionFactory.openSession();
try {
    // Print tracks that came from CDs
    List tracks = tracksFromMedia(SourceMedia.CD, session);
    for (ListIterator iter = tracks.listIterator() ;
...
```

Running this version produces output like Example 8-21.

Example 8-21. Results of querying by example for tracks from CDs

```
    [java] Track: "Adagio for Strings (ATB Remix)" (ATB, Samuel Barber, William
Orbit) 00:07:39, from Compact Disc
    [java] Track: "Adagio for Strings (Ferry Corsten Remix)" (Samuel Barber, Wi
lliam Orbit, Ferry Corsten) 00:06:35, from Compact Disc
    [java] Track: "Gravity's Angel" (Laurie Anderson) 00:06:06, from Compact Di
sc
    [java] Track: "Russian Trance" (PPK) 00:03:30, from Compact Disc
```

 You might think this is something of a contrived example, in that we didn't actually have a handy `Track` object around to use as an example and had to create one in the method. Well, perhaps, but there *is* a valuable reason to use this approach: it gives you even more compile-time checking than pure criteria queries. While any criteria query protects against syntactic runtime errors in HQL queries, you can still make mistakes in your property names, which won't be caught by the compiler, since they're just strings. When building example queries, you actually set property values using the mutator methods of the entity classes. This means if you make a typo, Java catches it at compile time.

As you might expect, you can use examples with subcriteria for associated objects, too. We could rewrite `tracksWithArtistLike( )` so that it uses an example `Artist` rather than building its criterion "by hand." We'll need to call `enableLike( )` on our `example`. Example 8-22 shows a concise way of doing this.

Example 8-22. Updating the artist name query to use an example artist
```
public static List tracksWithArtistLike(String namePattern, Session session)
{
    Criteria criteria = session.createCriteria(Track.class);
    Example example = Example.create(new Artist(namePattern, null, null));
    criteria.createCriteria("artists").add(example.enableLike()).addOrder(
        Order.asc("name").ignoreCase());
    return criteria.list();
}
```

This produces exactly the same output as when we were constructing the inner criteria "by hand." Remember that if you want to try running this you'll need to switch main( ) back to the way it was in Example 8-17.

A great variety of queries that power the user interface and general operation of a typical data-driven Java application can be expressed as criteria queries, and they provide advantages in readability, compile-time type checking, and even (surprisingly) compactness. As far as new database APIs go, I'd call this a winner.

> Criteria queries are pretty neat, aren't they? I liked them a lot more than I expected even in Hibernate 2, and they are more powerful now.

Property-Oriented Criteria Factories

We've already seen that there is often more than one way to express what you want using the criteria API, depending on your stylistic preferences, or the way you think about things. The Property class offers another bunch of alternatives of which you should be aware. We will not explore this class in depth because it is just another way of setting up criteria, but it is important to explain how it works, so you won't be confused if you run across examples, or feel baffled while scanning Hibernate's dense JavaDoc. (And, frankly, after one or two examples, you'll undoubtedly get the idea well enough that you may decide to adopt this approach yourself.)

Property is another factory for criteria, much like Restrictions, which we've been using in this chapter (and Order and Projection, for that matter). You can create essentially all the query refinements available with those other factories by using Property instead. Rather than starting with the kind of constraint in which you're interested, and then naming the property to which you want to apply it, you instead start with the property and pick a constraint.

As before, you start by creating Criteria on the object you want to query. But instead of saying, for example:

> Enough abstraction! Show some examples!

```
criteria.add(Restrictions.le("playTime", length));
```

you can say:

```
criteria.add(Property.forName("playTime").le(length));
```

It's really very similar—just a slightly different emphasis—as when you have more than one way to phrase the same concept in English. There are a bunch of methods in

Property that give you criteria, orderings, and projections. You can't construct a Property instance using new( )—you need to either start with the forName( ) static factory, or use an existing Property instance and call getProperty( ) on it to traverse to one of its component properties.

Here are a few more examples to show how this approach fits in. Where we had used statements like:

```
criteria.addOrder(Order.asc("name").ignoreCase());
```

we could instead have used:

```
criteria.addOrder(Property.forName("name").asc().ignoreCase());
```

And with projections, the approach we'd followed, such as:

```
criteria.setProjection(Projections.max("playTime"));
```

could equally well have been expressed as:

```
criteria.setProjection(Property.forName("playTime").max());
```

So, take your pick. Sometimes the kind of problem you're solving, or the thrust of the rest of the code, will evoke one style or the other. Or perhaps you'll just like one better and stick with it. But at least you're now aware you might run into both, and should be able to understand any criteria expression. These factory methods are all summarized in Appendix B.

> This is almost an embarrassment of riches!

Overwhelmed with options yet? No? Well, when criteria queries don't quite do the job, or you want an even more extreme alternative to all the choices you've seen in this chapter—especially if you're comfortable with the concision of SQL—you can turn to the full power of HQL. We investigate that in the next chapter.

What about…

…sneaking a little SQL in with your other criteria to take advantage of database-specific features or your mad DBA skillz? Using subqueries, or detached criteria that can be set up before you have a Hibernate session? Plugging in your own Java code to filter the results as the query is performed? All of these things and more are possible, but beyond the scope of this book. If you're ready for them, the *Advanced query options* chapter in *Java Persistence with Hibernate* is a good overview, and the Hibernate JavaDoc and source code are the definitive references.

## CHAPTER 9

A Look at HQL

We have already used HQL queries a few times in previous chapters. It's worth spending a little time looking at how HQL differs from SQL and some of the useful things you can do with it. As with the rest of this book, our intention is to provide a useful introduction and some examples, not a comprehensive reference.

As we mentioned back in Chapter 7, JPA's query language is a subset of HQL. So if you learn HQL, you'll be able to read JPA query language (QL) quite well, although if you're trying to *write* queries in the JPA you may well be tempted to go beyond its capabilities. That's a small price to pay for being able to use Hibernate most of the time.

> As noted at the end of Chapter 7, the examples in this chapter rely on the use of XML mapping files, so if you changed things around to work with annotations, you'll probably want to download the code examples to start over in this chapter's folder.

Writing HQL Queries

We've already shown that you can get by with fewer pieces in an HQL query than you might be used to in SQL (the queries we've been using, such as those in Chapter 3, have generally omitted the **select** clause). In fact, the only thing you really *need* to specify is the class in which you're interested. Example 9-1 shows a minimal query that's a perfectly valid way to get a list of all Track instances persisted in the database.

Example 9-1. The simplest HQL query

```
from Track
```

HQL stands for Hibernate Query Language. And SQL? It depends who you ask.

There's not much to it, is there? This is the HQL equivalent of Example 8-1, in which we built a criteria query on the Track class and supplied no criteria.

By default, Hibernate automatically "imports" the names of each class you map, which means you don't have to provide a fully qualified package name when you want to use it, the simple class name is enough. As long as you've not mapped more than one class with the same name, you don't need to use fully qualified class names in your queries. You are certainly free to do so if you prefer—as we often have in this book to help readers remember that the queries are expressed in terms of Java data beans and their properties, *not* database tables and columns (which you'd find in SQL). Example 9-2 produces precisely the same result as our first query.

Example 9-2. Explicit package naming, but still pretty simple

```
from com.oreilly.hh.data.Track
```

If you do have more than one mapped class with the same name, you can either use the fully qualified package name to refer to each, or you can assign an alternate name for one or both classes using an `import` tag in their mapping documents. You can also turn off the auto-import facility for a mapping file by adding `auto-import=false` to the top-level `hibernate-mapping` tag's attributes.

 You're probably used to queries being case-insensitive, since SQL behaves this way. For the most part, HQL acts the same, with the important exceptions of class and property names. Just as in the rest of Java, these are case-sensitive, so you must get the capitalization right.

Let's look at an extreme example of how HQL differs from SQL, by pushing its polymorphic query capability to its logical limit.

How do I do that?

A powerful way to highlight the fundamental difference between SQL and HQL is to consider what happens when you query `from java.lang.Object`. At first glance, this might not even seem to make sense! In fact, Hibernate supports queries that return polymorphic results. If you've got mapped classes that extend each other, or have some shared ancestor or interface, whether you've mapped the classes to the same table or to different tables, you can query the superclass. Since every Java object extends `Object`, this query asks Hibernate to return every single entity it knows about in the database.

We can test this by making a quick variant of our query test. Copy *QueryTest.java* to *QueryTest3.java*, and make the changes shown in Example 9-3 (most of the changes, which don't show up in the example, involve deleting example queries we don't need here).

If you're using Eclipse, you should jump ahead and read the section about the Hibernate Tools in Chapter 11, then come back to this chapter: the HQL Editor introduced there is a *much* easier way to play with all the different kinds of queries we're going to look at. It makes experimentation so efficient that you'll come up with your own variants and learn in more depth.

Example 9-3. Look, Toto, we're not in SQL anymore

```java
package com.oreilly.hh;

import org.hibernate.*;
import org.hibernate.cfg.Configuration;
import org.hibernate.criterion.*;

import com.oreilly.hh.data.*;

import java.util.*;

/**
 * Retrieve all persistent objects
 */
public class QueryTest3 {

    /**
     * Look up and print all entities when invoked from the command line.
     */
    public static void main(String args[]) throws Exception {
        // Create a configuration based on the properties file we've put
        // in the standard place.
        Configuration config = new Configuration();
        config.configure();

        // Get the session factory we can use for persistence
        SessionFactory sessionFactory = config.buildSessionFactory();

        // Ask for a session using the JDBC information we've configured
        Session session = sessionFactory.openSession();
        try {
            // Print every mapped object in the database
            List all = session.createQuery("from java.lang.Object").list(); ❶
            for (Object obj : all) {
                System.out.println(obj); ❷
            }
        } finally {
            // No matter what, close the session
            session.close();
        }

        // Clean up after ourselves
        sessionFactory.close();
    }
}
```

❶   This simple line invokes the odd and powerful query.

❷   Then all that's left to do is iterate over and print what we've found. We can't do much more than call **toString( )** on the objects we get back because we don't know what they might be. **Object** is not very deep as a shared interface.

There's one more step we need to take before we can run this. Add another target to *build.xml*, as shown in Example 9-4.

> As usual, these examples assume you've set up the environment by following the preceding chapters. You can also just use the downloadable sample source for this chapter. If you were following along through Chapter 7 and replaced your mapping files with annotations, you will need to either go back to your Chapter 6 code or download this chapter's code, since these examples rely on features of the mapping files.

Example 9-4. Invoking the über-query

```
<target name="qtest3" description="Retrieve all mapped objects"
        depends="compile">
  <java classname="com.oreilly.hh.QueryTest3" fork="true">
   <classpath refid="project.class.path"/>
  </java>
</target>
```

To be sure you've got all the sample data created, run *ant schema ctest atest*. You can then test the new query by running *ant qtest3*. You'll see results like those in Example 9-5.

Example 9-5. Everything Hibernate can find

```
% ant qtest3
Buildfile: build.xml

prepare:

usertypes:

codegen:
[hibernatetool] Executing Hibernate Tool with a Standard Configuration
[hibernatetool] 1. task: hbm2java (Generates a set of .java files)

compile:
    [javac] Compiling 4 source files to /Users/jim/Documents/Work/OReilly/svn_hi
bernate/current/examples/ch09/classes

qtest3:
    [java] com.oreilly.hh.data.Artist@8a137c [name='PPK' actualArtist='null' ]
    [java] com.oreilly.hh.data.Artist@79e4c [name='The Buggles' actualArtist='n
ull' ]
    [java] com.oreilly.hh.data.Artist@29ae5e [name='Laurie Anderson' actualArti
st='null' ]
    [java] com.oreilly.hh.data.Artist@76a9b6 [name='William Orbit' actualArtist
```

```
='null' ]
    [java] com.oreilly.hh.data.Artist@801919 [name='Ferry Corsten' actualArtist
='null' ]
    [java] com.oreilly.hh.data.Artist@efe4ac [name='Samuel Barber' actualArtist
='null' ]
    [java] com.oreilly.hh.data.Artist@8e13ab [name='ATB' actualArtist='null' ]
    [java] com.oreilly.hh.data.Artist@ad44f6 [name='Pulp Victim' actualArtist='
null' ]
    [java] com.oreilly.hh.data.Artist@8aaed5 [name='Martin L. Gore' actualArtis
t='null' ]
    [java] com.oreilly.hh.data.Album@a1644b [title='Counterfeit e.p.' tracks='[
com.oreilly.hh.data.AlbumTrack@132f26 [track='com.oreilly.hh.data.Track@d8f246 [
title='Compulsion' volume='Volume[left=100, right=100]' sourceMedia='CD' ]' ], c
om.oreilly.hh.data.AlbumTrack@5ae101 [track='com.oreilly.hh.data.Track@9eab7 [ti
tle='In a Manner of Speaking' volume='Volume[left=100, right=100]' sourceMedia='
CD' ]' ], com.oreilly.hh.data.AlbumTrack@6a16ae [track='com.oreilly.hh.data.Trac
k@10cf62 [title='Smile in the Crowd' volume='Volume[left=100, right=100]' source
Media='CD' ]' ], com.oreilly.hh.data.AlbumTrack@f7309a [track='com.oreilly.hh.da
ta.Track@9f332b [title='Gone' volume='Volume[left=100, right=100]' sourceMedia='
CD' ]' ], com.oreilly.hh.data.AlbumTrack@97cf78 [track='com.oreilly.hh.data.Trac
k@d86cae [title='Never Turn Your Back on Mother Earth' volume='Volume[left=100,
right=100]' sourceMedia='CD' ]' ], com.oreilly.hh.data.AlbumTrack@b5d53a [track=
'com.oreilly.hh.data.Track@c74b55 [title='Motherless Child' volume='Volume[left=
100, right=100]' sourceMedia='CD' ]' ]]' ]
    [java] com.oreilly.hh.data.Track@e74d83 [title='Russian Trance' volume='Vol
ume[left=100, right=100]' sourceMedia='CD' ]
    [java] com.oreilly.hh.data.Track@5d8362 [title='Video Killed the Radio Star
' volume='Volume[left=100, right=100]' sourceMedia='VHS' ]
    [java] com.oreilly.hh.data.Track@5c9ab5 [title='Gravity's Angel' volume='Vo
lume[left=100, right=100]' sourceMedia='CD' ]
    [java] com.oreilly.hh.data.Track@b0e76a [title='Adagio for Strings (Ferry C
orsten Remix)' volume='Volume[left=100, right=100]' sourceMedia='CD' ]
    [java] com.oreilly.hh.data.Track@28ea3f [title='Adagio for Strings (ATB Rem
ix)' volume='Volume[left=100, right=100]' sourceMedia='CD' ]
    [java] com.oreilly.hh.data.Track@2af08b [title='The World '99' volume='Volu
me[left=100, right=100]' sourceMedia='STREAM' ]
    [java] com.oreilly.hh.data.Track@164feb [title='Test Tone 1' volume='Volume
[left=50, right=75]' sourceMedia='null' ]
    [java] com.oreilly.hh.data.Track@d8f246 [title='Compulsion' volume='Volume[
left=100, right=100]' sourceMedia='CD' ]
    [java] com.oreilly.hh.data.Track@9eab7 [title='In a Manner of Speaking' vol
ume='Volume[left=100, right=100]' sourceMedia='CD' ]
    [java] com.oreilly.hh.data.Track@10cf62 [title='Smile in the Crowd' volume=
'Volume[left=100, right=100]' sourceMedia='CD' ]
    [java] com.oreilly.hh.data.Track@9f332b [title='Gone' volume='Volume[left=1
00, right=100]' sourceMedia='CD' ]
    [java] com.oreilly.hh.data.Track@d86cae [title='Never Turn Your Back on Mot
her Earth' volume='Volume[left=100, right=100]' sourceMedia='CD' ]
    [java] com.oreilly.hh.data.Track@c74b55 [title='Motherless Child' volume='V
olume[left=100, right=100]' sourceMedia='CD' ]

BUILD SUCCESSFUL
Total time: 9 seconds
```

What just happened?

Well, it's pretty remarkable if you think about it, because Hibernate had to do several separate SQL queries in order to obtain the results for us. A whole lot of work went on behind the scenes to hand us that list of every known persisted entity. Although it's hard to imagine a situation where you'll actually need to do something exactly like this, it certainly highlights some of the interesting capabilities of HQL and Hibernate.

There are certainly times when slightly less comprehensive queries will be very useful to you, so it's worth keeping in mind that table-spanning polymorphic queries are not only possible, but easy to use.

There are some limitations that come into play when you run an HQL query that requires multiple separate SQL queries to implement. You can't use order by clauses to sort the entire set of results, nor can you use the Query interface's scroll( ) method to walk through them.

What about...

...associations and joins? These are easy to work with as well. You can traverse associations by simply following the property chain, using periods as delimiters. To help you refer to a particular entity in your query expressions, HQL lets you assign aliases, just like SQL. This is particularly important if you want to refer to two separate entities of the same class, for example:

```
from com.oreilly.hh.Track as track1
```

which is equivalent to:

```
from com.oreilly.hh.Track track1
```

The version you'll use will most likely depend on what you're used to, or the style guidelines established for your project.

We'll see examples of joins later, once we introduce enough other HQL elements to make them interesting.

Selecting Properties and Pieces

The queries we've been using so far have returned entire persistent objects. This is the most common use of an object/relational mapping service like Hibernate, so it should come as no surprise. Once you've got the objects, you can use them in whatever way you need to within the familiar realm of Java code. There are circumstances where you might want only a subset of the properties that make up an object, though, such as producing reports. HQL can accommodate such needs, in exactly the same way you'd use ordinary SQL—projection in a select clause.

How do I do that?

Suppose we want to change *QueryTest.java* to display only the titles of the tracks that meet our search criteria, and we want to extract only that information from the database in the first place. We'd start by changing the query of Example 3-11 to retrieve only the `title` property. Edit *Track.hbm.xml* to make the query look like Example 9-6.

Example 9-6. Obtaining just the titles of the short tracks

```
<query name="com.oreilly.hh.tracksNoLongerThan">
  <![CDATA[
      select track.title from com.oreilly.hh.Track as track
      where track.playTime <= :length
  ]]>
</query>
```

Make sure the `tracksNoLongerThan( )` method in *QueryTest.java* is set up to use this query. (If you edited it to use criteria queries in Chapter 8, change it back to the way it was in Example 3-12. To save you the trouble of hunting that down, it's reproduced in Example 9-7.)

Example 9-7. HQL-driven query method, using the query mapped in Example 9-6

```
public static List tracksNoLongerThan(Time length, Session session) {
    Query query = session.getNamedQuery(
                      "com.oreilly.hh.tracksNoLongerThan");
    query.setTime("length", length);
    return query.list();
}
```

Finally, the `main( )` method needs to be updated, as shown in Example 9-8, to reflect the fact that the query method is now returning the title property rather than entire `Track` records. This property is defined as a `String`, so the method now returns a `List` of `String`s.

Example 9-8. Changes to QueryTest's main( ) method to work with the title query

```
// Print the titles of tracks that will fit in five minutes
List titles = tracksNoLongerThan(Time.valueOf("00:05:00"),
                                 session);
for (ListIterator iter = titles.listIterator() ;
     iter.hasNext() ; ) {
    String title = (String)iter.next();
    System.out.println("Track: " + title);
}
```

Those changes are pretty simple, and the relationship between the return type of the query and the `List` elements we see in Java is straightforward. Depending on what data you've set up, running this version using *ant qtest* will result in output similar to Example 9-9. (If you've not got any data, or you want it to look just like this, recreate the test data before displaying it by running *ant schema ctest atest qtest*.)

Example 9-9. Listing just the titles of tracks no more than five minutes long

```
qtest:
     [java] Track: Russian Trance
     [java] Track: Video Killed the Radio Star
     [java] Track: Test Tone 1
     [java] Track: In a Manner of Speaking
     [java] Track: Gone
     [java] Track: Never Turn Your Back on Mother Earth
     [java] Track: Motherless Child
```

What about...

...returning more than one property? You can certainly do this, and the properties can come from multiple objects if you're using a join, or if your query object has components or associations (which are, after all, a very convenient form of object-oriented join). As you'd expect from SQL, all you do is list the properties you'd like, separated by commas. As a simple example, let's get the IDs as well as the titles for our tracks in this query. Tweak *Track.hbm.xml* so the query looks like Example 9-10.

Example 9-10. Selecting multiple properties from an object

```xml
<query name="com.oreilly.hh.tracksNoLongerThan">
  <![CDATA[
      select track.id, track.title from com.oreilly.hh.Track as track
      where track.playTime <= :length
  ]]>
</query>
```

We don't need to change the query method at all; it still invokes this query by name, passes in the same named parameter, and returns the resulting list. But what does that list contain now? We'll need to update our loop in `main( )` so that it can show both the IDs and the titles.

In situations like this, when it needs to return multiple, separate values for each "row" in a query, each entry in the `List` returned by Hibernate will contain an array of objects. Each array contains the selected properties, in the order they're listed in the query. So we'll get a list of two-element arrays; each array will contain an `Integer` followed by a `String`.

Example 9-11 shows how we can update `main( )` in *QueryTest.java* to work with these arrays.

Example 9-11. Working with multiple, separate properties in query results

```java
// Print IDs and titles of tracks that will fit in five minutes
List titles = tracksNoLongerThan(Time.valueOf("00:05:00"),
                                 session);
for (ListIterator iter = titles.listIterator() ;
     iter.hasNext() ; ) {
    Object[] row = (Object[])iter.next();
    Integer id = (Integer)row[0];
    String title = (String)row[1];
```

```
            System.out.println("Track: " + aTitle + " [ID=" + id + ']');
    }
```

Running *ant qtest* after these changes produces output like Example 9-12.

Example 9-12. Listing titles and IDs

```
qtest:
    [java] Track: Russian Trance [ID=1]
    [java] Track: Video Killed the Radio Star [ID=2]
    [java] Track: Test Tone 1 [ID=7]
    [java] Track: In a Manner of Speaking [ID=9]
    [java] Track: Gone [ID=11]
    [java] Track: Never Turn Your Back on Mother Earth [ID=12]
    [java] Track: Motherless Child [ID=13]
```

I hope that while looking at this example you thought, "that's an awkward way to work with `Track` properties." If you didn't, compare Example 9-11 with the corresponding code in Example 3-7. The latter is more concise and natural, and it prints even more information about the tracks. If you're extracting information about a mapped object, you're almost always better off taking full advantage of the mapping capability to extract an actual instance of the object, so you can work with its properties with the full expressive and type-safe capabilities of Java.

So, why did we try this at all? Well, there are situations where retrieving multiple values in an HQL query can make sense: you might want just one property from each of a couple of mapped classes, for example. Or you might want to return a group of related classes by listing the class names in the `select` clause. For such cases it's worth knowing this technique. There may also be significant performance benefits if your mapped object has dozens of large (or non-lazily associated) properties, and you're only interested in one or two.

> Was this some sort of cruel joke?

There is another surprising trick you can use to impose a good object structure even when you're building reports that select a bunch of properties from disparate mapped objects. HQL lets you construct and return an arbitrary object within your `select` clause. So you could create an ad-hoc reporting class whose properties reflect the values needed by your report, and return instances of this class in the query instead of cryptic `Object` arrays. If we'd defined a `TrackSummary` class with `id` and `title` properties and an appropriate constructor, our query could have used:

```
    select new TrackSummary(track.id, track.title)
```

instead of:

```
    select track.id, track.title
```

and we wouldn't have needed any of the array manipulation in the code that works with the results. (Again, in this case, it would still have made more sense to simply return the entire `Track`, but this is useful when you're working with properties from multiple objects or even synthetic results like aggregate functions, illustrated later.)

Sorting

It should come as no surprise that you can use a SQL-style "order by" clause to control the order in which your output appears. We've alluded to this several times in earlier chapters, and it works just like you'd expect. You can use any property of the objects being returned to establish the sort order, and you can list multiple properties to establish subsorts within results for which the first property values are the same.

How do I do that?

Sorting is very simple: you list the values that you want to use to sort the results. As usual, where SQL uses columns, HQL uses properties. For Example 9-13, let's update the query in Example 9-10 so that it displays the results in reverse alphabetical order.

Example 9-13. Addition to Track.hbm.xml that sorts the results backwards by title

```
<query name="com.oreilly.hh.tracksNoLongerThan">
  <![CDATA[
      select track.id, track.title from com.oreilly.hh.Track as track
      where track.playTime <= :length
      order by track.title desc
  ]]>
</query>
```

> As in SQL, you specify an ascending sort using "asc" and a descending sort with "desc."

The output from running this is as you'd expect. See Example 9-14.

Example 9-14. Titles and IDs in reverse alphabetical order

```
% ant qtest
Buildfile: build.xml

prepare:
    [copy] Copying 1 file to /Users/jim/Documents/Work/OReilly/svn_hibernate/cu
rrent/examples/ch09/classes

usertypes:
...

qtest:
    [java] Track: Video Killed the Radio Star [ID=2]
    [java] Track: Test Tone 1 [ID=7]
    [java] Track: Russian Trance [ID=1]
    [java] Track: Never Turn Your Back on Mother Earth [ID=12]
    [java] Track: Motherless Child [ID=13]
    [java] Track: In a Manner of Speaking [ID=9]
    [java] Track: Gone [ID=11]

BUILD SUCCESSFUL
Total time: 9 seconds
```

Working with Aggregate Values

Especially when writing reports, you'll often want summary information from the database: "How many? What's the average? The longest?" HQL can help with this, by offering aggregate functions like those in SQL. In HQL, of course, these functions apply to the properties of persistent classes.

How do I do that?

Let's try some of this in our query test framework. First, add the query in Example 9-15 after the existing query in *Track.hbm.xml*.

Example 9-15. A query collecting aggregate information about tracks

```
<query name="com.oreilly.hh.trackSummary">
  <![CDATA[
      select count(*), min(track.playTime), max(track.playTime)
      from Track as track
  ]]>
</query>
```

I was tempted to try asking for the average playing time as well, but (as I discovered in Chapter 8) unfortunately HSQLDB doesn't know how to calculate averages for non-numerical values, and this property is stored in a column of type date.

Next we need to write a method to run this query and display the results. Add the code in Example 9-16 to *QueryTest.java*, after the tracksNoLongerThan( ) method.

Example 9-16. A method to run the trackSummary query

```
/**
 * Print summary information about all tracks.
 *
 * @param session the Hibernate session that can retrieve data.
 **/
public static void printTrackSummary(Session session) {
    Query query = session.getNamedQuery("com.oreilly.hh.trackSummary");
    Object[] results = (Object[])query.uniqueResult();
    System.out.println("Summary information:");
    System.out.println("      Total tracks: " + results[0]);
    System.out.println("   Shortest track: " + results[1]);
    System.out.println("    Longest track: " + results[2]);
}
```

Since we're only using aggregate functions in the query, we know we'll only get one row of results back. This is another opportunity to use the uniqueResult( ) convenience method offered by the Query interface. It saves us the trouble of getting back a list and extracting the first element. As discussed in "Selecting Properties and Pieces" earlier in this chapter, since we've asked for multiple distinct values, that result will be an Object array, whose elements are the values we requested in the same order we put them in the query. (The ugliness of this code, with its cryptic, numeric array references, should be more convincing than the TrackSummary example when it comes to illustrating why you might want to create "reporting objects" for use in your queries. Where in ordinary SQL you would name columns and request them by name from your ResultSet, in HQL you declare classes and create instances in your queries.)

We also need to add a line to main( ) to call this method. We can put it after the end of the loop in which we print details about selected tracks, as shown in Example 9-17.

Example 9-17. Addition to main( ) in QueryTest.java to display the new summary information

```
        ...
            System.out.println("Track: " + aTitle + " [ID=" + anID + ']');
        }
        printTrackSummary(session);
    } finally {
        // No matter what, close the session
        ...
```

With these additions, we get new output when running *ant qtest*. See Example 9-18.

Example 9-18. The summary output

```
        ...
    qtest:
         [java] Track: Video Killed the Radio Star [ID=2]
         [java] Track: Test Tone 1 [ID=7]
         [java] Track: Russian Trance [ID=1]
         [java] Track: Never Turn Your Back on Mother Earth [ID=12]
         [java] Track: Motherless Child [ID=13]
         [java] Track: In a Manner of Speaking [ID=9]
         [java] Track: Gone [ID=11]
         [java] Summary information:
         [java]         Total tracks: 13
         [java]       Shortest track: 00:00:10
         [java]        Longest track: 00:07:39

    BUILD SUCCESSFUL
    Total time: 9 seconds
```

That was pretty easy. Let's try something trickier—pulling information from joined tables. Tracks have a collection of artists associated with them. Suppose we want to get summary information about the tracks associated with a particular artist, rather than for all tracks. Example 9-19 shows what we'd add to the query.

Example 9-19. Summarizing tracks associated with an artist

```
    <query name="com.oreilly.hh.trackSummary">
      <![CDATA[
        select count(*), min(track.playTime), max(track.playTime)
        from Track as track
        where :artist in elements(track.artists)
      ]]>
    </query>
```

We've added a where clause to narrow down the tracks we want to see, using a named parameter, *artist*. HQL provides another use for the in operator. While you can use it in the normal SQL sense to give a list of possible values for a property, you can also do what we've done here. This statement tells Hibernate we are interested in tracks whose artists collection contains a specified value. To call this version of the query, beef up printTrackSummary( ) a little, as shown in Example 9-20.

Example 9-20. Enhancing printTrackSummary() to work with a specific artist

```java
/**
 * Print summary information about tracks associated with an artist.
 *
 * @param artist the artist in whose tracks we're interested.
 * @param session the Hibernate session that can retrieve data.
 **/
public static void printTrackSummary(Artist artist, Session session) {
    Query query = session.getNamedQuery("com.oreilly.hh.trackSummary");
    query.setParameter("artist", artist);
    Object[] results = (Object[])query.uniqueResult();
    System.out.println("Summary of tracks by " + artist.getName() + ':');
    System.out.println("      Total tracks: " + results[0]);
    System.out.println("   Shortest track: " + results[1]);
    System.out.println("    Longest track: " + results[2]);
}
```

There wasn't much to that, was there? Finally, the line that calls this method needs another parameter to specify an artist. Use the handy getArtist( ) method in *CreateTest.java* once again. Change the method call in *QueryTest.java*'s main( ) method to look like it does in Example 9-21.

Example 9-21. Calling the enhanced printTrackSummary()

```java
    ...
        System.out.println("Track: " + title + " [ID=" + id + ']');
    }
    printTrackSummary(CreateTest.getArtist("Samuel Barber",
                                           false, session), session);
} finally {
    // No matter what, close the session
    ...
```

Now when you run *ant qtest* you'll see information that looks like Example 9-22.

Example 9-22. Running the summary query for tracks by Samuel Barber

```
qtest:
    [java] Track: Video Killed the Radio Star [ID=2]
    [java] Track: Test Tone 1 [ID=7]
    [java] Track: Russian Trance [ID=1]
    [java] Track: Never Turn Your Back on Mother Earth [ID=12]
    [java] Track: Motherless Child [ID=13]
    [java] Track: In a Manner of Speaking [ID=9]
    [java] Track: Gone [ID=11]
    [java] Summary of tracks by Samuel Barber:
    [java]       Total tracks: 2
```

```
[java]      Shortest track: 00:06:35
[java]       Longest track: 00:07:39
```

What just happened?

This took so little effort that it's worth taking a minute to appreciate how much Hibernate actually did for us. The `getArtist( )` method we called returned the `Artist` instance corresponding to Samuel Barber. We were able to pass this entire object as a named parameter to our HQL query, and Hibernate knows enough about how to put together join queries using the `Artist`'s `id` property and the `TRACK_ARTISTS` table to implement the complicated condition we expressed so concisely in Example 9-10.

> Just try doing something like that with vanilla SQL!

The results we got reflect the two remixes of "Adagio for Strings" in the sample data. They don't show up in the detailed track list because they're both longer than five minutes.

Writing Native SQL Queries

Given the power and convenience of HQL, and the way it dovetails so naturally with the objects in your Java code, why wouldn't you want to use it? Well, there might be some special feature supported by the native SQL dialect of your project's database that HQL can't exploit. If you're willing to accept the (serious) fact that using this feature will make it harder to change databases in the future, Hibernate will let you write queries in that native dialect while still helping you write expressions in terms of properties and translate the results to objects. (If you didn't want this help, you could just use a raw JDBC connection to run a plain SQL query, of course.)

Another circumstance in which it might be nice to meet your database halfway is if you're in the process of migrating an existing JDBC-based project to Hibernate, and you want to take small steps rather than thoroughly rewriting each query right away.

How do I do that?

If you're embedding your query text inside your Java source code, you use the `Session` method `createSQLQuery( )` instead of Example 3-7's `createQuery( )`. Of course, you know better than to code like that, so I won't even show you an example. The better approach is to put the query in a mapping document like Example 3-11. The difference is that you use a `sql-query` tag rather than the `query` tag we've seen up until now. You also need to tell Hibernate the mapped class you want to return, and the alias that you're using to refer to it (and its properties) in the query.

As a somewhat contrived example, suppose we want to know all the tracks that end exactly halfway through the last minute they're playing (in other words, the time display on the jukebox would be *h:mm*:30). An easy way to do that would be to take advantage of HSQLDB's built-in SECOND function, which gives you the seconds part of a Time value. Since HQL doesn't know about functions that are specific to HSQLDB's SQL dialect, this will push us into the realm of a native SQL query. Example 9-23 shows what it would look like; add this after the HQL queries in *Track.hbm.xml*.

Example 9-23. Embedding a native SQL dialect query in a Hibernate mapping

```
<sql-query name="com.oreilly.hh.tracksEndingAt">
  <return alias="track" class="com.oreilly.hh.data.Track"/>
  <![CDATA[
      select {track.*}
      from TRACK as {track}
      where SECOND({track}.PLAYTIME) = :seconds
  ]]>
</sql-query>
```

The return tag tells Hibernate we're going to be using the alias track in our query to refer to a Track object. That allows us to use the shorthand {track.*} in the query body to refer to all the columns from the TRACK table we need in order to create a Track instance. (Notice that everywhere we use the alias in the query body we need to enclose it in curly braces. This gets us "out of" the native SQL environment so we can express things in terms of Hibernate-mapped classes and properties.)

The where clause in the query uses the HSQLDB SECOND function to narrow our results to include only tracks whose length has a specified number in the seconds part. Happily, even though we're building a native SQL query, we can still make use of Hibernate's nice named query parameters. In this case we're passing in a value named *seconds* to control the query. (You don't need to use curly braces to tell Hibernate you're using a named parameter, even in an SQL query; its parser is smart enough to figure this out.)

The code that uses this mapped SQL query is no different than our previous examples using HQL queries. The getNamedQuery( ) method is used to load both kinds, and they both implement the Query interface. So our Java method invoking this query should look familiar. Add the code in Example 9-24 after the printTrackSummary( ) method in *QueryTest.java*.

Example 9-24. Calling a native SQL mapped query

```
/**
 * Print tracks that end some number of seconds into their final minute.
 *
 * @param seconds, the number of seconds at which we want tracks to end.
 * @param session the Hibernate session that can retrieve data.
 **/
public static void printTracksEndingAt(int seconds, Session session) {
    Query query = session.getNamedQuery("com.oreilly.hh.tracksEndingAt");
    query.setInteger("seconds", seconds);
    List results = query.list();
    for (ListIterator iter = results.listIterator() ; iter.hasNext() ; ) {
        Track track = (Track)iter.next();
        System.out.println("Track: " + track.getTitle() +
                          ", length=" + track.getPlayTime());
```

```
        }
    }
```

Finally, add some lines to `main()` that call this method. Example 9-25 shows them added after the invocation of `printTrackSummary()`.

Example 9-25. Calling printTracksEndingAt() to display tracks ending at a half minute

```
    ...
        printTrackSummary(CreateTest.getArtist("Samuel Barber",
                                        false, session), session);
        System.out.println("Tracks ending halfway through final minute:");
        printTracksEndingAt(30, session);
    } finally {
        // No matter what, close the session
    ...
```

These changes produce the additional output shown in Example 9-26 when *ant qtest* is run.

Example 9-26. Sample output from the native SQL query

```
    qtest:
        [java] Track: Video Killed the Radio Star [ID=2]
    ...
        [java] Summary of tracks by Samuel Barber:
        [java]         Total tracks: 2
        [java]      Shortest track: 00:06:35
        [java]       Longest track: 00:07:39
        [java] Tracks ending halfway through final minute:
        [java] Track: Russian Trance, length=00:03:30

    BUILD SUCCESSFUL
    Total time: 10 seconds
```

There's certainly more tedium and attention to detail on multiple levels required when using a native SQL query compared to an HQL query (especially when your query starts getting complex or referring to multiple tables), but it's nice to know that it is possible on the occasions where you really need one.

What about...

...stored procedures? The `sql-query` mapping is also your entry point to working with database stored procedures from Hibernate, starting with Hibernate 3. (If this doesn't mean anything to you, don't worry; it just means you don't need to worry about it yet, you'll know when you do.) There are some definite limitations to the kinds of queries you can call and values they can return, and these differ from database to database. See the Hibernate manual[*] for the gory details.

---

[*] *http://www.hibernate.org/hib_docs/v3/reference/en/html_single/#sp_query*

...well, lots of other things? You undoubtedly suspect this chapter barely scratches the surface of what you can do with HQL. That's definitely true. When you start combining some of these capabilities, and working with collections, associations, and powerful expressions, you can achieve some remarkable things. We can't possibly cover them all in this introduction, so you'll want to take a close look at the HQL section and examples in the Hibernate reference documentation, and do some experimentation on your own.

When you look through the Hibernate Query Language[†] chapter in the reference documentation, be sure to look at the interesting things you can use in expressions, especially as they apply to collections. Don't miss the way you can use array bracket notation to select elements of indexed collections—you can even put arithmetic expressions inside the brackets.

The "Tips and Tricks" section that follows the longer examples gives some useful advice about working efficiently in different database environments, and using a variety of Hibernate interfaces to achieve useful results in ways you might not think of, especially if you're coming from a SQL background.

You may also want to peruse the books mentioned in Appendix E. Hopefully, this discussion has helped you get a grounding in the basics, and it will serve as a starting point, anchor, and even incentive for the explorations on which you will embark!

> This isn't your father's SQL....

[†] *http://www.hibernate.org/hib_docs/v3/reference/en/html/queryhql.html*

## PART II

Playing Nice with Others

Our examples so far have focused on a very narrow set of tools beyond Hibernate: Ant, the Maven Ant Tasks, the Hibernate Tools, and HSQLDB as our relational database. This has served us very well in providing a platform for getting quickly to the "meat" of Hibernate and focusing on exploring its features. In the real world, though, you'll often want to use Hibernate in different ways and in conjunction with other useful packages.

Luckily, that's very easy! So let's change gears and start introducing some new faces, like the popular MySQL database and the Eclipse IDE. Then we'll discuss Maven in more depth than we could when it was just a stepping stone towards getting the examples working, showing you ways it can help if you adopt more than the Ant Tasks. Finally, we highlight Spring and Stripes, two very useful projects that pair nicely with Hibernate.

## CHAPTER 10

Connecting Hibernate to MySQL

Setting Up a MySQL Database

As nifty and self-contained as HSQLDB is, your project may not be in the market for an embedded Java database. In fact, you're likely going to want to interface with some existing, external database server. Luckily, that's just as easy (assuming you have the database already up and running, which is certainly beyond the scope of this walk-through).

To highlight this flexibility in database choices, let's take a look at what we'd change in Chapter 2 if we wanted to connect Hibernate to a MySQL database.

> This example assumes you've already got a working MySQL instance, and can administer it.

How do I do that?

Connect to your MySQL server and set up a new database to play with, as shown in Example 10-1.

Example 10-1. Setting up the MySQL database notebook_db

```
% mysql -u root -p
Enter password:
Welcome to the MySQL monitor.  Commands end with ; or \g.
Your MySQL connection id is 3 to server version: 5.0.21

Type 'help;' or '\h' for help. Type '\c' to clear the buffer.

mysql> CREATE DATABASE notebook_db;
Query OK, 1 row affected (0.03 sec)

mysql> GRANT ALL ON notebook_db.* TO 'jim'@'janus.reseune.pvt' IDENTIFIED BY 's3
cret';
Query OK, 0 rows affected (0.02 sec)

mysql> quit;
Bye
```

Make a note of the database name you create, as well as the user and password that grant access to it. You will need to enter these into *hibernate.cfg.xml*, as shown later in Example 10-3. (And hopefully you'll use a more robust password than this in your real databases!) If your database server is a different machine than where you're running the examples, put the example machine's hostname in the GRANT line rather than localhost (or use '%' to indicate any host is acceptable if you're on a secure private network).

Connecting to MySQL

Next, we'll need a JDBC driver capable of connecting to MySQL. We can get this by adding another dependency in *build.xml*, as shown in Example 10-2. It's fine to have drivers for several different databases available to your code; they won't conflict with each other, since the Hibernate configuration file specifies which driver class to use. (If you're curious about how to get this driver "by hand," you can download[*] Connector/J from the MySQL site). If you want to avoid confusion on the part of future readers of the file, though, feel free to delete the hsqldb dependency, as well as the db target since data will no longer be showing up in HSQLDB to be viewed by that GUI.

Example 10-2. Adding the MySQL driver to our project dependencies in build.xml

```
...
    <artifact:dependencies pathId="dependency.class.path">
      <dependency groupId="hsqldb" artifactId="hsqldb" version="1.8.0.7"/>
      <dependency groupId="mysql" artifactId="mysql-connector-java"
                  version="5.0.5"/>
      <dependency groupId="org.hibernate" artifactId="hibernate"
                  version="3.2.5.ga">
...
```

Speaking of the configuration file, it's time to edit *hibernate.cfg.xml* to use the new driver and database we've just made available. Example 10-3 shows how to set up a connection to my own MySQL instance using the database created by Example 10-1 earlier. You'll need to tweak these values to correspond to your own server, your database, and the login credentials you chose. (If you're using MM.MySQL, the older incarnation of the MySQL JDBC driver, the driver_class will need to be com.mysql.jdbc.Driver.)

Also, delete the jdbc.batch_size property towards the bottom of the file. The MySQL driver doesn't have any problems reporting actual errors from inside batches, unlike the HSQLDB driver we've been using, and there is an even larger performance penalty from turning off batches when talking to an out-of-process database.

---

[*] *http://www.mysql.com/products/connector/j/*

Example 10-3. Changes to hibernate.cfg.xml to connect to the new MySQL database

```
<?xml version='1.0' encoding='utf-8'?>
<!DOCTYPE hibernate-configuration PUBLIC
        "-//Hibernate/Hibernate Configuration DTD 3.0//EN"
        "http://hibernate.sourceforge.net/hibernate-configuration-3.0.dtd">

<hibernate-configuration>
  <session-factory>

    <!-- SQL dialect -->
    <property name="dialect">org.hibernate.dialect.MySQL5Dialect</property>

    <!-- Database connection settings -->
    <property name="connection.driver_class">com.mysql.jdbc.Driver</property>
    <property
        name="connection.url">jdbc:mysql://localhost/notebook_db</property>
    <property name="connection.username">jim</property>
    <property name="connection.password">s3cret</property>
    <property name="connection.shutdown">true</property>

...
```

 If you're running MySQL on a different machine than on the one on which you're testing the examples, the third property definition here will need to reflect your database server name. Also, the `connection.shutdown` property is no longer needed, but it won't hurt anything if you leave it in.

Trying It Out

Once this is all set, you can rerun the schema-creation example that was set up in "Cooking Up a Schema" way back in Chapter 2. This time it will build the schema on your MySQL server rather than in the embedded HSQLDB world. You'll see output like what's shown in Example 10-4, although it will be longer than the example, in which we've cut out some of the repetitive and boring output, and highlighted a few particularly salient bits that prove our new settings have taken effect. (Note that we're starting with a separate *ant prepare* invocation, since this is the first time we're working in this chapter's example directory, and we need the right files in the class path before Ant first starts up to run the **schema** target.)

Example 10-4. Schema creation when connecting to MySQL

```
% ant prepare
Buildfile: build.xml
Downloading: mysql/mysql-connector-java/5.0.5/mysql-connector-java-5.0.5.pom
Transferring 1K
Downloading: mysql/mysql-connector-java/5.0.5/mysql-connector-java-5.0.5.jar
Transferring 500K

prepare:
```

```
       [mkdir] Created dir: /Users/jim/svn/oreilly/hibernate/current/examples/ch10/
classes
        [copy] Copying 5 files to /Users/jim/svn/oreilly/hibernate/current/examples
/ch10/classes

BUILD SUCCESSFUL
Total time: 3 seconds

% ant schema
Buildfile: build.xml

prepare:

usertypes:
       [javac] Compiling 2 source files to /Users/jim/svn/oreilly/hibernate/current
/examples/ch10/classes

codegen:
[hibernatetool] Executing Hibernate Tool with a Standard Configuration
[hibernatetool] 1. task: hbm2java (Generates a set of .java files)
[hibernatetool] 16:46:38,403  INFO Environment:514 - Hibernate 3.2.5
[hibernatetool] 16:46:38,415  INFO Environment:547 - hibernate.properties not fo
und
[hibernatetool] 16:46:38,419  INFO Environment:681 - Bytecode provider name : cg
lib
[hibernatetool] 16:46:38,434  INFO Environment:598 - using JDK 1.4 java.sql.Time
stamp handling
[hibernatetool] 16:46:38,561  INFO Configuration:1460 - configuring from file: h
ibernate.cfg.xml
[hibernatetool] 16:46:38,740  INFO Configuration:553 - Reading mappings from res
ource : com/oreilly/hh/data/Track.hbm.xml
[hibernatetool] 16:46:38,932  INFO HbmBinder:300 - Mapping class: com.oreilly.hh
.data.Track -> TRACK
...
[hibernatetool] 16:46:39,110  INFO HbmBinder:1422 - Mapping collection: com.orei
lly.hh.data.Artist.tracks -> TRACK_ARTISTS
[hibernatetool] 16:46:39,239  INFO Configuration:1541 - Configured SessionFactor
y: null
[hibernatetool] 16:46:39,411  INFO Version:15 - Hibernate Tools 3.2.0.b9

compile:
       [javac] Compiling 9 source files to /Users/jim/svn/oreilly/hibernate/current
/examples/ch10/classes

schema:
[hibernatetool] Executing Hibernate Tool with a Standard Configuration
[hibernatetool] 1. task: hbm2ddl (Generates database schema)
[hibernatetool] 16:46:41,502  INFO Configuration:1460 - configuring from file: h
ibernate.cfg.xml
[hibernatetool] 16:46:41,515  INFO Configuration:553 - Reading mappings from res
ource : com/oreilly/hh/data/Track.hbm.xml
...
[hibernatetool] 16:46:41,629  INFO Configuration:1541 - Configured SessionFactor
y: null
[hibernatetool] 16:46:41,659  INFO Dialect:152 - **Using dialect: org.hibernate.di**
```

alect.MySQL5Dialect
[hibernatetool] 16:46:41,714 INFO SchemaExport:154 - Running hbm2ddl schema exp
ort
[hibernatetool] 16:46:41,716 INFO SchemaExport:179 - exporting generated schema
 to database
[hibernatetool] 16:46:41,725 INFO DriverManagerConnectionProvider:41 - Using Hi
bernate built-in connection pool (not for production use!)
[hibernatetool] 16:46:41,726 INFO DriverManagerConnectionProvider:42 - Hibernat
e connection pool size: 1
[hibernatetool] 16:46:41,727 INFO DriverManagerConnectionProvider:45 - autocomm
it mode: false
[hibernatetool] 16:46:41,745 INFO DriverManagerConnectionProvider:80 - **using dr
iver: com.mysql.jdbc.Driver at URL: jdbc:mysql://localhost/notebook_db**
[hibernatetool] 16:46:41,746 INFO DriverManagerConnectionProvider:86 - **connecti
on properties: {user=jim, password=****, shutdown=true}**
[hibernatetool] alter table ALBUM_ARTISTS drop foreign key FK7BA403FC76BBFFF9;
...
[hibernatetool] alter table TRACK_COMMENTS drop foreign key FK105B2688E424525B;
[hibernatetool] drop table if exists ALBUM;
[hibernatetool] drop table if exists ALBUM_ARTISTS;
[hibernatetool] drop table if exists ALBUM_COMMENTS;
[hibernatetool] drop table if exists ALBUM_TRACKS;
[hibernatetool] drop table if exists ARTIST;
[hibernatetool] drop table if exists TRACK;
[hibernatetool] drop table if exists TRACK_ARTISTS;
[hibernatetool] drop table if exists TRACK_COMMENTS;
[hibernatetool] create table ALBUM (ALBUM_ID integer not null auto_increment, TI
TLE varchar(255) not null, numDiscs integer, added date, primary key (ALBUM_ID))
;
[hibernatetool] create table ALBUM_ARTISTS (ALBUM_ID integer not null, ARTIST_ID
 integer not null, primary key (ALBUM_ID, ARTIST_ID));
[hibernatetool] create table ALBUM_COMMENTS (ALBUM_ID integer not null, COMMENT
varchar(255));
[hibernatetool] create table ALBUM_TRACKS (ALBUM_ID integer not null, TRACK_ID i
nteger, disc integer, positionOnDisc integer, LIST_POS integer not null, primary
 key (ALBUM_ID, LIST_POS));
[hibernatetool] create table ARTIST (ARTIST_ID integer not null auto_increment,
NAME varchar(255) not null unique, actualArtist integer, primary key (ARTIST_ID)
);
[hibernatetool] create table TRACK (TRACK_ID integer not null auto_increment, TI
TLE varchar(255) not null, filePath varchar(255) not null, playTime time, added
date, VOL_LEFT smallint, VOL_RIGHT smallint, sourceMedia varchar(255), primary k
ey (TRACK_ID));
[hibernatetool] create table TRACK_ARTISTS (TRACK_ID integer not null, ARTIST_ID
 integer not null, primary key (TRACK_ID, ARTIST_ID));
[hibernatetool] create table TRACK_COMMENTS (TRACK_ID integer not null, COMMENT
varchar(255));
[hibernatetool] create index ALBUM_TITLE on ALBUM (TITLE);
[hibernatetool] alter table ALBUM_ARTISTS add index FK7BA403FC76BBFFF9 (ARTIST_I
D), add constraint FK7BA403FC76BBFFF9 foreign key (ARTIST_ID) references ARTIST
(ARTIST_ID);
[hibernatetool] alter table ALBUM_ARTISTS add index FK7BA403FCF2AD8FDB (ALBUM_ID
), add constraint FK7BA403FCF2AD8FDB foreign key (ALBUM_ID) references ALBUM (AL
BUM_ID);
[hibernatetool] alter table ALBUM_COMMENTS add index FK1E2C21E4F2AD8FDB (ALBUM_I

```
D), add constraint FK1E2C21E4F2AD8FDB foreign key (ALBUM_ID) references ALBUM (A
LBUM_ID);
[hibernatetool] alter table ALBUM_TRACKS add index FKD1CBBC78E424525B (TRACK_ID)
, add constraint FKD1CBBC78E424525B foreign key (TRACK_ID) references TRACK (TRA
CK_ID);
[hibernatetool] alter table ALBUM_TRACKS add index FKD1CBBC78F2AD8FDB (ALBUM_ID)
, add constraint FKD1CBBC78F2AD8FDB foreign key (ALBUM_ID) references ALBUM (ALB
UM_ID);
[hibernatetool] create index ARTIST_NAME on ARTIST (NAME);
[hibernatetool] alter table ARTIST add index FK7395D347A1422D3B (actualArtist),
add constraint FK7395D347A1422D3B foreign key (actualArtist) references ARTIST (
ARTIST_ID);
[hibernatetool] create index TRACK_TITLE on TRACK (TITLE);
[hibernatetool] alter table TRACK_ARTISTS add index FK72EFDAD8E424525B (TRACK_ID
), add constraint FK72EFDAD8E424525B foreign key (TRACK_ID) references TRACK (TR
ACK_ID);
[hibernatetool] alter table TRACK_ARTISTS add index FK72EFDAD876BBFFF9 (ARTIST_I
D), add constraint FK72EFDAD876BBFFF9 foreign key (ARTIST_ID) references ARTIST
(ARTIST_ID);
[hibernatetool] alter table TRACK_COMMENTS add index FK105B2688E424525B (TRACK_I
D), add constraint FK105B2688E424525B foreign key (TRACK_ID) references TRACK (T
RACK_ID);
[hibernatetool] 16:46:42,630  INFO SchemaExport:196 - schema export complete
[hibernatetool] 16:46:42,631  INFO DriverManagerConnectionProvider:147 - cleanin
g up connection pool: jdbc:mysql://localhost/notebook_db
[hibernatetool] 9 errors occurred while performing <hbm2ddl>.
[hibernatetool] Error #1: com.mysql.jdbc.exceptions.MySQLSyntaxErrorException: T
able 'notebook_db.album_artists' doesn't exist
[hibernatetool] Error #1: com.mysql.jdbc.exceptions.MySQLSyntaxErrorException: T
able 'notebook_db.album_artists' doesn't exist
[hibernatetool] Error #1: com.mysql.jdbc.exceptions.MySQLSyntaxErrorException: T
able 'notebook_db.album_comments' doesn't exist
[hibernatetool] Error #1: com.mysql.jdbc.exceptions.MySQLSyntaxErrorException: T
able 'notebook_db.album_tracks' doesn't exist
[hibernatetool] Error #1: com.mysql.jdbc.exceptions.MySQLSyntaxErrorException: T
able 'notebook_db.album_tracks' doesn't exist
[hibernatetool] Error #1: com.mysql.jdbc.exceptions.MySQLSyntaxErrorException: T
able 'notebook_db.artist' doesn't exist
[hibernatetool] Error #1: com.mysql.jdbc.exceptions.MySQLSyntaxErrorException: T
able 'notebook_db.track_artists' doesn't exist
[hibernatetool] Error #1: com.mysql.jdbc.exceptions.MySQLSyntaxErrorException: T
able 'notebook_db.track_artists' doesn't exist
[hibernatetool] Error #1: com.mysql.jdbc.exceptions.MySQLSyntaxErrorException: T
able 'notebook_db.track_comments' doesn't exist

BUILD SUCCESSFUL
Total time: 8 seconds
```

What just happened?

Hibernate configured itself to work with MySQL's specific features, examined the mapping document for our Track class, connected to the MySQL server, and executed the commands necessary to build a database schema for persisting our examples. (As before, there are several SQL exceptions reported at the end which, like Hibernate, you can ignore; they came from Hibernate's attempts to drop foreign keys that didn't yet exist, since this was the first time we were attempting to create the schema.)

Again, don't worry about the errors that appear at the end; these are caused by Hibernate's preemptive attempts to drop tables in case the schema already partially existed. Even though it reports them, it doesn't consider them a problem either, and proceeds with the rest of the schema creation task, reporting success in the end.

It's interesting to compare this with the HSQLDB version, Example 2-7. The output is almost the same, but there are clear differences in the SQL used to actually create the tables. This is what Hibernate means by SQL "dialects."

Looking at the Data

Back on the server, you can fire up the MySQL client again and confirm that the Track mapping schema has been created, as shown in Example 10-5.

Example 10-5. Checking the newly created MySQL schema

```
% mysql -u jim -p
Enter password:
Welcome to the MySQL monitor.  Commands end with ; or \g.
Your MySQL connection id is 21 to server version: 5.0.27

Type 'help;' or '\h' for help. Type '\c' to clear the buffer.

mysql> use notebook_db
Reading table information for completion of table and column names
You can turn off this feature to get a quicker startup with -A
Database changed

mysql> show tables;
+-----------------------+
| Tables_in_notebook_db |
+-----------------------+
| ALBUM_ARTISTS         |
| ALBUM_COMMENTS        |
| ALBUM_TRACKS          |
| ARTIST                |
| TRACK_ARTISTS         |
| TRACK_COMMENTS        |
| album                 |
| track                 |
+-----------------------+
8 rows in set (0.00 sec)

mysql> describe track;
+-------------+--------------+------+-----+---------+----------------+
| Field       | Type         | Null | Key | Default | Extra          |
+-------------+--------------+------+-----+---------+----------------+
| TRACK_ID    | int(11)      | NO   | PRI | NULL    | auto_increment |
| TITLE       | varchar(255) | NO   | MUL |         |                |
| filePath    | varchar(255) | NO   |     |         |                |
```

```
| playTime   | time         | YES |     | NULL    |                |
| added      | date         | YES |     | NULL    |                |
| VOL_LEFT   | smallint(6)  | YES |     | NULL    |                |
| VOL_RIGHT  | smallint(6)  | YES |     | NULL    |                |
| sourceMedia| varchar(255) | YES |     | NULL    |                |
+------------+--------------+-----+-----+---------+----------------+
8 rows in set (0.03 sec)

mysql> select * from TRACK;
Empty set (0.00 sec)

mysql> describe album_tracks;
+----------------+----------+------+-----+---------+-------+
| Field          | Type     | Null | Key | Default | Extra |
+----------------+----------+------+-----+---------+-------+
| ALBUM_ID       | int(11)  | NO   | PRI |         |       |
| TRACK_ID       | int(11)  | YES  | MUL | NULL    |       |
| disc           | int(11)  | YES  |     | NULL    |       |
| positionOnDisc | int(11)  | YES  |     | NULL    |       |
| LIST_POS       | int(11)  | NO   | PRI |         |       |
+----------------+----------+------+-----+---------+-------+
5 rows in set (0.00 sec)

mysql> quit;
Bye
```

It's not surprising to find the table empty. But if you run *ant ctest* from your example directory and then try the select query again, you'll see data like that in Example 10-6. One configuration file is the only change we need to make to completely switch the database with which Hibernate is working. This has come in handy more than a few times on production projects when clients change their minds about where they want data, or if multiple developers prefer to work on different operating systems.

Example 10-6. Looking at the TRACK table after running ctest

```
mysql> select * from track;
+----------+---------------------------------------------+-----------------------
--+----------+------------+----------+-----------+--------------+
| TRACK_ID | TITLE                                       | filePath
  | playTime | added      | VOL_LEFT | VOL_RIGHT | sourceMedia |
+----------+---------------------------------------------+-----------------------
--+----------+------------+----------+-----------+--------------+
|        1 | Russian Trance                              | vol2/album610/track02.mp
3 | 00:03:30 | 2007-09-22 |      100 |       100 | CD           |
|        2 | Video Killed the Radio Star                 | vol2/album611/track12.mp
3 | 00:03:49 | 2007-09-22 |      100 |       100 | VHS          |
|        3 | Gravity's Angel                             | vol2/album175/track03.mp
3 | 00:06:06 | 2007-09-22 |      100 |       100 | CD           |
|        4 | Adagio for Strings (Ferry Corsten Remix)    | vol2/album972/track01.mp
3 | 00:06:35 | 2007-09-22 |      100 |       100 | CD           |
|        5 | Adagio for Strings (ATB Remix)              | vol2/album972/track02.mp
3 | 00:07:39 | 2007-09-22 |      100 |       100 | CD           |
|        6 | The World '99                               | vol2/singles/pvw99.mp3
  | 00:07:05 | 2007-09-22 |      100 |       100 | STREAM       |
```

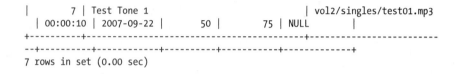

```
 |       7 | Test Tone 1                      | vol2/singles/test01.mp3
   | 00:00:10 | 2007-09-22 |      50 |      75 | NULL            |
 +----------+------------------------------------------------+------------------------
 --+----------+-----------+----------+----------+------------+
 7 rows in set (0.00 sec)
```

What about...

...a graphical way to work with MySQL? If you'd rather be in an environment like the graphical interface we illustrated for HSQLDB, you'll want to check out the MySQL GUI tools that can be downloaded at *http://dev.mysql.com/downloads/gui-tools/5.0.html*.

...connecting to Oracle, or another favorite, shared, or legacy database that doesn't happen to be MySQL or HSQLDB? You've probably already figured out that it's just as easy. All you need to do is change the `hibernate.dialect` property in your *hibernate.cfg.xml* to reflect the kind of database you want to use. There are many dialects available, covering nearly every free and commercial database I can think of; the ones available at the time of writing this book are listed in Appendix C, but check the Hibernate documentation for the latest list. If you need to work with a more obscure database, you may have to write your own dialect to support it, but that seems unlikely (and check to see if anyone's already started that effort).

Once you've got the dialect chosen, you'll also need to set the `hibernate.connection` properties (`driver`, `URL`, `username`, and `password`) to the proper values for establishing a JDBC connection to your chosen database environment. If you're porting an existing project to use Hibernate, you'll be able to obtain these from the code or configuration of that project. And, naturally, you'll need to include the database's JDBC driver as a dependency for your project during build and runtime.

Of course, if you're connecting to an existing or shared database, you won't be using Hibernate to create the schema. Instead, you'll write the mapping document to reflect the existing schema, either by hand or with the help of the Hibernate Tools (which we explore more deeply in Chapter 11), or a third-party package like Middlegen[†], and then start working with the data in the form of persistent objects.

You can even use Hibernate to talk to multiple different databases at the same time; you just need to create multiple `SessionFactory` instances with separate configurations. This goes beyond the simple, automatic configuration demonstrated here, but there are examples in the Hibernate reference documentation. Of course, a persistent object can only be associated with a single session at a time, which means it can only be linked to a single database at once. With clever, careful coding, though, you can copy or move objects between different database systems, even with a different schema to represent them. That's *way* out of scope for this book, though!

[†] *http://boss.bekk.no/boss/middlegen/*

## CHAPTER 11

Hibernate and Eclipse: Really Using the Hibernate Tools

Installing the Hibernate Tools in Eclipse

If you're working with Eclipse as your Java development environment (as so many of us are* these days), you can take far deeper advantage of the Hibernate Tools than we have been in the rest of the book (where we just used them to add Hibernate-related capabilities to our Ant builds).

How do I do that?

Before diving in, make sure you're running a recent enough version of Eclipse. The current release of the Hibernate Tools requires at least Eclipse 3.3 and WTP 2.0. So here's an excuse to upgrade if you've been putting it off.

The easiest way to install the Hibernate Tools into Eclipse is through Eclipse's normal *update site* mechanism. Start by telling Eclipse where to find Hibernate Tools, by choosing the Find and Install option in the Software Update menu, as shown in Figure 11-1.

We want to install something completely new, rather than update an existing plug-in, so choose Search for new features to install, and click Next.

Eclipse doesn't automatically know about the Hibernate Tools update site, so we need to explain where to find it. Click on New Remote Site, as shown in Figure 11-2.

Enter something descriptive like "Hibernate Tools" for the name of the new update site. As you'll see later in Figure 11-4, Eclipse now wants us to specify the URL at which the update site can be found. We'll have to do a little hunting to figure that out...

Switch to a web browser, open up the Hibernate web site at *http://hibernate.org*, and click on Hibernate Tools in the navigation menu on the lefthand side. (Or you can cut

---

* *http://www.oreillynet.com/onjava/blog/2004/06/ive_been_eclipsed.html*

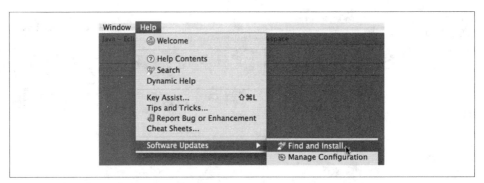

Figure 11-1. Updating features in Eclipse

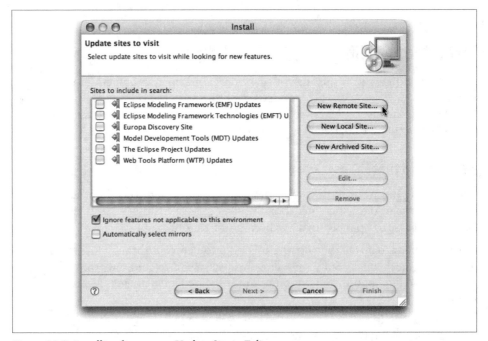

Figure 11-2. Installing from a new Update Site in Eclipse

to the chase by opening *http://tools.hibernate.org* directly.) Once you're there, you can read a bit about the tools, and follow various documentation links. We did that for a while, trying to figure out how to install the tools directly into Eclipse, and eventually noticed what we'd been missing: there's an update site link right on the Tools page. Copy that URL to your clipboard, as shown in Figure 11-3 (you can right-click or Control-click on the link to get the menu to appear).

If you're paying close attention, you may have noticed that the version of the Hibernate Tools mentioned on this page is newer than the beta 9 we've been using elsewhere in the book. Congratulations—you've spotted an example of how difficult it is to write

Hibernate Tools for Eclipse and Ant

Project Lead:	Max R. Andersen
Contributors:	Mark Hobson, Marshall Culpepper, David Channon, Joe Hudson and others
Latest release:	3.2.0.GA (What's New?)
Release date:	12.12.2007
Update site:	Hibernate Tools only & JBoss Tools
Nightly Build:	JBoss Tools
Documentation:	Reference, Viewlets, Build & Contr
Requirements:	Eclipse WTP 3.3/2.x or Ant, Decen

for an overview of the Hibernate 2.x toolset), imple
for integration into the build cycle. Hibernate Tools i
Studio. See the documentation and screenshots for

The following features are available within Eclipse:

Mapping Editor: An editor for Hibernate XML mapp
completion and syntax highlighting. The editor even
completion for class names, property/field names, table names and column

Open Link in New Window
Open Link in New Tab

Download Linked File
Download Linked File As...
Add Link to Bookmarks...

Copy Link

Inspect Element

Figure 11-3. Getting the Hibernate Tools Update Site URL

New Update Site

Name: Hibernate Tools

URL: ıttp://download.jboss.org/jbosstools/updates/stable

Cancel   OK

Figure 11-4. Configuring a new Update Site in Eclipse

about things that change as quickly as large open-source projects! At the time of this writing, the stable release is too new to be available through the Maven repository, so we're leaving the rest of the book alone. The changes in the new release don't affect the other chapters, in any case, but the latest version *is* necessary to work with the current release of Eclipse (3.3, also known as Europa, at the moment) and to enable some of the nicer features you'll see in this chapter.

So, paste the URL for the update site into the New Update Site window in Eclipse. You should see something like Figure 11-4. Click OK to enable the new site.

As you can see from Figure 11-5, Eclipse makes the reasonable assumption that you want to use the update site you just configured, so click Finish to contact that site and see what can be installed from there.

The window that pops up (Figure 11-6) is simple and promising enough. All we need to do is check the single checkbox next to Hibernate Tools, and install away, right?

Unfortunately, as soon as we check the Hibernate Tools checkbox, we run into a snag. There's an error message displayed at the top of the window, and the Next button is grayed out and unavailable to us.

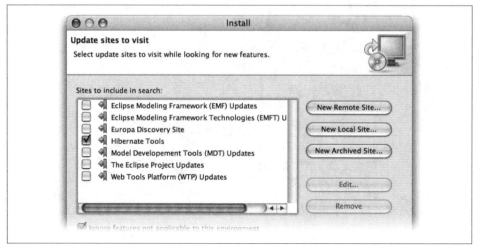

Figure 11-5. New Update Site is ready to use

Figure 11-6. Installing the Hibernate Tools: we need to dig deeper

What went wrong?

Eclipse won't let us proceed, because the SeamTools feature (one of the 10 plug-ins that make up the Hibernate Tools group) requires another plug-in, `org.eclipse.data tools.connectivity.feature`, which is not installed by default. Unfortunately, we need to backtrack a bit. Click Cancel, then start over with the Find and Install menu

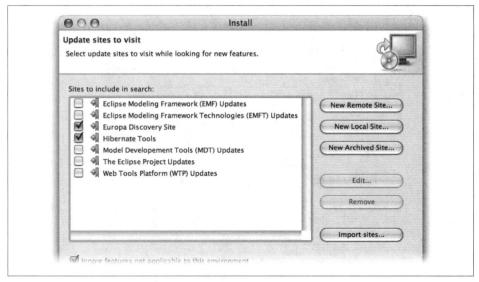

Figure 11-7. Enabling the Eclipse Discovery Site

option as you did at the beginning of this section. Once again, choose Search for new features to install, and click Next. This time, also enable the Europa Discovery Site, as shown in Figure 11-7, before clicking Finish.

Pick a mirror appropriate to your location from the list of choices and click OK (unless you've configured Eclipse to pick one automatically, which will save you this step). This time you'll see two groups of plug-ins available, the Europa Discovery Site and the Hibernate Tools. Once again, choose the Hibernate Tools group for installation. As before, you'll see an error at the top of the window, but this time we have the opportunity to fix that. One option would be to select the entire Europa Discovery Site group, but that would install a great deal more than is actually required, adding a great deal of unnecessary bloat to your Eclipse configuration.

So we want to figure out the minimal set of plug-ins we need from the Europa Discovery Site. Leaving the Hibernate Tools plug-in selected, expand the Europa Discovery Site group, but don't try to select anything. Although it is possible to manually find and select the plug-in which is being reported as a requirement for the Hibernate Tools, this leads to a lot of tedious research and trial and error to figure out exactly which combination of plug-ins is required to get things working (we tried it, and once we found the plug-in that provided data tools connectivity feature mentioned in the first error, we found it had dependencies of its own, and wasn't the only thing missing in the first place). Just as we were gritting our teeth in preparation for trying to write up a comprehensible explanation of how to select exactly what you need, we noticed the Select the Required button on the right. You can use it to automatically select the plug-ins you need. But our experimentation revealed that it only works if you first expand the disclosure triangle corresponding to the site from which the required plug-ins will

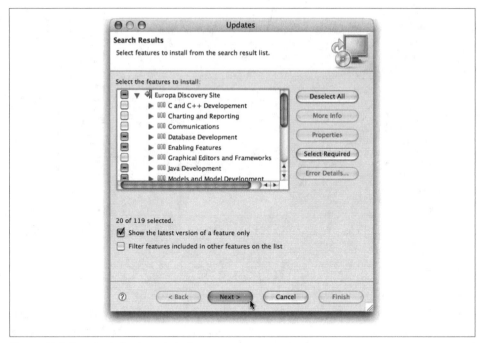

Figure 11-8. Required plug-ins selected

be downloaded. It did nothing at all until we expanded the Europa Discovery site. Once that was done, clicking Select Required automatically selected just the plug-ins required to resolve the dependency errors. So, do that now, since you've got the Hibernate Tools selected and the Europa Discovery site expanded. You will end up with something like Figure 11-8, although the exact number of things to be installed will depend on what you might have already installed yourself in the past.

The important point is that we no longer have an error message blocking our ability to install the Hibernate Tools! So click Next to install this set of plug-ins. Accept the licenses that appear in the following dialog and click Next again. Another dialog window pops up showing you that there are a related set of optional features that you can also install. Since we don't need them to work with the Hibernate Tools, just click Next in the Optional Features dialog to continue installing the precise set we requested.

The default installation locations (which will vary based on where Eclipse lives on your machine) are almost always fine, so unless you have special reasons to put them elsewhere, click Finish in the Installation dialog to go ahead and install the plug-ins.

The Update Manager will run for a while as the updates are downloaded. Eventually, a Feature Verification dialog will pop up. For each feature being installed, this will report whether or not it seems to be cryptographically signed by an organization that is trusted by the Eclipse project. Some of them will be; others (like the Hibernate Tools themselves) will lack valid signatures. This is common for third-party Eclipse plug-ins.

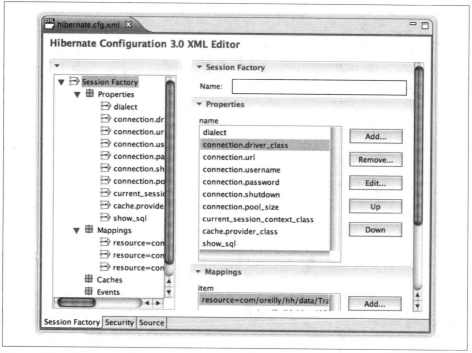

Figure 11-9. Hibernate configuration editor

Eclipse presents this situation as a warning, and wants to make sure you're willing to install a plug-in under those circumstances. Since I have had confidence in the sites from which I've downloaded them, I've always proceeded with the installation, anyway. If you feel the same way (and, basically, if you want to use the Hibernate Tools, you'll have to), click Install to proceed. (If you don't want to be asked for each plug-in, click Install All to accept them in bulk). The Update Manager will proceed with the installation. When it finishes with everything, it will suggest that you restart Eclipse. Go ahead and click Yes, to be safe, and wait for Eclipse to come back.

Now what?

It's immediately clear that Eclipse knows more about Hibernate than it used to. The icon for the Hibernate configuration file now gets a little Hibernate logo as part of it, and double-clicking on it or a mapping file opens a special editor that makes it easier to create and update such files, without seeing the underlying XML (Figure 11-9).

Figure 11-10. Autocompletion of property names in the Hibernate configuration editor

Of course, you can still view the XML if you're productive that way, by clicking on the Source tab at the bottom of the editor—and you'll find that you now get completion assistance for the various Hibernate-related elements and their values when working with the source, as shown in Figure 11-10. This goes beyond the XML editor's normal completion abilities for element names, which it can perform by analyzing the XML DTD, since the DTD says nothing about property names other than that they're text.

> This will certainly save me many trips to the reference documentation whether or not I'm working in source view!

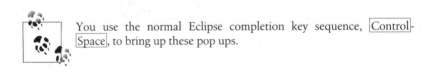 You use the normal Eclipse completion key sequence, Control-Space, to bring up these pop ups.

The editor for mapping documents is shown in Figure 11-11. These two editors seem quite powerful and useful; it's worth playing around with them for a while to get a feel for how they work and what they can do. By themselves they'd make a worthwhile addition to Eclipse for working with Hibernate.

To explore some of the other things you can do with the Hibernate Tools, they need to be activated for a project. If you're starting a new project, you can choose to create a new Hibernate configuration file. If you've got an existing Hibernate project, as we did working up this chapter, you can skip that part and simply create a new Hibernate console.

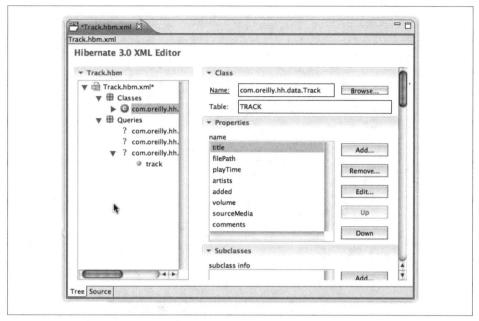

Figure 11-11. Hibernate mapping editor

Creating a Hibernate Console Configuration

With the project selected in the Project Explorer, choose File→New→Other, expand the Hibernate section that was added by the tools (Figure 11-12), and select Hibernate Console Configuration. (This is where you'll also be able to choose to create a new configuration file, or XML mapping, as well as reverse engineering configuration files, which we won't cover in this book.) Click Next to proceed with setting up the tools for your project.

The Hibernate Console Configuration window appears (Figure 11-13). Tell the tools how to find your Hibernate configuration file by clicking on the corresponding Browse button, and locating the file within the project. (This is automatically set up for you when you use the configuration file wizard to create it in the first place, and the latest version of the tools seems to be smart enough to find it automatically in the project structure we've been using for the code examples in this book.)

> If you're still using old-school properties files to configure Hibernate, you'd use the "Property file" field, found above the one we used in this example.

The rest of the settings on this tab can be left as they are for most projects, but we do need to adjust the class path since we're using the Maven Tasks for Ant to manage our dependencies, and the Hibernate Tasks won't magically know how to find the database driver inside the Maven repository. So we need to click on the Classpath tab and tell it manually. On that tab we'll click on the "Add External JARS" button, as shown in Figure 11-14.

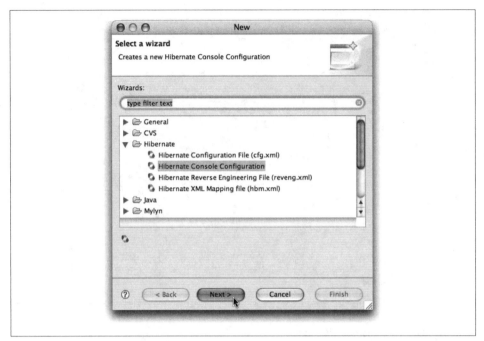

Figure 11-12. New Eclipse wizards offered by the Hibernate Tools

In the file selection dialog that results, we navigate inside our Maven repository (which can be found as described toward the end of "Setting Up a Project Hierarchy" in Chapter 1) to find the MySQL driver. In this case, under Mac OS X, the driver is found in ~/.m2/repository/mysql/ mysql-connector-java/5.0.5/mysql-connector-java-5.0.5.jar. Building on the previous chapter, we're continuing to work with MySQL. The Hibernate Tools are much more comfortable connecting to an external database; trying to work with an embedded in-memory database, the way we were using HSQLDB, isn't a good idea, since the tools assume they are free to keep connections to the database open, which will force you to always quit Eclipse when you want to do other things with the database, like running the **db** task through *ant* to view its contents. A standalone database like MySQL, on the other hand, has no problems with multiple simultaneous connections.

> You can use HSQLDB in a shared mode as well, supporting multiple connections, but that is outside the scope of this book, and you'd still need to decide where and how to run the "server" JVM.

After selecting the driver JAR, click Open (Figure 11-15).

 If you are using a proprietary database such as Oracle, you might need to download the JDBC Driver manually. Only freely distributable software is available in the Maven repository.

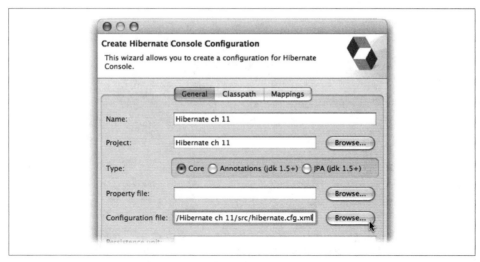

Figure 11-13. Setting up a Hibernate Console configuration

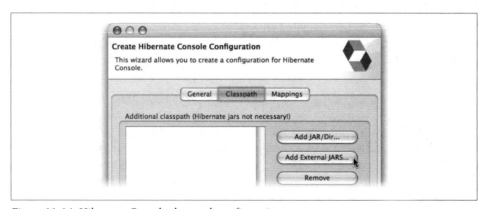

Figure 11-14. Hibernate Console class path configuration

With the class path thus augmented (see Figure 11-16), we are ready to click Finish to establish our Hibernate Console configuration.

The Hibernate Tools ask us if we want to enable Hibernate support for our project (see Figure 11-17). Hurrah, that's what we were after! We eagerly click OK.

More Editing Support

Now that we've got the Hibernate Tools enabled for our project, what kinds of things can we do? Well, now, when you're editing a mapping file, the XML editor gains the ability to auto-complete table and column names for you (Figure 11-18). This explains

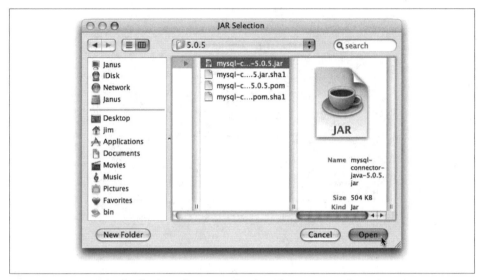

Figure 11-15. Locating the database driver JAR for the Hibernate Console configuration

why a project needs to be associated with a Hibernate Console configuration: the Hibernate Tools actually maintain a Hibernate session which can be used to inspect the database schema, and provide relevant assistance based on the actual project environment.

We've shown completion of column names in the TRACK table here, but you can complete table names as well (up in the class definition as well as in association definitions). Also, assuming you've already created the Java objects that will form your model, completion help is available for property names and class names, with JavaDoc support (as in Figure 11-19). Completion for property types is also always available, although that's even easier to pick in the nonsource view, where it is a drop-down menu.

 We did run into one "gotcha" in playing with database-driven completion. Even though SQL is usually case-insensitive when it comes to matching table and column names, the Hibernate Tools are not, and we couldn't get completion to work properly until we noticed that our track table had been created in all lowercase, and our mapping document had been referring to it in uppercase. Fixing the mapping document to match the actual database capitalization got things working.

Another useful Eclipse feature is available here as well. The [F3] key, which is used to navigate to the declaration of a variable, method, or class, works within the mapping editor to take you to the Java source for the class or property you're mapping.

Figure 11-16. Hibernate Console class path configuration completed

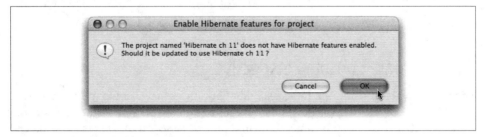

Figure 11-17. Hibernate features ready to go

We were surprised and pleased to discover (Figure 11-20) that even our custom type mappings were available, at the bottom of the type completion menu, which did not seem to be the case in the GUI mapping editor.

Figure 11-18. Autocompletion of column names in the Hibernate mapping editor

But wait, there's more!

These abilities mingle in with your normal Eclipse use, right in the Java perspective. But there are more tricks available once you open the Hibernate Console perspective, which you can do by clicking on the Open Perspective button in the toolbar and picking the Other choice, or choosing Window→Open Perspective→Other. Either approach yields the Open Perspective dialog shown in Figure 11-21. Choose Hibernate Console and click OK.

The Hibernate Console Perspective

The first thing to notice is the Hibernate Configurations view shown in Figure 11-22. We've expanded the "Hibernate ch 11" configuration we created at the start of this section, and dove down into some of the mappings, classes, and database schema entries it makes available for inspection. Notice the little graphical markers for identifiers, many-to-one, and one-to-many relationships. A wealth of information is available right in this view. We opened the drop-down menu to show that it offers access to several interesting features (and explains the purpose of the buttons to the left of the menu).

On the prosaic side, this menu offers us a way to edit our configuration, create new configurations for other Hibernate projects, and to refresh the view if we've changed things from outside Eclipse. More powerfully, the Run Schema Export option lets us

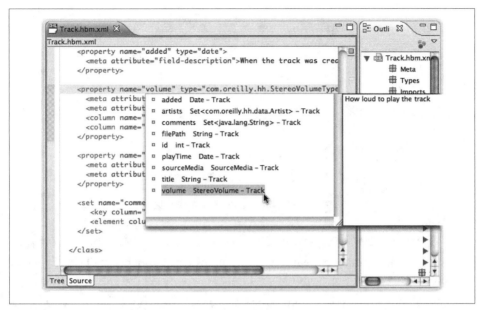

Figure 11-19. Autocompletion of property names in the Hibernate mapping editor

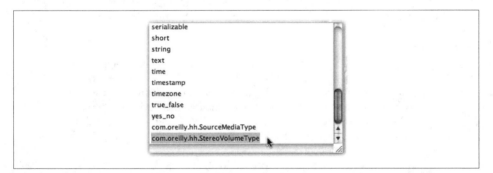

Figure 11-20. Custom type mappings available for completion

achieve the same result for which we wrote the **schema** Ant task in Chapter 2, by simply selecting a configuration entry and running it.

The menu also gives us a hint about the purposes of the mysterious-looking buttons just to the left of it. Let's explore what these do in more depth, starting with the HQL Editor choice. Figure 11-23 shows the view that opens upon picking that choice or clicking the button. It seems like a place we could explore HQL, but a quick attempt at table completion using Control-Space yields the error message, "Configuration not available nor open." Although I think "or" would be more correct, we seem to need to associate the window with a Hibernate Console configuration. Fair enough—that

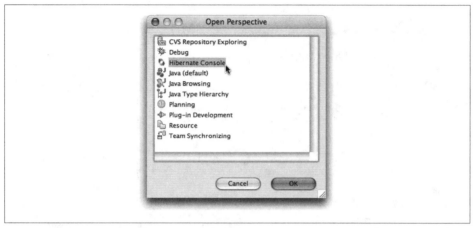

Figure 11-21. Opening the Hibernate Console perspective

makes sense—and although the interface is a bit distorted under Mac OS X, the menu at the top seems like a good candidate solution.

Sure enough, it's a menu of configurations. Once we choose our Hibernate ch 11 configuration in the menu, the editor's special powers come to life and completion works (see Figure 11-24). This is looking promising as a way to put together named queries for pasting into mapping documents, isn't it? Let's see what else it can do.

 If you get the same error message about an unavailable configuration even after selecting it, this probably means the Hibernate Tools haven't opened a `SessionFactory` for it yet. You can force this by right-clicking the configuration in the Hibernate Configurations view, and choosing Create SessionFactory (see Figure 11-25). Some other actions, like drilling down deeper into the Configurations, Session Factory, and Database tree nodes, seem to do the trick, too.

Completion help while authoring queries is certainly nice (it can complete property names, HQL keywords, and function names, too), but the real power of the tool comes from the fact that you can actually run queries and see their results—to convince yourself the query is right, your data is right, or just to learn more about HQL and your data model. Clicking on the big green Run HQL button at the top left of the editor view gives instant gratification, as in Figure 11-26.

Go ahead and try a bunch of queries. Add some projections, orderings, and aggregate functions—what a great opportunity to really learn about the query capabilities mentioned in Chapter 9! But, before moving on to the next editor type, there's another trick or two to discover....

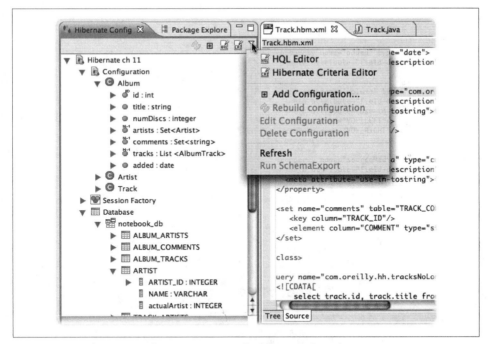

Figure 11-22. Hibernate Configurations view in the Hibernate Console perspective

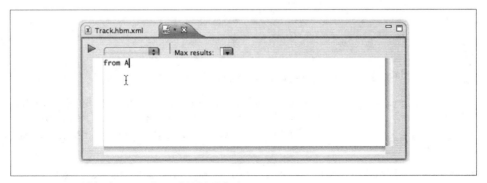

Figure 11-23. A blank, unconfigured HQL Editor view

 If you run queries against large tables, you may want to set a limit on the maximum number of results returned using the second menu at the top of the editor view. Since they all get loaded into memory, you might risk crashing Eclipse if you don't. Our toy examples in this book are no trouble at all, of course.

The Properties view sitting below the Hibernate Configurations view has been behaving pretty normally so far, showing things like XML element attributes while we were

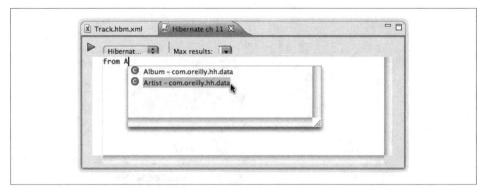

Figure 11-24. The HQL Editor view once connected to a Hibernate Console configuration

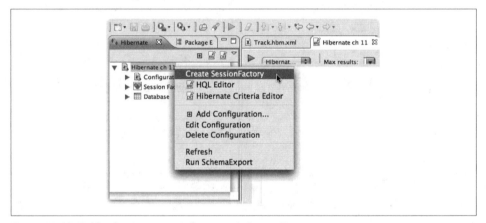

Figure 11-25. Explicitly opening a configuration's SessionFactory

editing mapping files, stuff you've probably seen in Eclipse before. Check out what happens when we click on one of the rows in our Hibernate Query Result view—Figure 11-27 shows the result of clicking on the William Orbit line in our **Artist** query results.

You can see all the Hibernate properties of the selected result object, and drill down through associations and collections by expanding the corresponding disclosure triangle. Again, try some experimentation on your own. (We probably didn't even have to bother suggesting that....)

> What an awesome prototyping, exploration, learning, and debugging tool!

You may also have wondered what the Query Parameters view hovering to the right of the HQL editor is all about. (If you haven't, maybe the view is not showing; open it by choosing Window→Show View→Other, and picking Query Parameters from the Hibernate section.) This lets you play with queries containing named parameters. Figure 11-28 shows an example; we pasted in the **tracksNoLongerThan** named query from Chapter 3 to play with, then discovered that clicking the ":P+" button in the Query

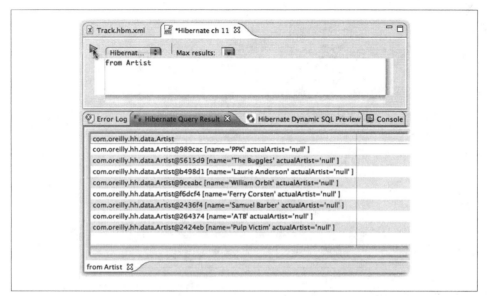

Figure 11-26. The Run HQL button and its results

Parameters view populated the list with the (single) parameter in our query. We had to set the Type to **time** (that column is a drop-down), and with the help of the format cue below the list, entered a time in the Value column, clicked the green Run button at the top left of the query editor, and got the expected results in the Hibernate Query Result view at the bottom.

It's hard to imagine a much easier interface for experimenting with HQL queries! And hardcore SQL geeks will be intrigued by this next trick (although you may well have already tried it for yourselves if you're following along in Eclipse): the Hibernate Dynamic SQL Preview which you can see next to the query result tab in Figure 11-28; if it's not showing in your own Eclipse, open it by choosing Window→Show View→Other, and picking Hibernate Dynamic SQL Preview from the Hibernate section. Choosing this view reveals the actual SQL that is use to perform a HQL query we've entered in the query editor, as shown in Figure 11-29.

This view is very interesting because it really is dynamic, as the title suggests. If you have it open while you are editing a query in the HQL editor, you can watch the corresponding SQL evolving as you type. It is potentially quite instructive. For example, consider the very simple but natural HQL query in Figure 11-30, and the resulting SQL.

 As one of our technical reviewers pointed out, this can also be a very valuable communication tool between Java developers who aren't particularly SQL-savvy and DBAs who have no interest in hearing about HQL or JDBC.

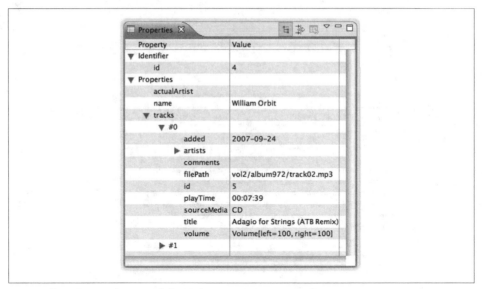

Figure 11-27. Browsing query results in the Properties view

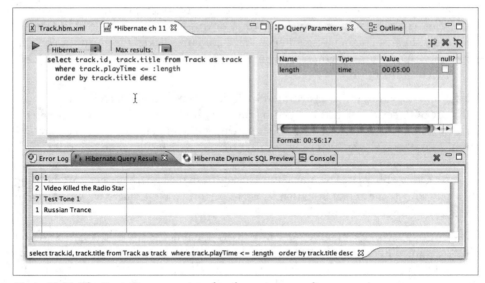

Figure 11-28. The Query Parameters interface for setting named parameters

Finally, the Criteria Editor view, accessed through the last unexplored button, is shown in Figure 11-31. It does what by now you probably expect. It provides a way for you to prototype Criteria queries, providing Java code completion (and the variable `session` is predefined to contain the Hibernate Console configuration's session for use by the query).

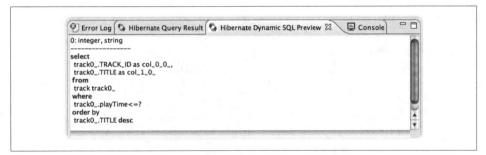

Figure 11-29. The Dynamic SQL Preview

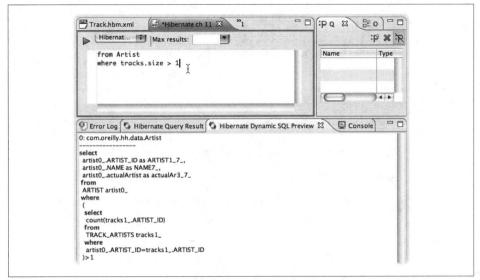

Figure 11-30. Seeing terse HQL as full SQL

 If you find that completion isn't working for you, remember to check that a valid Hibernate Console configuration is chosen in the menu next to the Run button, just like with the HQL Editor. Also, make sure Eclipse thinks the Criteria Editor view is selected (that it has a blue border). I sometimes managed to get it into a state where I was typing into it, but the query results view had the blue border, and none of the keyboard commands related to completion or editing worked the way they should.

What about...

...code generation features? These are available, too, and we didn't even notice the most direct way of accessing them at first. They were already available before we enabled the

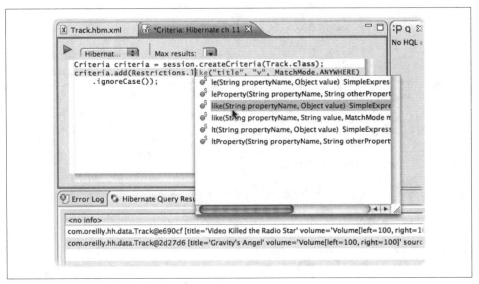

Figure 11-31. The Hibernate Tools' Criteria Editor

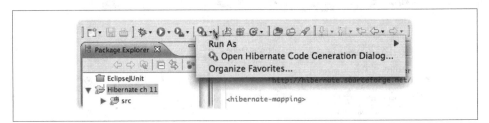

Figure 11-32. Code generation menu offered by the Hibernate Tools

tools for any specific project, although they couldn't do much until we at least created one Hibernate Console configuration. A closer look at the Eclipse toolbar reveals a new menu offered by the Hibernate Tools (see Figure 11-32).

This new menu snuck in there so subtly, it took a while to see it. This menu is the "front door" to a graphical way of setting up and running the code generation features of the Hibernate Tools.

Code Generation

Let's take a look at how we would replicate the codegen Ant target we created back in Chapter 2. To avoid sending you off on a page-flipping side trip, that target is reproduced as Example 11-1 here.

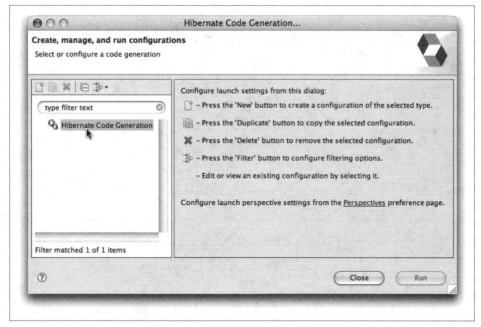

Figure 11-33. Preparing to create a new Hibernate code generation configuration

Example 11-1. Our code generation Ant task revisited

```
<!-- Generate the java code for all mapping files in our source tree -->
<target name="codegen" depends="usertypes"
        description="Generate Java source from the O/R mapping files">
  <hibernatetool destdir="${source.root}">
    <configuration configurationfile="${source.root}/hibernate.cfg.xml"/>
    <hbm2java jdk5="true"/>
  </hibernatetool>
</target>
```

To reconstruct this within Eclipse, we started by choosing Open Hibernate Code Generation Dialog from the menu shown in Figure 11-32. The window that appears (Figure 11-33), like many of the Eclipse tools, provides a way of setting up a variety of named configurations you can run.

 You seem to need to click on the Hibernate Code Generation label before the "New" button becomes active to create a new configuration.

Once we figured out how to activate it, we clicked on the "New" button (the one that looks like a little page with a plus sign at the top right corner) to set up a configuration to generate our data objects. That opens a configuration window with many options, some of which you can see in Figure 11-34.

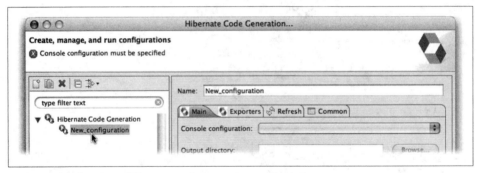

Figure 11-34. Creating a Hibernate code generation configuration

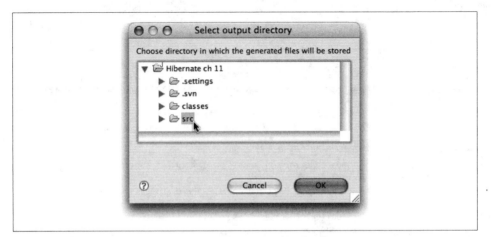

Figure 11-35. Specifying the output directory for our generated code

We assigned the configuration the name "Generate Ch 11 Model," chose our Hibernate Console configuration, and browsed to the project's *src* directory (see Figure 11-35), so the Main tab ended up looking like Figure 11-36.

> Of course, if you have more projects open in your Eclipse workspace, you'll see more root choices in this browse dialog.

We only need to worry about the Name and the top two choices in the Main tab, since we're not trying to do fancy reverse-engineering based on existing data. (That's a powerful feature you may want to explore on your own someday, when a big legacy schema lands on your lap that you need to make available in Java.) So we're ready to move on to the Exporters tab. Clicking on that reveals the interface shown in Figure 11-37, once we've filled it in to reproduce the behavior of our Ant target.

We checked Use Java 5 syntax, the graphical equivalent of the `jdk5=true` attribute setting in the Ant task, and then chose the Domain code (.java) exporter. Notice that although we're not using them here, there are a bunch of other generators available to

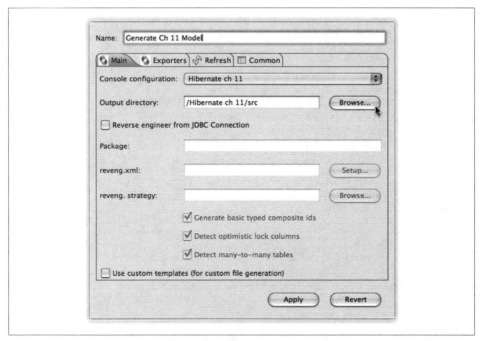

Figure 11-36. *Main code generation configuration to replicate our codegen Ant target*

us, for creating mapping files, the overall Hibernate configuration file, and even some web documentation of the database schema. Also, you can create some data access objects (DAO code) to make it easier to load and manipulate your model objects in a standardized, convenient way. Although beyond the scope of this book, these are all options you might want to explore on your own, or at least keep in the back of your mind for when they might come in handy.

In case you're wondering about the purpose of the Properties section at the bottom of the tab, it's basically a cop-out to let you set parameters for each of the exporters that have not (yet?) been exposed through a graphical interface. Clicking on any of the exporters (the name, not the checkbox) shows any properties that have been manually set for that generator, and activates the Add and Remove buttons so you can edit them. Refer to the documentation of the generator to find out what properties are available, and what they do.

> Which kind of defeats the purpose of offering a GUI.... At least they cover the common cases.

For the purposes of our current task, to reproduce what we previously did in our *build.xml* file, these are the correct settings. In fact, that's all we'd really need to set up. While we're in here, though, it's worth looking at some Eclipse-specific options, too.

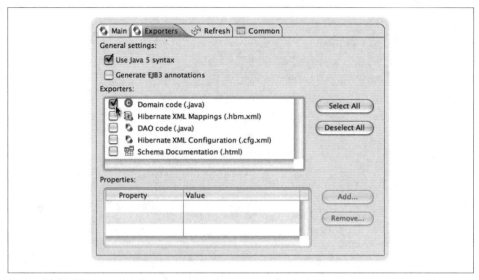

Figure 11-37. Exporters configuration to replicate our codegen Ant target

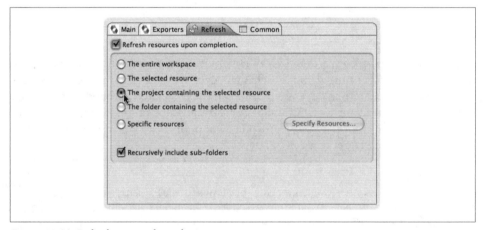

Figure 11-38. Refresh options for code generation

The Refresh tab (see Figure 11-38) lets you control which Eclipse resources are automatically refreshed after running the exporters.

We chose to turn on refreshing, but just for the project into which we're generating code. That seems appropriate for what we're doing.

Finally, the default settings on the Common tab seemed fine, so we left them alone, and hit Apply.

Our configuration appeared in the list on the left (see Figure 11-39). At this point we can either run it by selecting it there and clicking the Run button (seen at the bottom

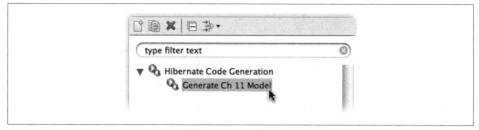

Figure 11-39. Our code generation configuration is ready to be run

right in Figure 11-34) or, if we think we'll be running it often, we can set it up as a favorite in the toolbar menu so it appears right at the top of that menu. For now, we'll just test it by running it from this dialog by selecting it and clicking Run.

Running it doesn't cause anything flashy to happen, although the status bar at the bottom right of the Eclipse window briefly shows background activity (we left the Launch in background setting checked in the Common configuration, so that's what we'd expect). To see if it really did anything, we can pull up one of the generated classes, such as *Album.java*, and take a look. The code in Example 11-2 shows the beginning of the Album source generated by the Hibernate Tools.

Example 11-2. Start of the Album source generated by the Hibernate Tools in Eclipse

```
package com.oreilly.hh.data;

// Generated Jan 5, 2008 6:36:04 PM by Hibernate Tools 3.2.0.CR1

import java.util.ArrayList;
import java.util.Date;
import java.util.HashSet;
import java.util.List;
import java.util.Set;

/**
 *       Represents an album in the music database, an organized list of tracks.
 *       @author Jim Elliott (with help from Hibernate)
 *
 */
public class Album implements java.io.Serializable {

    private int id;

    private String title;

    private Integer numDiscs;

    private Set<Artist> artists = new HashSet<Artist>(0);
...
```

Both the time stamp and the tools version number tell us that this class has been newly generated. (Recall that we're using version 3.2.0.b9 from Maven for the Ant tasks—who knew the delay getting the latest version into Maven would have a side benefit?)

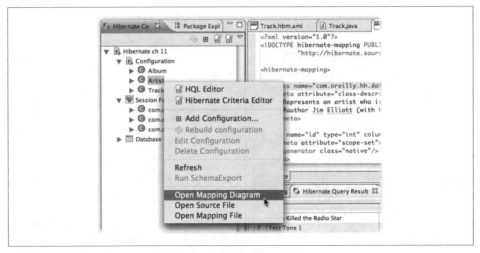

Figure 11-40. Opening a mapped object's model diagram

Other than that, the results look just like what we obtained from Ant. Not too exciting, perhaps, but actually just what we'd like to see.

So where, does this leave us? Having tools like this built into Eclipse can be huge time savers during the design and exploration phases of a project. Being able to put together queries—with schema-aware completion assistance, property browsing and real-time SQL display—is a great way to develop an understanding of the data and the model objects. It's certainly much faster and more convenient than throwing together stand-alone example classes like our various query tests earlier in the book, then compiling, running, and tweaking them. You can try many more variations much more quickly, and with none of the tedious boilerplate (what little is left when using Hibernate, anyway) needed to get the environment set up.

Mapping Diagrams

For most of the time this book was being written, the Hibernate Tools were in beta, and this last feature was disabled. Luckily, right before we went to press, version 3.2 was finally released, with mapping diagrams available. A graphical view of the object and data models can be a great aid to understanding, and now you can produce these right inside Eclipse. To create one, choose a mapped class in the Hibernate Configurations view and bring up its contextual menu (right-click or [Control]-click on the element, as shown in Figure 11-40), and choose Open Mapping Diagram.

This produces a new view like the one in Figure 11-41. We've chosen a simple class here so the diagram fits on the page, but with a big screen you can view and scroll around through a complex set of associations in a very informative way. You can drag elements of the diagram around if you don't like the way it was laid out, and you can

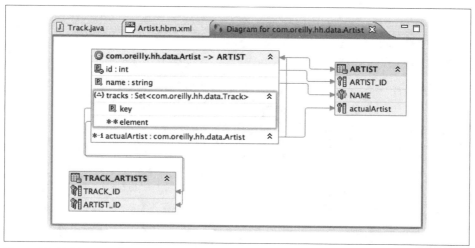

Figure 11-41. Mapping diagram for the Artist class

use contextual menus within the diagram to open source files and mapping documents for elements that interest you.

Obviously, schema-aware XML and query editing, with GUI options for building mappings and Hibernate configurations, are incredibly useful capabilities—they augment one of the main benefits of using Eclipse in the first place. Diagrams to help visualize and understand the data model are icing on the cake. And, given the ability to dynamically interact with the Hibernate session, generate code with a button click, and run queries right in the IDE, it's possible to get quite far without even setting up an Ant build file. If you're thinking along those lines, and interested in getting rid of the clumsy requirement to manually add Maven resources to the class path, the next chapter will be right up your alley.

## CHAPTER 12

Maven in More Depth

If you download our code examples from the O'Reilly website, you'll notice that every chapter's example directory contains a mysterious *pom.xml* file which we haven't mentioned yet. This *pom.xml* is the configuration for a build tool called *Apache Maven*, a widely used alternative to Apache Ant. A full introduction to Maven is outside the scope of this book, but we did think that it was important enough to include some instructions for installing and using Maven with Hibernate. This chapter is an attempt at the shortest introduction to Maven on record, focusing on using Maven and the Hibernate3 plug-in. Along the way, we'll introduce some of the core concepts in Maven.

What Is Maven?

Maven is a declarative build tool. Instead of defining a set of procedural steps to build a project, you describe your project using a *Project Object Model* (POM) in a *pom.xml* file. All the heavy lifting is done by Maven plug-ins, which are a set of goals that know how to read your POM and accomplish a task. For example, there are default Maven plug-ins that compile code, create JAR files, assemble WAR files, create web sites, sign JAR files, run code metrics, execute unit tests, read Hibernate mapping files, and more. All you need to do to use Maven is tell it where the source code is and what your dependencies are—Maven is smart enough to figure out what to do next. The alternative to Maven is to define an explicit build procedure using a tool like Apache Ant. Maven provides a declarative approach to building and testing a project, and, as noted above, is quickly gaining popularity as an alternative to Ant.

All of this convenience does come at a cost. Maven knows what to do with your project's source code, configuration, and unit tests because it makes some assumptions. Out of the box, Maven is assuming a standard project layout and is also making assumptions about your project's build lifecycle. So before you jump into Maven, we want to make sure that you are fully aware of some of the core assumptions it makes.

> Maven will save you time if you take the time to learn it and its conventions.

One is the definition of a project. In Maven a project consists of source code and resources which produce a single *artifact*. This single artifact can be something like a JAR or a WAR, but the important thing to know is that one project produces one artifact. Another important assumption is that (for the most part) you'll be using the standard directory layout. Most of Maven's initial assumptions can be changed in the *pom.xml*. As one example, if you don't store your source code in *src/main/java*, you can specify another directory in the *pom.xml*.

If you'd like to use Maven, but you have a few projects that don't exactly fit Maven's assumptions, you don't have to abandon Ant. In fact, Maven provides an easy mechanism for calling out to an existing Ant build file. Most of the examples in this book were built around an Ant build file, with the exception of the examples for this chapter. If you download the example code for this book, you'll notice that this particular example has a different directory layout than the other chapters. Let's explore that structure, known as the *Standard Directory Layout* in Maven.

> If you don't like Maven's conventions, you may want to use an alternate program.

For a longer introduction, read *Maven: The Definitive Guide*[*] from Sonatype.

Maven's standard directory layout

The ideal build tool would just automatically know what to do with a set of *.java* files. Such a system would have some built-in intelligence allowing you to simply write some source code, put a simple file in the root directory, run the build, and go home early. It would recognize that your project contains some Java source code and that you want to generate a JAR file from it. If you wanted to generate a WAR file, you could provide some gentle hints that modified the default behavior.

This ideal has been realized with Maven, in part, because Maven provides a set of strong conventions that obviate most configuration. This is known as *convention over configuration* and it is an idea that has become very popular in the past few years with frameworks like Ruby on Rails, which allow you to write very complex web applications without hacking at a huge number of configuration files. (Stripes, which we introduce in Chapter 14, takes a similar approach in the Java world.) Convention over configuration is the reason why your Apple laptop tends to just work out of the box, and it is the reason why you don't have to read a car's manual before driving it to know that the gas pedal is on the right and the brake on the left. By the same token (if you've followed the conventions), Maven knows where your source code, unit tests, site documentation, and configuration are without you having to take precious time out of your day to tell it these things. Example 12-1 shows what a Maven project's directory layout looks like.

---

[*] *http://www.sonatype.com/book/index.html*

Example 12-1. Maven's standard directory layout content

pom.xml

> Every project must have a *pom.xml* file (a POM). POM files are described in detail in "A Maven Project Object Model" later in this chapter.

src/

> Source material of various kinds lives in subdirectories.

src/main/java/

> Java source code which is to be included in the resulting artifact (JAR file, WAR file, etc.) is rooted here.

src/main/resources/

> This location contains *resources* for the project: non-Java source code, things like *log4j.properties*, *hibernate.cfg.xml*, localization files, or Hibernate mapping files that get built into the deliverable.

src/test/java/

> Unit tests (either TestNG or JUnit tests) are rooted here.

src/test/resources/

> Contains the resources used only during testing.

src/site/

> Site documentation is organized here.

target/

> Everything generated from a build, be it source, bytecode, or the final product, will end up in *target*. *target* is a build product so it can be deleted at whim and excluded from version control.

There are a few other standard directories such as *src/main/webapp*, *src/main/config*, *src/main/assembly*, and *src/main/filters*, which we're not going to discuss much beyond saying that they serve different purposes for people making full use of Maven to create complex applications. For example, *src/main/webapp* would be the document root of a web application if we were generating a WAR artifact. *src/main/assembly* is used to house assembly descriptors which we would need if we were creating a custom archive for a command-line application. The directories listed in Example 12-1 should be present in every Maven project—they are the lowest common denominator.

Although it seems like a relatively simple idea, the industry hasn't yet agreed on a standard directory layout for something like a Java project—in fact, one of the most common objections to Maven is that people don't like the directory structure. You can easily customize this structure, and if you look at some of the other chapters in this book, you'll see we adopted our own directory layout. There are some drawbacks to this approach—for example, some of the chapter examples are not completely compatible with the Maven Hibernate3 plug-in because of subtle problems with using a custom directory layout. I would caution you against trying to adapt Maven to your project's custom layout, but rather to try to adapt your project to Maven's standard layout before customizing. There are some simple differences which won't cause any problems with Maven, like storing resources under *src/main/java*, or configuring Maven to store source code in *src/java* instead of *src/main/java*. Problems start to crop up when you do things like generate Java code from Hibernate mapping files and store that code in *src/main/java*. Just as Maven has standards for things like source code, it also has some conventions for *generated* source code (that ends up in *target/generated-source*, which is included in the list of "compile source roots" so it will be compiled along with the source you wrote yourself).

If you just read this section and you are thinking, "Well, we have a better directory layout," there's a good chance Maven is not for you. If you try to fiddle with some of Maven's core assumptions, you'll spend a few days hitting up against a series of frustrating obstacles. In the end, it won't work, you'll start loudly cursing Maven, and then you'll blog about how much you hate it because you didn't agree with the basic assumptions. In case you haven't noticed, the first few sections of this chapter are trying to save you some time. I can attest that Maven has saved me countless days of effort and has paid dividends in the form of efficiency, but I've also watched people approach Maven from the wrong direction only to come away with nothing but invective for the project. Adapt to it; don't try to make it adapt to you. It has opinions, and if you start questioning those opinions, it'll bite you.

> The theme of this chapter is either "Adopt Maven's Conventions" or "You will be assimilated. Resistance is futile."

Installing Maven

You can download a binary release of Maven from *http://maven.apache.org/down load.html*. Download the current release of Maven in a format that's convenient for you to work with. Pick an appropriate place for it to live, and expand the archive there. If you've expanded the archive into something like the directory */usr/local/maven-2.0.8*, you may want to create a symbolic link to make it easier to work with and to avoid the need to change any environment configuration whenever you upgrade to a newer version:

```
/usr/local % ln -s maven-2.0.8 maven
/usr/local % export M2_HOME=/usr/local/maven
/usr/local % export PATH=${PATH}:${M2_HOME}/bin
```

Once Maven is situated, you need to do a couple of things to make it work correctly. You need to add its *bin* directory in the distribution (in this example, */usr/local/maven/ bin*) to your command path. You also need to set the environment variable M2_HOME to the top-level directory you installed (in this example, */usr/local/maven*). Details about how to perform these steps under different operating systems can be found in *Maven: The Definitive Guide*.

Building, Testing, and Running a Project

Assuming that you've downloaded the examples from this book's site[†], you should change directories into the *ch12* example, and run the *mvn test*. You'll see results like Example 12-2.

Example 12-2. Telling Maven to test our project

```
$ mvn test
[INFO] Scanning for projects... ❶
[INFO] -------------------------------------------------------------------------
---
[INFO] Building Harnessing Hibernate: Chapter Twelve: Maven
[INFO]    task-segment: [test]
[INFO] -------------------------------------------------------------------------
---
[INFO] [resources:resources]
[INFO] Using default encoding to copy filtered resources.
[INFO] [compiler:compile] ❷
[INFO] Compiling 9 source files to ~\examples\ch12\target\classes
[INFO] Preparing hibernate3:hbm2ddl
[WARNING] Removing: hbm2ddl from forked lifecycle, to prevent recursive invocati
on.
[INFO] [resources:resources]
[INFO] Using default encoding to copy filtered resources.
[INFO] [hibernate3:hbm2ddl {execution: generate-ddl}] ❸
[INFO] Configuration XML file loaded:
~/examples/ch12/src/main/resources/hibernate.cfg.xml
20:16:05,580  INFO org.hibernate.cfg.annotations.Version - Hibernate Annotations
 3.2.0.GA
20:16:05,595  INFO org.hibernate.cfg.Environment - Hibernate 3.2.0.cr5
20:16:05,598  INFO org.hibernate.cfg.Environment - hibernate.properties not foun
d
20:16:05,599  INFO org.hibernate.cfg.Environment - Bytecode provider name : cgli
b
20:16:05,603  INFO org.hibernate.cfg.Environment - using JDK 1.4 java.sql.Timest
amp handling
[INFO] Configuration XML file loaded:
~/examples/ch12/src/main/resources/hibernate.cfg.xml
20:16:05,684  INFO org.hibernate.cfg.Configuration - configuring from url:
~/examples/ch12/src/main/resources/hibernate.cfg.xml
20:16:05,808  INFO org.hibernate.cfg.Configuration - Configured SessionFactory:
null
(schema export omitted)
20:16:07,172  INFO org.hibernate.tool.hbm2ddl.SchemaExport - schema export compl
ete
20:16:07,173  INFO org.hibernate.connection.DriverManagerConnectionProvider - cl
eaning up connection pool: jdbc:hsqldb:data/music
[INFO] [resources:testResources]
[INFO] Using default encoding to copy filtered resources.
[INFO] [compiler:testCompile] ❹
[INFO] Compiling 2 source files to ~\examples\ch12\target\test-classes
```

[†] *http://www.oreilly.com/catalog/9780596517724/*

```
20:16:08,194  INFO org.hibernate.connection.DriverManagerConnectionProvider - cl
eaning up connection pool: jdbc:hsqldb:data/music
[INFO] [surefire:test] ❺
[INFO] Surefire report directory: ~\examples\ch12\target\surefire-reports


-------------------------------------------------------
 T E S T S
-------------------------------------------------------
Running com.oreilly.hh.ArtistTest
Hibernate: insert into ARTIST (ARTIST_ID, actualArtist_ARTIST_ID, NAME) values (
null, ?, ?)
Hibernate: call identity()
Tests run: 1, Failures: 0, Errors: 0, Skipped: 0, Time elapsed: 1.345 sec

Results :

Tests run: 1, Failures: 0, Errors: 0, Skipped: 0
```

The command generated quite a bit of activity. Let's take a look at what just happened:

❶   First, what does *mvn test* mean? On the command line we're invoking Maven and giving it the name of a target stage in the Maven Build Lifecycle. The Maven Build Lifecycle is a set of stages that Maven passes through during a build. Maven plug-ins are registered to execute during lifecycle stages: code is compiled in the compile stage, tests are executed in the test stage, and JARs are created in the package stage. For a complete list of stages, see "The Maven Build Lifecycle" later in this chapter.

❷   To get to the test stage we have to first pass through the compile stage. The Maven Compiler plug-in is registered to run during the compile stage. Maven plug-ins consist of goals, and we can see that the compile goal is executed and that nine source files are compiled, with the byte code sent to *target/classes*. How can we tell that the Compiler plug-in executed the compile goal? The string [compiler:compile] gives us that information: throughout the Maven output you'll see similar strings. The portion of the string before the colon is the *plug-in identifier*, and the portion after is the *goal identifier* of the goal being executed. Note that the warning log statement a few lines down from compiler:compile is to be expected; you can safely ignore it for now.

❸   Next, we see that we're executing the hbm2ddl goal of the Hibernate3 plug-in. This is not a default plug-in—you have to explicitly add it to Maven, but you don't have to provide it with much configuration. It assumes the location of *hibernate.cfg.xml* in *src/main/resources*. We'll explore more of the Hibernate3 Maven plug-in in "Using the Maven Hibernate3 Plug-in", below.

❹   Next, we compile the unit tests. The Compiler plug-in has a goal named testCompile. The test bytecode is stored in *target/test-classes*.

❺ Lastly, the Surefire plug-in executes the `test` goal which scans for classes that extend of JUnit's `TestCase` class. In this example, we've written a simple JUnit test that inserts a value into the `ARTIST` table.

That was it—Maven just compiled the source code, created a HSQLDB database, compiled the unit tests, and ran a unit test that inserted a row in a database. If you want to repeat the example, delete the *data* directory or the unit test will try to insert a row into the database that violates the unique constraint on an artist's name. To clean your project, run *mvn clean*:

```
$ mvn clean
[INFO] Scanning for projects...
[INFO] ------------------------------------------------------------------------
---
[INFO] Building Harnessing Hibernate: Chapter Twelve: Maven
[INFO]    task-segment: [clean]
[INFO] ------------------------------------------------------------------------
---
[INFO] [clean:clean]
[INFO] Deleting directory ~\examples\ch12\target
[INFO] Deleting directory ~\examples\ch12\target\classes
[INFO] Deleting directory ~\examples\ch12\target\test-classes
[INFO] Deleting directory ~\examples\ch12\target\site
```

If you were going to use classes from this project in another project, you'd want to generate a JAR to include in the class path. To generate a JAR artifact, run *mvn package*:

```
$ mvn package
[INFO] Scanning for projects...
[INFO] ------------------------------------------------------------------------
---
[INFO] Building Harnessing Hibernate: Chapter Twelve: Maven
[INFO]    task-segment: [package]
[INFO] ------------------------------------------------------------------------
---
...skipping output...
[INFO] [jar:jar]
[INFO] Building jar: ~\examples\ch12\target\hib-dev-ch12-2.0-SNAPSHOT.jar
```

A good deal of output was removed from that example—it was exactly the same as the output from *mvn test*, after which came the output of the Jar plug-in's `jar` goal which we did show. The Jar plug-in is bound to the **package** phase of the Maven Build Lifecycle and it creates a JAR artifact in *target* named *hib-dev-ch12-2.0-SNAPSHOT.jar*.

Generating IDE Project Files using Maven

You created a database, compiled code, tested it, and packaged the results in the previous section, but that's not all you can do with Maven. Maven has a number of plug-ins which are not directly tied to the regular Maven lifecycle. One common feature of any project is the presence of configuration files for an Integrated Development Environment (IDE). Often a team will standardize on a single development environment like IntelliJ, Eclipse, NetBeans, or Emacs JDE, and the configuration files for the tools will be distributed as a part of the project. If an organization has standardized on a single set of tools, storing IDE configuration files in version control might make some sense.

Storing IDE configuration in version control doesn't make much sense when an organization doesn't use a single set of tools, or—in the case of most Open Source projects—the individuals working on a project have little or no direct communication or power to coordinate such choices as development platform and IDEs. Even if you don't believe in allowing individual developers to make independent choices about tool sets, there's an advantage to generating your IDE configuration files from Maven. Often these configuration files contain the same dependency information, identifiers, and settings that you will be storing in your *pom.xml*. Not generating your IDE configuration from your *pom.xml* means that you'll be storing and maintaining two copies of this information.

> Most people have preferences when it comes to development tools, so generating IDE projects from the POM allows for individuals to use the tools with which they are most productive.

To generate a set of Eclipse configuration files, run *mvn eclipse:eclipse* from the *ch12* example directory:

```
$ mvn eclipse:eclipse
[INFO] Scanning for projects...
[INFO] Searching repository for plugin with prefix: 'eclipse'.
[INFO] ------------------------------------------------------------------------
---
[INFO] Building Harnessing Hibernate: Chapter Twelve: Maven
[INFO]    task-segment: [eclipse:eclipse]
[INFO] ------------------------------------------------------------------------
---
[INFO] Preparing eclipse:eclipse
[INFO] No goals needed for project - skipping
[INFO] [eclipse:eclipse]
[INFO] Using source status cache: ~\examples\ch12\target\mvn-eclipse-cache.prope
rties
[INFO] Wrote settings to ~\examples\ch12\.settings\org.eclipse.jdt.core.prefs
[INFO] Wrote Eclipse project for "hib-dev-ch12" to ~\examples\ch12.
```

Maven just used the information in *pom.xml* to generate Eclipse project files (*.project* and *.classpath*) in the project's directory. To import this project into Eclipse, select File→Import.... In the Import dialog, expand the General section, choose Existing Projects into Workspace and click Next. Select the root directory by browsing to the *examples* directory and click Next again. Eclipse will then crawl through the selected directory and all subdirectories searching for *.project* files. After your project has been imported, you will need to add a Java Classpath Variable named M2_REPO which points to ~/.m2/repository. To do this, go to the Eclipse Preferences. Under Java / Build Path / Classpath Variables, you will see a list of existing Classpath Variables including ECLIPSE_HOME. Add a new Classpath Variable named M2_REPO and point it to your local Maven 2 repository, which should be in ~/.m2/repository.

You will only need to add the M2_REPO Classpath Variable once, and if you would prefer not to go through the process of adding the variable through the Eclipse Preferences, you can use the Maven Eclipse plug-in to add the Classpath Variable to your Eclipse Workspace like this:

```
/home/tobrien $ mvn -o eclipse:add-maven-repo \
                          -Declipse.localRepository=~/.m2/repository \
                          -Declipse.workspace\=~/eclipse
```

All of the chapter examples in this book include a *pom.xml* file, but not all of them are completely compatible with Maven. The one thing you can reliably do in every chapter, though, is generate Eclipse project files using *mvn eclipse:eclipse*. Try it! Change to any other chapter example directory, and run *mvn eclipse:eclipse*, then import that chapter. Or, if you want to generate Eclipse project files for all of the chapters at once, change directories to the parent directory of the chapter examples and run *mvn eclipse:eclipse* from there. Running from the *examples* directory will execute the Eclipse plug-in's eclipse goal against all of the submodules, one for each chapter for which code examples exist.

In addition to Eclipse projects, you can also generate projects for IntelliJ's Idea IDE. To do so, execute the idea goal of the Idea plug-in as follows:

```
$ mvn idea:idea
[INFO] Scanning for projects...
[INFO] Searching repository for plugin with prefix: 'idea'.
[INFO] ------------------------------------------------------------------------
---
[INFO] Building Harnessing Hibernate: Chapter Twelve: Maven
[INFO]    task-segment: [idea:idea]
[INFO] ------------------------------------------------------------------------
---
[INFO] Preparing idea:idea
[INFO] No goals needed for project - skipping
[INFO] [idea:idea]
[INFO] jdkName is not set, using [java version1.6.0_02] as default.
```

The idea goal creates three files in the project directory: *hib-dev-ch12.iml*, *hib-dev-ch12.ipr*, and *hib-dev-ch12.iws*. Using these files, you can import this project into Idea.

Generating Reports with Maven

We've built a project; now let's generate some simple reports. One report that might be useful is an HTML page that displays the results of the unit tests. Did they succeed or fail? Which tests failed? You'll also want JavaDoc for your code, and maybe annotated source to use during code reviews. All of these are generated when you run *mvn site*:

```
$ mvn site
[INFO] Scanning for projects...
[INFO] ------------------------------------------------------------------------
---
```

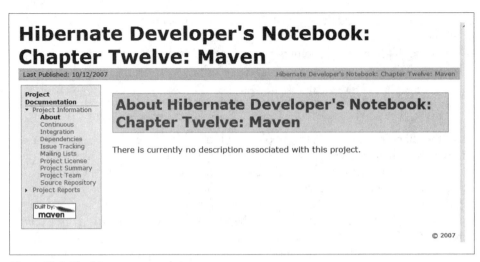

Figure 12-1. The Maven-generated site

```
[INFO] Building Harnessing Hibernate: Chapter Twelve: Maven
[INFO]    task-segment: [site]
[INFO] ------------------------------------------------------------------------
---
[INFO] Setting property: classpath.resource.loader.class => 'org.codehaus.plexus
.velocity.ContextClassLoaderResourceLoader'.
[INFO] Setting property: velocimacro.messages.on => 'false'.
[INFO] Setting property: resource.loader => 'classpath'.
[INFO] Setting property: resource.manager.logwhenfound => 'false'.
[INFO] ************************************************************
[INFO] Starting Jakarta Velocity v1.4
[INFO] [site:site]
Constructing Javadoc information...
Standard Doclet version 1.6.0_02
Building tree for all the packages and classes...
Generating ~/examples/ch12/target/site/apidocs\index.html...
[INFO] Generate "Source Xref" report.
[INFO] Generate "Continuous Integration" report.
[INFO] Generate "Dependencies" report.
[INFO] Generate "Issue Tracking" report.
[INFO] Generate "Project License" report.
[INFO] Generate "Mailing Lists" report.
[INFO] Generate "About" report.
[INFO] Generate "Project Summary" report.
[INFO] Generate "Source Repository" report.
[INFO] Generate "Project Team" report.
[INFO] Final Memory: 23M/42M
```

I removed a good deal of output from the above snippet. If you run *mvn site*, you'll see pages and pages of activity. Maven was creating a project web site and generating a few useful reports. Let's take a quick look at the results.

Maven generates a simple web site that lists a number of reports and pages about the project. The default site template doesn't look great, as you can see in Figure 12-1, but

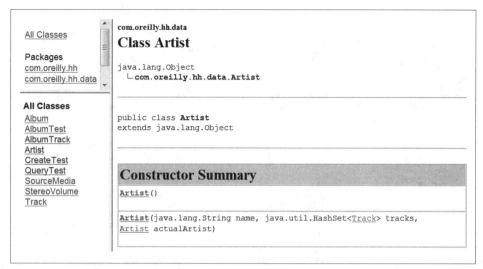

Figure 12-2. Project JavaDoc within the site

it provides a basic web site in case you want to publish information about a project online. If you configure your project's POM correctly, you can generate a simple page listing the project contributors, the license, and a link to an issue management tool (like Bugzilla, JIRA, or Trac). If you are creating an open source project, this information provides a solid foundation for a public, developer-focused web site. Even if you are working in a closed environment it can still be useful to a team of developers. While the look and feel of the default Maven site leaves much to be desired, it can be customized with stylesheets and templates stored under the *src/site* directory. If you click on Project Reports in the left-hand navigation menu, you can view some useful reports. You can also browse your project's JavaDoc, as shown in Figure 12-2.

You can browse the results of the unit tests, by clicking on the Surefire report (see Figure 12-3).

Since this project only defined a single unit test, there's not much to see in the Surefire report. If your project contained a substantial number of tests, this would allow people to check the overall quality of the code. If you find a problem with a unit test, or if you need to conduct a code review for some particularly bad code, you can also browse the annotated, cross-referenced source code using the JXR report (see Figure 12-4).

The JXR report can be useful to explore during a code review. There are a multitude of other reports available, as well: test coverage reports with Clover, JDepend reports, DocBook, and PDF generation, among others.

Without telling you much about how Maven is working, we've just compiled, built a database, tested, packaged, and documented some simple example code. In the next section, we're going to take a look at the single file that makes all this possible: *pom.xml*. You'll start to get a sense of how Maven can be configured and customized.

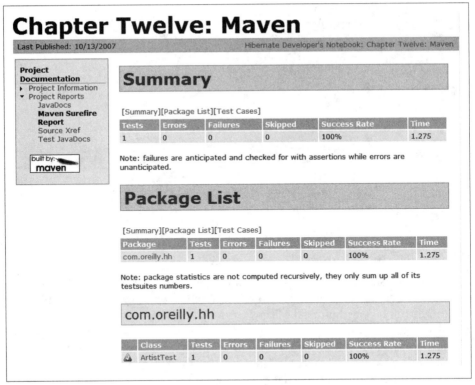

Project Documentation
▸ Project Information
▾ Project Reports
   JavaDocs
   Maven Surefire Report
   Source Xref
   Test JavaDocs

built by: maven

Summary

[Summary][Package List][Test Cases]

Tests	Errors	Failures	Skipped	Success Rate	Time
1	0	0	0	100%	1.275

Note: failures are anticipated and checked for with assertions while errors are unanticipated.

Package List

[Summary][Package List][Test Cases]

Package	Tests	Errors	Failures	Skipped	Success Rate	Time
com.oreilly.hh	1	0	0	0	100%	1.275

Note: package statistics are not computed recursively, they only sum up all of its testsuites numbers.

com.oreilly.hh

Class	Tests	Errors	Failures	Skipped	Success Rate	Time
⚠ ArtistTest	1	0	0	0	100%	1.275

Figure 12-3. Unit test results in the project site

A Maven Project Object Model

This is it. This is the only configuration file you need to write for Maven to work. Every Maven project has a *pom.xml* file, and it describes the project's attributes and dependencies, and contains any custom build configuration. Example 12-3 shows the *pom.xml* that made the previous build possible.

Example 12-3. Maven Project Object Model (POM)

```
<project xmlns="http://maven.apache.org/POM/4.0.0" ❶
        xmlns:xsi="http://www.w3.org/2001/XMLSchema-instance"
        xsi:schemaLocation="http://maven.apache.org/POM/4.0.0
           http://maven.apache.org/xsd/maven-4.0.0.xsd">
   <modelVersion>4.0.0</modelVersion>
   <groupId>com.oreilly.hh</groupId> ❷
   <artifactId>hib-dev-ch12</artifactId>
   <version>2.0-SNAPSHOT</version>
   <name>Harnessing Hibernate: Chapter Twelve: Maven</name>
   <packaging>jar</packaging> ❸
   <dependencies> ❹
     <dependency>
       <groupId>junit</groupId>
```

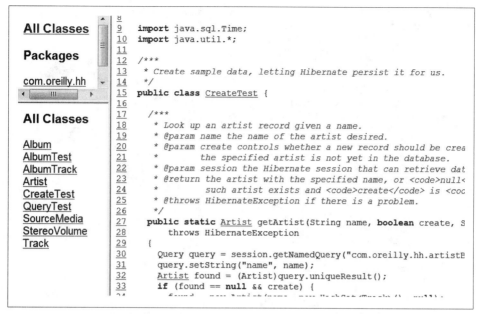

```
  8
  9  import java.sql.Time;
 10  import java.util.*;
 11
 12  /***
 13   * Create sample data, letting Hibernate persist it for us.
 14   */
 15  public class CreateTest {
 16
 17    /***
 18     * Look up an artist record given a name.
 19     * @param name the name of the artist desired.
 20     * @param create controls whether a new record should be crea
 21     *        the specified artist is not yet in the database.
 22     * @param session the Hibernate session that can retrieve dat
 23     * @return the artist with the specified name, or <code>null<
 24     *        such artist exists and <code>create</code> is <coc
 25     * @throws HibernateException if there is a problem.
 26     */
 27    public static Artist getArtist(String name, boolean create, S
 28         throws HibernateException
 29    {
 30       Query query = session.getNamedQuery("com.oreilly.hh.artistE
 31       query.setString("name", name);
 32       Artist found = (Artist)query.uniqueResult();
 33       if (found == null && create) {
```

Figure 12-4. Cross-referenced HTML source code

```xml
        <artifactId>junit</artifactId>
        <version>3.8.1</version>
        <scope>test</scope>
      </dependency>
      <dependency>
        <groupId>hsqldb</groupId>
        <artifactId>hsqldb</artifactId>
        <version>1.8.0.7</version>
      </dependency>
      <dependency>
        <groupId>org.hibernate</groupId>
        <artifactId>hibernate</artifactId>
        <version>3.2.5.ga</version>
        <exclusions>
          <exclusion>
            <groupId>javax.transaction</groupId>
            <artifactId>jta</artifactId>
          </exclusion>
        </exclusions>
      </dependency>
      <dependency>
        <groupId>org.apache.geronimo.specs</groupId>
        <artifactId>geronimo-jta_1.1_spec</artifactId>
        <version>1.1</version>
      </dependency>
      <dependency>
        <groupId>log4j</groupId>
        <artifactId>log4j</artifactId>
        <version>1.2.14</version>
```

```
        </dependency>
        <dependency>
          <groupId>org.hibernate</groupId>
          <artifactId>hibernate-annotations</artifactId>
          <version>3.3.0.ga</version>
        </dependency>
        <dependency>
          <groupId>org.hibernate</groupId>
          <artifactId>hibernate-commons-annotations</artifactId>
          <version>3.3.0.ga</version>
        </dependency>
      </dependencies>
      <build>
        <extensions> ❺
          <extension>
            <groupId>hsqldb</groupId>
            <artifactId>hsqldb</artifactId>
            <version>1.8.0.7</version>
          </extension>
          <extension>
            <groupId>log4j</groupId>
            <artifactId>log4j</artifactId>
            <version>1.2.14</version>
          </extension>
        </extensions>
        <plugins>
          <plugin> ❻
            <groupId>org.apache.maven.plugins</groupId>
            <artifactId>maven-compiler-plugin</artifactId>
            <configuration>
              <source>1.5</source>
              <target>1.5</target>
            </configuration>
          </plugin>
          <plugin> ❼
            <groupId>org.codehaus.mojo</groupId>
            <artifactId>hibernate3-maven-plugin</artifactId>
            <version>2.0</version>
            <executions>
              <execution>
                <id>generate-ddl</id>
                <phase>process-classes</phase>
                <goals>
                  <goal>hbm2ddl</goal>
                </goals>
              </execution>
            </executions>
          </plugin>
        </plugins>
      </build>
      <reporting> ❽
        <plugins>
          <plugin>
            <artifactId>maven-javadoc-plugin</artifactId>
          </plugin>
```

```
      <plugin>
        <groupId>org.codehaus.mojo</groupId>
        <artifactId>jxr-maven-plugin</artifactId>
      </plugin>
      <plugin>
        <artifactId>maven-surefire-report-plugin</artifactId>
      </plugin>
    </plugins>
  </reporting>
</project>
```

This is all the configuration we need to compile, test, and generate a web site:

❶ The document element is `project`. We supply the `xsi:schemaLocation` that defines the Maven POM version 4 schema. If you need a comprehensive reference, load this XML schema into a tool like XMLSpy—the schema is well documented.

❷ Next we define a set of identifiers common to every Maven project: a `groupId`, an `artifactId`, and a `version`. These three properties are the unique "coordinates" of a Maven project. Throughout this POM you'll notice that dependencies, extensions, and plug-ins are all referred to using one or more of these properties.

❸ `packaging` for this project is `jar`. Setting the packaging format to `jar` tells Maven that the project expects to generate a JAR file as a result of its build. Maven has a set of predefined packaging formats such as `pom`, `jar`, and `war`. If no packaging is declared in a POM, the default value is `jar`.

❹ The `dependencies` element tells Maven what external libraries this project depends upon. The dependencies in a Maven POM work exactly the same as the dependencies we've been using in the Maven Ant Task, and if you compare the contents of dependencies in this *pom.xml* with the ones in *build.xml* you'll see that we're including the same dependencies as Chapter 7's *build.xml*: JUnit, HSQLDB, Hibernate minus JTA, a replacement JTA from Apache Geronimo, and Hibernate Annotations.

❺ The `build` element is where we define build customizations. It is here that we can configure custom behavior for plug-ins, and configure plug-ins that might not be available with the default Maven install. Since the Hibernate3 plug-in is going to be configured to use HSQLDB, we add the `hsqldb` and `log4j` libraries as `extensions` under the `build` element. The contents of the `extension` element are the `groupId`, `artifactId`, and `version` values for any dependencies which need to be on the class path during plug-in execution.

❻ The first `plugin` element configures the compiler plug-in to set the source and target to Java 5.

❼ Here we're configuring the Hibernate3 Maven plug-in from the Mojo project at Codehaus‡. At the time we wrote this book, the latest release of the Hibernate3

‡ *http://mojo.codehaus.org/maven-hibernate3/hibernate3-maven-plugin/*

plug-in was 2.0. This plug-in configuration identifies the common location of *hibernate.cfg.xml* and also adds a property to tell `hbm2ddl` not to drop an existing database when we generate our schema. The Ant-based example executed the `hbm2ddl` goal during a build after the compilation phase, but this POM ties `hbm2ddl` to the `process-classes` phase in Maven. We'll explore the phases of the Maven Build Lifecycle in more detail in "The Maven Build Lifecycle" later in this chapter.

❽ Finally, the reporting section configures the report generators which are executed during site generation. Maven plug-ins which generate reports have a `report` goal which is called during site generation. To include a report, a plug-in must be included under the `reporting` element.

Notice the difference between this *pom.xml* file and a *build.xml* from another chapter. In the *build.xml* we're explicitly telling Ant what to do, where and when to do it, and what to do it to. In Maven, we're just pointing out the dependencies and specifying what goals we need executed. Maven plug-ins know what to do—the compile plug-in knows to look in *src/main/java* for source and *src/test/java* for tests. The Hibernate3 plug-in "knows" that our *hibernate.cfg.xml* file is in *src/main/resources*. If we stored our *hibernate.cfg.xml* file in a different location, we could tell the plug-in that, but, why bother overriding a convention that makes sense? We'll take a closer look at the Hibernate3 plug-in in the "Using the Maven Hibernate3 Plug-in" section later in this chapter.

Parent/child Project Object Models

This chapter's example uses a single, stand-alone *pom.xml* to ease the introduction to Maven. Almost all of the other chapters' examples are involved in what is called a *multimodule* Maven project, in which each submodule depends on a parent module. Let's take a look at the example for Chapter 7. In the *ch07* directory you'll find a *pom.xml* whose contents are shown in Example 12-4. The first thing you will notice is how small it is: where are all of the dependencies?

Example 12-4. The pom.xml file for Chapter 7

```
<?xml version="1.0" encoding="UTF-8"?>
<project xmlns="http://maven.apache.org/POM/4.0.0"
    xmlns:xsi="http://www.w3.org/2001/XMLSchema-instance"
    xsi:schemaLocation="http://maven.apache.org/POM/4.0.0
      http://maven.apache.org/maven-v4_0_0.xsd">
    <parent>
        <groupId>com.oreilly.hh</groupId>  ❶
        <artifactId>hib-dev-parent</artifactId>
        <version>2.0-SNAPSHOT</version>
    </parent>
    <modelVersion>4.0.0</modelVersion>
    <artifactId>hib-dev-ch7</artifactId>  ❷
    <packaging>jar</packaging>  ❸
    <name>Harnessing Hibernate: Chapter Seven</name>
```

```
          <version>2.0-SNAPSHOT</version>
          <build>
            <plugins>
              <plugin>
                <groupId>org.codehaus.mojo</groupId>
                <artifactId>hibernate3-maven-plugin</artifactId>
                <version>2.0-alpha-3-SNAPSHOT</version>
                <executions>
                  <execution>
                    <id>generate-ddl</id>
                    <phase>process-classes</phase>
                    <goals>
                      <goal>hbm2ddl</goal>
                    </goals>
                  </execution>
                </executions>
                <configuration>
                  <components>
                    <component>
                      <name>hbm2ddl</name> ❹
                      <implementation>annotationconfiguration</implementation>
                    </component>
                  </components>
                </configuration>
              </plugin>
            </plugins>
          </build>
          <dependencies> ❺
            <dependency>
              <groupId>org.hibernate</groupId>
              <artifactId>hibernate-annotations</artifactId>
              <version>3.3.0.ga</version>
            </dependency>
            <dependency>
              <groupId>org.hibernate</groupId>
              <artifactId>hibernate-commons-annotations</artifactId>
              <version>3.3.0.ga</version>
            </dependency>
          </dependencies>
        </project>

  </project>
```

This *pom.xml* is deceptively simple because it inherits the bulk of its configuration from
the parent project's POM (which we'll get to in a second). Let's examine the contents
of this simple POM:

❶   We link this project to a parent project defined by a `groupId`, an `artifactId`, and
    a `version`. These three properties are common to all projects defined in Maven—
    they are the unique "coordinates" of a Maven project. We'll take a look at the
    parent project in the next example, but for now, all you need to know is that
    examples/ch07/pom.xml inherits all of the properties from the POM defined in
    examples/pom.xml.

❷ We define the `artifactId` as `hib-dev-ch07`. We're overriding a property from the parent POM and providing a value unique to this project. As noted, all projects must have a unique combination of `groupId`, `artifactId`, and `version`, and this simply makes sure that the *ch07* example has a unique `artifactId`. Note that this *pom.xml* doesn't define a `groupId`; it doesn't need to as it inherits the `groupId` from the parent *pom.xml*.

❸ Next we override the `packaging` property for this project's POM. Maven has a set of predefined packaging formats such as `pom`, `jar`, and `war`. Setting the packaging format for the *ch07* example to `jar` simply tells Maven that the project expects to generate a JAR as a result of its build.

❹ We're configuring the Maven Hibernate3 plug-in, much as we did in this chapter's example directory. The difference here is that we're configuring the Hibernate3 plug-in to use annotation-based configuration, since Chapter 7 is all about annotations. This configuration pulls Hibernate's mapping information from a set of annotated model classes stored in *src/main/java*. Maven compiles the Java source into *target/classes*, and the Maven Hibernate3 plug-in then scans the resulting bytecode for `@Entity` annotations. Finally, this mapping information is used by the `hbm2ddl` goal to generate an HSQLDB database.

❺ We declare the dependencies for this submodule as being Hibernate Annotations and Hibernate Commons Annotations. These new dependencies are in addition to any dependencies defined by the parent project.

The Chapter 7 POM references a parent POM. Where is this parent POM defined? Go to the parent directory of *ch07*, and you'll find a (much larger) *pom.xml* file. This is the file that defines all the properties shared by each of the chapter example POMs. Let's take a look at this parent *pom.xml*, shown in Example 12-5.

Example 12-5. The shared, top-level pom.xml

```
<?xml version="1.0" encoding="UTF-8"?>
<project xmlns="http://maven.apache.org/POM/4.0.0"
    xmlns:xsi="http://www.w3.org/2001/XMLSchema-instance"
    xsi:schemaLocation="http://maven.apache.org/POM/4.0.0
      http://maven.apache.org/maven-v4_0_0.xsd">

    <modelVersion>4.0.0</modelVersion>
    <groupId>com.oreilly.hh</groupId> ❶
    <artifactId>hib-dev-parent</artifactId>
    <packaging>pom</packaging> ❷
    <name>Harnessing Hibernate: Parent Project</name>
    <version>2.0-SNAPSHOT</version>
    <modules> ❸
      <module>ch01</module>
      <module>ch02</module>
      <module>ch03</module>
      <module>ch04</module>
      <module>ch05</module>
      <module>ch06</module>
```

```
        <module>ch07</module>
        <module>ch08</module>
        <module>ch09</module>
        <module>ch10</module>
        <module>ch11</module>
        <module>ch12</module>
        <module>ch13</module>
        <module>ch14</module>
</modules>
<build>
    <extensions> ❹
        <extension>
            <groupId>hsqldb</groupId>
            <artifactId>hsqldb</artifactId>
            <version>1.8.0.7</version>
        </extension>
        <extension>
            <groupId>log4j</groupId>
            <artifactId>log4j</artifactId>
            <version>1.2.14</version>
        </extension>
    </extensions>
    <resources>
        <resource>
            <directory>src</directory> ❺
        </resource>
    </resources>
    <sourceDirectory>src</sourceDirectory>
    <plugins>
        <plugin>
            <groupId>org.apache.maven.plugins</groupId>
            <artifactId>maven-compiler-plugin</artifactId> ❻
            <configuration>
                <source>1.5</source>
                <target>1.5</target>
            </configuration>
        </plugin>
        <plugin>
            <groupId>org.codehaus.mojo</groupId>
            <artifactId>hibernate3-maven-plugin</artifactId> ❼
            <version>2.0</version>
            <configuration>
                <components>
                  <component>
                    <name>hbm2java</name>
                    <implementation>configuration</implementation>
                  </component>
                </components>
                <componentProperties>
                    <drop>false</drop>
                    <configurationfile>
                      src/hibernate.cfg.xml
                    </configurationfile>
                    <jdk5>true</jdk5>
                </componentProperties>
```

```
            </configuration>
        </plugin>
      </plugins>
    </build>
    <dependencies> ❽
      <dependency>
        <groupId>hsqldb</groupId>
        <artifactId>hsqldb</artifactId>
        <version>1.8.0.7</version>
      </dependency>
      <dependency>
        <groupId>org.hibernate</groupId>
        <artifactId>hibernate</artifactId>
        <version>3.2.5.ga</version>
        <exclusions>
          <exclusion>
            <groupId>javax.transaction</groupId>
            <artifactId>jta</artifactId>
          </exclusion>
        </exclusions>
      </dependency>
      <dependency>
        <groupId>org.apache.geronimo.specs</groupId>
        <artifactId>geronimo-jta_1.1_spec</artifactId>
        <version>1.1</version>
      </dependency>
      <dependency>
        <groupId>log4j</groupId>
        <artifactId>log4j</artifactId>
        <version>1.2.14</version>
      </dependency>
    </dependencies>
  </project>
```

This parent POM contains much more information than the child POMs. It defines all of the common dependencies, directory overrides, and plug-in configuration shared by the individual chapter examples that use it. Once again, let's go through this parent POM section-by-section:

❶ The `groupId` element defines the group identifier which will be shared by all the subprojects. The standard practice for a `groupId` is to use a reverse fully-qualified domain name (which you own, or with which the project is associated), followed by domain-specific identifiers. This is especially important if you want to publish your artifacts in a Maven repository.

❷ In the parent POM the `packaging` is set to `pom`. This just means that the project exists solely to provide a POM; this project isn't providing a JAR file or a WAR file, just a POM.

❸ The parent POM defines a list of `modules`. This section lists every chapter example directory that contains a *pom.xml*, and if you look in every directory you'll notice a *pom.xml* that references this parent POM. Specifying all of the modules in the parent POM gives us the ability to build all of the chapters (or modules) at once.

❹ `extensions` configures the class path used by the plug-ins. The parent *pom.xml* defines the same extensions we saw in Example 12-3.

❺ Here we're customizing the location of our project's classpath resources. In a normal Maven project we wouldn't need to define this property—we would rely on the default value of `${basedir}/src/main/resources` (where `${basedir}` is the directory which contains the *pom.xml* file). In this book (since it's a book about Hibernate, not Maven), we're adapting the Maven build to the existing chapter examples, and we have to define the classpath resource directory as *src/*. In addition to customizing the location of the classpath resources, we also need to customize the location of the source code. In a standard Maven project, we wouldn't define this property in the *pom.xml* and we would use the default value of `${basedir}/src/main/java`.

❻ This section configures the compiler plug-in to target Java 5.

❼ The Hibernate3 plug-in is configured with a few global options. Setting `drop` to `false` will prevent the `hbm2ddl` goal from dropping an existing database. Setting `jdk5` to `true` will cause the `hbm2java` goal to generate properties using Java 5 generics (for example, `Set<Album>` rather than just `Set`). We also configure the default location for our *hibernate.cfg.xml* using `configurationFile` since it's not where Maven wants it to be. The `component` entry for `hbm2java` sets the `implementation` to `configuration`, which means that the default behavior will be to scan the main resources directory for *.hbm.xml* mapping files. We saw in Example 12-4 that the *pom.xml* in *ch07* overrides this configuration for the `hbm2ddl` component to use annotations for Hibernate configuration instead.

❽ Lastly, the top-level POM defines a set of dependencies which are shared by all chapter examples. They are HSQLDB 1.8.0.7, Hibernate 3.2.5.ga, the JTA library via the Apache Geronimo project, and Log4J 1.2.14. Compare the contents of this `dependencies` element with the contents of the Maven Ant Task configuration in any chapter's *build.xml* script.

Let's run the examples in *ch07* as an example. First, delete the data directory if it exists, and then run *mvn install*. This will compile the source code, generate the database from the annotations on the model, and package the *ch07* example in a JAR file. After we run the build, we can run `CreateTest`, `QueryTest`, and `AlbumTest` just as we would have done with Ant. Example 12-6 shows how.

Example 12-6. Using Maven to run the Chapter 7 tests

```
~/examples/ch07 $ mvn exec:java -Dexec.mainClass=com.oreilly.hh.CreateTest
[INFO] Scanning for projects...
[INFO] Searching repository for plugin with prefix: 'exec'.
[INFO] ------------------------------------------------------------------------
---
```

```
[INFO] Building Harnessing Hibernate: Chapter Seven
[INFO]     task-segment: [exec:java]
[INFO] ------------------------------------------------------------------------
---
[INFO] Preparing exec:java
[INFO] No goals needed for project - skipping
[INFO] [exec:java]

~/examples/ch07 $ mvn exec:java -Dexec.mainClass=com.oreilly.hh.QueryTest
[INFO] Scanning for projects...
[INFO] Searching repository for plugin with prefix: 'exec'.
[INFO] ------------------------------------------------------------------------
---
[INFO] Building Harnessing Hibernate: Chapter Seven
[INFO]     task-segment: [exec:java]
[INFO] ------------------------------------------------------------------------
---
[INFO] Preparing exec:java
[INFO] No goals needed for project - skipping
[INFO] [exec:java]
Track: "Russian Trance", 00:03:30
Track: "Video Killed the Radio Star", 00:03:49
Track: "Test Tone 1", 00:00:10

~/examples/ch07 $ mvn exec:java -Dexec.mainClass=com.oreilly.hh.AlbumTest
(output omitted)
```

We're using a plug-in goal which is not normally attached to a lifecycle phase—
exec:java. This goal takes the parameter exec.mainClass from the command line and
executes the main( ) method in the named class.

The Maven Build Lifecycle

We've talked about the lifecycle in the previous sections of this chapter, so by now
you've gathered that there is a compile phase, a test phase, a package phase, and an
install phase. In Example 12-3 we attached the hbm2ddl goal to the process-classes
phase, and we mentioned that this phase follows the compile phase. If this all seems
like Voodoo, don't worry—we'll briefly explain the phases in the lifecycle and the order
in which they're executed. When you run Maven from the command line you have the
choice of specifying the name of a phase or of executing a plug-in goal explicitly. When
you specify a phase, Maven will execute all of the phases in the Maven lifecycle up to
and including the specified phase. As Maven progresses through the Build Lifecycle it
triggers plug-in goals which have been attached to the current phase. If, on the other
hand, you request a plug-in goal explicitly, Maven will only execute that single plug-in
goal.

Here's a list of all the Maven phases, in the order in which they occur. The phases that
are important to our examples are explained in some detail, whereas other phases have
been combined to save some space:

validate
> Validates the POM.

generate-sources
> Generates any source code. The Hibernate3 plug-in has an `hbm2java` goal which we could use to generate Java from XML-based mappings (as we did in previous chapters). If we wanted to do that, it would make sense for us to attach `hbm2java` to this phase.

process-sources, generate-resources, process-resources
> In addition to generating source code, you can process the output of the source generation, generate resources (like properties files, images, sounds, or other such noncode elements of a package), and process resources.

compile
> The Compiler plug-in runs the `compile` goal, which compiles all of the source code in the compile source root directories. Plug-ins can add directories to the compile source root—for example, the Hibernate3 plug-in's `hbm2java` goal generates source code from *.hbm.xml* files and puts the generated source in *target/generated-source*. The Hibernate3 plug-in then adds this *target/generated-source* directory to the compile source roots so that it is included in the compilation.

process-classes
> Post-processes the results of the compilation. We've hooked the `hbm2ddl` goal to the `process-classes` task because the `hbm2ddl` task is configured to use the annotations on our object model, which get compiled into the model class files. The Hibernate3 plug-in is configured to scan the generated bytecode for the presence of the `@Entity` annotation. Because the classes have to be compiled for this scan to take place, we've hooked this goal to the `process-classes` phase which follows the `compile` phase.

generate-test-sources, process-test-sources,
generate-test-resources, process-test-resources
> These are analogous to the similarly named `generate-sources` through `process-resources` phases, and allow you to generate unit tests and any resources they might need.

test-compile
> The Compiler plug-in is invoked again to compile the test sources with the `test Compile` goal. For our example, it is as simple as compiling a single class in *src/test/java*. The `testCompile` goal compiles all of the source code in the test source root directories. Again, it isn't as simple as saying everything in *src/test/java* is compiled because plug-ins have the opportunity to generate source code for unit tests (and add directories to the test source root) in the previous four lifecycle phases.

test
> The Surefire plug-in scans the output of the `test-compile` for classes that extend JUnit's `TestCase` class, and uses JUnit to execute these unit tests. (It can also run TestNG tests.)

prepare-package

Provides a hook for goals that need to prepare the project to be packaged.

package

For our example project, we're just spitting out a JAR file in *target*. The default behavior for jar packaging is to create a file named *${artifactId}-${version}.jar*. You can customize that name if you need to, but in general it is always better avoid customizations if possible.

pre-integration-test, integration-test, post-integration-test

Unit tests don't usually connect to a database—in fact it would feel odd to write a unit test that did this. (I'd call this a functional or integration test.) If you need to perform a series of integration tests, use these three phases to define the relevant goals.

verify

verify is a placeholder phase for you to define goals for checking the quality of the generated output.

install

In our project, the install phase simply copies the generated artifact to a *~/.m2/repository/${groupId}/${artifactId}/${version}/${artifactId}-${version}.jar* file. If you were creating a more complex set of projects with interdependencies—say project A defined a persistence library that project B depended on—then Project B would define a dependency on Project A using the groupId, artifactId, and version, and Maven would attempt to resolve Project A's artifact in your local repository when building Project B. install enables this by installing artifacts into your local repository.

deploy

Used to publish your project's artifact, site, and reports to an external repository. This is a phase that is used by projects to publish artifacts to a remote Maven repository. A remote Maven repository can be a public Maven repository or a private, internal Maven repository for your organization.

Using the Maven Hibernate3 Plug-in

This chapter uses the Maven Hibernate3 Plug-in[§] from the Mojo project hosted by Codehaus. Mojo was created to provide a place outside of the Apache Software Foundation (ASF) for people to develop Maven plug-ins. Codehaus doesn't have as many rules as the ASF; it is easier for someone interested in a few plug-ins to start contributing to Mojo than it would be if all of these Maven plug-ins were hosted within the Maven project at the ASF. Another reason for hosting Mojo at Codehaus is that some Maven plug-ins use technologies with licenses that are not compatible with the Apache Software License. A plug-in at Mojo can depend on a GPL dependency, and can itself be

[§] *http://mojo.codehaus.org/maven-hibernate3/hibernate3-maven-plugin/*

released under a non-Apache Software License. In the Apache Software Foundation, everything needs to be released under the Apache Software License.

To use the Maven Hibernate3 plug-in, all you need to do is to include the plug-in element from Example 12-7 in your project's *pom.xml*.

Example 12-7. Using the Maven Hibernate3 plug-in

```
<project xmlns="http://maven.apache.org/POM/4.0.0"
         xmlns:xsi="http://www.w3.org/2001/XMLSchema-instance"
         xsi:schemaLocation="http://maven.apache.org/POM/4.0.0
            http://maven.apache.org/xsd/maven-4.0.0.xsd">
   ...pom content skipped...
   <build>
     <plugins>
       <plugin>
         <groupId>org.codehaus.mojo</groupId>
         <artifactId>hibernate3-maven-plugin</artifactId>
         <version>2.0</version>
       </plugin>
     </plugins>
   </build>
   ...pom content skipped...
</project>
```

The Hibernate3 plug-in defines the following goals (know as components for configuration purposes):

hibernate3:hbm2cfgxml
> Generates a *hibernate.cfg.xml* file based on an existing database schema. You would use this goal to build a Hibernate configuration from an existing database.

hibernate3:hbm2ddl
> Generates SQL DDL based on your Hibernate mappings (using either annotations or *.hbm.xml* files). In our example it generates an HSQLDB database.

hibernate3:hbm2doc
> Produces an HTML report which describes the Object Model and the database schema and how the two relate to each other. The generated report has the look and feel of JavaDoc.

hibernate3:hbm2hbmxml
> Generates *.hbm.xml* mapping documents from an existing database schema. If you have a set of database tables you can use this task to generate mapping files and the next goal to generate Java classes.

hibernate3:hbm2java
> Generates Java source code from Hibernate mappings. This goal can be used to generate Java from *.hbm.xml* files or it can be used to generate Java classes that correspond to the tables in an existing database.

For more information about Maven plug-ins you can read the online documentation on the Maven web site[||], and for information about the Hibernate3 Maven plug-in, take a look at the Mojo project[#].

 Mojo is a project for people who want to write Maven plug-ins that are outside of the set of Core plug-ins distributed with Apache Maven. If you have a good idea for a Maven plug-in, you should consider participating in the Mojo project.

Configuring the Hibernate3 plug-in

The Maven Hibernate3 plug-in provides a number of configuration points. Here's a list of some of its important configuration options:

propertyfile
> If you don't specify your JDBC connection information in your Hibernate configuration file, you can specify the JDBC connection parameters in a *database.properties* file. Defaults to *src/main/resources/database.properties*.

configurationfile
> The Hibernate configuration file. Defaults to *src/main/resources/hibernate.cfg.xml*.

jdk5
> Generate Java 5 source code. Enables the use of generics and enums when generating code to match Hibernate mappings. Defaults to `false`.

ejb3
> Generate source code with annotations. Defaults to `false`.

drop
> Drop a database before executing `hbm2ddl`. Defaults to `false`.

create
> Create a database when executing `hbm2ddl`. Defaults to `true`.

outputfilename
> Configures the output filename for a Hibernate3 plug-in goal.

implementation
> Configures the source of the Hibernate mappings. Valid values are `configuration`, `annotationconfiguration`, `jpaconfiguration`, and `jdbcconfiguration`.

There are a few more configuration parameters—for a full list, please see the Component Properties[*] page on the Maven Hibernate3 project web site.

[||] *http://maven.apache.org*

[#] *http://mojo.codehaus.org*

[*] *http://mojo.codehaus.org/maven-hibernate3/hibernate3-maven-plugin/componentproperties.html*

Each configuration point can be configured for a particular component (i.e. hbm2java or hbm2ddl), and each configuration point can also be configured across all components. Since Example 12-3 doesn't supply any configuration properties, Hibernate is executed with the default options to read Hibernate mappings from *.hbm.xml* files. In Example 12-4 the plug-in configuration overrides the implementation for the hbm2ddl goal to read the mappings from the annotated class files. This is worthy of a bit more discussion.

> The Hibernate3 plug-in is under active development at Mojo. Don't forget to check the project's web site for updates.

The implementation property is somewhat special. It refers to the way in which the Hibernate3 plug-in derives Hibernate mapping information. There are four choices: configuration scans your source directories for *.hbm.xml* mapping files; annotation configuration scans your compiled classes for Hibernate Annotations; jdbcconfiguration uses reverse engineering to generate Hibernate mappings directly from an existing database. jpaconfiguration is similar to annotationconfiguration with the exception that it will look for a *persistence.xml* and not a *hibernate.cfg.xml* configuration file. Each goal has a default implementation selection depending on the context in which it is run. For example, the hbm2ddl goal defaults to configuration when it is running in JDK 1.4, and it defaults to annotationconfiguration when it is running in Java SE 5. For the full list of default implementations for Hibernate3 goals, see the Component Configuration[†] page on the Maven Hibernate3 project web site.

Generating Hibernate mapping documentation

The Maven Hibernate3 plug-in has a task that creates documentation for a set of Hibernate Mappings. This documentation resembles JavaDoc and details the structure of the database tables and the corresponding Java model objects. To generate this document, run the hbm2doc goal of the Hibernate3 plug-in after running install:

```
~/examples/ch12 $ mvn install
(output omitted)

~/examples/ch12 $ mvn hibernate:hbm2doc
[INFO] Scanning for projects...
[INFO] Searching repository for plugin with prefix: 'hibernate3'.
[INFO] ------------------------------------------------------------------------
---
[INFO] Building Harnessing Hibernate: Chapter Twelve: Maven
[INFO]    task-segment: [hibernate3:hbm2doc]
[INFO] ------------------------------------------------------------------------
---
[INFO] [hibernate3:hbm2doc]
[INFO] using annotationconfiguration task.
[INFO] Configuration XML file loaded: file:/Users/tobrien/svnw/hibernate-book/cu
rrent/examples/ch12/src/main/resources/hibernate.cfg.xml
[INFO] src/main/resources/database.properties not found within the project. Tryi
```

[†] *http://mojo.codehaus.org/maven-hibernate3/hibernate3-maven-plugin/components.html*

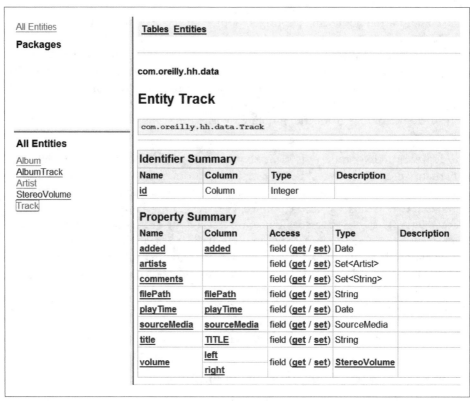

Figure 12-5. Entity documentation for Track produced by hbm2doc

```
ng absolute path.
[INFO] No hibernate properties file loaded.
[INFO] -------------------------------------------------------------------------
[INFO] BUILD SUCCESSFUL
[INFO] -------------------------------------------------------------------------
```

After the `hbm2doc` goal is completed, there will be an HTML document in *target/hiber nate3/javadoc/index.html*. Open this page in a browser and you will see a set of HTML documents that detail the Hibernate mapping. You can browse the Hibernate mappings from the database table perspective or the entity perspective. The entity perspective shown in Figure 12-5 allows you to see which tables are related to specific entity objects, and the table perspective shown in Figure 12-6 allows you to click on a database table and see which entity object maps to a specific table.

Becoming a Maven Maven

Maven will save you time. It will, I promise. If you adopt Maven with the right approach, you won't have to worry about maintaining someone's idea of a clever (read:

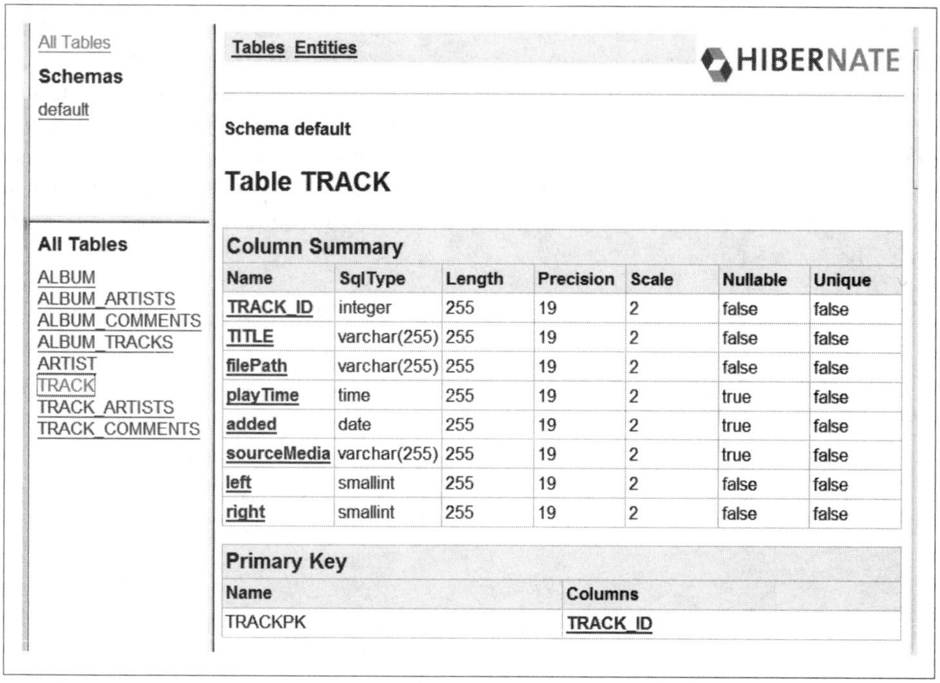

All Tables
Schemas
default

All Tables
ALBUM
ALBUM_ARTISTS
ALBUM_COMMENTS
ALBUM_TRACKS
ARTIST
TRACK
TRACK_ARTISTS
TRACK_COMMENTS

Tables Entities

HIBERNATE

Schema default

Table TRACK

Column Summary

Name	SqlType	Length	Precision	Scale	Nullable	Unique
TRACK_ID	integer	255	19	2	false	false
TITLE	varchar(255)	255	19	2	false	false
filePath	varchar(255)	255	19	2	false	false
playTime	time	255	19	2	true	false
added	date	255	19	2	true	false
sourceMedia	varchar(255)	255	19	2	true	false
left	smallint	255	19	2	false	false
right	smallint	255	19	2	false	false

Primary Key

Name	Columns
TRACKPK	TRACK_ID

Figure 12-6. Table documentation for TRACK produced by hbm2doc

over-engineered) procedural build system. But, as with any technology, Maven has some remaining issues: the documentation is still a bit rough, and there are plug-ins (like the Hibernate3 plug-in) which are not yet fully documented.

No technology is easy to introduce to a team, especially not one that makes assumptions about things like build structure or database design. I've seen teams reject Hibernate on the grounds that Hibernate collection mappings would violate the standards of a database administrator. I've seen organizations reject Hibernate because it doesn't create SQL that is up to the standards of the development team. I've dealt with very abstract criticism of Hibernate that sounded like it came from a modern art critic ("Relational databases are an outmoded construct"). Maven is no stranger to similar irrational objections. There are those among us who, for whatever reason, don't want to use time-saving technologies that might require them to adopt a standard. If you decide to adopt Maven as a build tool, make sure that everyone is on board with the idea of a declarative build before starting a migration to it.

> If the Mojo Hibernate3 plug-in documentation is frustrating you, blame Tim. He's working with the Mojo maintainer to improve that plug-in right now. Hopefully, by the time you read this, that plug-in will be fully documented. If not, feel free to send him hate mail.

In the next chapter I'm going to introduce another technology that provides a set of standards and conventions that will save you even more time. You've just started to see how Maven can take care of the build while you sit back and relax. Chapter 13 will show you how the Spring Framework takes most of the coding out of using Hibernate. There's a danger to all of this time saving technology—you are going to run out of tedious things to do while procrastinating. With Maven making the build effortless and Spring making Hibernate effortless, there's a good chance your boss might find out just how easy your job is and start piling on the work. If you are worried about running out of tedious things to do like managing builds or writing cookie-cutter code, I'd suggest ignoring both this chapter and the next. On the other hand, you could adopt Maven and Spring and use the extra time to take more breaks, go home early, or just read more online books at Safari.

## CHAPTER 13

Put a Spring in your Step: Hibernate with Spring

What Is Spring?

If you've been paying attention to Java programming over the last few years, you've probably heard of the Spring Framework. The Spring Framework is an *Inversion of Control* (IoC) container with a number of additional integrated features and modules. To some it is just an IoC container; to others it is an entire platform for application development. (We will expand on what is meant in the next section.)

Created by Rod Johnson in 2000, Spring rose to prominence as an alternative to Enterprise Java Beans (EJBs). Between 2000 and 2004, Sun Microsystems released a series of (somewhat terrible) specifications for EJBs. EJBs were difficult to understand, *develop*, and deploy without writing volumes of repetitive code and/or using proprietary tools to shield yourself from the underlying technology. Rod's seminal text, *Expert One-on-One J2EE Design and Development*, published by WROX in 2002, introduced a large number of developers to the idea of replacing EJBs with a simple IoC container and a number of APIs that served to isolate your programs from the rougher edges in Sun's APIs. Instead of interacting directly with the JDBC, JMS, or the JTA APIs, you could use templates and helpers within Spring. While Sun's core enterprise APIs are still important to know, a side-effect of using Spring was to lessen the choke-hold Sun had on defining and proposing new libraries and applications. Instead of programming to JDBC or JNDI directly, you could write your program to operate within Spring's container which was relatively agnostic about what underlying technology you might choose to implement persistence or messaging or whatever you were trying to do. Spring wasn't the only project to try to break through Sun's monopoly on setting standards in the Java space, but it has unarguably been the most successful.

You might write a few of your persistence layer objects to interact with JDBC directly, but you also might choose to implement a few using some custom proprietary code from Oracle, and you may write the rest using Hibernate. Spring enables this choice by providing an agnostic IoC container and a collection of useful abstractions. The discussion surrounding enterprise development no longer revolves around Sun and the various standards produced by the Java Community Process (JCP); instead, Spring has encouraged a proliferation of choice by providing a common "bus" to which most new projects can build. Look at Spring's integration with web frameworks for an example: Wicket, Struts 2 (was WebWork), Stripes, GWT, and Tapestry all provide first-class Spring integration, and Spring's documentation details integration with JavaServer Faces, Tapestry, and WebWork. Spring provides out-of-the-box integration for various Object Relational Mapping frameworks, including Hibernate, JDO, Oracle TopLink, iBatis SQL Maps, and JPA. Spring is the platform that enables a "freedom of choice" for implementation, and almost every new open source library or project must, in some way, integrate with the Spring Framework to become relevant to the large audience of developers who use it. The consensus among many is that while Sun might tell you that Java is a "platform," it is really just a language—Spring is the real platform. After you read this chapter, you'll have an idea of how Spring takes much of the work out of using Hibernate.

What is inversion of control?

There's no single definition of IoC, but a central concept is *Dependency Injection*. From Wikipedia:

> ...a pattern in which responsibility for object creation and object linking is removed from [the objects] and transferred to a factory.

Spring, the lightweight container, assumes responsibility for wiring together a set of components, and injects dependencies either via JavaBean properties or constructor arguments. Using Spring you develop a series of simple pieces, and then you tell Spring how to wire them together to create a larger system. This comes in very handy if your architecture relies on reusable "components." In this chapter, our Data Access Objects (DAOs) are implemented as components (or beans) in a Spring Application Context and our example classes depend on these components as bean properties. If we wanted to reuse our DAOs in another system such as a command-line utility or a web application, those systems would depend on the same components as bean properties, and Spring would take responsibility for wiring our components together based on an XML description of our program's construction.

Spring encourages reusability by taking on the responsibility of gluing together a set of focused components. Your DAOs don't care what they are connected to or what components are using them; they are focused solely on providing an interface to whatever component depends on them. If you are interested in a longer description of both Dependency Injection and Inversion of Control, you should read Martin Fowler's *Inversion of Control Containers and the Dependency Injection Pattern*[*].

---

[*] *http://martinfowler.com/articles/injection.html*

Combining Spring and Hibernate

Now that you know what Spring is all about, let's get back to Hibernate. This chapter focuses on the DAO pattern, transaction abstractions, and helpers provided by the Spring Framework.

What can you expect from this chapter? While using Spring with Hibernate is straightforward, there are a few steps we need to take before we can really take advantage of Spring's Hibernate integration. First, because Spring is an IoC container, we need to modify the examples from the previous chapters and create objects to "wire together." We'll be exploring the DAO pattern in the next section. After we've created one, we will modify our current set of examples to implement a common interface Test to which we will apply a Transactional annotation. Then we will create a Spring application context by writing an XML document which tells Spring what objects to create and what objects to wire together. Finally, we will write a command-line program that loads our Spring application context and starts an example program.

Adding the Spring framework as a project dependency

> Enough with this introduction. Let's get to the code.

To use Spring in the example project, we'll need to add another dependency to the build. Open up *build.xml* and add the dependency highlighted in bold in Example 13-1.

Example 13-1. Adding Spring as a dependency

```
<artifact:dependencies pathId="dependency.class.path">
  <dependency groupId="hsqldb" artifactId="hsqldb" version="1.8.0.7"/>
  <dependency groupId="org.hibernate" artifactId="hibernate" version="3.2.4.sp1">
    <exclusion groupId="javax.transaction" artifactId="jta" />
  </dependency>
  <dependency groupId="org.hibernate" artifactId="hibernate-tools" version="3.2.0.
beta9a" />
  <dependency groupId="org.hibernate" artifactId="hibernate-annotations" version="
3.3.0.ga" />
  <dependency groupId="org.hibernate" artifactId="hibernate-commons-annotations" v
ersion="3.3.0.ga" />
  <dependency groupId="org.apache.geronimo.specs" artifactId="geronimo-jta_1.1_spe
c" version="1.1" />
  <dependency groupId="log4j" artifactId="log4j" version="1.2.14" />
  <dependency groupId="org.springframework" artifactId="spring" version="2.5"/>
</artifact:dependencies>
```

Great—now when we run the Ant build, we're going to notice that the Maven Ant task will download *spring-2.5.jar* from one of the Maven repositories.

Writing a Data Access Object

A Data Access Object (DAO) is a common pattern which helps to isolate your application's code from the code that accesses and manipulates records in a database. In a larger architecture, a DAO provides a boundary between two separate architectural layers. We are introducing DAO objects in the context of the Spring Framework to give you a sense of how you can fit Hibernate into an overall system architecture, and we are introducing DAO objects because they represent a common pattern you will encounter in any real-world system that needs to interact with a database.

What is a Data Access Object?

I'm always surprised when an author writes a twenty page description of the DAO pattern, its advantages, and its disadvantages. If you read the Sun J2EE blueprint, you'll read a thick document explaining DAO creation patterns using factories and how the DAO pattern fits into the larger approach to enterprise application development. We're going to skip much of the formality and just sum up the DAO pattern in two simple bullet points. The DAO pattern:

- Consolidates all persistence operations (create, read, update, delete) into a single interface usually organized by table or object type.
- Provides one or more swappable implementations of this interface which can use any number of different persistence APIs and underlying storage media.

Or, if you are looking for an even more compact definition: "DAOs hide all the gory details of persistence behind an interface."

When you use an Object/Relational Mapping (ORM) framework such as Hibernate, you are usually approaching the database as a set of objects. The examples in this book revolve around three objects: Artist, Album, and Track, and the DAO objects we are going to create mirror these three objects: ArtistDAO, AlbumDAO, and TrackDAO. Figure 13-1 shows a class diagram of the ArtistDAO we will be creating shortly.

In this diagram, your application's logic is represented as the class YourClass. Your Class would have a reference to an ArtistDAO interface which provides four simple methods:

Artist persist(Artist artist)
    Saves the state of an Artist object to the database. This method will insert a new row or update an existing row depending on the state of the artist parameter. The contract for this method is to check the id property of the artist parameter. If the id property is null, insert a new row into the ARTIST table, and if the id property is not null, update the matching row in the database. This method returns a persisted Artist object; in other words, if you pass this method an Artist object with a null id property, it will create a new row in the database, and return an Artist

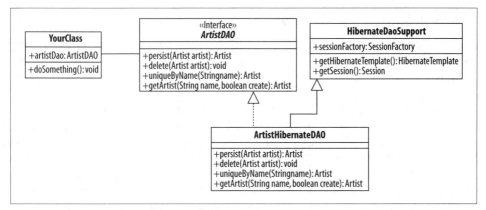

Figure 13-1. Isolating application and persistence code with a Data Access Object

object with a non-`null` `id` property containing the identifier of the newly inserted row.

`void delete(Artist artist)`
Deletes the matching row from the database.

`Artist uniqueByName(String name)`
Returns a single `Artist` with a `name` property equal to the `name` parameter.

`Artist getArtist(String name, boolean create)`
Finds the `Artist` with a matching `name` property. If the `create` parameter is `true`, and a matching `Artist` cannot be found, this method will create and persist a new `Artist` with the supplied `name` parameter.

While `YourClass` is coded to the `ArtistDAO` interface, you are really invoking an implementation of the `ArtistDAO` interface—`ArtistHibernateDAO`. This implementation of `ArtistDAO` extends Spring's `HibernateDaoSupport` class which contains all the necessary magic to make writing Hibernate code as painless as possible. Using this `HibernateDao Support`, you can avoid writing all of the exception handling, transaction management, and session management code that you've seen in the previous chapters. In fact, I think you'll be surprised (and maybe a bit disappointed) at how easy it is to Hibernate in Spring.

> This book uses the following naming convention. A DAO interface is defined in the `com.oreilly.hh.dao` package, and its class name is the name of the related object with "DAO" appended (for example, `Artist DAO`). The Hibernate-specific implementation of this interface is named `ArtistHibernateDAO` and is placed in the `com.oreilly.hh.dao.hibernate` package.

Why would I want to use a DAO?

There are a few reasons, but first and foremost is increased flexibility. Since you are coding to an interface, you can easily swap in a new implementation if you need to use a different O/R mapping service or storage medium. In the introduction I mentioned that Spring provides an integration layer that can work with any number of object-relational mapping technologies, from iBatis SQL Maps to Oracle's TopLink to Hibernate, but Spring also provides a rich set of abstractions that make executing SQL with JDBC straightforward. In most of the applications with which I've worked, Hibernate provided most of the persistence logic, but it didn't solve every problem. There are times when you need to execute SQL directly, and Spring provides classes like `JDBCTemplate` to make this very easy. When you put a DAO interface between your application's logic and the persistence layer, you've made it easier to swap in other implementations for a particular DAO class or method when the need arises.

This flexibility and isolation goes both ways—it is easier to replace both the implementation of a specific DAO class, and it is easier to reuse your persistence layer when you need to rewrite or upgrade your application logic. Take a situation many readers of this book find themselves in right now: your team has been maintaining a legacy system written in Struts 1.*x*, and you want to upgrade the application to Stripes or Struts 2. If the persistence code is tightly coupled to the web framework code, you will likely find it impossible to rewrite one without rewriting the other.

Following the DAO pattern might seem unnecessary for a simple application, but more often than not, you have a need to reuse persistence code across multiple projects. Creating a set of DAO objects might seem contrary to the agile orthodoxy, but it is an investment in complexity that tends to pay off over time. If your system is anything more than a simple "Hello World" example, you'll probably want to take some time to separate your persistence logic from your application.

Writing the ArtistDAO interface

Without delay, let's jump into writing the code for this example. The first thing we need to do is write the `ArtistDAO` interface. Create an interface in the `com.oreilly.hh.dao` package named `ArtistDAO` and put the code shown in Example 13-2 in this new interface.

Example 13-2. The ArtistDAO interface

```
package com.oreilly.hh.dao;

import com.oreilly.hh.data.Artist;

/**
 * Provides persistence operations for the Artist object
 */
public interface ArtistDAO {
```

```
/**
 * Persist an Artist instance (create or update)
 * depending on the value of the id
 */
public Artist persist(Artist artist);

/**
 * Remove an Artist from the database
 */
public void delete(Artist artist);

/**
 * Return an Artist that matches the name argument
 */
public Artist uniqueByName(String name);

/**
 * Returns the matching Artist object.   If the
 * create parameter is true, this method will
 * insert a new Artist and return the newly created
 * Artist object.
 */
public Artist getArtist(String name, boolean create);
}
```

All right, that was relatively easy; all we're talking about here is a few simple methods to implement. Let's take a look at how we implement this logic using the `Hibernate DaoSupport` class.

Implementing the ArtistDAO interface

The next step is to write an implementation for the `ArtistDAO`. We are going to write an `ArtistHibernateDAO` which implements the `ArtistDAO` interface and extends Spring's `HibernateDaoSupport` class. `HibernateDaoSupport` provides access to your Hibernate `Session` object and it also provides access to a `HibernateTemplate` which can be used to simplify almost any operation you can accomplish with the Hibernate `Session` object. To implement `ArtistDAO`, create a new class in the `com.oreilly.hh.dao.hibernate` package to contain the Hibernate-specific implementation of `ArtistDAO` shown in Example 13-3.

Example 13-3. Implementing the ArtistDAO interface

```
package com.oreilly.hh.dao.hibernate;

import java.util.HashSet;

import org.apache.log4j.Logger;
import org.hibernate.Query;
import org.springframework.orm.hibernate3.support.HibernateDaoSupport;

import com.oreilly.hh.dao.ArtistDAO;
import com.oreilly.hh.data.Artist;
```

```
import com.oreilly.hh.data.Track;

/**
 * Hibernate-specific implementation of the ArtistDAO interface. This class
 * extends the Spring-specific HibernateDaoSupport to provide access to
 * the SessionFactory and the HibernateTemplate.
 */
public class ArtistHibernateDAO extends HibernateDaoSupport
                                implements ArtistDAO {

  private static Logger log =
    Logger.getLogger(ArtistHibernateDAO.class);

  /* (non-Javadoc)
   * @see com.oreilly.hh.dao.ArtistDAO#persist(com.oreilly.hh.data.Artist)
   */
  public Artist persist(Artist artist) { ❶
    return (Artist) getHibernateTemplate().merge(artist);
  }

  /* (non-Javadoc)
   * @see com.oreilly.hh.dao.ArtistDAO#delete(com.oreilly.hh.data.Artist)
   */
  public void delete(Artist artist) { ❷
    getHibernateTemplate().delete(artist);
  }

  /* (non-Javadoc)
   * @see com.oreilly.hh.dao.ArtistDAO#uniqueByName(java.lang.String)
   */
  public Artist uniqueByName(final String name) { ❸
    return (Artist) getHibernateTemplate().execute(new HibernateCallback() {
      public Object doInHibernate(Session session) {
        Query query = getSession().getNamedQuery("com.oreilly.hh.artistByName");
        query.setString("name", name);
        return (Artist) query.uniqueResult();
      }
    });
  }

  /* (non-Javadoc)
   * @see com.oreilly.hh.dao.ArtistDAO#getArtist(java.lang.String, boolean)
   */
  public Artist getArtist(String name, boolean create) { ❹
    Artist found = uniqueByName( name );
    if (found == null && create) {
      found = new Artist(name, new HashSet<Track>(), null);
      found = persist(found);
    }
    if (found != null && found.getActualArtist() != null) {
      return found.getActualArtist();
    }
    return found;
  }
}
```

---

❶ This `persist()` method simply calls out to the `merge()` method of `HibernateTemplate`. The implementation of `merge()` looks at the `id` property of the *artist* parameter. If the `id` is `null`, `merge()` inserts a new row into the `ARTIST` table, and returns a new instance of `Artist` that has a populated `id` property. If the id is not `null`, `merge()` finds the matching row and updates it with the contents of the *artist* parameter.

❷ `delete()` simply passes the artist parameter to the `delete()` method in `HibernateTemplate`. This method expects an object with a non-`null` `id` and deletes the corresponding row in the `ARTIST` table.

❸ `uniqueByName()` is where things start to get more interesting. This is the first time in this class that we've referenced the `Session` object we've been using throughout this entire book. We're using `getSession()` to retrieve a `NamedQuery`. This named `Query` is defined in the `Artist` class using the `@NamedQuery` annotation. We then proceed to set the named parameter *name* and retrieve a unique result. If there is no matching `Artist` in the database, `uniqueResult()` returns `null`. I'll bet you also noticed that we're using an anonymous instance of `HibernateCallback` and passing that to the `HibernateTemplate` object. For more information about `HibernateCallback`, see "How do I do that?" later in this chapter.

❹ The `getArtist()` method really just rolls up calls to the other methods in `Artist` `DAO`. This method attempts to retrieve an `Artist` by name by calling `uniqueByName()`. If no `Artist` is found and the create parameter is `true`, `getArtist()` creates a new instance of `Artist` with a `null` id and calls `persist()`. If no matching `Artist` is found and create is `false`, the method will return `null`. If a found or newly created `Artist` has a non-`null` `actualArtist` property, this method will return the value of `artist.getActualArtist()`. (The purpose of this step is explained in "Reflexive Associations" in Chapter 5.)

What HibernateDaoSupport provides

`HibernateDaoSupport` gives us a hook to the `SessionFactory` without having to know anything about how the Hibernate environment was created or configured. When we subclass `HibernateDaoSupport` our class then has access to a Hibernate `Session` via `getSession()` and a `HibernateTemplate` via `getHibernateTemplate()`. You already know what you can do with a Hibernate `Session` object (that's why you read the previous 10 chapters). The interesting bits of the Spring/Hibernate integration are supplied by the `HibernateTemplate` class. Let's delve into the details of this class.

To quote from the JavaDoc for `HibernateTemplate`: "This class can be considered [an] alternative to working with the raw Hibernate 3 Session API." `HibernateTemplate` simplifies tasks that would otherwise be accomplished using the `Session` object, and it also translates `HibernateException`s to more general `DataAccessException`s. You use `HibernateTemplate` in one of two ways: you can call a set of simple helper functions such as `load()`, `save()`, `delete()`, or you can execute a `HibernateCallback` instance using the execute() method. The most common way you'll find yourself using HibernateTemplate is through the simple helper functions—you only need to create a HibernateCallback object when you want to execute some Hibernate-specific code within the HibernateTemplate.

What is a DataAccessException? When we introduced the DAO pattern, it was an attempt to shield application code from the specifics of any one persistence API or library. It wouldn't help us if our technology-neutral DAO threw a Hibernate-specific ObjectNotFoundException, so HibernateTemplate is responsible for handling any Hibernate-specific exceptions which may occure inside it. The Stripes API provides a simple way to tolerate such implementation-specific exceptions by wrapping them in its own generalized data access exceptions.

HibernateTemplate and HibernateCallback are the real workhorses that will help us avoid writing lines and lines of unnecessary Java code. Let's use them both to reimplement the examples from the previous chapters.

How do I do that?

Before we use HibernateTemplate and HibernateCallback we need to run through a quick survey of the methods available to us.

HibernateTemplate provides a number of simple convenience methods that can turn multiple lines of direct Hibernate Session API code into simple one-liners. Let's take a look at some examples of convenience methods to simplify querying a database table. Example 13-4 shows some examples of querying and finding objects.

Example 13-4. HibernateTemplate's find() helpers

```
HibernateTemplate tmpl = getHibernateTemplate();

// All of these lines Find Artist with name 'Pavement'
List artists = tmpl.find("from com.oreilly.hh.data.Artist a " +
                         "  where a.name = 'Pavement'"); ❶

String name = "Pavement";
List artists = tmpl.find("from com.oreilly.hh.data.Artist a " +
                         "  where a.name = ?", name); ❷

List artists = tmpl.findByNamedParam("from com.oreilly.hh.data.Artist a " +
                                     "  where a.name = :name", "name", name); ❸

// Assuming that there is a NamedQuery annotation "Artist.byName" on the
// Artist class
List artists = tmpl.findByNamedQuery("Artist.byName", name); ❹

Artist artist = new Artist();
artist.setName("Pavement");
List artists = tmpl.findByExample(artist); ❺

// If we want to iterate through the result
```

```
Iterator artists = tmpl.iterate("from com.oreilly.hh.data.Artist " +
                        "  where a.name = ?", name); ❻

// The following lines find all Artists
List artists = tmpl.find("from com.oreilly.hh.data.Artist"); ❼
List artists = tmpl.loadAll(Artist.class);
```

The find methods are relatively straightforward:

❶   There is a simple find( ) that takes an HQL query with no parameters.

❷   This version of the method takes an HQL query and a single additional parameter. A similar version takes a query and an array of additional parameters: List find (String hql, Object[] params). These support the use of unnamed query parameters, but as we discussed in Chapter 3, there are better ways of writing queries.

❸   The findByNamedParameter( ) method can handle queries with named parameters.

❹   There is a findByNamedQuery( ) that allows you to quickly invoke a predefined HQL query, in this case named Artist.byName.

❺   You can tie into Hibernate's query-by-example capabilities using findByExample( ).

❻   If you want to iterate through some results, you can call the iterate( ) method. When you call iterate( ), Hibernate retrieves all of the IDs for matching rows and initializes elements as you iterate through the returned Iterator.

❼   Lastly, if you just want to load all the rows from a given table, you can call find( ) or loadAll( ).

> As discussed in "Better Ways to Build Queries" in Chapter 3, named queries are a good way to keep the query definitions out of your DAO code. If you are using Annotations, you define named queries using the @NamedQuery annotation. See Chapter 7 for more details on this annotation.

If we already know the value of the ID for a particular persistent object, HibernateTemplate provides helper methods for loading an object by an ID, as shown in Example 13-5.

Example 13-5. Loading objects with HibernateTemplate
```
// Identifier of Artist to load
Integer id = 1;

// Load an Artist object, return persistent Artist object
Artist artist = getHibernateTemplate().load(Artist.class, id);

// Populate the object passed in as a parameter.  Using the
// object's type to specify the class
```

```
Artist artist = new Artist();
getHibernateTemplate().load(artist, id);
```

In the first example, we call the load( ) function with a Class and a Serializable ID value. Hibernate will then retrieve the row from the database and return an instance of the requested object. Instead of a Class object, you can also pass an object instance, Hibernate will use the type of the parameter to determine the class to retrieve.

We've examined the helpers on HibernateTemplate for querying and the helpers for loading. What about modifying rows in the database? Example 13-6 shows some examples that insert or update rows in the database.

Example 13-6. Saving and updating with HibernateTemplate

```
// Persist a new instance in the database
Artist a  = new Artist();
a.setName("Fischerspooner");
getHibernateTemplate().save(a);

// Load, modify, update a row in the database
Artist a = getHibernateTemplate().load(Artist.class, 1);
a.setName("Milli Vanilli");
getHibernateTemplate().update(a);

// Either insert or update depending on the identifier
// of the object; associate resulting object with Session
Artist a = getHibernateTemplate().merge(a);
```

save( ) and update( ) are straightforward; both of these methods correspond to the similarly named methods on the Hibernate Session object. save( ) generates a new ID and inserts a new row in the table, and update( ) updates the matching row in the table. merge( ) is a bit more flexible: it examines the id of the parameter and calls either save( ) or update( ) depending on whether the ID is null.

You can also execute any arbitrary code that uses a Hibernate Session with a HibernateCallback. Before I try to explain exactly what this means, let's take a look at Example 13-7.

Example 13-7. Writing a HibernateCallback

```
final String name = "Pavement";

Artist artist = (Artist) getHibernateTemplate().execute(new HibernateCallback() {
  public Object doInHibernate(Session session) {
    Criteria criteria = session.createCriteria(Artist.class);
    criteria.add(Restrictions.like("name", name));
    return criteria.uniqueResult();
  }
});
```

So what exactly is happening here? This example instantiates an anonymous inner class, which implements the HibernateCallback interface and passes it to the execute( ) method in HibernateTemplate. The HibernateCallback interface defines a single method `doInHibernate( )`, which is executed with a Hibernate `Session`. The body of this method (as implemented in our anonymous inner class) uses the Hibernate `Criteria` API to generate a query that retrieves an `Artist` by name.

Why would we use the callback method when we could have easily obtained a reference to the Hibernate `Session` and created the same `Criteria` object? Even though we can access the `Session` object directly in `HibernateDaoSupport` using the `getSession( )` method, we want to avoid direct calls to the Hibernate API because we don't want to throw any Hibernate-specific exceptions (not even a `RuntimeException`). Remember your application is accessing this DAO via an interface, and it doesn't know or care about the Hibernate-specific `ObjectNotFoundException` or about an exception in your HQL. Instead of accessing the `Session` object directly with `getSession( )`, you can and should shield the rest of your application from such gory plumbing details by using a `HibernateCallback` to run any Hibernate API calls within the `HibernateTemplate`.

Where are the other DAOs?

Because they're all very similar, it's not worth wasting paper listing and talking about the others. You wouldn't want to type in all that code anyway, so download the code examples if you'd like to look at them.

Creating an Application Context

When we introduced Spring we discussed how it would assume responsibility for creating and connecting the components in our application. For Spring to do this, we need to tell it about the various components (which Spring calls *beans*) in our system and how they are connected to each other. We do this using an XML document that describes the class of each bean, assigns it an ID, and establishes its relationships to other beans. Why the ID? In this context, an ID is a unique logical name for the bean, which is what you use to express relationships with other beans, and to request beans at runtime. In our example Spring configuration file we use logical names such as `artist Dao` and `albumDao.` Each ID refers to a single component defined in the file.

This XML document is then used by Spring to create an `ApplicationContext` object from which we can retrieve our components by name. Figure 13-2 is a diagram of our application's `ApplicationContext`.

From Figure 13-2 you can see that we have three test components that are connected to three DAO objects, and the DAO objects all have a reference to the `sessionFactory` object which is responsible for creating a Hibernate `Session` object and connecting to the database. This application is described by the Spring configuration file shown in Example 13-8, which you should name *applicationContext.xml* and place in the *src* directory.

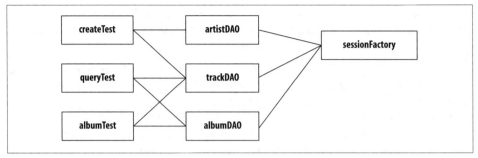

Figure 13-2. Our Spring application context

Example 13-8. Spring applicationContext.xml

```xml
<?xml version="1.0" encoding="UTF-8"?>
<beans xmlns="http://www.springframework.org/schema/beans"
       xmlns:xsi="http://www.w3.org/2001/XMLSchema-instance"
       xmlns:tx="http://www.springframework.org/schema/tx"
       xsi:schemaLocation=
         http://www.springframework.org/schema/beans http://www.springframework.
org/schema/beans/spring-beans-2.0.xsd
         http://www.springframework.org/schema/tx http://www.springframework.org
/schema/tx/spring-tx-2.0.xsd"
       default-lazy-init="true"> ❶
  <bean id="sessionFactory" ❷
        class="org.springframework.orm.hibernate3.annotation.AnnotationSessionFa
ctoryBean">
     <property name="annotatedClasses"> ❸
       <list>
         <value>com.oreilly.hh.data.Album</value>
         <value>com.oreilly.hh.data.AlbumTrack</value>
         <value>com.oreilly.hh.data.Artist</value>
         <value>com.oreilly.hh.data.StereoVolume</value>
         <value>com.oreilly.hh.data.Track</value>
       </list>
     </property>
     <property name="hibernateProperties"> ❹
       <props>
         <prop key="hibernate.show_sql">false</prop>
         <prop key="hibernate.format_sql">true</prop>
         <prop key="hibernate.transaction.factory_class">org.hibernate.transaction
.JDBCTransactionFactory</prop>
         <prop key="hibernate.dialect">org.hibernate.dialect.HSQLDialect
</prop>
         <prop key="hibernate.connection.pool_size">0</prop>
         <prop key="hibernate.connection.driver_class">org.hsqldb.jdbcDriver</prop
>
         <prop key="hibernate.connection.url">jdbc:hsqldb:data/music;shutdo
wn=true</prop>
         <prop key="hibernate.connection.username">sa</prop>
         <prop key="hibernate.connection.password"></prop>
       </props>
     </property>
  </bean>
```

```
<!-- enable the configuration of transactional behavior based on annotations --
>
<tx:annotation-driven transaction-manager="transactionManager"/> ❺
<bean id="transactionManager"
      class="org.springframework.orm.hibernate3.HibernateTransactionManager">
  <property name="sessionFactory">
    <ref local="sessionFactory"/>
  </property>
</bean>

<bean class="org.springframework.beans.factory.annotation.RequiredAnnotationBean
PostProcessor"/> ❻

<!-- Define our Data Access beans -->
<bean id="albumDAO" class="com.oreilly.hh.dao.hibernate.AlbumHibernateDAO"> ❼
  <property name="sessionFactory" ref="sessionFactory"/>
</bean>

<bean id="artistDAO" class="com.oreilly.hh.dao.hibernate.ArtistHibernateDAO">
  <property name="sessionFactory" ref="sessionFactory"/>
</bean>

<bean id="trackDAO" class="com.oreilly.hh.dao.hibernate.TrackHibernateDAO">
  <property name="sessionFactory" ref="sessionFactory"/>
</bean>

<!-- Define our Test beans -->
<bean id="createTest" class="com.oreilly.hh.CreateTest"> ❽
  <property name="trackDAO" ref="trackDAO"/>
  <property name="artistDAO" ref="artistDAO"/>
</bean>

<bean id="queryTest" class="com.oreilly.hh.QueryTest">
  <property name="trackDAO" ref="trackDAO"/>
</bean>

<bean id="albumTest" class="com.oreilly.hh.AlbumTest">
  <property name="albumDAO" ref="albumDAO"/>
  <property name="artistDAO" ref="artistDAO"/>
  <property name="trackDAO" ref="trackDAO"/>
</bean>
</beans>
```

All right, that was quite a bit of XML to read through, wasn't it? There are a lot of interesting things going on in this file, so let's go over each section with a fine-toothed comb:

❶   The top-level element is beans, and we have to declare some important *namespaces* for Spring to work properly. The *http://www.springframework.org/schema/beans* namespace is the default namespace that describes the elements for declaring beans, and the *http://www.springframework.org/schema/tx* namespace is used to define the annotation-driven transaction configuration, described later in this chapter. The `default-lazy-init` attribute controls the default behavior of the Spring IoC container: if this default setting is `true`, Spring will instantiate components only when they are requested. If `default-lazy-init` is set to `false`, Spring will instantiate beans during the initialization of the `ApplicationContext`.

❷ `sessionFactory` is a bean that takes care of generating `Session` objects and dealing with connections to a JDBC `DataSource`. In general, the `sessionFactory` would work with a `DataSource`, and we would configure a Commons DBCP or C3P0 connection pool along side our `SessionFactory` in the *applicationContext.xml*. To keep this example contained, the `sessionFactory` contains properties that configure the JDBC connection directly.

❸ As in the *hibernate.cfg.xml* file, we are defining all of the annotated classes that Hibernate needs to process.

❹ The `hibernateProperties` element configures Hibernate. We'll delve into more of the details of this section in "Hibernate configuration properties" later in this chapter.

❺ The transactional annotation configuration is described in detail in "Transactions: the test interface" later in this chapter. The `tx:annotation-driven` element and the definition of the `transactionManager` allow us to use the `Transactional` annotation to define the scope and nature of any transactions in our application.

❻ The `RequiredAnnotationBeanPostProcessor` is an unnamed component; its presence activates the enforcement of the `Required` annotation on setter methods. If you put the `Required` attribute on the setter of a required bean property, Spring will validate that this property was set after initializing a bean. This is used in the test classes to make sure that Spring has configured our DAO dependencies.

❼ The DAO objects are all defined here: `albumDAO`, `artistDAO`, and `trackDAO`.

❽ The test beans are all defined here: `createTest`, `queryTest`, and `albumTest`.

Hibernate configuration properties

Taking a closer look at the `hibernateProperties` in Example 13-8, you will notice that there are a number of interesting configuration properties. Let's examine each of them:

`hibernate.connection.driver_class`, `hibernate.connection.url`, `hibernate.connection.username`, `hibernate.connection.password`
> These configuration properties take care of configuring the JDBC connection to the database. These properties should be familiar from previous chapters; the values in *applicationContext.xml* are the same as the values we used earlier in *hibernate.cfg.xml* and *hibernate.properties*.

`hibernate.connection.pool_size`
> This property sets the size of the internal Hibernate connection pool. Instead of using the Hibernate connection pool, you could also use Hibernate's built-in

support for Apache Commons DBCP or C3P0, both of which are good choices if you are deploying a production system. If this property is set to a nonzero value, Hibernate will attempt to recycle and reuse connections to the database.

This is an interesting case, because we're setting the pool_size to zero, because I want to turn off connection pooling for this example to making working with HSQLDB a little easier. HSQLDB expects a SHUTDOWN command when the last connection is terminated, and because I don't want to write and configure a special shutdown hook, I'm simply making sure that my JDBC Connection object is closed when I'm done with it.

`hibernate.dialect`

Here we set the Hibernate dialect. For a list of available dialects, see Appendix C.

`hibernate.transaction.factory_class`

In this example, we're using the JDBC driver to manage our transactions. In a more complex deployment environment using JTA we might configure this with `org.hibernate.transaction.JTATransactionFactory` if we were using container-managed transactions.

`hibernate.show_sql`, `hibernate.format_sql`

If show_sql is set to true, Hibernate will print out the SQL it is executing. This can be very helpful if you are trying to debug Spring and figure out how a specific mapping is trying to access the database table. If format_sql is true, the SQL statement is formatted; if format_sql is false, the SQL is printed on one line.

Putting It All Together

All of this Spring configuration is useless if we don't know how to create a Spring ApplicationContext and run our code. In this section, we're going to adapt the CreateTest, QueryTest, and AlbumTest classes used in previous examples to implement a Test interface rather than expecting them to be run from the command line directly, and create a TestRunner to execute these test objects from our Spring ApplicationContext.

Transactions: the test interface

Later in this chapter, we'll write a class named TestRunner which knows how to retrieve a bean from a Spring ApplicationContext, which is expected to implement the Test interface, and execute that bean's run( ) method. The beans it uses will be adaptations of the CreateTest, QueryTest, and AlbumTest classes from the previous chapters. To work in this new way, we'll have them each implement a common interface called Test, shown in Example 13-9.

Example 13-9. The Test interface

```
package com.oreilly.hh;
import org.springframework.transaction.annotation.Transactional;
```

```
/**
 * A common interface for our example classes.  We'll need this
 * because TestHarness needs to cast CreateTest, QueryTest, or
 * AlbumTest to a common interface after it retrieves the bean
 * from the Spring application context.
 */
public interface Test {
    /**
     * Runs a simple example
     */
    @Transactional(readOnly=false)
    public void run();
}
```

This Test interface serves as a common interface for use by TestRunner, and it also gives us a convenient method to annotate with the Transactional annotation. The Transactional annotation takes care of binding a Session to the current Thread, starting a transaction, and either committing the transaction if the method returns normally, or rolling it back if there is an exception.

For more information about the @Transactional annotation, please see Appendix D.

How do I activate the transactional annotation?

To turn on the processing of the Transactional annotation, we used this chunk of configuration in our *applicationContext.xml*:

```
<!-- enable the configuration of transactional behavior based on annotations -->
<tx:annotation-driven transaction-manager="transactionManager"/>
<bean id="transactionManager"
      class="org.springframework.orm.hibernate3.HibernateTransactionManager">
   <property name="sessionFactory">
     <ref local="sessionFactory"/>
   </property>
</bean>
```

The *tx:annotation-driven* element simply activates the Transactional annotation and points it to a PlatformTransactionManager. HibernateTransactionManager is an implementation of the Spring Framework's PlatformTransactionManager. It takes care of binding a Hibernate Session from the sessionFactory to the current Thread using SessionFactoryUtils. Since our DAO objects all extend HibernateDaoSupport and use the HibernateTemplate, these persistent objects are able to participate in transactions and obtain the same thread-bound Session object. This isn't just useful for dealing with transactions, it is essential when we're working with lazy associations.

The Transactional annotation ensures that the same Session will remain open and bound to the current Thread during the execution of the annotated method. Without this annotation, Hibernate would create a new Session for every operation that needed a Session, and you would be unable to fetch any associations of the objects you had retrieved using Hibernate.

Why is this? Let's back track a bit to topics we brought up in Chapter 5. Recall that in Hibernate 3, associations between mapped objects default to lazy loading. Unless you change this explicitly for a particular class or association, related objects are not retrieved from the database until you've traversed to a particular object. For example, if you retrieve an `Album` object from the database, the `List` of `AlbumTrack` objects is not retrieved until you call the `album.getAlbumTracks( )` method. To accomplish this, Hibernate does two things:

1. Hibernate returns a "proxy" object that stands in for the not-yet-loaded object. When you retrieve a `Track` object, the object returned is a `Track`, but associated collections such as `track.getArtists( )` are instances of `PersistentSet.`

2. A `PersistentSet` is something Hibernate manages, and you don't normally need to think much about it. What is pertinent to this discussion is that it is an implementation of `PersistentCollection` and it contains a reference to a `Session` object. In other words, that `PersistentSet` is involved in fetching the related `Artists` on an as-needed basis. You'll get a `Track` back, but you won't fetch any `Artist` objects until you call `track.getArtists( )`, and they need to come through the `Session`.

Fetching lazy associations only works if the `PersistentSet` is referencing an active `Session`. Without an open session, attempting to traverse a lazy association will throw an exception. In a web application, you might use something like Spring's `OpenSessionInViewFilter` to make sure you have a reference to a `Session` throughout a single request. In this application, we're relying on the `Transactional` annotation to make sure that all of the code in any `run( )` method implementation has access to the same Hibernate `Session` object.

Adapting CreateTest, QueryTest, and AlbumTest

Now that we've got our `Test` interface defined and set up to provide a stable transaction environment to its implementations, we can revise `CreateTest`, `QueryTest`, and `AlbumTest`. First is the adaptation of `CreateTest` shown in Example 13-10.

Example 13-10. CreateTest adapted for use in our Spring context

```
package com.oreilly.hh;

import java.sql.Time;
import java.util.*;
import com.oreilly.hh.dao.*;
import com.oreilly.hh.data.*;

/**
 * Create sample data, letting Hibernate persist it for us.
 */
public class CreateTest implements Test {

    private ArtistDAO artistDAO;
    private TrackDAO trackDAO;
```

```
/**
 * Utility method to associate an artist with a track
 */
private static void addTrackArtist(Track track, Artist artist) {
    track.getArtists().add(artist);
}

/* (non-Javadoc)
 * @see com.oreilly.hh.Test#run()
 */
public void run() {
    StereoVolume fullVolume = new StereoVolume();

    Track track = new Track("Russian Trance", "vol2/album610/track02.mp3",
            Time.valueOf("00:03:30"), new HashSet<Artist>(), new Date(),
            fullVolume, SourceMedia.CD, new HashSet<String>());
    addTrackArtist(track, artistDAO.getArtist("PPK", true));
    trackDAO.persist(track);
}

public ArtistDAO getArtistDAO() { return artistDAO; }
public void setArtistDAO(ArtistDAO artistDAO) {
    this.artistDAO = artistDAO;
}

public TrackDAO getTrackDAO() { return trackDAO; }
public void setTrackDAO(TrackDAO trackDAO) {
    this.trackDAO = trackDAO;
}
}
```

Notice that CreateTest has two private member variables, artistDAO and trackDAO, both of which are made visible with accessor methods as bean properties. Then we have a simple run() method, as mandated by the Test interface, which in this case creates an instance of Track, associates an Artist with the Track, and then persists the Track object with a call to trackDAO.makePersistent(). That's it—no try/catch/finally blocks and no mention of a transaction. We've offloaded almost everything to the Spring framework with the help of our DAO. Example 13-11 is an excerpt from *applicationContext.xml* in which an instance of this CreateTest class is created as a bean with the ID createTest, and the bean properties artistDAO and trackDAO are populated with references to the DAO beans.

Example 13-11. Configuring the createTest bean
```
<bean id="createTest" class="com.oreilly.hh.CreateTest">
  <property name="trackDAO" ref="trackDAO"/>
  <property name="artistDAO" ref="artistDAO"/>
</bean>
```

Compare this implementation of CreateTest to the original version in Example 3-3. You can hardly compare them. The non-Spring version of CreateTest had to take care of Session creation, transaction management, exception handling, and configuration.

The new version doesn't even mention the Session object. In fact, there's nothing Hibernate-specific in this latest CreateTest: the DAOs prevent our application logic from having to deal directly with the underlying persistence mechanism. In other words, once you get your mind around the Spring Framework and get it set up, it is an order of magnitude easier than working with Hibernate directly. See Example 13-12.

Example 13-12. QueryTest adapted for use with Spring

```
package com.oreilly.hh;

import java.sql.Time;
import java.util.List;
import org.apache.log4j.Logger;
import com.oreilly.hh.dao.TrackDAO;
import com.oreilly.hh.data.Track;

/**
 * Retrieve data as objects
 */
public class QueryTest implements Test {

    private static Logger log = Logger.getLogger(QueryTest.class);

    private TrackDAO trackDAO;

    public void run() {
        // Print the tracks that will fit in five minutes
        List<Track> tracks = trackDAO.tracksNoLongerThan(
            Time.valueOf("00:05:00"));
        for (Track track : tracks) {
            // For each track returned, print out the
            // title and the playTime
            log.info("Track: \"" + track.getTitle() + "\", "
                    + track.getPlayTime());
        }
    }

    public TrackDAO getTrackDAO() { return trackDAO; }
    public void setTrackDAO(TrackDAO trackDAO) {
        this.trackDAO = trackDAO;
    }
}
```

The reimplementation of QueryTest also defines a private member variable referencing the TrackDAO object, and the run() method invokes the method trackDAO.tracksNoLongerThan(), passing it a Java.sql.Time instance of 5 minutes. This code then loops through the results and prints out the Track's title and playTime properties using Log4J. See Example 13-13.

Example 13-13. Reimplementing AlbumTest

```
package com.oreilly.hh;

import java.sql.Time;
```

```
import java.util.*;
import org.apache.log4j.Logger;
import com.oreilly.hh.dao.*;
import com.oreilly.hh.data.*;

/**
 * Create sample album data, letting Hibernate persist it for us.
 */
public class AlbumTest implements Test {

    private static Logger log = Logger.getLogger( AlbumTest.class );

    private AlbumDAO albumDAO;  ❶
    private ArtistDAO artistDAO;
    private TrackDAO trackDAO;

    public void run() {
        // Retrieve (or create) an Artist matching this name
        Artist artist = artistDAO.getArtist("Martin L. Gore", true);  ❷

        // Create an instance of album, add the artist and persist it
        // to the database.
        Album album = new Album("Counterfeit e.p.", 1,
            new HashSet<Artist>(), new HashSet<String>(),
            new ArrayList<AlbumTrack>(5), new Date());
        album.getArtists().add(artist);
        album = albumDAO.persist(album);  ❸

        // Add two album tracks
        addAlbumTrack(album, "Compulsion", "vol1/album83/track01.mp3",
                    Time.valueOf("00:05:29"), artist, 1, 1);
        addAlbumTrack(album, "In a Manner of Speaking",
                    "vol1/album83/track02.mp3", Time.valueOf("00:04:21"),
                        artist, 1, 2);

        // persist the album
        album = albumDAO.persist( album );  ❹

        log.info(album);
    }

    /**
     * Quick and dirty helper method to handle repetitive portion of creating
     * album tracks. A real implementation would have much more flexibility.
     */
    private void addAlbumTrack(Album album, String title, String file,
                                Time length, Artist artist, int disc,
                                int positionOnDisc) {
        // Create a new Track object and add the artist
        Track track = new Track(title, file, length, new HashSet<Artist>(),
                                new Date(), new StereoVolume(), SourceMedia.CD,
                                new HashSet<String>());
        track.getArtists().add(artist);

        // Persist the track to the database
```

```
    track = trackDAO.persist(track);

    // Add a new instance of  AlbumTrack with the persisted
    // album and track objects
    album.getTracks().add(new AlbumTrack(track, disc, positionOnDisc));
  }

public AlbumDAO getAlbumDAO() { return albumDAO; }
public void setAlbumDAO(AlbumDAO albumDAO) {
  this.albumDAO = albumDAO;
}

public ArtistDAO getArtistDAO() { return artistDAO; }
public void setArtistDAO(ArtistDAO artistDAO) {
  this.artistDAO = artistDAO;
}

public TrackDAO getTrackDAO() { return trackDAO; }
public void setTrackDAO(TrackDAO trackDAO) {
  this.trackDAO = trackDAO;
}
}
```

AlbumTest is more complex than either CreateTest or QueryTest because it deals with the creation and persistence of multiple objects and the side-effects of cascading. Let's step through the code:

❶ Just as CreateTest and QueryTest did, the AlbumTest class defines a series of private fields that reference all of the DAO objects it needs: trackDAO, artistDAO, and albumDAO.

❷ AlbumTest retrieves an Artist using artistDAO.getArtist( ), which creates a new Artist if it cannot find the artist you've requested.

❸ The Album instance is persisted. This creates a row in the database and returns an Album object with a non-null id property. We're persisting the Album record now so we can use the new instance of Album to create Track objects and then relate them to the new Album object. For this to work properly, we're going to need to make sure that our Album and Track objects have non-null id properties.

❹ We then add a series of Track objects. To create the Track objects, we first create a new instance of Track, and then persist the Track object with trackDAO.persist( ). In the addAlbumTrack( ) method, we create Track objects and combine them with Albums in the AlbumTrack relationship object. The tracks property on Album has a OneToMany relationship with cascade set to CacscadeType.ALL, so when we persist the album object again, it will automatically create rows in ALBUM_TRACKS.

That's the extent of our Test implementations. The general recipe here was to migrate all of the persistence code to our DAOs and then to migrate our standalone CreateTest, QueryTest, and AlbumTest classes to beans with properties referencing these DAOs, with the actual test code moved into a `run( )` method as required by the `Test` interface. This lets the Spring Framework wire all of our components together. In the next section we'll see how all of this is executed.

TestRunner: loading a Spring ApplicationContext

All this code is useless if we don't have a way of loading a Spring `ApplicationContext` and executing our `Test` objects. For this, we'll create a `TestRunner` class with a static `main( )` method to be executed from our Ant *build.xml*. Example 13-14 is a complete listing of `TestRunner`. This class takes care of loading our Spring `ApplicationContext`, retrieving a `Test` implementation, and executing it.

Example 13-14. Loading a Spring application context

```
package com.oreilly.hh;

import org.apache.log4j.Logger;
import org.apache.log4j.PropertyConfigurator;
import org.springframework.context.ApplicationContext;
import org.springframework.context.support.ClassPathXmlApplicationContext;

/**
 * A simple harness to run our tests.  Configures Log4J,
 * creates an ApplicationContext, retrieves a bean from Spring
 */
public class TestRunner {

  private static Logger log;

  public static void main(String[] args) throws Exception {
    // Configure Log4J from a properties file
    PropertyConfigurator.configure(
      TestRunner.class.getResource("/log4j.properties")); ❶
    log = Logger.getLogger(TestRunner.class);

    // Load our Spring Application Context
    log.info( "Initializing TestRunner..." );
    log.info( "Loading Spring Configuration..." );
    ApplicationContext context = ❷
      new ClassPathXmlApplicationContext("applicationContext.xml");

    // Retrieve the test name from the command line and
    // run the test.
    String testName = args[0];
    log.info( "Running test: " + testName );
    Test test = (Test) context.getBean(testName); ❸
    test.run();
  }
}
```

`TestRunner` takes care of three things for us, as noted in the JavaDoc:

❶   Configure Log4J by referencing *log4j.properties* at the root of the class path.

---

❷ Create a Spring `ApplicationContext` object using the `ClassPathXmlApplication`
`Context` object. The `ClassPathXmlApplicationContext` constructor takes a `String`
that specifies the path of the Spring XML configuration on the class path. In this
instance, our *applicationContext.xml* is at the root of the class path (right next to
our *log4j.properties* file).

❸ Lastly, we get the name of the bean from the command-line arguments, and we
retrieve this `Test` object from the `ApplicationContext`. As you can see, it's very
easy to retrieve a named bean from the `ApplicationContext`: just call `context.get`
`Bean(name)` and cast the result to the expected type.

Running CreateTest, QueryTest, and AlbumTest

To run `TestRunner` and retrieve the appropriate bean from our Spring
`ApplicationContext`, we need to modify our Ant *build.xml* script. Find the targets named
`ctest`, `qtest`, and `atest`, and change them to contain the following XML, as shown in
Example 13-15.

Example 13-15. Executing TestRunner from Ant

```
<target name="atest" description="Creates and persists some album data" depends=
"compile">
  <java classname="com.oreilly.hh.TestRunner" fork="true">
    <classpath refid="project.class.path" />
    <arg value="albumTest"/>
  </java>
</target>

<target name="ctest" description="Creates and persists some sample data"
        depends="compile">
  <java classname="com.oreilly.hh.TestRunner" fork="true" failonerror="true">
    <classpath refid="project.class.path" />
    <arg value="createTest"/>
  </java>
</target>

<target name="qtest" description="Runs a query" depends="compile">
  <java classname="com.oreilly.hh.TestRunner" fork="true">
    <classpath refid="project.class.path" />
    <arg value="queryTest"/>
  </java>
</target>
```

The `TestRunner` class uses its first command-line argument as the name of the bean to
retrieve from the Spring `ApplicationContext`. In the *build.xml* we are invoking
`TestRunner` and passing in the name of the bean (from *applicationContext.xml*) as an
argument.

To create the test database, run *ant schema* as usual, and to insert data into the database,
run our new version of *ant ctest*:

```
% ant schema
% ant ctest
Buildfile: build.xml

prepare:

compile:

ctest:
     [java]  INFO TestRunner:20 - Initializing TestRunner...
     [java]  INFO TestRunner:21 - Loading Spring Configuration...
     [java]  INFO TestRunner:25 - Running test: createTest

BUILD SUCCESSFUL
Total time: 3 seconds
```

Run *ant qtest* to invoke the new QueryTest example and confirm that everything we put together worked as expected:

```
% ant qtest
Buildfile: build.xml

prepare:

compile:

qtest:
     [java]  INFO TestRunner:20 - Initializing TestRunner...
     [java]  INFO TestRunner:21 - Loading Spring Configuration...
     [java]  INFO TestRunner:25 - Running test: queryTest
     [java]  INFO QueryTest:25 - Track: "Russian Trance", 00:03:30
     [java]  INFO QueryTest:25 - Track: "Video Killed the Radio Star", 00:03:49
     [java]  INFO QueryTest:25 - Track: "Test Tone 1", 00:00:10

BUILD SUCCESSFUL
Total time: 3 seconds
```

Finally, we can run the new AlbumTest example. Type *ant atest*, and you should see the following output:

```
% ant atest
Buildfile: build.xml

prepare:

compile:

atest:
     [java]  INFO TestRunner:16 - Initializing TestRunner...
     [java]  INFO TestRunner:17 - Loading Spring Configuration...
     [java]  INFO TestRunner:21 - Running test: albumTest
     [java]  INFO AlbumTest:40 - Persisted Album: 1
     [java]  INFO AlbumTest:59 - Saved an album named Counterfeit e.p.
     [java]  INFO AlbumTest:60 - With 2 tracks.
```

```
BUILD SUCCESSFUL
Total time: 2 seconds
```

It worked! Now what?

The Spring Framework and Hibernate complement each other quite nicely, and if you are about to adopt Hibernate for a large application, you should consider basing your application on the Spring Framework. Once you've invested the time to learn the framework, we're certain you'll find yourself writing less transaction handling, connection management, and Hibernate session management code. The less time you have to spend on these tasks, the more time you can devote to your application's specific requirements and logic. Portability is another reason to use Spring (or any IoC container, for that matter) and to start using patterns like the DAO. While Hibernate is the first choice among persistence libraries today, there's no telling what the next decade will bring. If you isolate your Hibernate-specific code from the rest of your application, it'll be that much easier to experiment with the next technology that comes down the road.

Take care not to be deceived by the simplicity of Hibernate when coupled with Spring. The authors of this book unanimously agreed that while Hibernate was a great thing, it can sometimes be difficult to debug and diagnose for any number of reasons: a single-character typo, a badly mapped table, a slightly incorrect flush mode, or some arcane incompatibility with a JDBC driver. Spring makes Hibernate easy because it

> Use Spring. It takes care of the tedious work. But don't use it as an excuse not to learn the details of Hibernate.

provides some useful abstractions—you gain simplicity, but it takes you that much further away from executing a SQL statement against a database. While you might not have to write your own transaction handling code, there will be times when these abstractions can make it more difficult to diagnose the root cause of an error. Don't get me wrong—I would not use Hibernate without Spring, but you'll be better able to diagnose problems is you have a solid grounding in the details of Hibernate.

In the next chapter, we'll show you how to take the next step—how to integrate Hibernate into a web application framework called Stripes. In this web application, you'll see how Spring serves as a neutral broker between Stripes and Hibernate. As you read that chapter, you should keep in mind the fact that most of the popular web application frameworks in use today have some facility for direct integration with Spring. If you use Struts 2, Wicket, or Spring MVC, many of the concepts remain the same. Spring is something of a Rosetta Stone for software, and once you adopt it you have access to all the libraries which were designed to interoperate with Spring. Use Spring as your foundation, and you'll have an easier time swapping in different technologies as your requirements change. Among some of the possibilities are writing DAO components in JRuby or Groovy instead of Java, integrating a cron-like facility using Quartz, and exposing service objects as SOAP endpoints using libraries like Apache CXF.

## CHAPTER 14

The Finishing Touch: Stripes with Spring and Hibernate

Over the last several years, Java web frameworks have been popping up all over the place. For a while, Struts was the *de facto* Java framework for web applications but people are now realizing that there are all sorts of options available. Java Server Faces (JSF) has a reasonable share of the enterprise space, and Spring MVC rides along with the Spring Framework into many installations, but developers who discover Stripes are often drawn to this alternative. Stripes doesn't quite carry the same name recognition that Spring does at this point, but as you know, marketing success doesn't always directly correlate with quality. Stripes is one of those projects that does a lot of great things despite its relative anonymity.

If you've had much experience with some of the web frameworks out there, you probably noticed a handful of ways to get Java code wired together with URLs and form submissions. Most of these ways require complicated XML and Java code to get anything nontrivial to work. These frameworks are so complicated and difficult to use that many people have turned away from using Java entirely for web applications because of the toll it seemed to take on implementation speed. Those people who turned away from Java frameworks also turned away from the great libraries already written in Java and from a feature-rich language. It's our feeling that Java has a lot to offer, and Stripes eases the development pains traditionally associated with Java web development by making good use of Java's features and a consistent architecture.

Despite most developers' better judgement, Struts has ruled the Java web landscape for quite some time. Tim Fennell created Stripes as an alternative to the Struts web framework because he was frustrated with all the stuff that went into *struts-config.xml* as well as the sheer number of files he needed to work with to accomplish simple tasks[*]. By targeting Java 5 and Servlet 2.4 from the start of the project, he was able to make some improvements over the status quo in Java web development.

---

[*] See *http://stripesframework.org/display/stripes/Stripes+vs.+Struts*

Most of the tedious tasks of Struts are replaced in Stripes with sensible defaults, reflection, annotations, and type inference with generics. The result is a clean, easily understood, and easy-to-extend development framework that puts the fun back into Java web development.

Earn Your Stripes

The stated goal of the Stripes project[†] is to make life easy for developers. To that end, convention is preferred over configuration and when your application needs to stray from the defaults, there are ways to go about overriding those defaults. Just like in the Spring chapter, we're not going to be able to fully flesh out all the developer-friendly features Stripes has to offer, but hopefully you'll gain an understanding of what Stripes is, and of at least one way we've found to make it work with Spring and Hibernate.

There are a few basic pieces of Stripes applications about which it's best to know upfront. `DispatcherServlet` and `StripesFilter` are both implemented by Stripes, while you're responsible for `ActionBean`s and views.

DispatcherServlet

In a Stripes application, there is usually only one implementation of the J2EE `HttpServlet` interface. That implementation is provided for you by Stripes' `DispatcherServlet`. The `DispatcherSerlvet` looks at an incoming request URL, figures out which `ActionBean` to instantiate, and what methods to invoke on that `ActionBean`. It's worthwhile to think of the Dispatcher as the "manager" of your application. As requests are coming into the application, the Dispatcher examines them and figures out how to delegate responsibility to the appropriate part of the application. By convention, the `DispatcherServlet` is mapped to `*.action` URLs.

StripesFilter

The `StripesFilter` wraps around all the HTTP requests being processed by your application. The `StripesDispatcher` doesn't get a chance to run when a JSP is requested directly, so it's the responsibility of `StripesFilter` to provide some of the features of Stripes to JSPs and `ActionBean`s, so they can operate in similar ways. The `StripesFilter` performs multipart form handling, locale selecting, flash scope management, as well as last stop exception handling.

ActionBeans

You really see Stripes shine when you're writing `ActionBean`s. The interface only requires a getter and setter for a property named `context` that will be an instance of

[†] *http://stripesframework.org/*

ActionBeanContext. The DispatcherServlet uses reflection on the ActionBeans, along with the HTTP request parameters and annotations in the ActionBean, to determine the methods to be run.

In addition to setContext( ) and getContext( ), your ActionBeans will contain methods that return Resolutions and property accessors for interaction with views. You'll see what we mean when we start building the example. Your ActionBeans will not be doing things like calling HttpRequest.getParameter( ), since binding request parameters to objects will be taken care of automatically by Stripes.

Views

Stripes uses JSP as its view technology. When your ActionBean forwards the request to a JSP, Stripes provides the JSP with a reference to the ActionBean so it can use the JSTL Expression Language to get data out of the ActionBean. Conversely, JSPs can invoke an ActionBean's event handler with the useActionBean tag to prepare the request for display (by formatting attributes, for example). Stripes also provides a simple JSP tag library that helps link the application together and present forms.

Prepare Tomcat

We're assuming you have a working Apache Tomcat environment in which to play. You'll need to make sure you have a user that has the manager role in that Tomcat environment, and the place to do so is $CATALINA_HOME/conf/tomcat-users.xml. You'll want to get your tomcat-users.xml file to look something like Example 14-1.

Example 14-1. tomcat-users.xml with a manager defined

```
<?xml version='1.0' encoding='utf-8'?>
<tomcat-users>
  <role rolename="manager"/>
  <role rolename="tomcat"/>
  <role rolename="role1"/>
  <user username="tomcat" password="tomcat" roles="tomcat,manager"/>
  <user username="both" password="tomcat" roles="tomcat,role1"/>
  <user username="role1" password="tomcat" roles="role1"/>
</tomcat-users>
```

If you had to add a manager role to your *tomcat-users.xml*, go ahead and restart Tomcat. Then you can get started creating the Stripes application.

Create the Web Application

Now that you've got a running Tomcat instance, the next step is to create a web application. We'll start by creating the directory structure for our web application inside your project directory, as demonstrated in Example 14-2, so you can start with that directory if you created it by hand, or you can download the code examples from the book's web site.

Example 14-2. Command to create the web application structure

```
$ mkdir -p webapp/WEB-INF
```

To get started, lets put a *web.xml* and an *index.jsp* in our application so we can get something deployed. Every J2EE web application needs a *web.xml* file, so we'll start there. Later on we'll fill this file out with `Filters` and `Servlets`, but for now we're going with a bare bones *web.xml* in *webapp/WEB-INF*, like the one shown in Example 14-3.

Example 14-3. A minimal webapp/WEB-INF/web.xml

```
<?xml version="1.0" encoding="UTF-8"?>
<web-app xmlns="http://java.sun.com/xml/ns/j2ee"
  xmlns:xsi="http://www.w3.org/2001/XMLSchema-instance"
  xsi:schemaLocation="http://java.sun.com/xml/ns/j2ee
  http://java.sun.com/xml/ns/j2ee/web-app_2_4.xsd" version="2.4">
</web-app>
```

A web application isn't much to look at without at least one view, so we'll start with a very basic *index.jsp* file in our application's root directory, *webapp/*. Again, we're not going for style points just yet; we just need something there so that we'll know when things are working. The code shown in Example 14-4 will do the trick.

Example 14-4. A basic JSP in webapp/index.jsp

```
<?xml version="1.0"?>
<%@ page contentType="text/html;charset=UTF-8" language="java"%>
Hello World
```

There are a number of ways to deploy applications to Tomcat these days and you're obviously welcome to do whatever you prefer in this regard. I prefer sending Tomcat the context information with the Ant `deploy` task. You can specify the `docBase` in the application context so that Tomcat will find your application in your development location. With this technique, you will only have to deploy the application once. Deploying to Tomcat can take some time, so your compile and test cycles will be faster than if you deployed every time.

There are a handful of things that Tomcat needs to know about an application in order to run it. A way to provide that information to Tomcat is by sending it a context file (as in Example 14-5). The main thing we need Tomcat to know is the location of the application.

Example 14-5. A sample tomcat-context.xml

```
<?xml version="1.0" ?>
<Context
    docBase="/home/rfowler/current/examples/ch14/webapp" ❶
    debug="0"
    reloadable="true" ❷
```

```
      >
</Context>
```

❶ The docBase attribute specifies where the application resides on the Tomcat server's filesystem. You need to change the value to the actual location of the application on your computer.

❷ The reloadable attribute of the Context specifies whether or not Tomcat should watch the application for class file changes and reload the application context if a change is noticed. Turning reloading on takes a step out of our development cycle, but is a waste of CPU cycles once an application is moved into production.

Now that you've written a context file, it's time to update *build.xml* so that you can deploy the application. There are a few dependencies you need to add to the build in this chapter and we're going to stick them all in at once, as shown in Example 14-6.

Example 14-6. New Tomcat dependencies in build.xml

```
...
<artifact:dependencies pathId="dependency.class.path"
                       filesetid="dependency.fileset">
  <dependency groupId="hsqldb" artifactId="hsqldb" version="1.8.0.7"/>
  <dependency groupId="mysql" artifactId="mysql-connector-java"
              version="5.0.5"/>
  <dependency groupId="org.hibernate" artifactId="hibernate"
              version="3.2.5.ga">
    <exclusion  groupId="javax.transaction" artifactId="jta" />
  </dependency>
  <dependency groupId="org.hibernate" artifactId="hibernate-tools"
              version="3.2.0.beta9a"/>
  <dependency groupId="org.apache.geronimo.specs"
              artifactId="geronimo-jta_1.1_spec" version="1.1"/>
  <dependency groupId="log4j" artifactId="log4j" version="1.2.14" />
  <dependency groupId="javax.servlet" artifactId="jstl" version="1.1.1" />
  <dependency groupId="taglibs" artifactId="standard" version="1.1.1" />
   <dependency groupId="org.hibernate" artifactId="hibernate-annotations"
              version="3.3.0.ga" />
  <dependency groupId="org.hibernate"
              artifactId="hibernate-commons-annotations"
              version="3.3.0.ga" />
  <dependency groupId="org.springframework" artifactId="spring"
              version="2.5"/>
  <dependency groupId="commons-dbcp" artifactId="commons-dbcp"
              version="1.2.2"/>
  <dependency groupId="net.sourceforge.stripes" artifactId="stripes"
              version="1.4.3" /> ❶
  <dependency groupId="tomcat" artifactId="servlet-api" version="5.5.12" /> ❷
  <dependency groupId="tomcat" artifactId="catalina-ant"
              version="5.5.15" /> ❸
  <dependency groupId="tomcat" artifactId="jasper-compiler"
              version="5.5.15" />
  <dependency groupId="tomcat" artifactId="jasper-runtime"
              version="5.5.15" /> ❹
```

```
</artifact:dependencies>
...
```

❶   The `stripes` artifact provides the jars needed to use the Stripes framework.

❷   The `servlet-api` artifact provides the libraries that contain the J2EE Servlet in-
        terfaces and support classes. The `HttpServletRequest` and `HttpServletResponse`
        classes are both provided by this artifact.

❸   The `catalina-ant artifactId` provides some Ant tasks used to interact with a
        running Apache Tomcat instance. Shortly, you'll add a new target to the build
        file that leverages Tomcat's `deploy` task from this artifact.

❹   The `jasper-compiler` and `jasper-runtime` artifacts are required by the Tomcat
        `deploy` tag in addition to the `catalina-ant` artifact.

While we're in there, the next steps are to set up the Catalina Ant tasks with a `task
def` and define the new `target` for deploying the application. Ant's `deploy` task will send
Tomcat the *tomcat-context.xml* file (Example 14-5) along with authentication information and the context path. See Example 14-7.

Example 14-7. Ant target for deploying our application

```
...
<taskdef name="hibernatetool"
        classname="org.hibernate.tool.ant.HibernateToolTask"
        classpathref="project.class.path" />
<!-- Teach Ant how to use Tomcat's deploy task -->
<taskdef name="deploy" classpathref="dependency.class.path"
        classname="org.apache.catalina.ant.DeployTask"/>
 <target name="db" description="Runs HSQLDB database management UI
against the database file--use when application is not running">
  <java classname="org.hsqldb.util.DatabaseManager"
        fork="yes">
    <classpath refid="project.class.path"/>
    <arg value="-driver"/>
    <arg value="org.hsqldb.jdbcDriver"/>
    <arg value="-url"/>
    <arg value="jdbc:hsqldb:${data.dir}/music"/>
    <arg value="-user"/>
    <arg value="sa"/>
  </java>
</target>

...
<target name="qtest3" description="Retrieve all mapped objects"
        depends="compile">
  <java classname="com.oreilly.hh.QueryTest3" fork="true" failonerror="true">
   <classpath refid="project.class.path"/>
  </java>
</target>
<target name="deploy">
  <deploy url="http://localhost:8080/manager" ❶
        username="tomcat" password="tomcat" ❷
```

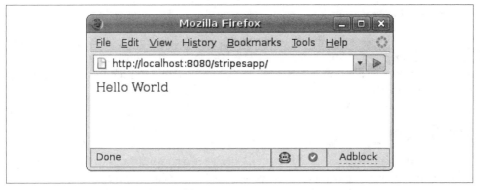

Figure 14-1. Tomcat says "Hello World"

```
            path="/stripesapp" ❸
            config="${basedir}/tomcat-context.xml" /> ❹
    </target>
    ...
```

❶   The `url` attribute of the `deploy` task specifies the URL of the manager servlet that comes with Apache Tomcat.

❷   The `username` and `password` attributes specify the authentication information of the user with the `manager` role that you configured in Example 14-1.

❸   The `path` attribute tells Tomcat the context path into which the application should be deployed.

❹   The `config` attribute specifies the context file to send Tomcat. This is the file we wrote in Example 14-5.

With all that in place, you should be able to run the *ant deploy* command as shown in Example 14-8 and then access our simple application with a web browser.

Example 14-8. Deploy the application

```
$ant deploy
Buildfile: build.xml

deploy:
   [deploy] OK - Deployed application at context path /stripesapp

BUILD SUCCESSFUL
Total time: 3 seconds
```

That "OK" in the preceding example means that Tomcat accepted the new application. Point your browser to *http://localhost:8080/stripesapp* and see if your application exists and is running. Tomcat will evaluate and return *index.jsp* from the web application's root by default. Therefore, the application should say "Hello World," as shown in Figure 14-1.

What just happened?

We've just spun through a whole bunch of tasks that don't necessarily have anything to do with Stripes or Hibernate, but we've laid the groundwork to get started with Stripes. You now have a working Apache Tomcat installation along with a working web application that we'll build on.

Add Stripes

To make our project work in a web context, there are a couple things we want to change in our `compile` task. Up to this point, we've been using Ant to start our applications, so Ant has been providing appropriate class paths to our code. So far this has worked great, but Tomcat's class loader management is complicated enough that it'll be easiest to just copy our dependencies into the *WEB-INF/lib* directory of our application. We also want the compile task to place files in *WEB-INF* so Tomcat can find them. See Example 14-9.

Example 14-9. Compile task updated for web application

```
...
<property name="source.root" value="src"/>
<property name="class.root" value="webapp/WEB-INF/classes"/> ❶
<property name="data.dir" value="webapp/WEB-INF/data"/> ❷
...
<target name="compile" depends="prepare"
        description="Compiles all Java classes">
  <javac srcdir="${source.root}"
         destdir="${class.root}"
         debug="on"
         optimize="off"
         deprecation="on">
    <classpath refid="project.class.path"/>
  </javac>
  <filter token="docroot" value="${basedir}/webapp" /> ❸
  <copy todir="webapp/WEB-INF" filtering="true" overwrite="true">
    <fileset dir="src" includes="applicationContext.xml" />
  </copy> ❹
  <copy todir="webapp/WEB-INF/lib" flatten="true">
    <fileset refid="dependency.fileset" />
  </copy> ❺
</target>
...
```

❶   Since we're changing our application into a J2EE web application, we need to put our classes into the *webapp/WEB-INF/classes* directory. The easiest way to do that is by changing the `class.root` property value.

❷   HSQLDB won't be able to just find the database in the relative path of *data* any more since the current working directory isn't guaranteed. Therefore, we need to provide a full path to the database to Hibernate. To do that, create a `data.dir` property that you'll use when copying the *applicationContext.xml* file.

❸ The ant `filter` task specifies that the `@docroot@` token be replaced with the location of the web application while copying *applicationContext.xml*.

❹ Spring's *applicationContext.xml* file needs to be copied into the *webapp/WEB-INF* directory so that Tomcat can find it.

❺ Now that the application is no longer being started by Ant, we can't rely on Java libraries being found in the local Maven repository. The J2EE specification says that an application's JAR files go into the *WEB-INF/lib* directory, so this step copies the files we need out of the Maven local repository into *WEB-INF/lib*.

To make the filter with the token `docroot` do anything useful, we need to put the `@docroot@` token into *src/applicationContext.xml* (which we set up in Chapter 13). Example 14-10 shows the change.

Example 14-10. Database location change in applicationContext.xml

```
...
<property name="hibernateProperties">
    <props>
        <prop key="hibernate.show_sql">true</prop>
        <prop key="hibernate.format_sql">true</prop>
        <prop key="hibernate.transaction.factory_class">org.hibernate.transact
ion.JDBCTransactionFactory</prop>
        <prop key="hibernate.dialect">org.hibernate.dialect.HSQLDialect</prop>
        <prop key="hibernate.connection.autocommit">false</prop>
        <prop key="hibernate.connection.release_mode">after_transaction</prop>
        <prop key="hibernate.connection.shutdown">true</prop>
        <prop key="hibernate.connection.driver_class">org.hsqldb.jdbcDriver</
prop>
        <prop key="hibernate.connection.url">jdbc:hsqldb:@docroot@/WEB-INF/dat
a/music</prop>
        <prop key="hibernate.connection.username">sa</prop>
        <prop key="hibernate.connection.password"></prop>
        <prop key="hibernate.current_session_context_class">thread</prop>
        <prop key="hibernate.jdbc.batch_size">0</prop>
    </props>
</property>
...
```

Now that our build environment has been updated, we can start using Stripes. There are a number of changes to be made to our *web.xml* in order to get Spring, Hibernate, and Stripes to all work together. There's a lot in Example 14-11, but it's all there for a reason. I've pointed out the important things to watch for afterward.

Example 14-11. web.xml updated for Stripes integration

```
<?xml version="1.0" encoding="UTF-8"?>

<web-app xmlns="http://java.sun.com/xml/ns/j2ee"
  xmlns:xsi="http://www.w3.org/2001/XMLSchema-instance"
```

```
xsi:schemaLocation="http://java.sun.com/xml/ns/j2ee
        http://java.sun.com/xml/ns/j2ee/web-app_2_4.xsd"
version="2.4">
<listener>
    <listener-class>
       org.springframework.web.context.ContextLoaderListener
    </listener-class> ❶
</listener>
<context-param>
    <param-name>contextConfigLocation</param-name>
    <param-value>/WEB-INF/applicationContext.xml</param-value>
</context-param>
<!-- Hibernate OpenSession Filter -->
<filter>
  <filter-name>hibernateFilter</filter-name> ❷
  <filter-class>
     org.springframework.orm.hibernate3.support.OpenSessionInViewFilter
  </filter-class>
  <init-param>
    <param-name>singleSession</param-name>
    <param-value>true</param-value>
  </init-param>
  <init-param>
    <param-name>sessionFactoryBeanName</param-name>
    <param-value>sessionFactory</param-value>
  </init-param>
  <init-param>
      <param-name>flushMode</param-name>
      <param-value>ALWAYS</param-value>
  </init-param>
</filter>
<filter>
  <display-name>Stripes Filter</display-name> ❸
  <filter-name>StripesFilter</filter-name>
  <filter-class>
    net.sourceforge.stripes.controller.StripesFilter
  </filter-class>
  <init-param>
    <param-name>ActionResolver.PackageFilters</param-name>
    <param-value>com.oreilly.*</param-value>
  </init-param>
  <init-param>
    <param-name>ActionResolver.UrlFilters</param-name>
    <param-value>WEB-INF/classes</param-value>
  </init-param>
  <init-param>
      <param-name>Interceptor.Classes</param-name>
      <param-value>
          net.sourceforge.stripes.integration.spring.SpringInterceptor,
          net.sourceforge.stripes.controller.BeforeAfterMethodInterceptor
      </param-value>
  </init-param>
</filter>
<filter-mapping>
  <filter-name>hibernateFilter</filter-name>
```

```
      <url-pattern>*.jsp</url-pattern>
      <dispatcher>REQUEST</dispatcher>
   </filter-mapping>
<filter-mapping>
    <filter-name>hibernateFilter</filter-name>
    <url-pattern>*.action</url-pattern>
    <dispatcher>REQUEST</dispatcher>
</filter-mapping>

<filter-mapping>
    <filter-name>StripesFilter</filter-name>
    <url-pattern>*.jsp</url-pattern>
    <dispatcher>REQUEST</dispatcher>
</filter-mapping>
<filter-mapping>
    <filter-name>StripesFilter</filter-name>
    <url-pattern>*.action</url-pattern>
    <dispatcher>REQUEST</dispatcher>
</filter-mapping>
<servlet>
    <servlet-name>StripesDispatcher</servlet-name> ❹
    <servlet-class>
      net.sourceforge.stripes.controller.DispatcherServlet
    </servlet-class>
    <load-on-startup>1</load-on-startup>
</servlet>
<servlet-mapping>
    <servlet-name>StripesDispatcher</servlet-name>
    <url-pattern>*.action</url-pattern>
</servlet-mapping>
</web-app>
```

❶ The ContextLoaderListener filter initializes the Spring Framework for the web application.

❷ The hibernateFilter is provided by Spring to get a Hibernate session wrapped around all of the request processing. Using this feature spares us from having to manage Hibernate sessions ourselves. This is nice because proper session management can be one of the trickiest parts of writing Hibernate-backed web applications.

❸ The Stripes Filter is mapped around *.action and *.jsp HTTP requests. It provides some basic form handling and configuration services that are needed when either JSPs or ActionBeans are invoked.

❹ The StripesDispatcher servlet is mapped to *.action and determines which methods to call in which ActionBean, as well as handling the Resolutions that are returned by these event methods.

Before you can start using Stripes, there's one last prerequisite to install in order for it to work correctly. The *StripesResources.properties* file sits in the *classes* directory and provides some formatting strings that Stripes needs. For this example it's easiest to just grab the *StripesResources.properties* file out of the *examples/ch14/src* directory of the

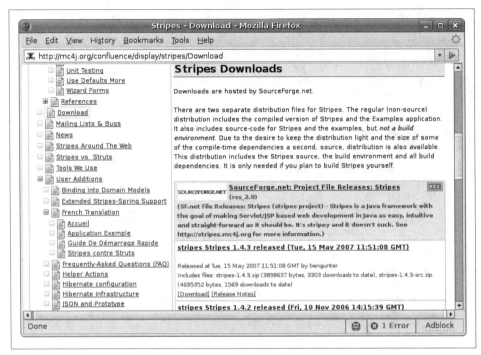

Figure 14-2. Stripes download page

book's example code download, but you can also get it from the Stripes download page‡. Click on the Download button in the Stripes 1.4.3 section about halfway down the page, as shown in Figure 14-2, and proceed through the gauntlet of SourceForge downloading with which we're all so familiar. Once you've downloaded *stripes-1.4.3.zip*, unzip it and copy *stripes-1.4.3/lib/StripesResources.properties* into your *src* directory. You can look at it if you'd like, but that file is just a dependency as far as this chapter is concerned.

It's finally time to write a little code. First we'll write a couple of JSPs, then follow that up with an `ActionBean`. The JSPs we're writing here should look pretty familiar if you've done any JSP coding at all in the last few years. The pieces you probably won't recognize are the tags with the `stripes:` prefix. The Stripes tag library is written to complement JSTL and provides features that will help your application classes and views work together. Example 14-12 shows the source code of a page that lets us edit `Albums`.

Example 14-12. Our album editing view, webapp/albums/edit.jsp

```
<%@ page contentType="text/html;charset=UTF-8" language="java"%>
<%@ taglib prefix="c" uri="http://java.sun.com/jsp/jstl/core"%>
<%@ taglib prefix="stripes" uri="http://stripes.sourceforge.net/stripes.tld"%> ❶
<stripes:useActionBean
```

‡ *http://www.stripesframework.org/display/stripes/Download*

```
      beanclass="com.oreilly.hh.web.AlbumActionBean"
      var="actionBean" event="edit" /> ❷
<h1>Album Edit Page</h1>
<stripes:form action="/Album.action" > ❸
  <stripes:errors />
  <stripes:hidden name="album.id"></stripes:hidden> ❹
  <table>
     <tr>
         <td>Title:</td>
         <td><stripes:text name="album.title" /></td> ❺
     </tr>
     <tr>
         <td>Discs:</td>
         <td><stripes:text name="album.numDiscs" /></td>
      </tr>
   </table>

   <h2>Album Comments</h2>
     <c:choose>
       <c:when test="${actionBean.album.id != null }">
         <stripes:link href="/albums/edit_comment.jsp">
             <stripes:param name="album.id" value="${actionBean.album.id }" />
             Add A Comment
         </stripes:link>
         <c:if test="${empty actionBean.album.comments}" >
         There are no album comments yet.
         </c:if>
       </c:when>
       <c:otherwise>
           Please add the album before entering comments.
       </c:otherwise>
     </c:choose>
   <ul>
   <c:forEach items="${actionBean.album.comments }" var="comment">
       <li>${comment }</li>
   </c:forEach>
   </ul>
  <br />
  <stripes:submit name="save" value="Save"></stripes:submit> ❻
</stripes:form>
```

As you can see, this is a pretty normal looking JSP file, though there are a few things worth looking at more closely:

❶   The taglib declaration pulls in the Stripes tag library, so our code on the page can take advantage of them using the prefix "**stripes:**".

❷   This **useActionBean** tag tells Stripes to initialize the **AlbumActionBean** and run its **edit** event if this hasn't taken place (such as the case where the browser is requesting the JSP directly, rather than through an action URL). The **edit** event will load the **Album** object from the database so the form can be populated.

❸ Stripes' `form` outputs a normal HTML as well as a handful of things behind the scenes. The `action` attribute specifies the `ActionBean` to which the form will be submitted.

❹ The Stripes `hidden` tag works much like the normal HTML hidden `input` tag. The benefit of using the Stripes version is that it does automatic population.

❺ The Stripes `text` tag creates an text input field, as you would expect. As with the `hidden` tag, it automatically populates the value.

❻ The Stripes `submit` tag emits a typical submit button. The thing to be aware of here is that the `name` of the submit tag is the `ActionBean` event handling method that will be called when the form submits. In this case, `AlbumActionBean.save( )` will be called. (Events and their handlers are explained further in the `Action Bean` discussion later in this chapter.)

 Stripes also has a `label` tag that can help with localization and keeping your code concise. We're not using it here so we can get to the Hibernate stuff. Luckily the Stripes Documentation[§] on this is pretty easy to follow.

While we're at it, lets also write a JSP for listing the albums in our database so we have a landing page and a way to see what is in there. While there is less to look at in Example 14-13 than there was in *edit.jsp*, pay attention to the Stripes `link` tag toward the end.

Example 14-13. An album list view, webapp/albums/list.jsp

```
<%@ page contentType="text/html;charset=UTF-8" language="java"%>
<%@ taglib prefix="c" uri="http://java.sun.com/jsp/jstl/core"%>
<%@ taglib prefix="stripes"
   uri="http://stripes.sourceforge.net/stripes.tld"%>
<stripes:useActionBean beanclass="com.oreilly.hh.web.AlbumActionBean"
   var="actionBean" event="list" />
<table>
  <tr>
    <th>title</th>
    <th>discs</th>
    <th>action</th>
  </tr>
  <c:forEach items="${actionBean.albums}" var="album">
    <tr>
      <td>${album.title }</td>
      <td>${album.numDiscs }</td>
      <td><stripes:link href="/albums/edit.jsp">
        <stripes:param name="album.id" value="${album.id }" />
          edit
        </stripes:link></td>
```

§ *http://www.stripesframework.org/display/stripes/Documentation*

```
      </tr>
    </c:forEach>
  </table>
  <stripes:link href="/albums/edit.jsp">new</stripes:link>
```

The `stripes:link` tag helps you link your application together with HTML anchors. It features attributes that can build URLs to `ActionBean` event handlers as well as JSPs.

Write up an ActionBean

Now it's time to write an `ActionBean`. You can think of the `ActionBean` as the Controller in a Model, View, Controller (MVC) pattern. Example 14-14 shows a first pass at our `AlbumActionBean`, and should give you a pretty good feel for what one involves.

The methods in this class fall into two basic categories: property accessors and event handlers. The property accessors work just like any other Java Bean's setters and getters, so they should look familiar. On the other hand, the methods that return `Resolution`s won't look quite so familiar, but the concept is pretty simple. When a request comes in to the `StripesDispatcher`, part of the HTTP request indicates the name of event whose handler can process the request. After Stripes runs through its `BindingAndValidation` lifecycle stage, the event handler method indicated by the request is called (the `StripesDispatcher` uses reflection to find a public method whose name matches the event, and which returns a `Resolution`). The `Resolution` returned by the event handler is then evaluated by the `StripesDispatcher` (it's usually a forward or redirect). Example 14-14 shows our *AlbumActionBean.java*.

Example 14-14. The album controller, AlbumActionBean.java

```java
package com.oreilly.hh.web;

import java.util.List;

import org.apache.log4j.Logger;

import net.sourceforge.stripes.action.*;
import net.sourceforge.stripes.integration.spring.SpringBean;
import net.sourceforge.stripes.validation.*;

import com.oreilly.hh.dao.AlbumDAO;
import com.oreilly.hh.data.Album;

/**
 * Class that implements the web based front end of our Jukebox.
 *
 */
public class AlbumActionBean implements ActionBean {
    /**
     * Logger
     */
    private static Logger log = Logger.getLogger(AlbumActionBean.class);
    /**
```

```
 * The ActionBeanContext provided to this class by Stripes DispatcherServlet.
 */
private ActionBeanContext context;
/**
 * The list of Album objects we will display on the Album list page.
 */
private List<Album> albums;
/**
 * The Album we are providing a form for on the edit page.
 */
private Album album;
/**
 * The Data Access Object for our Albums.
 */
private AlbumDAO albumDAO;

public ActionBeanContext getContext() { ❶
    return context;
}

public void setContext(ActionBeanContext aContext) {
    context = aContext;
}

/**
 * The default event handler that displays a list of Albums.
 * @return a forward to the Album list jsp.
 */
@DefaultHandler
public Resolution list() { ❷
    albums = albumDAO.list(); ❸
    return new ForwardResolution("/albums/list.jsp");
}

/**
 * The event handler for handling edits to an Album
 * @return a forward to the Album edit jsp.
 */
public Resolution edit() {
    if(album != null) { ❹
        album = albumDAO.get(album.getId());
    }
    return new ForwardResolution("/albums/edit.jsp");
}

/**
 * The event handler for saving an Album.
 * @return a redirect to the Album list jsp.
 */
public Resolution save() {
    albumDAO.persist(album);
    log.debug("Redirecting to list!");
    return new RedirectResolution("/albums/list.jsp");
}
```

```
    /**
     * A getter for the view to retrieve the list of Albums.
     * @return a list of Albums
     */
    public List<Album> getAlbums() { ❺
        return albums;
    }


    /**
     * A setter for the DispatcherServlet to call that provides the album to save.
     * @param anAlbum
     */
    @ValidateNestedProperties({ ❻
        @Validate(field = "title", required= true, on = {"save"} ),
        @Validate(field = "numDiscs", required= true, on = {"save"})
    })
    public void setAlbum(Album anAlbum) {
        log.debug("setAlbum");
        album = anAlbum;
    }

    /**
     * A getter for the edit view to call.
     * @return an Album
     */
    public Album getAlbum() {
        return album;
    }

    /**
     * A method Spring will call that provides this class with an AlbumDAO instance.
     * @param anAlbumDAO The AlbumDAO object
     */
    @SpringBean("albumDAO") ❼
    public void injectAlbumDAO(AlbumDAO albumDAO) {
        this.albumDAO = albumDAO;
    }
}
```

❶ The only requirements imposed by the ActionBean interface are implementations of the setContext( ) and getContext( ) methods, which provide a way for the bean to get information about the Stripes environment in which it is operating.

❷ Public methods that return Resolutions are called event handlers in Stripes. They are automatically bound to URLs that the browser will be able to reach. This method, for instance will be chosen by the Dispatcher at the path /stripesapp/ Album.action?save=.

❸ The AlbumDao.list( ) method doesn't exist yet, so we'll need to add it to the AlbumDAO interface (from Chapter 13) as well as the AlbumHibernateDAO implementation.

❹ "If the album isn't `null`, then load the album" seems like backwards logic but what's happening is that while Stripes is binding the request to objects in the `ActionBean`, it sees an `album.id` parameter and creates a new `Album` with that `id` value for us, and then calls this method. But what we really want is to load an `Album` from the database to edit, so that's what we're doing here.

❺ Public getters and setters in the `ActionBean` will be called by Stripes whenever form data that matches the naming scheme of the bean properties is found in the request. For instance, `setAlbum()` will be called by Stripes when `album.id`, `album.title`, and `album.numDiscs` are request parameters. In the other direction, the getter will be used to pre-populate values when rendering the form to the browser (that's how those `stripes:text` tags and such in Example 14-12 work).

❻ Stripes provides validation annotations to mark how fields should look when event handlers are called. We won't go into detail on that here, but you can find more information in the Stripes documentation[‖] online.

❼ The `SpringBean` annotation is what tells Stripes to look in the Spring context for the value to insert here. We don't use a public setter as is typical in Spring applications because such methods could be called by a hacker formatting a web request properly—you want to prevent that for security reasons. It's generally a good idea to use some other naming convention for methods that Spring will call[#].

As I mentioned earlier, `AlbumDAO` needs both a `list()` method that returns all the `Album`s and a `get()` method that retrieves one `Album` based on its id. To implement this, we need to make tweaks to both our `AlbumDAO` interface and our `AlbumHibernateDAO` implementation. Example 14-15 shows our updated *AlbumDAO.java*, with changes highlighted in bold.

Example 14-15. Adding the list() and get() definitions to AlbumDAO

```
package com.oreilly.hh.dao;

import java.util.List;

import com.oreilly.hh.data.Album;

public interface AlbumDAO {
    public Album persist( Album album );
    public void delete(Album album);
    public List<Album> list();
    public Album get(Integer id);
}
```

Example 14-16 highlights the changes needed in *AlbumHibernateDAO.java*.

‖ http://www.stripesframework.org/display/stripes/Validation+Reference

http://www.stripesframework.org/display/stripes/Spring+with+Stripes

---

Example 14-16. Adding list( ) and get( ) implementations to AlbumHibernateDAO

```
package com.oreilly.hh.dao.hibernate;

import java.util.List;

import org.springframework.orm.hibernate3.support.HibernateDaoSupport;

import com.oreilly.hh.dao.AlbumDAO;
import com.oreilly.hh.data.Album;

public class AlbumHibernateDAO extends HibernateDaoSupport implements AlbumDAO {

    public Album persist(Album album) {
        album = (Album) getHibernateTemplate().merge(album);
        getSession().flush();
        return album;
    }

    public void delete(Album album) {
        getHibernateTemplate().delete(album);
    }
    @SuppressWarnings("unchecked")
    public List<Album> list() {
        return getHibernateTemplate().loadAll(Album.class);
    }

    public Album get(Integer id) {
        return (Album)getHibernateTemplate().load(Album.class, id);
    }
}
```

The HibernateTemplate.loadAll( ) method used in Example 14-16 does the same thing Session.loadAll( ) does; it returns a list of all the persisted objects of the provided class. The benefits of the HibernateTemplate class were discussed in Chapter 13.

Now that we've got a couple views, an **ActionBean**, and appropriate DAO changes in place, we should be able to compile and experience the application. See Example 14-17.

Example 14-17. Compiling our Stripes application

```
$ ant compile
Buildfile: build.xml
Overriding previous definition of reference to project.class.path

prepare:

compile:
    [javac] Compiling 20 source files to
    /home/rfowler/Hibernate Book/examples/ch12/webapp/WEB-INF/classes
    [copy] Copying 1 file to /home/rfowler/Hibernate Book/examples/ch12/webapp/
WEB-INF

BUILD SUCCESSFUL
Total time: 2 seconds
```

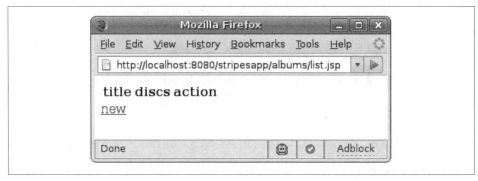

Figure 14-3. Our ActionBean lives!

When you deployed the application in Example 14-5, one of the attributes of the `Context` element was `reloadable=true`. That is in there so that when you provide new versions of classes in your web application's *WEB-INF/classes* directory, Tomcat will reload the context. Assuming that you still have Tomcat running, if you wait a few moments, the context should reload automatically. Once that process finishes, you should be able to point your browser to *http://localhost:8080/stripesapp/albums/ list.jsp* and see something similar to Figure 14-3.

There's nothing in our database right now, so this page doesn't list any albums, but clicking on the "new" link will bring us to the editing page we wrote in Example 14-12, as shown in Figure 14-4.

As you might hope, entering valid data in the form and submitting it will save the values into the database and return you to the list view, as illustrated in Figure 14-5. If so, you've just integrated Hibernate, Stripes and Spring successfully! Take a moment to think about the database work you've done in this chapter. The exciting part is that there wasn't much. You added `list( )` and `edit( )` to `AlbumDAO` and `AlbumHibernate DAO`, and used the `AlbumDAO` object to load and persist the `Album`. You'll also notice that there isn't any code dealing directly with `HTTPServletResponse` or `HTTPServletRequest` objects—Stripes has been kind enough to take care of all that tedious work for you.

What just happened?

So far we've built a simple web application with Stripes, Spring, and Hibernate. At this point we can list albums, create new ones, and edit them. The `AlbumActionBean` class is working with Stripes and the Hibernate DAOs that we wrote in Chapter 13 to save objects and provide objects to the views.

Figure 14-4. Loading the Edit page

What's next?

Now that we've taken a look at how to get basic inserting, updating, and listing working, we need to circle back a little bit to be able to handle associations in our application. Right now, associations are not taken into consideration at all.

Dealing with Associations

Because our example doesn't deal with any associations, we avoided some complexity that goes into typical applications. As it turns out, calling merge( ) as the DAO objects do in their persist( ) methods actually persists whatever you send it. If the object you are persisting doesn't also include all the objects associated with it, the previously persisted version gets overwritten and loses those associations. For example, if an Album had two comments, but was saved with an empty set of comments, the pre-existing comments would be lost.

Let's implement an event handler and view for adding and editing Album comments. That way you'll be able to see the problem we're trying to solve before we actually go about solving it. First, we'll add an *editComments.jsp* file with the contents of Example 14-18 that will provide a form to add comments to the Albums.

Figure 14-5. The list view with something to display

Example 14-18. A comment editor, webapp/albums/edit_comment.jsp

```
<%@ page contentType="text/html;charset=UTF-8" language="java"%>
<%@ taglib prefix="c" uri="http://java.sun.com/jsp/jstl/core"%>
<%@ taglib prefix="stripes" uri="http://stripes.sourceforge.net/stripes.tld"%>
<stripes:useActionBean beanclass="com.oreilly.hh.web.AlbumActionBean" var="act
ionBean" event="edit" />
<h1>Add a comment for the album <span style="font-style: italic">${actionBean.
album.title }</span></h1>
<stripes:form action="/Album.action" >
    <stripes:hidden name="album.id" />
    Comment: <stripes:text name="comment" />
    <br />
    <stripes:submit name="saveComment" value="Save" />
</stripes:form>
```

This JSP should look somewhat familiar since it follows the same pattern as Example 14-12. As you can tell from the **stripes:form** tag, this page submits to the AlbumActionBean we've already written. Since the **stripes:submit** tag is named saveComment, we need to add a public method named **saveComment( )** in AlbumAction Bean that returns a Resolution. Since the **stripes:text** tag's name is comment, we also need to create **setComment( )** and **getComment( )** property accessors in the bean. Example 14-19 shows these additions to *AlbumActionBean.java*.

Example 14-19. Additions to AlbumActionBean.java to support comments

```
...
/**
 * Event handler to save a comment to the Album
 * @return redirect to the edit Album page.
 */
public Resolution saveComment() {
    Album a = albumDAO.get(album.getId());
    a.getComments().add(comment);
    albumDAO.persist(a);
    RedirectResolution r = new RedirectResolution("/albums/edit.jsp");
```

```
        r.addParameter("album.id", album.getId());
        return r;
    }

    /**
     * @return the comment
     */
    public String getComment() {
        return comment;
    }

    /**
     * @param aComment the comment to set
     */
    public void setComment(String aComment) {
        comment = aComment;
    }
    ...
```

After you recompile and work with the new feature a little bit, you may notice a pretty major bug with the application. If you add some comments to an Album, then try updating the same Album's title or number of discs, you'll notice that the comments disappear. The reason for this bug is that every time the `saveAlbum()` method is being called, Stripes is creating a new Album object, and we're then telling Hibernate to save that new object. The new object has no comments but it does have an ID, so Hibernate is updating the persisted Album to have no comments.

There are a couple of ways to save objects that have associations. One is to set the `inverse` flag to true so that when you update the object, any changes to the associations would be ignored. This wouldn't work for album comments, however, because comments are just `String`s in our model, rather than full-blown entities, so there is no way to call `setAlbum()` on a comment. Another way to manage this problem would be to actually load the object with all its current associations from the database before Stripes calls any setters on the bean, thereby having the associated objects already populated in the object before Stripes starts tinkering with it. This sounds more promising; let's try it.

It is worth thinking a little bit about the lifecycle of Stripes handling a request. The Stripes Lifecycle Documentation[*] does a good job of explaining what's happening in detail, so head there if you hanker for additional information. In a nutshell, after the event handler is resolved, there is a stage called `BindingAndValidation` where the applicable setters on the `ActionBean` are called. Stripes provides an "interceptor" mechanism through which we can insert our own code to do stuff before `BindingAndValidation` runs.

---

[*] *http://stripesframework.org/display/stripes/Lifecycles+Etc.*

Interceptors: a powerful way to extend stripes

To tell our interceptor when to run, we'll create our own annotation to use in our action beans. This will make our extension fit very naturally with the way the rest of Stripes works.

Interceptors and Aspect Oriented Programming (AOP) are shunned by some because debugging AOP software has traditionally been difficult. In some AOP applications it can be hard to figure out what code is running and when. With the advent of features such as Java 5 Annotations, however, it's possible to do a lot more in a self-documenting way—without resorting to extra-linguistic tricks—so I encourage you to keep an open mind about Stripes' interceptor implementation. Indeed, both Stripes and Spring make very effective use of this approach. Stripes uses a pattern of interceptors that inspect `ActionBean`s for annotations and act on those annotations. This is how Spring-based dependency injection is achieved in Stripes, and it also enables particular `ActionBean` methods to be called at appropriate lifecycle stages. It is fairly simple to follow this pattern to add our own functionality, so that's what we're going to do to add a mechanism for loading data beans before the binding and validation stage.

If you haven't written an annotation before, the syntax will feel unfamiliar, but the ideas are reasonably straightforward. The code in Example 14-20 is saying that developers will be able to mark methods with the `@LoadBean` annotation and provide the name of a member to load before `BindingAndValidation` happens. (The annotation itself doesn't provide those semantics, it just supports the syntax—our Interceptor code in Example 14-22 is what uses the annotation to implement the desired meaning.) Example 14-20 shows our new annotation, which should be saved as *LoadBean.java*.

Example 14-20. Creating a LoadBean annotation

```
package com.oreilly.hh.web;

import java.lang.annotation.*;
/**
 * An annotation used to mark methods with a bean to load.
 *
 * @author  Ryan Fowler
 */
@Retention(RetentionPolicy.RUNTIME) ❶
@Target({ElementType.METHOD}) ❷
@Documented ❸
public @interface LoadBean { ❹
    /**
     * The name of the bean to load.
     */
    String value(); ❺
}
```

❶   The `@RetentionPolicy` on this annotation is `RunTime`—this tells Java to keep the annotation around in compiled classes so that our `Interceptor` can see it during runtime. Yes, you use lots of annotations to write annotations.

❷ The `@Target` annotation specifies what element types the `LoadBean` annotation can be applied to. Our interceptor will look at the annotation when running specific `ActionBean` event handlers. Since event handlers are methods in the `ActionBean`, our target type is `ElementType.METHOD`.

❸ The `@Documented` annotation specifies that the LoadBean annotation should be documented by JavaDoc.

❹ The annotation definition syntax looks unsettling at first because of the `@interface` specifier. The competing desires of adding new features to Java but not adding new keywords resulted in reusing the `interface` keyword for defining an annotation. Those two desires were technically met, but the readability of annotation definitions suffered.

❺ The `value( )` definition is just specifying that the annotation has one argument, and that argument's name is `value`. The reason to use the name `value` is that people can use the shorthand of `@LoadBean("memberName")` instead of the slightly longer `@LoadBean(value="memberName")`. This is a convention supported by the annotation mechanism.

At this point we should apply this annotation to the relevant event handler in our `AlbumActionBean` to tell our interceptor what it needs to do. The `@LoadBean` annotation later tells our interceptor to load the `Album` bean before the setters on `Album` get called by Stripes. Example 14-21 shows the new, still-sleek version of `AlbumAction Bean.save( )`.

Example 14-21. New AlbumActionBean.save( ) event handler

```
...
    /**
     * The event handler for saving an Album.
     * @return a redirect to the Album list jsp.
     */
    @LoadBean("album")
    public Resolution save() {
        albumDAO.persist(album);
        log.debug("Redirecting to list!");
        return new RedirectResolution("/albums/list.jsp");
    }
...
```

OK, so this sounds great, but how does the magic interceptor work? In order to get that `Album` bean loaded, we need something that runs before the `BindingAndValidation` stage to do the loading. As we hinted earlier, Stripes provides an interceptor execution feature that provides just the hook we need. To use this feature, we write a class that implements the Stripes `Interceptor` interface, and then tell Stripes about it using an `init-param` for the `StripesFilter`. We tag that class with an `@Intercepts` annotation to tell Stripes what lifecycle stages it is interested in, and implement the `intercept( )` method that will be called at those points of execution.

In our intercept( ) method, we check the event handler for a @LoadBean annotation. If that annotation exists, we try to load the object that is named by the annotation's value attribute using Spring and Hibernate. Once all that is done, the interceptor instructs Spring to continue on with what it has to do next by calling ExecutionContext.proceed( ) and returning whatever value that returns. Example 14-22 shows the source of *LoadObjectInterceptor.java*.

Example 14-22. The object loading interceptor

```
package com.oreilly.hh.web;

import java.lang.reflect.Method;

import javax.servlet.http.HttpServletRequest;

import org.apache.log4j.Logger;
import org.springframework.orm.hibernate3.HibernateTemplate;

import net.sourceforge.stripes.action.Resolution;
import net.sourceforge.stripes.controller.*;
import net.sourceforge.stripes.integration.spring.*;
import net.sourceforge.stripes.util.bean.BeanUtil;

@Intercepts({LifecycleStage.BindingAndValidation}) ❶
public class LoadObjectInterceptor extends SpringInterceptorSupport
    implements Interceptor {

    HibernateTemplate hibernateTemplate;
    private Logger log = Logger.getLogger(LoadObjectInterceptor.class);

    public Resolution intercept(ExecutionContext ctx) throws Exception { ❷
        Method handler = ctx.getHandler();
        LoadBean loadProperty = handler.getAnnotation(LoadBean.class); ❸
        if(loadProperty != null && loadProperty.value() != ""
                && loadProperty.value() != null ) { ❹
            String propertyName = loadProperty.value();
            String idName = propertyName+".id";
            HttpServletRequest request = ctx.getActionBeanContext().getRequest(); ❺
            String idValue = request.getParameter(idName);
            Class<?> propertyClass =
                BeanUtil.getPropertyType(propertyName, ctx.getActionBean()); ❻

            if(idValue != null && idValue != "" ) {
                Object o = hibernateTemplate.get(propertyClass,
                                        Integer.valueOf(idValue)); ❼

                BeanUtil.setPropertyValue(propertyName,
                                    ctx.getActionBean(),
                                    propertyClass.cast(o)); ❽
            }
        }
        Resolution resolution = ctx.proceed(); ❾
        return resolution;
    }
```

```
@SpringBean("hibernateTemplate") ❿
public void injectHibernateTemplate(HibernateTemplate aHibernateTemplate) {
    this.hibernateTemplate = aHibernateTemplate;
}
```
}

❶ Stripes already knows that this class is meant to be an `Interceptor` because it's in the list provided in *web.xml*. However, it's the `@Intercepts` annotation that tells Stripes which lifecycle stages this particular class will intercept.

❷ The `intercept()` method is the one that gets called at the lifecycle stages in which we've expressed an interest. This is the method in which we will do our data loading. The first thing we need to do is find out about the event handler that Spring has chosen, so we can look for our `@LoadBean` annotation. Spring makes this easy, through the `ExecutionContext.getHandler()` method, which returns the `Method` object representing that event handler.

❸ Java 5's annotation support extends nicely to reflection, so we can call `Method.getAnnotation()` in this simple way to find the `@LoadBean` annotation on the event handler method, if there is one.

❹ `getAnnotation()` will return `null` if there is no annotation of the requested type, so the Interceptor checks to see if the `@LoadBean` annotation was found and if its value was populated enough to try continuing with the Hibernate load. `Load Bean.value()` returns the value attached to the annotation on the event handler. In the case of Example 14-21, `propertyName` will be set to `album`.

The unspoken naming convention we've been following is that the `id` property of our data beans will always be named `id`. Given the way Stripes builds request parameters, this means that we can figure out the parameter containing the ID of the bean we're supposed to load by simply appending the string ".`id`" to the name of the bean we found in the `@LoadBean` annotation. In the case of Example 14-21, the relevant request parameter would be `album.id`.

❺ We have the name of the request parameter we're interested in loading, so we can look for that parameter in the request, which we find through `ExecutionContext.getActionBeanContext().getRequest()`.

❻ Before the interceptor can load the object using Spring's `HibernateTemplate`, it needs to know what type of object it's trying to load. Stripes provides a utility class for working with beans named `BeanUtil` to simplify this type of interaction with beans. `BeanUtil.getPropertyType()` returns a `Class` object telling us exactly what we need to know.

❼ Armed with both the ID and type we are trying to load, we're ready to have Hibernate do its thing. We can pass both right to the `HibernateTemplate.get()` method and load our data. Notice that this Interceptor is completely general—it doesn't need our class-specific DAOs, and will work with any data bean that is bound to a Hibernate-mapped object, in any application we might write using these frameworks.

❽   BeanUtil also provides a setPropertyValue( ) method that lets us assign a value to a property in an object. We need to cast the object we retrieved from Hibernate into the property's class beforehand because otherwise the setter on the ActionBean will fail.

❾   The ExecutionContext.proceed( ) method returns a Resolution that points Stripes to the next thing it needs to do.

❿   Just like the ActionBeans, classes that inherit from SpringInterceptorSupport can have their dependencies injected by Spring. In this case, we're getting the HibernateTemplate class from Spring.

Now we need to let Stripes know that it should run the LoadObjectInterceptor that we've just created. We've already placed the SpringInterceptor in *web.xml* to provide Spring bean injection. Place the LoadObjectInterceptor line in between the SpringInterceptor and BeforeAfterMethodInterceptor entries in the Interceptor.Classes init-param, as shown in Example 14-23.

Example 14-23. Adding our Interceptor to StripesFilter in web.xml

```
...
<filter>
    <display-name>Stripes Filter</display-name>
    <filter-name>StripesFilter</filter-name>
    <filter-class>
      net.sourceforge.stripes.controller.StripesFilter
    </filter-class>
    <init-param>
      <param-name>ActionResolver.PackageFilters</param-name>
      <param-value>com.oreilly.*</param-value>
    </init-param>
    <init-param>
      <param-name>ActionResolver.UrlFilters</param-name>
      <param-value>WEB-INF/classes</param-value>
    </init-param>
    <init-param>
      <param-name>Interceptor.Classes</param-name>
      <param-value>
          net.sourceforge.stripes.integration.spring.SpringInterceptor,
          com.oreilly.hh.web.LoadObjectInterceptor,
          net.sourceforge.stripes.controller.BeforeAfterMethodInterceptor
      </param-value>
    </init-param>
</filter>
...
```

Back in Chapter 13, the DAO objects extended HibernateDAOSupport but our LoadObjectInterceptor can't do that since it needs to extend Stripes' SpringInterceptorSupport for dependency injection to work. For that reason, we added injectHibernateTemplate() to `LoadObjectInterceptor`, and need to define a `HibernateTemplate` bean with the id `hibernateTemplate` in our *applicationContext.xml*, as shown in Example 14-24.

Example 14-24. Addition to applicationContext.xml to inject HibernateTemplate in our Interceptor

```
...
<bean id="hibernateTemplate" class="org.springframework.orm.hibernate3.Hibernate
Template">
    <property name="sessionFactory">
        <ref bean="sessionFactory"/>
    </property>
    <property name="cacheQueries">
        <value>true</value>
    </property>
</bean>
...
```

After another *ant compile*, Tomcat should reload the context, and your application should handle the album comments problem that we uncovered earlier. Before the `AlbumActionBean`'s save event handler is called, the `LoadObjectInterceptor.intercept()` method is called. Since there is a `@LoadBean` annotation on the `AlbumActionBean.save()` method, the `LoadObjectInterceptor` tries to load an `Album` with the id provided in the request's `album.id` parameter. Assuming this all works, when Stripes starts calling setters on the `Album`, the associations are already in the `Album`, so they don't get removed when `persist()` is called.

Part of what makes this example so interesting is that it shows you how to add capabilities to Stripes that feel very "Stripesy"—they work behind the scenes, and are triggered by simple, compact annotations.

We've shown you one of many ways to integrate Hibernate with Stripes. Stripes' helpful features, modern coding techniques, and reasonable extension points make it a pleasant web framework to work with. Most web applications need a persistence mechanism of some sort, and Hibernate's ORM features combined with Stripes' automatic object population make for a powerful combination. The projects weren't necessarily written to work with each other, but the integration goes pretty smoothly and—especially with some glue from Spring—things fit together quite nicely.

You may be able to apply some of the techniques explored in this chapter to other Java tasks. Using an interceptor to examine the metadata annotations stored in classes that are being acted on is a technique we've found helpful for things like adding security features to our applications.

Hibernate Types

Hibernate makes a fundamental distinction between two different kinds of data in terms of how they relate to the persistence service: *entities* and *values*.

An entity is something with its own independent existence, regardless of whether it's currently reachable by any object within a Java virtual machine. Entities can be retrieved from the database through queries, and they must be explicitly saved and deleted by the application. (If cascading relationships have been set up, the act of saving or deleting a parent entity can also save or delete its children, but this is still explicit at the level of the parent.)

Values are stored only as part of the persistent state of an entity. They have no independent existence. They might be primitives, collections, enumerations, or custom user types. Since they are entirely subordinated to the entity in which they exist, they cannot be independently versioned, nor can they be shared by more than one entity or collection.

Notice that a particular Java object might be either an entity or a value—the difference is in how it is designed and presented to the persistence service. Primitive Java types are always values.

Basic Types

Here is a smattering of information about the built-in types, showing how they relate Java classes to SQL column types. We present samples of the variability between databases, but are not trying to show every variant; check out the source code for all the dialect implementations in `org.hibernate.dialect` for the definitive details (look for `registerColumnType( )` calls).

Hibernate's basic types fall into a number of groupings:

Simple numeric and Boolean types
> These correspond to the primitive Java types that represent numbers, characters, and Boolean values, or their wrapper classes. They get mapped to appropriate SQL

column types (based on the SQL dialect in use). They are: boolean, byte, charac ter, double, float, integer, long, short, true_false, and yes_no. The last two are alternate ways to represent a Boolean value within the database; true_false uses the values "T" and "F," whereas yes_no uses "Y" and "N."

String type

The Hibernate type string maps from java.lang.String to the appropriate string column type for the SQL dialect (usually VARCHAR, but in Oracle VARCHAR2 is used).

Time types

Hibernate uses date, time, and timestamp to map from java.util.Date (and sub-classes) to appropriate SQL types (e.g., DATE, TIME, TIMESTAMP). The timestamp implementation uses the current time within the Java environment; you can use the database's notion of the current time instead by using dbtimestamp.

If you prefer working with the more convenient java.util.Calendar class, there is no need to translate to and from Date values in your own code; you can map it directly with calendar (which stores the date and time as a TIMESTAMP) or calendar_date (which considers only the date, as a DATE column).

Arbitrary precision numeric

The Hibernate type big_decimal provides a mapping between java.math.BigDeci mal to the appropriate SQL type (usually NUMERIC, but Oracle uses NUMBER). Hiber-nate's big_integer maps java.math.BigInteger (usually to BIGINT, but Informix calls it INT8 and Oracle again uses NUMBER).

Localization values

The types locale, timezone, and currency are stored as strings (VARCHAR or VARCHAR2, as noted above), and mapped to the Locale, TimeZone, and Currency classes in the java.util package. Locale and Currency are stored using their ISO codes, while TimeZone is stored using its ID property.

Class names

The type class maps instances of java.lang.Class using their fully qualified names, stored in a string column (VARCHAR, or VARCHAR2 in Oracle).

Byte arrays

The type binary stores byte arrays in an appropriate SQL binary type.

Any serializable object

The type serializable can be used to map any serializable Java object into a SQL binary column. This is the fallback type used when attempting to persist an object that doesn't have a more specific appropriate mapping (and for which you do not want to implement a UserType custom mapping; see the next section). The SQL column type is the same as is used for binary, described later.

JDBC large objects

The types blob and clob provide mappings for the Blob and Clob classes in the java.sql package. If you are dealing with truly large values, your best bet is to declare the properties as either Blob or Clob—even though this introduces an explicit JDBC dependency to your data object, it easily allows Hibernate to leverage JDBC features to lazily load the property value only if you need it.

If you are not worried that the data is too huge, you can spare yourself this direct JDBC interface, declare the property type as `String` or `byte[ ]`, and map it using `text` or `binary`. These correspond to SQL column types of `CLOB` and `VARBINARY` (`RAW` in Oracle, `BYTEA` in PostgreSQL), respectively, and the values are loaded immediately into the properties when the object is loaded.

Custom Value Types

In addition to mapping your objects as entities, you can also create classes that are mapped to the database as values within other entities, without their own independent existence. This can be as simple as changing the way an existing type is mapped (because you want to use a different column type or representation), or as complex as splitting a value across multiple columns.

Although you can do this on a case-by-case basis within your mapping documents, the principle of avoiding repeated code argues for encapsulating types you use in more than one place into an actual reusable class. Your class will implement either `org.hibernate.UserType` or `org.hibernate.CompositeUserType`. This technique is illustrated in Chapter 6.

This is also how you map Java 5's `enum` types (and hand-coded instances of the type-safe enumeration pattern in from previous Java versions). You can use a single, reusable custom type mapping for all enumerations, as discussed in Chapter 6.

"Any" Type Mappings

This final kind of mapping is very much a free-for-all. Essentially, it allows you to map references to any of your other mapped entities interchangeably. This is done by providing two columns, one which contains the name of the table to which each reference is being made, and another which provides the ID within that table of the specific entity of interest.

You can't maintain any sort of foreign key constraints in such a loose relationship. It's rare to need this kind of mapping at all. One situation in which you might find it useful is if you want to maintain an audit log that can contain actual objects. The reference manual also mentions web application session data as another potential use, but that seems unlikely in a well-structured application.

All Types

The following table shows each of the type classes in the `org.hibernate.types` package, along with the type name you would use for it in a mapping document, the most common SQL type(s) used in columns storing mapped values, and any relevant comments about its purpose. In many cases, more detailed discussion can be found earlier. To save space, the "Type" that appears at the end of each class name has been removed, except in the case of the Type interface implemented by all the others.

Type class	Type name	SQL type	Notes
AbstractBynary (perhaps a pun on byte/binary/array?)	N/A	N/A	Encapsulates the code used to bind streams of bytes into VARBINARY-style columns
AbstractCharArray	N/A	N/A	Encapsulates the code used to bind streams of characters into VARCHAR-style columns
AbstractComponent (interface)	N/A	N/A	Lets Component types store collections, have cascades, etc.
Abstract	N/A	N/A	Abstract skeleton used by the built-in types
Any	any	N/A	Supports "any" type mappings
Array	array	N/A	Maps a Java array as a persistent collection
Association(interface)	N/A	N/A	Supports associations between entities
Bag	bag	N/A	Maps collections with bag semantics
BigDecimal	big_decimal	NUMERIC	In Oracle, SQL type is NUMBER
BigInteger	big_integer	BIGINT	In Oracle, SQL type is NUMBER; Informix uses INT8.
Binary	binary	VARBINARY	Basic type for byte arrays, eagerly fetched (see above)
Blob	blob	BLOB	Link to JDBC support for lazily loaded byte arrays
Boolean	boolean	BIT	A basic and primitive type
Byte	byte	TINYINT	A basic and primitive type
CalendarDate	calendar_date	DATE	Maps Calendar, ignoring time
Calendar	calendar	TIMESTAMP	Maps Calendar, including time
Character	character	CHAR	A basic and primitive type
CharacterArray	N/A	VARCHAR	Maps Character[ ] properties
CharArray	N/A	VARCHAR	Maps char[ ] properties
CharBoolean	N/A	CHAR	Abstract skeleton used to implement yes_no and true_false types
Class	class	VARCHAR or VARCHAR2	Basic type that stores a class' name

Type class	Type name	SQL type	Notes
Clob	clob	CLOB	Link to JDBC support for lazily loaded char arrays
Collection	N/A	N/A	Supports all persistent collection types
Component	component	N/A	Maps the properties of a contained value class on to a group of columns
CompositeCustom	N/A	N/A	Adapts CompositeUserType implementations to the Type interface
Currency	currency	VARCHAR or VARCHAR2	Stores ISO code for a currency
Custom	N/A	N/A	Adapts UserType implementations to the Type interface
Date	date	DATE	A basic type
DbTimestamp	dbtimestamp	TIMESTAMP	A basic type, uses database notion of "now"
Discriminator(interface)	N/A	N/A	Marker interface for types that can be used for discriminator properties (to select the right mapped subclass)
Double	double	DOUBLE	A basic and primitive type
EmbeddedComponent	composite-element	N/A	Specializes ComponentType for declaration within a mapping
Entity	N/A	N/A	Represents a reference to another entity
Float	float	FLOAT	A basic and primitive type
Identifier(interface)	id	N/A	Marker interface for types that store identifiers of entities
IdentifierBag	idbag	N/A	Maps a Collection with bag semantics and surrogate identifier column
Immutable	N/A	N/A	Abstract superclass for immutable types; extends NullableType
Integer	integer	INTEGER	A basic and primitive type
List	list	N/A	Maps a Java List
Literal(interface)	N/A	N/A	Marker interface for types that store SQL literals
Locale	locale	VARCHAR or VARCHAR2	Stores ISO code for a locale
Long	long	LONG	A basic and primitive type
ManyToOne	many-to-one	N/A	An association between entities
Map	map	N/A	Maps a Java Map

Type class	Type name	SQL type	Notes
Meta	meta-type	N/A	Stores discriminator values for polymorphic mapping using any
Mutable	N/A	N/A	Abstract superclass for mutable types
Nullable	N/A	N/A	Abstract superclass for simple, one column types that can be null
OneToOne	one-to-one	N/A	An association between entities
OrderedMap	N/A	N/A	Extension of MapType to preserve SQL ordering
OrderedSet	N/A	N/A	Extension of SetType to preserve SQL ordering
Primitive	N/A	N/A	Abstract skeleton for mapping primitive Java types; extends ImmutableType
Serializable	serializable	Binary (see JDBC Large Objects earlier)	Catch-all mapping for serializable classes with no better alternative
Set	set	N/A	Maps a Java Set
Short	short	SMALLINT	A basic and primitive type
SortedMap	N/A	N/A	Extension of MapType to use Java Collections ordering
SortedSet	N/A	N/A	Extension of SetType to use Java Collections ordering
String	string	VARCHAR or VARCHAR2	A basic type
Text	text	CLOB	Eagerly fetches a CLOB into a String property (see above)
Time	time	TIME	A basic type
TimeZone	timezone	VARCHAR or VARCHAR2	Stores time zone ID
Timestamp	timestamp	TIMESTAMP	A basic type, uses JVM notion of "now"
TrueFalse	true_false	CHAR	Stores Booleans as "T" or "F"
Type(interface)	N/A	N/A	Superinterface of all these types
Version(interface)	N/A	N/A	Extends Type for version stamping
WrapperBinary	N/A	N/A	Seems unfinished
YesNo	yes_no	CHAR	Stores Booleans as "Y" or "N"

There is also a TypeFactory class which provides assistance in building the right Type implementation for a given need, such as when parsing a type name in a mapping document. Reading its source is interesting.

The Criteria API

Criteria queries start by obtaining a `Criteria` object from the `Session`, using the `createCriteria()` method to identify the primary class (and thus table) on which the query is to be performed. Restrictions, projections, and orderings are then attached to the query using the factories described below, making it a very powerful and convenient interface.

The Criterion Factory

Hibernate provides the class `org.hibernate.criterion.Restrictions` as a factory for creating the `Criterion` instances you use to narrow down the objects (rows) you want from criteria queries. `Restrictions` defines a bunch of static methods you can invoke to conveniently create each of the standard `Criterion` implementations available in Hibernate, using parameters you supply. These criteria are used to determine which persistent objects from the database are included in the results of your query. The following table provides a summary of the available options.

Method	Parameters	Purpose
allEq	Map *properties*	A shortcut for requiring several properties to have particular values. The keys of the supplied map are the names of the properties you want to constrain, while the values in the map are the target values each property must equal if an entity is to be included in the query results. The returned `Criterion` ensures that each named *property* has the corresponding value.
and	Criterion *lhs*, Criterion *rhs*	Builds a compound `Criterion` that requires both halves to be met in order for the whole to succeed. See also `conjunction()`.
between	String *property*, Object *low*, Object *high*	Requires the value of the named property to fall between the values of *low* and *high*.
conjunction	None	Creates a `Conjunction` object which can be used to build an "and" criterion with as many pieces as you need. Simply call its `add()` method

Method	Parameters	Purpose
		with each of the Criterion instances you want to check. The conjunction will be true if and only if all its component criteria are true. This is more convenient than building a tree of and( ) criteria "by hand." The add( ) method of the Criteria interface acts as though it contains a Conjunction.
disjunction	None	Creates a Disjunction object that can be used to build an "or" criterion with as many pieces as you need. Simply call its add( ) method with each of the Criterion instances you want to check. The disjunction will be true if any of its component criteria are true. This is more convenient than building a tree of or( ) criteria "by hand." See Example 8-10.
eq	String *property*, Object *value*	Requires the named property to have the specified value.
eqProperty	String *property1*, String *property2*	Requires the two named properties to have the same value.
ge	String *property*, Object *value*	Requires the named property to be greater than or equal to the specified value.
geProperty	String *property1*, String *property2*	Requires the first named property to be greater than or equal to the second.
gt	String *property*, Object *value*	Requires the named property to be greater than the specified value.
gtProperty	String *property1*, String *property2*	Requires the first named property to be greater than the second.
idEq	Object *value*	Requires the identifier property to be equal to the specified value.
ilike	String *property*, Object *value*	A case-insensitive "like" operator. See like.
ilike	String *property*, String *value*, Match Mode *mode*	A case-insensitive "like" operator for people who don't want to mess with "like" syntax and just want to match a substring. MatchMode is a type-safe enumeration with values START, END, ANYWHERE, and EXACT. This method adjusts the syntax of *value* to reflect the kind of matching specified by *mode*, then proceeds like the two-parameter ilike( ).
in	String *property*, Collection *values*	A shortcut for allowing the named property to have any of the values contained in the collection. This is more convenient than building up a disjunction( ) of eq( ) criteria "by hand."
in	String *property*, Object[ ] *values*	A shortcut for allowing the named property to have any of the values contained in the array. This is more convenient than building up a disjunction( ) of eq( ) criteria "by hand."
isEmpty	String *property*	Requires the named collection property to be empty (have zero length).
isNotEmpty	String *property*	Requires the named collection property to be have one or more elements.
isNotNull	String *property*	Requires the named property to have a value other than null.

Method	Parameters	Purpose
isNull	String *property*	Requires the named property to be `null`.
le	String *property*, Object *value*	Requires the named property to be less than or equal to the specified value. See Example 8-3.
leProperty	String *property1*, String *property2*	Requires the first named property to be less than or equal to the second.
like	String *property*, Object *value*	Requires the named property to be "like" the specified value (in the sense of the SQL `like` operator, which allows simple substring matching). See Examples 8-8 and 8-16.
like	String *property*, String *value*, Match Mode *mode*	A "like" operator for people who don't want to mess with "like" syntax and just want to match a substring. See `ilike( )` for more details.
lt	String *property*, Object *value*	Requires the named property to be less than the specified value.
ltProperty	String *property1*, String *property2*	Requires the first named property to be less than the second.
naturalId	None	Allows selection through a multicolumn "natural business key" mapped using `natural-id`.
ne	String *property*, Object *value*	Requires the named property to have any value other than the specified value.
neProperty	String *property1*, String *property2*	Requires the two named properties to have different values.
not	Criterion *expression*	Negates the supplied `Criterion` (if it matched, this one fails, and vice versa).
or	Criterion *lhs*, Criterion *rhs*	Builds a compound `Criterion` that succeeds if either of its halves matches. See also `disjunction( )`.
sizeEq	String *property*, int *size*	Requires the named collection property to have the specified number of elements.
sizeGe	String *property*, int *size*	Requires the named collection property to have at least the specified number of elements.
sizeGt	String *property*, int *size*	Requires the named collection property to have more than the specified number of elements.
sizeLe	String *property*, int *size*	Requires the named collection property to have no more than the specified number of elements.
sizeLt	String *property*, int *size*	Requires the named collection property to have fewer than the specified number of elements.
sizeNe	String *property*, int *size*	Requires the named collection property to have a different number of elements than *size*.
sqlRestriction	String *sql*	Applies a constraint expressed in the native SQL dialect of the underlying database system. This can be very powerful, but be aware it might lead to loss of portability.

Method	Parameters	Purpose
sqlRestriction	String *sql*, Object[] *values*, Type[] *types*	Applies a constraint expressed in the native SQL of the underlying database, with the supplied JDBC parameters. This can be very powerful, but be aware it might lead to loss of portability.
sqlRestriction	String *sql*, Object *value*, Type *type*	Applies a constraint expressed in the native SQL of the underlying database, with the supplied JDBC parameter. This can be very powerful, but be aware it might lead to loss of portability.

When specifying query text for the sqlRestriction( ) methods, any occurrences of the string "{alias}" within the query will be replaced by the actual alias of the table on which the query is being performed.

Many of these methods accept Criterion instances as arguments, allowing you to build compound criteria trees with as much complexity as you need. conjunction( ) and disjunction( ) return objects that make it even easier to add criteria, by returning objects with add( ) methods you can call as many times as you'd like to add criteria. If your query gets sufficiently complex, however, it might be easier to express and understand in HQL. There are also a few remaining kinds of queries that are not yet supported by this API, so you may not always be able to avoid HQL. But that's becoming increasingly rare—most of the kinds of bread-and-butter queries that come up all the time in application development are expressed very naturally and easily in this API, leading to readable and compact Java code that can be checked for correctness at compile-time.

The Projection Factory

Hibernate provides the class org.hibernate.criterion.Projections as a factory for creating the Projection instances you use to narrow down the properties (columns) you want from criteria queries, and requesting the calculation of aggregate values. Projections defines static methods you can invoke to conveniently create each of the standard Projection implementations available in Hibernate, using parameters you supply. These projections are used to narrow, group or transform the properties that get included in the results of your query. Here is a summary of the available options.

Method	Parameters	Purpose
alias	Projection *projection*, String *alias*	Assigns an alias (name) to the projection, so it can be referred to in other places within your Criteria query (such as for grouping, ordering, and the like).
avg	String *property*	Calculates the average of the named property.
count	String *property*	Calculates the number of times this property appears in the results.
countDistinct	String *property*	Calculates the number of distinct (different) values this property has within the results.

Method	Parameters	Purpose
distinct	Projection *projection*	Causes only unique values to be returned from the projection (eliminates duplicate values).
groupProperty	String *property*	Causes results to be grouped by the specified property (useful when calculating aggregate values). See Example 8-15.
id	None	Returns the object's identifier as an element of the projection (regardless of what the name of the identifier property may be).
max	String *property*	Calculates the largest value of the named property. See Example 8-15.
min	String *property*	Calculates the smallest value of the named property.
projectionList	None	Creates a new projection list, for requesting more than one projected value. See Example 8-14.
property	String *property*	Includes the value of the named property in the projection. See Example 8-13.
rowCount	None	Calculates the total number of results returned. See Example 8-15.
sqlGroupProjection	String *sql*, String *groupBy*, String[] *columnAliases*, Type[] *types*	Lets you use database-specific SQL code to perform the projection; *groupBy* can contain a SQL "GROUP BY" clause. You need to tell Hibernate the names and types of any column aliases your projection returns.
sqlProjection	String *sql*, String[] *columnAliases*, Type [] *types*	Lets you use database-specific SQL code to perform the projection; you can perform grouping using groupProperty( ) projections, above. You need to tell Hibernate the names and types of any column aliases your projection returns.
sum	String *property*	Calculates the arithmetic sum of the values of the named property.

The Order Factory

You can ask Hibernate (and thereby, the underlying database system) to sort your results in a particular order. The class org.hibernate.criterion.Order represents these ordering requests, and offers two static factory methods for creating the instances you need, which can then be added to your query. Once you've obtained your Order instance, you can call the nonstatic method ignoreCase( ) on it if you would like your results sorted in a case-insensitive way.

Method	Parameters	Purpose
asc	String *property*	Creates an ordering that will sort results in ascending order by the named property. See Example 8-6.
desc	String *property*	Creates an ordering that will sort results in descending order by the named property.

The Property Factory

In the methods we've been looking at so far, you start with the criterion, projection, or order you're interested in creating, and then supply the name of the property with which you want to work as a parameter. The Criteria API also lets you work in the opposite direction, starting with the property and then calling a method to build a criterion or projection based on it. The class `org.hibernate.criterion.Property` is a factory for creating the `Property` instances you use when you prefer this approach. `Property` defines a single static method, `forName( )`, which you can invoke to create an instance representing a particular property. Once you've got that instance, you can call one of the following methods to create criteria, projections and orderings based on the property it represents. Here is a list of the more commonly useful methods; the ones we omit have to do with detached criteria and subqueries, which are beyond the scope of this book. When you want to learn about them, see the *Advanced query options* chapter of *Java Persistence with Hibernate* or *Detached queries and subqueries*[*] in the online reference.

Method	Parameters	Purpose
asc	None	Creates an `Order` that will sort results in ascending order by the property.
avg	None	Creates a `Projection` that returns the average of the property's values.
between	Object *min*, Object *max*	Creates a `Criterion` that requires the property have a value between *min* and *max*.
count	None	Creates a `Projection` that returns the number of times the property appears in the results.[a]
desc	None	Creates an ordering that will sort results in descending order by the named property.
eq	Object *value*	Creates a `Criterion` that requires the property to equal the supplied value.[b]
eqProperty	Property *other*	Creates a `Criterion` that requires the property to equal another property, represented by *other*.
eqProperty	String *property*	Creates a `Criterion` that requires the property to equal another property, named by *property*.
ge	Object *value*	Creates a `Criterion` that requires the property to be greater than or equal to the specified value.[b]
geProperty	Property *other*	Creates a `Criterion` that requires the property to be greater than or equal to another property, represented by *other*.
geProperty	String *property*	Creates a `Criterion` that requires the property to be greater than or equal to another property, named by *property*.
getProperty	String *property*	Extracts the named component property of the current property (which is presumably a compound property). Returns another `Property` instance.

---

[*] *http://www.hibernate.org/hib_docs/v3/reference/en/html/querycriteria.html#querycriteria-detachedqueries*

Method	Parameters	Purpose
group	None	Creates a Projection that requests results be grouped by values of the property.
gt	Object *value*	Creates a Criterion that requires the property to be greater than the specified value.[b]
gtProperty	Property *other*	Creates a Criterion that requires the property to be greater than another property, represented by *other*.
gtProperty	String *property*	Creates a Criterion that requires the property to be greater than another property, named by *property*.
in	Collection *values*	Creates a Criterion that requires the supplied collection to contain the property.
in	Object[] *values*	Creates a Criterion that requires the property to be equal to any element of the array.
isEmpty	None	Creates a Criterion that requires the property to be empty (be a collection with length zero).
isNotEmpty	None	Creates a Criterion that requires the property to be a collection with at least one element.
isNotNull	None	Creates a Criterion that requires the property to have a non-null value.
isNull	None	Creates a Criterion that requires the property to have a null value.
le	Object *value*	Creates a Criterion that requires the property to be less than or equal to the specified value.[b]
leProperty	Property *other*	Creates a Criterion that requires the property to be less than or equal to another property, represented by *other*.
leProperty	String *property*	Creates a Criterion that requires the property to be less than or equal to another property, named by *property*.
like	Object *value*	Creates a Criterion that requires the property to be "like" the specified value (in the sense of the SQL like operator, which allows simple substring matching).[b]
like	String *value*, Match Mode *mode*	A version of "like" for people who don't want to mess with "like" syntax and just want to match a substring. MatchMode is a type-safe enumeration with values START, END, ANYWHERE, and EXACT. This method adjusts the syntax of *value* to reflect the kind of matching specified by *mode*, then proceeds like the single-parameter like( ) earlier.[b]
lt	Object *value*	Creates a Criterion that requires the property to be less than the specified value.[b]
ltProperty	Property *other*	Creates a Criterion that requires the property to be less than another property, represented by *other*.
ltProperty	String *property*	Creates a Criterion that requires the property to be less than another property, named by *property*.
max	None	Creates a Projection that returns the largest of the property's values.
min	None	Creates a Projection that returns the smallest of the property's values.
ne	Object *value*	Creates a Criterion that requires the property to have any value other than the specified value.[b]

Method	Parameters	Purpose
neProperty	Property *other*	Creates a Criterion that requires the property to have a different value than the *other*.
neProperty	String *property*	Creates a Criterion that requires the property to have a different value than the named *property*.

a The actual class returned, CountProjection, has a setDistinct( ) method you can call if you want to count distinct values.

b The actual class returned, SimpleExpression, has an ignoreCase( ) method you can call if you want comparison to be case-insensitive.

Hibernate SQL Dialects

Getting Fluent in the Local SQL

Hibernate ships with detailed support for many[*] commercial and free relational databases. While most features will work properly without doing so, it's important to set the `hibernate.dialect` configuration property to the right subclass of `org.hibernate.dialect.Dialect`, especially if you want to use features like `native` or `sequence` primary key generation or session locking. Choosing a dialect is also a very convenient way of setting up a whole raft of Hibernate configuration parameters you'd otherwise have to deal with individually.

Database system	Appropriate hibernate.dialect setting
Caché 2007.1	`org.hibernate.dialect.Cache71Dialect`
DB2	`org.hibernate.dialect.DB2Dialect`
DB2 AS/400	`org.hibernate.dialect.DB2400Dialect`
DB2 OS390	`org.hibernate.dialect.DB2390Dialect`
Derby	`org.hibernate.dialect.DerbyDialect`
Firebird	`org.hibernate.dialect.FirebirdDialect`
FrontBase	`org.hibernate.dialect.FrontbaseDialect`
H2	`org.hibernate.dialect.H2Dialect`
HSQLDB	`org.hibernate.dialect.HSQLDialect`
Informix	`org.hibernate.dialect.InformixDialect`
Ingres	`org.hibernate.dialect.IngresDialect`
Interbase	`org.hibernate.dialect.InterbaseDialect`
JDataStore	`org.hibernate.dialect.JDataStore`
Mckoi SQL	`org.hibernate.dialect.MckoiDialect`

[*] I never expected to bump into Caché again, having left the world of health care software to work in Java....

Database system	Appropriate hibernate.dialect setting
Mimer SQL	`org.hibernate.dialect.MimerSQLDialect`
Microsoft SQL Server	`org.hibernate.dialect.SQLServerDialect`
MySQL (versions prior to 5.x)	`org.hibernate.dialect.MySQLDialect`
MySQL (version 5.x and later)	`org.hibernate.dialect.MySQL5Dialect`
MySQL (prior to 5.x, using InnoDB tables)	`org.hibernate.dialect.MySQLInnoDBDialect`
MySQL (prior to 5.x, using MyISAM tables)	`org.hibernate.dialect.MySQLMyISAMDialect`
MySQL (version 5.x, using InnoDB tables)	`org.hibernate.dialect.MySQL5InnoDBDialect`
Oracle (any version)	`org.hibernate.dialect.OracleDialect`
Oracle 8i	`org.hibernate.dialect.Oracle8iDialect`
Oracle 9i or 10g	`org.hibernate.dialect.Oracle9Dialect`
Oracle 10g only (use of ANSI join syntax)	`org.hibernate.dialect.Oracle10gDialect`
Pointbase	`org.hibernate.dialect.PointbaseDialect`
PostgreSQL	`org.hibernate.dialect.PostgreSQLDialect`
Progress	`org.hibernate.dialect.ProgressDialect`
SAP DB	`org.hibernate.dialect.SAPDBDialect`
Sybase (or MS SQL Server)	`org.hibernate.dialect.SybaseDialect`
Sybase 11.9.2	`org.hibernate.dialect.Sybase11Dialect`
Sybase Anywhere	`org.hibernate.dialect.SybaseAnywhereDialect`
Teradata	`org.hibernate.dialect.TeradataDialect`
TimesTen 5.1	`org.hibernate.dialect.TimesTenDialect`
Unisys 2200 RDMS	`org.hibernate.dialect.RDMSOS2200Dialect`

If you don't see your target database here, check whether support has been added to
the latest Hibernate release. Most of the dialects are listed in the *SQL Dialects*[†] section
of the Hibernate reference documentation. If that doesn't pan out, see if you can find
a third-party effort to support the database, or consider starting your own!

[†] *http://www.hibernate.org/hib_docs/v3/reference/en/html/session-configuration.html#configuration-optional-
dialects*

Spring Transaction Support

Using the Spring Framework's Transactional Annotation

You can put the Transactional annotation on either concrete classes or interfaces, and it can be placed on a class or a method. If a class is annotated with Transactional, the settings apply to every method defined in that class. If a method is annotated with Transactional, the transaction settings apply to a single method. If the Transactional annotation is present on both a class and a method, the settings from the method annotation take precedence over the class annotation.

From the Transactional annotation you can control the isolation level of a transaction, the timeout, the propagation setting, and an array of exceptions which should cause the transaction to roll back. For example, if we wanted to always create a new transaction with a serializable isolation level that would time out if not completed in one minute and would roll back on a NumberFormatException, we'd write code like Example D-1.

> If these terms are unfamiliar, the tables might help explain them.

Example D-1. More control of transaction configuration

```
@Transactional(readOnly=false,
    propagation=Propagation.REQUIRES_NEW,
    isolation=Isolation.SERIALIZABLE,
    rollbackFor={NumberFormatException.class},
    timeout=60)
public abstract void run();
```

If you use the `Transactional` annotation, you need to be careful where you put the annotation. If you start using proxies in Spring, or if you start to delve into Spring's compelling support for Aspect-Oriented Programming (AOP), you may want to avoid putting `Transactional` on an interface, and you'll also want to be careful about putting `Transactional` on nonpublic methods. In this example, we put the `Transactional` annotation on an interface because we're not using any of Spring's AOP facilities. If you are troubleshooting a system where the `Transactional` annotation is being ignored, the first thing you will want to do is verify public visibility of the annotated method. There can be some very confusing situations that arise with proxies and AOP that you may encounter if you are using AspectJ or the older Spring AOP facilities. Once you start using Spring's AOP facilities, you should start putting @`Transactional` on concrete classes.

Transactional annotation attributes

Table D-1 lists the attributes for the `Transactional` annotation.

Table D-1. List of Transactional annotation attributes

Annotation property	Type	Description
isolation	Isolation	Transaction isolation settings. See Table D-3 below for more information about the available options.
noRollbackFor	Class[]	An array of exception classes (or class names) which will not cause a transaction rollback. You can specify an array of fully-qualified class names or an array of Class objects.
noRollbackForClassName	String[]	
propagation	Propagation	Transaction propagation configuration. See Table D-2 for more information about this setting.
readOnly	boolean	Specifies whether the transaction is read-only or read-write.
rollbackFor	Class[]	An array of exception classes (or class names) which will cause a transaction rollback. The default behavior is for RuntimeExceptions to trigger a rollback, while checked exceptions do not normally trigger a rollback. If you throw a checked exception and you want it to trigger a rollback, you'll need to add it to the rollbackFor attribute. You can specify an array of fully-qualified class names or an array of Class objects.
rollbackForClassName	String[]	
timeout	int	Number of seconds after which a transaction will time out. A timeout value of −1 specifies that the transaction has no timeout (an infinite timeout).

Transaction propagation

The `propagation` attribute tells Spring whether the operation requires a new transaction, a nested transaction, or can operate within an existing transaction. Table D-2 lists the valid values for the `propagation` attribute.

Table D-2. Values of the Propagation enumeration

Value	Description
Propagation.REQUIRED	Uses an existing transaction or creates a new one if none exists (this is the default).
Propagation.SUPPORTS	Will participate in an existing transaction, but won't create a new one if none exists.
Propagation.MANDATORY	Requires the presence of an existing transaction and throws an exception if none exists.
Propagation.REQUIRES_NEW	Creates a new transaction just for this method and suspends the current transaction if one exists.
Propagation.NOT_SUPPORTED	Persistence operations in the annotated method will not execute in a transaction. If called within an existing transaction, the transaction is suspended.
Propagation.NEVER	Throws an exception if the method is called within a transaction.
Propagation.NESTED	If called within an existing transaction, execute the annotated method in a nested transaction.

Propagation behavior will depend on your transaction provider. If you are using JTA, make sure you read the documentation carefully to see if nested transactions are supported.

Transaction isolation

The `isolation` attribute controls how the locks are acquired within a transaction and how transactions are affected by concurrent transactions and statements executed against the database. Table D-3 lists the valid values for the `isolation` attribute.

Table D-3. Values of the Isolation enumeration

Value	Description
Isolation.DEFAULT	Uses the default isolation level of the underlying database.
Isolation.SERIALIZABLE	Provides for the highest level of isolation, prevents dirty reads, nonrepeatable reads, and phantom reads. When using this isolation level even read operations may acquire locks in the database. When using this isolation level (or any isolation-level above READ_UNCOMMITTED) you should take care to avoid deadlocks between two concurrent transactions.
Isolation.REPEATABLE_READ	Prevents dirty reads and nonrepeatable reads. Does not protect against phantom reads.
Isolation.READ_COMMITTED	Prevents dirty reads. Nonrepeatable reads and phantom reads are possible.
Isolation.READ_UNCOMMITTED	Lowest level of isolation, one transaction will see uncommitted changes from a second transaction. Dirty reads, nonrepeatable reads, and phantom reads are all possible at this level.

It is often unrealistic to use SERIALIZABLE in a real world system without "serializing" all access to the database. You are often forced to use either REPEATABLE_READ or READ_COMMITTED and build in some logic to detect deadlocks and retry operations which have failed. A large multi-user application (like a web site) that uses serialization needs to be aware of transaction deadlock, and if you are using any isolation level higher than READ_UNCOMMITTED, you should make sure that your Transactional annotation defines a finite value for the timeout attribute. Isolation behavior depends on the database you are using. For example, MySQL with the InnoDB storage engine is going to have a slightly different interpretation of the isolation levels than different versions of Oracle, SQL Server, Derby, or HSQLDB.

Using a JTA Transaction Manager

In the examples in Chapter 13, we are using the HibernateTransactionManager because it is straightforward to use and readily available. If you need to use JTA to participate in distributed transactions or transactions that span multiple technologies (JDBC + JMS), you can use the substitute for transactionManager in your *applicationContext.xml* as shown in Example D-2.

Example D-2. Configuring a JTA transaction manager

```
<!-- enable the configuration of transactional behavior based on annotations -->
<tx:annotation-driven transaction-manager="transactionManager"/>
<bean id="transactionManager"
  class="org.springframework.transaction.jta.JtaTransactionManager" />
```

Where to Go Next

There are a number of ways you can dig deeper into the capabilities of Hibernate and the other ways it can be used. Here are some good choices; pick the ones that best suit your needs, learning style, and time frame.

Online Manuals

All of the tools mentioned in this book have good online documentation. If you have a basic idea of how to use the package, the online reference can give you the details you need to accomplish specific tasks. Look for the Documentation links prominently featured on each package's home page.

Books

A more complete and in-depth discussion of Hibernate can be found in *Java Persistence with Hibernate* by Christian Bauer and Gavin King (Manning Publications). As the creators of Hibernate, they're very familiar with the details, though they sometimes assume a fairly deep proficiency with database concepts.

To help gain that proficiency, you might also want to pick up *Java Database Best Practices* by George Reese (O'Reilly), or at least read the chapter we mentioned in Chapter 4 that is available online[*].

For an in-depth reference covering Apache Maven, read *Maven: The Definitive Guide*[†] from Sonatype. To learn more about Apache Ant, pick up a copy of *Ant: The Definitive Guide* by Jesse E. Tilly and Eric M. Burke (O'Reilly), or the more recent *Ant in Action* by Steve Loughran and Erik Hatcher (Manning).

For more information about the Spring Framework, pick up a copy of *Spring: A Developer's Notebook* by Bruce Tate and Justin Gehtland (O'Reilly) or a copy of

---

[*] *http://www.oreilly.com/catalog/javadtabp/chapter/ch02.pdf*

[†] *http://www.sonatype.com/book/index.html*

Professional Java Development with the Spring Framework by Rod Johnson, Juergen Hoeller, Alef Arendsen, Thomas Risberg, and Colin Samplaneau (WROX). While the authors of this book might be partial to the O'Reilly title, we wanted you to know that the WROX book is written by the people who created and maintain the Spring Framework.

Source Code

As with any open-source project, the ultimate arbiter of truth is the source code, and you can learn a lot by looking at it—and not just about the task you're directly focused on. And of course, as Java packages, the JavaDoc that gets generated from the source is a valuable reference. If you are working in Eclipse, it is well worth downloading the projects' source distributions, and telling Eclipse where the source trees are for each of the library JARs. This will enable full popup JavaDoc as you're completing class and method names and arguments, and enable you to dive into the source for each element by hitting F3, just as if it was part of your own project. We find this a terrific orientation and learning aid.

 If you are using Maven and running the eclipse:eclipse goal, you can download both source and JavaDocs using the following command:

```
mvn eclipse:eclipse -DdownloadSources=true  -DdownloadJavadocs=true
```

This may take some time to download all of the source and JavaDoc bundles for each dependency. Once you have the source and JavaDoc in your local Maven repository, you'll be able to view source code and JavaDoc for dependencies within the Eclipse IDE. Source and JavaDoc artifacts exist for most (but not all) widely-used open source libraries.

Dealing with Newer Releases

Changes are always a problem for a printed book, so you should expect to run into a few snags with new releases of all the software we cover. The examples in this new version of the book are based on the following specific versions of the various tools discussed:

- Ant 1.7.0 (least likely to be an issue)
- Eclipse 3.3.1.1
- Geronimo JTA 1.1 implementation
- Hibernate 3.2.5
- Hibernate Annotations 3.3.0.ga
- Hibernate Commons Annotations 3.3.0.ga
- Hibernate Tools 3.2.0 beta 9a (most places)

- Hibernate Tools 3.2.0.GA (Chapter 11)
- HSQLDB 1.8.0.7
- Log4J 1.2.14 (also highly unlikely to cause issues)
- Maven 2.0.8
- MySQL 5.0.21
- Spring Framework 2.5
- Stripes 1.4.3

Newer releases may change the way things work, sometimes in backward-incompatible ways. That's part of the fun in keeping up with active open source projects. The Maven specifications we provide should help you find the specific versions we used, which will help with the learning and experimentation process. You can then check the packages' release notes for ideas on when and how to move up to the latest and greatest.

You can also watch the Errata page on the book's site[‡] to see if anyone has encountered your issues and found a solution. If not, please submit your own discoveries to share with others!

Hibernate and HSQLDB each have an online support forum that can be valuable for dealing with incompatible changes, or just plain learning your way around the more complex aspects of the tools.

Getting Involved

One of the great things about open source is that you are not just using software, you are participating in a community. If you use Hibernate, Spring, Ant, Maven, or Stripes, you should sign up for the user mailing list to keep up with changes and new releases. If you need to customize the source code and you would like to contribute your changes back, all of these projects have very mature communities for integrating your changes. After you are comfortable with a technology, take some initiative and contribute a few documentation patches to the developer mailing list. Don't be afraid to get involved; open source thrives on independent initiative. You don't have to ask anyone's permission in contributing to these projects—all you have to do is show up and start participating.

To learn more about the community behind Hibernate, and to start participating in the project, go to the Hibernate website at *http://www.hibernate.org*. You can sign up for Hibernate user and developer mailing lists or read the support forums by following the instructions on this page: *http://www.hibernate.org/20.html*. The Hibernate team has a very active blog which you can read at *http://blog.hibernate.org/*. Add this blog to your favorite RSS reader—it is a great way to keep abreast of the related technologies (such as Seam and Hibernate Shards) which Gavin and others are actively developing.

[‡] *http://www.oreilly.com/catalog/9780596517724/*

The Spring Framework is associated with a company called Spring Source (*http://www.springsource.com*) which employs a number of core contributors to the Spring project. For more information about the Spring Framework community you can visit *http://www.springframework.org*. If you would like to sign up for mailing lists or get your hands on the source code to the Spring Framework, you'll want to read the information on the development page which is available at *http://www.springframework.org/development*. If you are really excited about the Spring Framework, you should consider attending Spring Source's annual conference, *The Spring Experience*. Information about Spring training is available on the Spring Source company web site, and information about The Spring Experience is available from the conference site, *http://www.thespringexperience.com/*.

Apache Ant and Apache Maven are two top-level projects operating within the Apache Software Foundation (ASF). For information on the large community of developers working within the Apache Software Foundation, check out the foundation's web site at *http://www.apache.org*. Apache is a massive organization that is responsible for some of the most widely used software projects in the world, from the ever-popular Apache web server and Tomcat application server to the Jakarta Commons libraries. To learn more about the development community surrounding Apache Maven, go to the project web site, *http://maven.apache.org*. To learn more about the development community surrounding Apache Ant, go to Ant's project web site at *http://ant.apache.org*. Both Ant and Maven have very active communities and offer high-traffic user and developer mailing lists.

Stripes' home page is located at *http://www.stripesframework.org/*. You'll find tutorials, reference documentation, and JavaDoc at that site. The interface to sign up for the SourceForge mailing lists is at *https://sourceforge.net/mail/?group_id=145476*. For Java language geeks, browsing through the source code of Stripes can be a fun experience since it's written by someone who clearly knows and uses Java's current feature set. I highly recommend downloading the Stripes source package and poking around, mostly just for fun.

Index

A

Abstract class, 330
AbstractBynary class, 330
AbstractCharArray class, 330
AbstractComponent interface, 330
ActionBean interface, 298
    writing ActionBeans, 311–315
ad-hoc reporting classes, 187
adding
    associated records (see lifecycle
        associations)
addOrder() method (Criteria), 172, 174, 178
add() method (Criteria), 166
aggregate functions, HQL, 189–192
aggregation with criteria queries, 163, 168,
       171–172
alias records, 108
aliases
    for projections, 172
    in HQL, 184
alias() method (Projections), 336
allEq() method (Restrictions), 333
and() method (Restrictions), 333
annotation-driven element
        (applicationContext.xml), 284, 286
AnnotationConfiguration class, 157
annotations, 139–161
    applied to model classes, 143–158
    cascading automatically, 158–161
    importing, 145
    obtaining, 141–143
    Stripes interceptors, 320–325
Ant
    community behind, 350

deploying Tomcat, 300–304
getting distribution of, 3–5
teaching to use Hibernate tools, 31
Ant configuration file (see build.xml)
Ant Tasks for Maven, 4
ANT_HOME enivironment variable, 8
Any class, 330
AOP (Aspect Oriented Programming), 320
Apache Ant distribution, getting, 3–5
Apache Geronimo project, 22
Apache Maven (see Maven)
Apache Tomcat environment, 299
    community behind, 350
    deploying using Ant, 300–304
application context, Spring, 281–285
    loading, 292
ApplicationContext objects, 281, 292
applicationContext.xml file, 305
    transactionManager bean, 346
    turning on Transactional annotation, 286–
       287
arbitrary mapping objects, 187
arbitrary precision numeric types, 328
Array class, 330
artifact dependencies (see dependencies)
artifact:dependencies element (build.xml), 16,
    21
artifactId attribute, artifacts, 21
artifactId element (pom.xml), 253, 255
artifacts (Maven), 21, 240, 302
    (see also specific artifact by name)
asc() method (Order), 166
asc() method (Projections), 337
asc() method (Property), 338
Aspect Oriented Programming (AOP), 320

We'd like to hear your suggestions for improving our indexes. Send email to *index@oreilly.com*.

assemble() method, 134
assembly directory, 241
Association interface, 330
associations, 87
   (see also collections)
   augmenting associations in, 92–103
   bidirectional (see bidirectional associations)
   cascade settings, 106
   criteria with, 173–174
   eager and lazy, 87–90, 287
   lifecycle associations, 104–107
   reflexive, 107–109
   Stripes with, 317–319
   traversing in queries, 184
@AttributeOverrides annotation, 151
auto-commit mode (JDBC), 55
auto-complete, 216, 219
auto-import atttribute, 180
auto-import facility, 180
avg() method (Projections), 336
avg() method (Property), 338

B

Bag class, 330
basedir attribute, project element, 15
batching, 45
bean element (applicationContext.xml), 283
BeanUtil class, 323
between() method (Property), 338
between() method (Restrictions), 333
bidirectional associations, 66, 80–84
   eager and lazy, 87–90, 287
BigDecimal class, 330
BigInteger class, 330
big_decimal type, 328
big_integer type, 328
Binary class, 330
binary releases of Hibernate Core, 10
binary type, 328
Blob class, 330
blob type, 328
books on Hibernate, 347
Boolean class, 330
Boolean types, 327
build element (pom.xml), 253
build.xml (Ant build file), 13–17
   creating database tables, 34–40
   defining dependencies in, 16, 21
     (see also dependences)

deploying applications to Tomcat, 301
   generating classes, 29–34
   Hibernate Annotations, 141–143
   pom.xml vs., 253, 254
building Maven projects, 243–245
built-in types, 327
byte arrays, 328
Byte class, 330

C

Calendar class, 330
CalendarDate class, 330
capitalization and auto-complete, 220
cascade annotations, 158–161
cascade attribute, 106, 161
catalina-ant artifact, 302
CDATA construct for queries, 61
Character class, 330
CharacterArray class, 330
CharArray class, 330
CharBoolean class, 330
class annotations (see annotations)
Class class, 330
class mapping (see mapping)
class names
   completion assistance for, 220
   in queries, 180
class path, 16
   Eclipse variables for, 246
   Hibernate Console, 217
   Maven projects, 259
class type, 328
class-description attribute, meta element, 28
class-path section (build.xml), 16
class.root property, 16
classes
   annotating, 143–158
   creating with mappings, 29–34
   importing, 48
classes directory, 13
   creating, 36
.classpath file (Eclipse), 246
Clob class, 331
clob type, 328
closing session factories, 51
code generation, build file, 29–34
   Eclipse features for, 229, 230–236
codegen target (build.xml), 31
   circular dependency with compile, 121

creating, 217–219

installing Hibernate Tools, 209–216

version of, 209

Eclipse configuration files, generating, 246

eclipse goal, 246

Eclipse IDE project files, 6

editing support with Hibernate Tools, 215, 219–222

ejb3 option (Hibernate3 Maven plug-in), 264

EJBs (Enterprise Java Beans), x, 269

@Embeddable annotation, 155

@Embedded annotation, 151

EmbeddedComponent class, 331

enableLike() method (Example), 176

EnhancedUserType interface, 138

Enterprise Java Beans (EJBs), 269

entities, 92, 327

Entity class, 331

entity-level annotations, 146

EntityManager interface (JPA), 143, 146

enum keyword, 112

enumerated type, defined, 112

enumerated types, persistent, 111, 112–126

creating custom mapping, 114–119

working with, 119–126

eqProperty() method (Property), 338

eqProperty() method (Restrictions), 334

eq() method (Property), 338

eq() method (Restrictions), 334

Europa Discovery Site, 213

event handlers, ActionBean interface, 311, 313

Example objects, 175

example, querying by, 175–177

excludeNone() method (Example), 175

excludeProperty() method (Example), 175

excludeZeroes() method (Example), 175

execute() method (HibernateTemplate), 277, 280

explicit package naming, 180

extension element (pom.xml), 253

extensions element (pom.xml), 259

F

F3 key (Eclipse), 220

field-description meta tag, 65

filter task, 305

findByExample() method (HibernateTemplate), 279

findByNamedParameter() method (HibernateTemplate), 279

findByNamedQuery() method (HibernateTemplate), 279

finding (see retrieving)

find() method (HibernateTemplate), 278

Float class, 331

fork attribute, java task, 17

form tag (Stripes), 310, 318

forName() method (Property), 178

fully qualified names in queries, 180

G

generate-resources stage (Maven Build Lifecycle), 261

generate-sources stage (Maven Build Lifecycle), 261

generate-test-resources stage (Maven Build Lifecycle), 261

generate-test-sources stage (Maven Build Lifecycle), 261

generating JAR artifacts (Maven), 245

generator tag, id element, 29

generics, 69

geProperty() method (Property), 338

geProperty() method (Restrictions), 334

getAnnotation() method (Method), 323

getContext() method (ActionBean), 299, 313

getHandler() method (ExecutionContext), 323

getHibernateTemplate() method (HibernateDaoSupport), 277

getNamedQuery() method (Session), 193

getPropertyType() method (BeanUtil), 323

getPropertyValue() method, 134

getProperty() method (Property), 338

getSupport() method (HibernateDaoSupport), 277

ge() method (Property), 338

ge() method (Restrictions), 334

GNU environment for Java, 5

goal identifier (Maven), 244

groupId attribute, artifacts, 21

groupId element (pom.xml), 253, 255, 258

groupProperty() method (Projections), 171, 337

groups of things (see collections)

group() method (Property), 339

gtProperty() method (Property), 339

merge() method (HibernateTemplate), 277, 280

Meta class, 332

meta element, 28

min() method (Projections), 337

min() method (Property), 339

modules element (pom.xml), 258

Mojo project, 253, 262, 264

multimodule Maven projects, 254–260

Mutable class, 332

mvn eclipse command, 246, 247

mvn idea command, 247

mvn package command, 245

mvn site command, 247–249

mvn test command, 244

MySQL, 199–207

    connecting to, 200–205

    Hibernate Tools with, 218

    setting up database, 199

MySQL driver, 218

N

named parameters, 60–61

    Hibernate Console with, 226

named queries, 60–61

    annotations and, 146

names, completion assistance for, 219

naming columns, 96

naming mapping files, 28

native SQL queries, 192–195

naturalId() method (Restrictions), 335

neProperty() method (Property), 340

neProperty() method (Restrictions), 335

NESTED attribute (propagation attribute), 345

NEVER attribute (propagation attribute), 345

ne() method (Property), 339

ne() method (Restrictions), 335

noRollbackFor attribute, Transactional annotation, 344

noRollbackForClassName attribute, Transactional annotation, 344

NOT_SUPPORTED attribute (propagation attribute), 345

not() method (Restrictions), 335

Nullable class, 332

nullSafeGet() method, 118, 134

nullSafeSet() method, 118, 134

O

O/R mapping, 25

object lifecycles, associations of, 104–107

object models, graphical view of, 236–237

object properties (see properties)

object-oriented programming, 25

objects

    annotating, 143–158

    associated with themselves (see reflexive associations)

    loading data into (see queries)

    loading into databases (see persistent objects, creating)

one-to-many mappings, 95

@OneToMany annotation, 154, 161

OneToOne class, 332

online documentation on Hibernate, 347

Order class, 166, 337

ordered collections, 90–91

OrderedMap class, 332

OrderedSet class, 332

ordering (see sorting)

org.hibernate.types package, 329

or() method (Restrictions), 335

outputfilename option (Hibernate3 Maven plug-in), 264

P

package names in queries, 180

package stage (Maven Build Lifecycle), 244, 260, 262

packaging element (pom.xml), 253, 256, 258

ParameterizedUserType interface, 138

parent/child POMs (Maven), 254–260

password attribute, deploy task, 303

path attribute, deploy task, 303

path element (build.xml), 16

persistent collections, creating, 71–77

persistent enumerated types, 111, 112–126

    creating custom mapping, 114–119

    working with, 119–126

persistent mapped objects, 49

persistent objects

    creating, 46–55

    deleting, 49, 59

    retrieving, 56–60

PersistentEnum interface, 114

PersistentSet class, 287

About the Authors

James Elliott is a senior software engineer at Berbee, with nearly two decades of professional experience as a systems developer. His involvement and fascination (some would say obsession) with computers started long before that, when his middle school in Mexico City somehow acquired a strange device labeled "Apple II." It's been a wild ride ever since.

Jim started designing with objects well before his work environments made that convenient. He has a passion for building high-quality tools and frameworks to simplify the tasks of other developers (not to mention his own), and he loves how using Java effectively can help in that effort, especially as the language matures.

After a globe-trotting childhood, Jim earned his bachelor's degree in computer science at Rensselaer Polytechnic Institute in upstate New York and his master's at the University of Wisconsin-Madison, with some interesting stints at Bell Laboratories (Murray Hill, birthplace of C and Unix). Although he succumbed to the allure of the real world shortly after completing his PhD qualifying exams, he was happy to find interesting work in Madison, where he lives with his partner Joe Buberger.

Ryan Fowler is a software engineer at Berbee. His programming life started in Basic on Apple II machines in elementary school at St. Stephen School in Grand Rapids, Michigan. After a hiatus, he returned to coding in the computer science department at Alma College in Alma, Michigan while earning his bachelor's degree. Ryan skis, sails, and rounds life out with some guitar playing when there's no snow or wind. Ryan lives in Madison, Wisconsin with his wife Sarah.

Tim O'Brien is both an Emacs partisan and a recent convert to the Apple Macintosh computer. Tim discovered programming on a TRS-80 in the early 1980s and went on to study electrical engineering at the University of Virginia. Tim works as an independent technologist, often partnering with Grassroots Technologies; most recently he developed hybrid architectures for various clients in the financial news, consumer protection, automotive, and educational publishing industries. In his free time Tim likes to sleep, write, and participate in open source documentation projects. Tim currently lives in Evanston, Illinois with his wife Susan and daughter Josephine.

Colophon

The animal on the cover of *Harnessing Hibernate* is a hedgehog, a small mammal in the family *Erinaceinae*. There are 16 hedgehog species in 5 genera, found throughout parts of Europe, Asia, Africa, and New Zealand. Some of these species are: the four-toed hedgehog (south-Saharan Africa); the long-eared hedgehog (Central Asia); the desert hedgehog (Africa and the Middle East); and the bare-bellied hedgehog (India). The different species vary in size, measuring 5 to 12 inches long and weighing 15 to 40 ounces. The most common domesticated hedgehog, known as the four-toed or African pygmy hedgehog, is smaller than its European cousins and has become a popular pet in many countries. The name *hedgehog* first came into use in the mid-15th century —"hedge" because it roots through undergrowth, and "hog" because of its pig-like snout. Hedgehogs are also known as urchins, hedgepigs, and furze-pigs.

The hedgehog's most distinctive feature is its spines, which grow everywhere on its body except its face, legs, and belly. When threatened, it rolls into a tight ball so that all of its spines point outward, presenting a barbed surface to predators. These spines are stiff, hollow hairs made of keratin and are very strong. Unlike a porcupine's quills, they do not fall out, except when a hedgehog sheds its baby spines during a process known as "quilling."

Hedgehogs eat small invertebrates such as frogs, slugs, and earthworms. Some hedgehogs have immunity to toxins and can eat bees, wasps, and venomous snakes. Being nocturnal, they sleep for most of the day in grass or under rocks or in holes in the ground. Although all hedgehogs can hibernate, not all do—hibernation depends on factors such as location, temperature, and abundance of food. In England, Bonfire Night celebrations on November 5th pose a particular risk to hedgehogs, who often sleep in the wood piles used for bonfires. Wildlife protection groups now warn the public to inspect their wood piles before lighting fires in order to protect hibernating hedgehogs.

The cover image is from J. G. Wood's *Animate Creation*. The cover font is Adobe ITC Garamond. The text font is Linotype Birka; the heading font is Adobe Myriad Condensed; and the code font is LucasFont's TheSansMonoCondensed.

Related Titles from O'Reilly

Java

Ajax on Java

Ant: The Definitive Guide,
  2nd Edition

Better, Faster, Lighter Java

Beyond Java

Eclipse

Eclipse Cookbook

Eclipse IDE Pocket Guide

Enterprise JavaBeans 3.0,
  5th Edition

Hardcore Java

Head First Design Patterns

Head First Design Patterns Poster

Head First Java, *2nd Edition*

Head First Servlets & JSP

Head First EJB

Hibernate: A Developer's
  Notebook

J2EE Design Patterns

Java 5.0 Tiger: A Developer's
  Notebook

Java & XML Data Binding

Java & XML, *3rd Edition*

Java Cookbook, *2nd Edition*

Java Data Objects

Java Database Best Practices

Java Enterprise Best Practices

Java Enterprise in a Nutshell,
  3rd Edition

Java Examples in a Nutshell,
  3rd Edition

Java Extreme Programming
  Cookbook

Java Generics and Collections

Java in a Nutshell, *5th Edition*

Java I/O, *2nd Edition*

Java Management Extensions

Java Message Service

Java Network Programming,
  3rd Edition

Java NIO

Java Performance Tuning,
  2nd Edition

Java RMI

Java Security, *2nd Edition*

JavaServer Faces

JavaServer Pages,
  3rd Edition

Java Servlet & JSP
  Cookbook

Java Servlet Programming,
  2nd Edition

Java Swing, *2nd Edition*

Java Web Services
  in a Nutshell

JBoss: A Developer's
  Notebook

JBoss at Work: A Practical Guide

Learning Java, *3rd Edition*

Mac OS X for Java Geeks

Maven: A Developer's
  Notebook

Programming Jakarta Struts,
  2nd Edition

QuickTime for Java: A
  Developer's Notebook

Spring: A Developer's
  Notebook

Swing Hacks

Tomcat: The Definitive Guide,
  2nd Edition

WebLogic: The Definitive Guide

Our books are available at most retail and online bookstores.
To order direct: 1-800-998-9938 • *order@oreilly.com* • *www.oreilly.com*
Online editions of most O'Reilly titles are available by subscription at *safari.oreilly.com*

70502